Sarah and Her Sisters

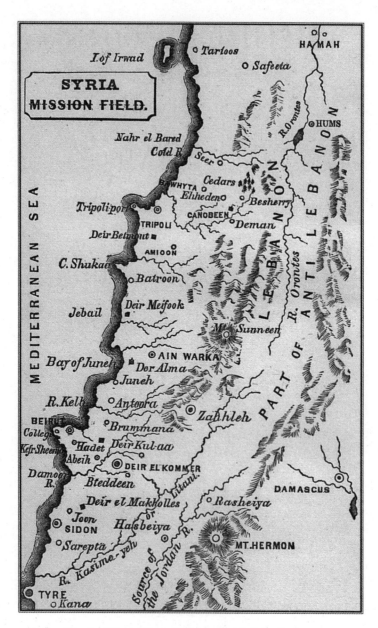

Fig. 1 – Map of Syria Mission Field, Frontispiece: *Bible Work in Bible Lands* by Rev. Isaac Bird, 1872.

Sarah and Her Sisters

American Missionary Pioneers
in Arab Female Education, 1834–1937

Robert D. Stoddard, Jr.

⊟ hachette
A. Antoine

All rights reserved.

Text © Robert Dick Stoddard Jr., 2019

© Hachette Antoine sal, 2020
Antoine Bldg, Street 402, Mkalles, Lebanon
P.O. Box 11-0656, Riad al-Solh, 1107 2050 Beirut, Lebanon
info@hachette-antoine.com
www.hachette-antoine.com
facebook.com/HachetteAntoine
instagram.com/HachetteAntoine
twitter.com/NaufalBooks

This book on the early history of Lebanese American University
was completed during the Presidency of Dr. Joseph G. Jabbra.

Cover design: Dalia Daher
Layout: Marie-Thérèse Merheb
Index: Leila Merhej
Printing: Arab Printing Press

ISBN 978-614-469-537-1
e-ISBN 978-614-469-538-8

For my kindred spirit, Judy,
and our dear friend,
Julinda Abu Nasr

Contents

Preface..9

Prologue: 1823–1834 13

Chapter One: Sarah Smith's Beirut Female School (1834–1836)................21

Chapter Two: Sarah's Successors in Beirut (1836–1858).............................75

Chapter Three: First Boarding Schools for Older Girls (1835–1862)..........91

Chapter Four: Syrian Female Seminary (1862–1867) 111

Chapter Five: Eliza Everett's Beirut Female Seminary (1868–1895) 129

Chapter Six: Testing Miss Everett's Heirs (1895–1904)..............................161

Chapter Seven: Decade of Progress and Promise (1904–1914).................191

Chapter Eight: Surrounded by Suffering (1914–1920)...............................219

Chapter Nine: Higher Education at Last (1920–1927) 243

Chapter Ten: Sarrafian House Women's College (1927–1933) 273

Chapter Eleven: AJCW's Ras Beirut Campus (1933–1937)........................309

Epilogue: (1937 to the present)...345

Author's Note 347

Acknowledgments 351

Appendix A: American Elementary & Secondary Teachers
in Syria/Lebanon 355

Appendix B: Native Teachers in Syria/Lebanon
(named in intermittent and incomplete records) 357

Appendix C: American Junior College for Women 1924–1937 359

Chronology (1809–1939)...363

Notes 369

Index 399

Preface

The title of this book warrants parsing. Sarah Huntington Smith had only one biological sister, but female Protestant missionaries in the nineteenth century considered themselves "sisters in Christ." Most of the "sisters" sent to Ottoman Syria were New England Congregationalists adhering to the Reformed Protestant doctrines of John Calvin. The earliest went to the Holy Land of Jesus to help their missionary husbands "save" the native "heathen" from their sins and eternal damnation by converting them to Protestantism. In order to be "saved," one had to be able to read the Bible. Thus, while there was a scattering of rudimentary schools for native girls, these women set about establishing American-style schools of a higher quality for "Arab" girls. (In their eyes, all the people in Ottoman Syria who spoke Arabic, regardless of their race, nationality, or religion, were "Arabs."[1])

Sarah and Her Sisters had its origins in 1999 when I was serving as a vice president of Lebanese American University, which was then celebrating its seventy-fifth year as a college. I found precious little history of the school on hand. Only in retirement did I find online the *Memoir of Sarah L. H. Smith, Late of the Mission in Syria*. That discovery led to my three lectures at LAU in January 2009 on Sarah Smith, the founder of the "Beirut Female School" to which LAU traditionally traced its roots, and her husband, Rev. Eli Smith, a scholar of Arabic. I was then challenged by Academic Dean Abdallah Sfeir and others to connect the dots from Sarah to the present university. Thus began a decade of research and writing on only the first of LAU's two centuries of history—more than enough for one volume.

My primary objectives are twofold. The first is to bring these faded historical figures out of the shadows to tell their own stories in their own words. Whereas their male counterparts had only limited success in making converts and establishing native churches, these missionary "sisters" succeeded in establishing a series of elementary and secondary schools for girls and the first college for women in the Arab world. Their forgotten stories deserve to be heard anew.

My second aim is to make these pioneering teachers known to Lebanese American University women and alumnae especially. They are the beneficiaries of the early missionaries' successes and are therefore indebted to them. LAU women are the great, great—now for six, seven, and eight generations—"granddaughters" of Sarah and her sisters. And their personal stories are the latest chapters in the history of female education in the region. I hope today's readers find these stories particularly relevant in an era when Malala Yousafzai courageously defies her Taliban attackers as she and others campaign for girls' schools in Afghanistan and the third world.

A good deal has been written about the motives, methods, and impact, for good or for ill, of the American missionaries. Scholars like Ussama Makdisi, who were brought up in the region, speak the language, and know much more about its history and culture than I, have written extensively about how the missionaries viewed and treated their native subjects. Their insights are enlightening and many ring true. But this book is not meant to be a scholarly analysis of these important and often contentious issues. Except for a brief author's note at the end of the book, this scrutiny and discussion must be carried on by others.

Professor Makdisi charges that Americans writing about the missionaries in Ottoman Syria tell their story "as if it were a continuation of their mission to native American Indians; as if all that mattered was the 'American' aspect to this story."[2] That perspective persists even today. As an American who has spent only limited time in the Near East, I am writing about Syria's residents from a mainly American point of view. I have accessed mostly American source materials, the bulk of them primary sources housed in the Presbyterian Historical Society in Philadelphia: Syria Mission and school reports, personal letters, diary entries, journal articles, and other records. In addition to Sarah's posthumous memoir, much was found in memoirs and writings of other missionaries, those of Henry H. Jessup especially. To the best of my knowledge, this is the first time these teachers and schools have been "connected" to this extent to tell the early history of American efforts toward female education in Syria-Lebanon as it relates to Lebanese American University.

Whatever their motives and methods, these "sisters" were unquestionably committed to their religious beliefs and passionate about educating indigenous females. They left families and friends behind for years, if not decades or a lifetime, to serve abroad. It took courage to sail thousands of arduous miles to a foreign port. It took discipline to master Arabic. It took determination to wage the uphill battle for female education in a patriarchal society that was opposed or at best indifferent to it. Teaching, administering schools, and supervising boarders day in and day out was hard work and took stamina. It was much more difficult to raise funds for educating females than for males. Then there were the personal sacrifices the missionary teachers made. Single women in their prime gave up hope for marriage and children of their own. They were all subject to prevalent diseases with only limited medical care available. Several made the ultimate sacrifice, literally giving their lives to teach Arab girls and young women.

Information regarding the native teachers who assisted the Americans is sketchy. Those few named in the records are listed in an appendix. Wherever possible their invaluable roles are highlighted in the text. The schools could not have functioned without them, but their contributions were, unfortunately, underacknowledged. They were assigned a second-class status and paid significantly less with fewer benefits than the Americans. (At least one native teacher spoke out against this differentiation, and when her supervisors refused to call her "Miss" rather than by her first name, she resigned and went to another school in Egypt.[3])

Just as Sarah and her sisters felt a strong sense of calling to enlighten the girls and women in Syria, I too have felt a calling to dig deeper and edify others who might share my curiosity. I have tried to be as true as possible to the beliefs, ideas, and intent of these missionaries and as accurate as possible in telling their stories. Nonetheless, I take full responsibility for any mistakes or inaccuracies made in interpreting and quoting from the primary sources they left behind. I hope this book will be of interest to scholars and general readers in church history and missiology. Those in the fields of women's studies, female education, and Near East studies may also gain a new perspective from these first-person accounts of the missionaries' work. Church women and advocates for World Mission who champion the education of girls in the developing world will find it of particular interest. There is more to be uncovered and shared about each of these "sisters," but I will be satisfied if, in the meantime, readers come to know them from their own words and gain new insights into how they advanced the welfare of girls and women throughout the Near East and the Arabic-speaking world.

Prologue
1823–1834

If a missionary were disposed to open a school, there are probably few places in Syria that would be more promising than Beyroot itself.

Pliny Fisk
July 10, 1823

The Rev. Pliny Fisk wrote this to "a lady in Connecticut" upon entering the city of Beirut for the first time.[1] Accompanied by the Rev. Jonas King, Fisk was one of the first three missionaries sent to Ottoman Syria (today's Syria, Lebanon, Israel/Palestine and Jordan) by the American Board of Commissioners for Foreign Missions (ABCFM). As ordained Congregational ministers trained at Andover Theological Seminary, they were to save the souls of Eastern Christians, Muslims, Jews, and pagans in the Holy Land by converting them to Protestantism. Unfortunately for the missionaries, neither Syria's Muslim majority nor its Jewish minority had any interest in the newcomers' religion. Moreover, their fellow Christians—Maronite and Latin Catholics, and Greek and Armenian Orthodox—were downright hostile to them. It was a tough assignment that would end with Fisk's premature death in two years.[2]

Since Fisk and King had arrived unaccompanied by wives, residents assumed them to be travelers merely passing through. But when the Reverends William Goodell and Isaac Bird disembarked from the Maltese brig *La Divina Providenza* in November 1823 with their wives, Abigail and Ann, the infant William Bird, Jr, and trunks of garments, household goods, and books, it was apparent to onlookers that they planned to stay. While their final destination was Jerusalem, British Consul Peter Abbot convinced them to rent a house and stay in Beirut for the winter before proceeding south.[3]

Set before the glorious, snow-capped mountains of Lebanon, the small port city *Bayrut al-mahrusa* (guarded place), with about 8,000 densely packed residents, was the size of a large Arab market town. Its skyline was punctuated by minarets, various church towers, and three- and four-story stone houses. Most of the large shoreline dwellings were inhabited by Europeans, foreign consuls, and wealthy merchants. The only public buildings were several inns, two hotels for foreigners, and the sultan's palace (*seraglio*), all scattered throughout a maze of narrow, winding streets and dark alleys bounded by three walls and the shoreline. Beyond the walls were sand dunes dotted by cemeteries and groups of houses indicating that the city was beginning to expand. Whereas Arab Sunni and Shiite Muslims and Druze were predominant throughout the region, Beirut had the largest concentration of Christians in the Levant, many having escaped war, famine, and regional instability and hoping to benefit from the city's renewed commerce with Europe.[4]

The Goodells and Birds made themselves as comfortable as possible in their chilly, damp residence with open windows and spent daylight hours studying Turkish, Arabic, Armenian, and Italian, which was in common use locally. Impatient to move on, Isaac Bird set out with Jonas King for Jerusalem in January, leaving the others to distribute Bibles in the four languages and preach their Protestant gospel to whomever would listen.

Curious to know why these strangely garbed men and unveiled ladies had come, native Syrians—women especially—came at first in great numbers to hear them. One unusual trait they observed was how the American men treated their wives, serving them first at the

Fig. 2 – Rev. Pliny Fisk, first American Protestant missionary to enter Beirut in 1823.

Fig. 3 – Later photos of Rev. Isaac and Ann Bird (left) and Rev. William and Abigail Goodell (right), the first missionary couples sent to Syria in 1823 by the ABCFM.

table and assisting them in every little thing. Conversely, the missionaries were shocked by how Syrian men of all sects appeared to treat their wives. "The women are treated as slaves," wrote Goodell. "When they go out they wrap themselves in a large white sheet and neither walk nor eat with their husbands. To ask a man about his wife's health is an almost unpardonable offense."

When the rented house became crowded with native women wanting to look at the two missionary wives, Abigail Goodell and Ann Bird took turns reading biblical passages to their visitors, presumably in halting Arabic from an early translation of the Bible into Arabic since the Syrian women knew no English. The women were then urged to read the verses back out loud. One woman doubted she could learn to read because a previous attempt to teach women at a convent resulted in only two becoming partially literate. Even though attendance was irregular, and some women were derided by friends, they made modest progress. Thus began the American wives' first efforts to educate Syrian females. In the process, they emphasized the importance of education and believed that they demonstrated their own intelligence and influence, how they instructed their own children, and how they communicated in writing and otherwise contributed to the overall welfare of their community.[5]

Five months in Jerusalem convinced Isaac Bird that the political unrest there made Beirut a more promising venue for missionary work. Returning to his wife and son, he joined forces with William Goodell, who was learning Arabic and Armenian from native tutors. Educating females may have been a priority for the wives, but their husbands' directive was to make converts. Since Syrian society was patriarchal and male-dominated, and since adherents had to be literate to read the Bible for themselves, their priority was to establish, as fast as possible, schools for boys that would combine a basic education with religious instruction. In this venture they were at first amazingly successful.[6]

Their schools were not, however, the first ones in Syria. The earliest known schools were run within some mosques. Young children, mostly boys, were taught in one-room *kuttab* (elementary schools). Older students could attend the more advanced *madrasas*. A higher religious education was available only in mosques in Damascus or Cairo's al-Azhar Mosque. Christian schools also existed in the region. Maronite Catholic priests were trained in a half-dozen seminaries, while Greek Orthodox clergy went to similar schools in Beirut, Damascus, and Jerusalem. The earliest *mission* schools were founded in the late sixteenth century by European Jesuits and operated until the dissolution of the order in 1773. The Jesuit presence was revived within the native Catholic community in the early 1800s with the opening of elementary and preparatory schools in Ain Turah and Ghazir for boys and in Beirut for girls. With this one exception, all were for males only and taught by males.[7]

Goodell and Bird faced fierce opposition from the local clerics—Greek and Maronite especially—who saw Protestant attempts at schooling as a threat to their authority. They warned their people not to "drink and disseminate the poisonous Protestant doctrine." Nevertheless, while their wives were taking in and teaching "six Arab children" daily, Goodell and Bird in 1825 engaged a Maronite priest, Assad Shidiak, to start a small Arabic grammar school for boys that within a year grew to fifty pupils. Several similar free schools were quickly established throughout Beirut and Mount Lebanon. A system of free schools in which teachers supervised older students as tutors developed rapidly, and soon 300 children were enrolled. By the end of 1826 there were thirteen schools with over 700 animated and promising students. The fact that "more than one hundred of them were girls" was, in William Goodell's opinion, "remarkable evidence of a change of sentiment in regard to the education of women." The boys and girls alike were found to be lively, punctual, and serious about learning, causing the local clerics to become increasingly alarmed and hostile.[8]

Successful as they were, the Protestant schools were overtaken by events. Twice in 1826 Beirut was plundered, first by invading Greeks rebelling against the Turks, and then by troops of the Egyptian general, Ibrahim Pasha. The schools in the city were closed, but the outlying ones remained open. The Mission's work was further hindered by a summer outbreak of the plague (Black Death) in 1827, causing Isaac Bird to take his family to the mountains until the threat had passed. The next crisis occurred when priests encouraged local tribal leaders to break up the schools. Some teachers were threatened and resigned. Then the Mission's honest and good-hearted agent, Tannoos Hadad, was arrested and imprisoned for "attempting to change the religion of the country by teaching children to read the New Testament and the Psalms." When a boy who testified against him admitted he was bribed, Hadad was freed, but his school remained closed. Tannoos was then engaged to teach Arabic to a young, newly arrived missionary, Eli Smith.

The remaining schools were closed abruptly with the outbreak of the first Egyptian-Ottoman War. In return for Egypt's assistance during the Greek war for independence, the Turks had promised Muhammad Ali Pasha control of Syria and Arabia. When that offer was withdrawn, Ali's son, Ibrahim Pasha, invaded Syria with superior forces, routing the Ottomans and taking control of the entire Levant, including Beirut and Mount Lebanon. All missionary operations were suspended. Grieving the loss of the schools that once flourished, the Goodells and Birds, plus Eli Smith and other members of the small Syria Mission, twenty-one in all, retreated to Malta aboard a small, two-masted ship on May 2, 1828.[9]

While the missionary couples remained in Malta, control of the Levant was wrenched from a weakened Sultan Mahmud II by Ibrahim Pasha. When peace and stability were restored in 1829, it was deemed safe for the Birds and the newly arrived Presbyterian couple, Rev. George and Matilda Whiting, to return to Beirut in May 1830 aboard a Maltese brig. With Ibrahim Pasha firmly in control as the new viceroy, the Syria Mission was reestablished in a more settled Beirut. Isaac Bird was allowed to purchase a desirable plot of land in 1831 and within a year built a substantial home affectionately named Burj Bird (Bird's Fortress). It initially housed his family, the Whitings, a few servants, and occasional visitors. The basement was turned into a school with classrooms and a dormitory for six boys. Otherwise, the Mission's educational outreach was not renewed until 1834, when William and Eliza Thomson, also Presbyterians, and the first medical missionary, Dr. Asa Dodge and his wife Martha, arrived in Beirut.

Before coming to Syria, Eliza Thomson had run a private girls' school in Princeton, New Jersey while William was attending Princeton Theological Seminary. Nevertheless, she and Martha Dodge were ill prepared to overcome the local prejudice against educating girls. With much apprehension, they assembled a few little girls in the mission house to teach them what they could on an irregular schedule for an hour or two a day. The women not only encountered indifference and prejudice against female education, but renewed resistance from local religious authorities who labeled them dangerous heretics whose influence would contaminate their followers. This unequivocal warning indicated that any such attempt to teach even little girls might be fruitless. Nevertheless, in persisting, they set the stage for the arrival of another "sister," Sarah Lanman Huntington Smith of Norwich, Connecticut, whose experience teaching Native American children would enable her to revolutionize female education in Syria.[10]

CHAPTER ONE

Sarah Smith's Beirut Female School (1834–1836)

"Could the females of Syria be educated and regenerated, the whole face of the country would change."

Sarah L. Smith to her parents
Bhamdoon, Syria, September 25, 1834

JANUARY 28, 1834 – BEIRUT, SYRIA

A heavily loaded skiff ground to a halt in the shallow waters of Beirut harbor. Its sole female occupant, dressed in a long, blue dress and matching bonnet, was immediately swept up and carried ashore in the arms of a burly, dusky-skinned porter clad only in pantaloons rolled above his knees. Gently lowered to the white sand beach, thirty-two-year-old Sarah Huntington Smith could hardly believe that her high-heeled ankle boots were, after a four-month voyage from Boston, at last touching "Syria's sacred shore." Nor could she ever imagine how, in her brief time in this "Bible land," her work would forevermore change the lives of the "benighted females" of Syria, let alone light a flame for female education that would spread throughout the Arabic-speaking world within a century.

Sarah and her husband of five months, the Reverend EliSmith, were warmly welcomed by the Reverend Isaac Bird and his wife Ann, fellow New Englanders who were the longest-serving American missionaries in Ottoman Syria. As porters, arguing loudly in Arabic, loaded the Smiths' baggage and trunks on to patiently waiting donkeys, Sarah was helped on to one of the small beasts. Riding side-saddle, she and Mrs. Bird began the trek uphill to the Mission House on the north side of the Cape of Beirut with their husbands walking ahead and their baggage following. Riding through the lower gate of the small walled city, up its narrow, winding cobbled streets and out the upper Bab Yaqoub (Gate of Jacob), the party emerged in Zuqaq al Blat, a hillside area of scattered houses surrounded by luxuriant gardens.[1]

Upon reaching the three-story Mission House known as Burj Bird, the newcomers were introduced to eight other missionary "brothers" and "sisters" who, like their predecessors, were sent by American Board of Foreign Missions (ABCFM) to the Holy Land of Jesus. Their mission was to bring the Protestant gospel to native Eastern Catholic and Orthodox Christians, whom they viewed as lapsed in the faith, as well as to Arab Muslims and Jews. In addition to the Birds were Reverend Asa Dodge, MD, and his wife Martha, also fellow Congregationalists, and two Presbyterian couples, Reverend George and Matilda Whiting and Reverend William and Eliza Thomson. Two other welcomers were the long-serving British Consul, Peter Abbott, and his Italian-born wife, Maria. Some of Eli's old friends among the natives greeted him so joyfully in Arabic that he felt as if he had returned home. Sarah, on the other hand, found the foreign language, setting, and culture taxing, and was overwhelmed by it all.[2]

The Smiths' arrival in Ottoman Syria coincided with a realignment of power throughout the Levant. Ibrahim Pasha, son of Muhammad 'Ali Pasha of Egypt, had recently taken control of Ottoman Syria by force, annexing today's Syria, Lebanon, and Israel/Palestine. The Turks' repeated failure to regain control marked the beginning of the end of the Ottoman Empire and the sultan's rule.[3]

Backed by his father, Ibrahim started modernizing the region and cleaning up Beirut. He appointed a council of twelve Muslims and Christians to help govern its residents; formed departments of public health and commerce and a police force; developed a road network and a postal system; and instituted new sanitary measures. Trees were planted, new roads built, and existing ones repaired and widened. A *lazaretto* (quarantine station) for visitors was constructed at the port to stem the spread of disease, and smallpox vaccine was distributed widely. Beirut became Syria's major port as the first steam ships exchanged the silk of Mount Lebanon for European goods. Ibrahim established Western consuls and provided diplomatic services, raising the United States consular agent to the rank of consul in 1836. An especially progressive measure was the advancement in education triggered in large measure by the educational work of the English, French, and American missionaries.[4]

Eli and Sarah moved into their own room in the Mission House they shared with the other American couples, servants, and visitors. Her first letter home described their bird's-eye view of the small, walled city laying "at the foot of the beautiful and famed Mount Lebanon; gardens towards the south with hedge-rows of cactus, or prickly pear, mulberry trees, sycamore, *kharoob*, palm and cypress and almond trees in full blossom, beauties beyond description." She was fascinated by the "bright yellow houses tinged with brown scattered among the gardens. Mount Lebanon, in all its grandeur, stretches from north to south while the snowy ridges of its lofty eminences, and numerous villages in its declivities give additional interest to the every-varying scenery. I will never tire of the scene spread before me. Beirut pleases me more than any place I have ever seen, including my own dear native town."[5]

NATIVE OF NORWICH

Sarah Lanman Huntington's "native town" was Norwich, Connecticut, where she was born on June 18, 1802 into one of its leading families. Norwich was a bustling river port thirteen miles upstream from Long Island Sound. Sarah's father Jabez, a successful banker and merchant, and her mother, Mary Lanman Huntington, were strict Calvinists who were descended from New England Puritans. Sarah had an older brother, Jedidiah; an older sister, Faith; and two younger brothers, Edward and Peter. Growing up in an affluent home, the four Huntington siblings were privileged to be among the New England Protestant elites.

A physically and emotionally delicate child cared for by the kindly "Mrs. Ewen," Sarah at the age of six was confined to bed with a protracted, unidentified illness. A year later, her mother Mary died giving birth to Sarah's younger brother Peter. Left with five children, Jabez married his late wife's blind sister, Sarah, whom young Sarah already loved as her aunt.

Little Sarah probably first attended the Chelsea Grammar School organized by her father and other prominent Norwich citizens. Here she was likely taught by the severe schoolmistress who told her, "If I did not love you, I should not whip you." Being privileged, she was at age nine one of only twenty-five girls able to attend a private female academy begun by Misses Nancy Hyde and Lydia Huntley. Themselves only in their late teens, these two believed the goal of education was usefulness and to acquire a degree of independence. Instruction included geography, natural and moral philosophy, and history. Grammar, logic, arithmetic, and penmanship took precedence over Bible reading, recitation, and spelling. Each girl kept a daily journal, a practice Sarah continued throughout her life. Unfortunately, the school closed after only one year due to Miss Hyde's unspecified terminal illness. Lydia went on to become the well-known poet and pioneer feminist, Lydia Huntley Sigourney, with whom Sarah maintained a lifelong friendship. Brief though it was, Sarah's exposure to these two young teachers certainly accounted for her love of systematic learning and study for the sake of acquiring useful knowledge and self-improvement.[6]

In 1817, fifteen-year-old Sarah continued her formal education at Mrs. Prousor's boarding school in Boston. Shunning enticements such as the theater, cotillions, and balls, she became absorbed in her studies but quite homesick. After only one year, she returned to Norwich, giving no thought to further education as there were then no colleges for women in America. Only white males of means, like her brothers Jedidiah and Peter, could aspire to go to the likes of Harvard and Yale.

Freed from formal schooling, Sarah took occasional trips throughout New England and the mid-Atlantic states, visiting family and friends, seeing the sights, and satisfying her thirst for adventure. They included trips to Boston, Hartford, Vermont, and New York. On a trip to New Hampshire with her brother Edward, Sarah, an avid walker and hiker, would be one of the "few ladies ever to reach the summit" of Mount Washington, the highest peak east of the Rocky Mountains.[7]

THE MAKING OF A MISSIONARY

Sarah's childhood and adolescence coincided with the Second Great Awakening, one of the most profound religious revivals in American history, which was sweeping the newly formed United States in the early 1800s. Revival meetings occurred throughout New England, congregations were growing, and new churches were being established. Renewed interest in religion led to the founding of new academies, colleges, and theological seminaries; most importantly for Sarah, it also stimulated the beginning of home and foreign missionary enterprises. The keen interest of students at Andover Theological Seminary in spreading the gospel abroad spurred Congregational, Presbyterian, and Dutch Reformed church leaders to establish the American Board of Commissioners for Foreign Missions of which Sarah's father, Jabez, was a founding member. Thus, the stage was set for young Sarah's future calling.[8]

Sarah faithfully attended Sabbath School and worship services at the Second Congregational Church in Norwich. At fourteen, she began teaching a class until, convinced of her own sinfulness, she resigned at age eighteen. The sudden death of a girlhood friend, and the urging of another friend that she commit herself to Christ, precipitated an agonizing, week-long spiritual struggle. This culminated in an intense religious experience in which Sarah "submitted herself" to Christ, her Savior. From then on she "rejoiced in all revivals of religion." Sure of her own faith, her primary purpose in life became winning others to Christ so they too might be saved. Starting with her two younger brothers, other relatives, and friends, she had mixed results.

While a senior at Yale, Sarah's brother Peter had his own conversion experience at a revival and fulfilled his sister's ardent prayers by deciding to enter the ministry. To earn money for his theological education, he became a private tutor in Natchez, Mississippi, but, sadly, fell ill with an unspecified disease that forced him to return home and give up all hope of the ministry. Sarah devoted herself to his care until he died on Christmas Eve, 1832. Devastated, she resolved to somehow fulfill his calling.

Sarah's Mohegan School

Unable as a female to become a minister, Sarah, in her early twenties, became interested in mission work. She first contemplated going west to teach Native American children, whom she viewed as "heathens" needing conversion, in a Foreign Mission Board school. (The ABCFM considered Indian tribes to be "foreign" nations even though they resided within the borders of the United States.) At the age of twenty-five she decided instead to minister to the remnant of the once numerous Mohegan Indian tribe living near her home before the Indian Removal Act forcibly removed them from their land. Signed by President Andrew Jackson on May 26, 1830 at the behest of southern lawmakers who coveted the Cherokee Nation's land in Georgia, the act dictated that all "uncivilized" (i.e., uneducated according to white men's standards) and "unchristian" American "aborigines" be moved west of the Mississippi River. Consequently, Sarah would begin her own mission and school to educate and convert the Mohegans to Christianity, thereby saving both their souls *and* their tribal land.[9]

Following the sound of axes coming from the nearby forest in 1827, Sarah found the remaining one hundred or so Mohegans. These impoverished men, women, and children—not to be confused with the Mohican Tribe of upper New York State—were, in her mind, illiterate and heathen. With the help of a friend from Norwich and in collaboration with three Mohegan women—Lucy Occum Tantaquidgeon, her daughter Lucy, and her granddaughter Cynthia—Sarah started a Sabbath School in the women's farmhouse that became a weekday school as well. After gaining the trust of the Mohegans and receiving Lucy Occum's gift of land for a meeting house, Sarah moved into a small cabin that served as her parlor, bedroom, kitchen, and temporary schoolroom and chapel. Although not formally trained, Sarah had an affinity for teaching and a natural affection for her pupils. She wrote to her former teacher, Lydia Huntley Sigourney, that the school had grown to "sixteen scholars with four or five more expected."[10]

With the help of friends in Norwich society, Sarah raised the first funds for the meetinghouse that would be both a church and a schoolhouse. A Connecticut congressman, who happened to be a cousin, helped her get $500 in federal funds to complete the project. By December 1830 Sarah was teaching about twenty pupils in the weekday school, including four adults. They studied simple arithmetic, reading, writing, and music, as well as millinery and tailoring for girls. Her school hours were 9:30 to 4:00 with a half hour allocated for recess. The Sabbath school grew to twice the size of

Fig. 4 – Mohegan chapel and schoolhouse
built by Sarah Huntington and friends in 1831.

Fig. 5 – Second Congregational Church, Norwich, CT, the Huntington
family church where Sarah and Eli were married in 1833.

the day school. Sarah's Mohegan mission was soon designated a "foreign mission" of the American Board.

When the Mohegan Meeting House was completed in 1831, Sarah turned the school over to a good friend, Miss Rebecca Williams of nearby Lebanon, Connecticut, who would be paid $400 a year by the U.S. government. As more Mohegans were educated and some converted to Christianity, they were no longer considered "uncivilized and unchristian" and therefore could not be evicted from their tribal land. To this day, the Mohegan tribe, which owns and operates the lucrative Mohegan Sun Casino on their 2,400-acre reservation in Connecticut, remains grateful to Sarah Lanman Huntington for the critical role she played in saving their ancestors from extinction and helping preserve their remaining tribal land. A wall plaque in the casino verifies the critical role Sarah played in their history. Tribal Council vice chairwoman Jayne Fawcett in 1996 told a *New York Times* reporter, "Sarah Huntington saved us."[11]

No Longer "Unfettered"

Sarah was well acquainted with the overseas work of the ABCFM. She first heard of the Syria Mission in a talk given in 1824 by a young missionary going to Palestine. Learning more of the need for overseas missionaries at a meeting of the local Foreign Missionary Society in 1831, she resolved that whenever her parents no longer needed her living at home, and if still "unfettered," she would go abroad as a missionary. Sarah's opportunity to do so came that very summer when she was introduced to the Reverend Eli Smith, a bachelor from North Fork, Connecticut, home on leave after spending five years in locations that must have sounded exotic to Sarah. He had operated the Mission Press in Malta, surveyed possible mission sites in Greece, learned Arabic in Syria, and nearly died of cholera while touring Asia Minor, Georgia, and Persia. Smith was to return to Syria, but not until he found a wife to take with him.[12]

Fig. 6 – Only known photo (Daguerreotype) of Sarah Huntington Smith c. 1833.

During Eli's first years abroad, the Mission Board changed its policy regarding the marital status of its exclusively male missionaries. From about 1833 on, they had to be married for several reasons. A wife would serve as a "spiritual companion," a confidant and helpmate who would oversee her husband's household, so he could devote his entire attention to preaching the gospel. She would enable him "to manage that powerful law of nature, which produces the family state." Missionary couples would demonstrate proper family relationships, bearing and raising children who were uniquely qualified to become future missionaries themselves. A well-educated wife could homeschool her own children and provide religious education for native children. Furthermore, since the females of Syria were "sequestered," or not allowed out of the house unless accompanied by a male member of the family, only missionary wives could reach them. Such women could educate and evangelize native women and girls.[13]

At age twenty-nine, Sarah, becoming resigned to spinsterhood, was interested to hear a young missionary, itinerating on his furlough in the spring of 1832, speak in Norwich on his experiences in the Near East and of the need for more missionaries to go there to save the souls of those in the Holy Land. She was thus surprised, but certainly not displeased, to receive shortly thereafter Rev. Eli Smith's unexpected proposal that she become his "helpmate" and return with him to Beirut. This was an answer to her prayer to become a missionary, if not a wife. With her father's hesitant blessing (Eli was of poorer stock, the son of a Connecticut farmer and part-time shoemaker), she readily accepted his offer and they were married in July by her pastor in the Second Congregational Church of Norwich. After spending the rest of the summer visiting family and friends in New England to say goodbye, the newlyweds embarked from Boston on September 21, 1831 aboard the two-masted brig *George*. Except for Sarah's violent seasickness, their journey to Malta and

Fig. 7 – The *Brig Herald*, built in Duxbury, Massachusetts, was similar to the *Brig George* on which Sarah and Eli Smith sailed from Boston to Malta, September 21 – November 14, 1833.

Fig. 8 – Eli and Sarah reached Beirut in January 1834 aboard a Trabacollo from Alexandria, Egypt, via Larnaca, Cyprus.

Fig. 9 – Beirut Harbor and Mount Lebanon drawn in 1834, the year Eli and Sarah landed and she first set foot on "Syria's sacred shore."

Settling In

Eli Smith's primary assignment was to relocate the Mission press in Malta to Beirut to better serve the Arabic-speaking world. There he was to renew his language study, translate mission materials into Arabic, develop a more readable Arabic type, and produce a better Bible in Arabic. Meanwhile, Sarah was to run their household, which at first consisted of only Eli, herself, and their servant, Ahmed, who had been brought from Malta. All of them were living within the shared confines of the Mission House. She was also expected, God willing, to bear and raise children to become missionaries. Otherwise, she was asked only to teach Sabbath school for English-speaking children and participate in the city's English-speaking society. However, as a relatively well educated woman who had already run her own mission school for Indian children, Sarah found this arrangement less than satisfying, and sought to become more useful.[15]

Her first obstacle was the language barrier. Having immersed himself in Arabic five years earlier while living with his tutor's family in a mountain village above Beirut, Eli quickly recovered his fluency. Sarah, on the other hand, had learned only the alphabet on their voyage. Since Eli was preoccupied with his work, she spent her mornings with a native tutor trying to learn the difficult language. In the evenings, she also studied Italian and French.

To occupy herself between Arabic lessons, Sarah began assisting Eliza Thomson, Martha Dodge, and Mrs. Gregory Wortabet, the wife of an Armenian priest, in conducting an informal class of illiterate Syrian girls in the Mission House. The women were attempting to teach the six or eight little girls, likely from ages four to seven or eight, some basic reading, writing, and arithmetic. Eliza was probably leading the efforts for she had taught previously in a female seminary while William attended Princeton Theological Seminary. Their main method of teaching the Arabic and English alphabets and numbers zero through nine was by showing the girls how to stitch on cloth stretched tightly across a wooden hoop as they themselves had been taught as girls in America—but only in English. The girls were then shown how to decorate their work with embroidered designs to create "samplers" that could be framed and displayed to demonstrate the girls' virtue, achievement, and industry. Assisting in the "sewing department," Sarah wrote home: "Our school continues to prosper, and I love the children exceedingly. Do pray that God will bless this incipient step to enlighten the females of this country. You cannot conceive of their deplorable ignorance."[16]

Fearing strong opposition by patriarchal Catholic and Orthodox clerics who still viewed the Protestants as dangerous heretics who threatened their authority and would contaminate their children, the class was limited to an hour or two on irregular days. Although it was a sincere effort to reach and teach uneducated girls, Isaac Bird was not optimistic that the four women could accomplish much since the Mission's previous common schools, mostly for boys, had only limited and short-lived success. But he and the other missionaries had to admit they had little or no access to the secluded females of Syria. That left it to Sarah Smith to prove that "acting on strong faith rather than cautious calculation" was the only way to overcome the long-standing cultural prejudices against wives and daughters that made the general population indifferent toward female education.[17]

"WIDE DOOR OF USEFULNESS"

As an experienced Sabbath School teacher, Sarah had no trouble starting a Sunday morning class for American and English children. Concerned that their children were otherwise growing up in Beirut "without proper instruction," their expatriate parents urged her to start a weekday school in English as well. But Sarah decided to free herself from as much housekeeping as possible and instead "devote herself exclusively to the *natives* for which a knowledge of the Arabic language was necessary." With Eli's encouragement and help, she and Martha Dodge began another Sabbath School for Syrian girls in the home of Eli's former Arabic tutor, Tannoos al Haddad. Some of the girls were also in the class that met in the Mission House some weekdays. To accelerate her communication skills, Sarah started a serious study of Arabic grammar.[18]

On outings accompanied by Eli or Ahmad, Sarah felt herself "surrounded by degraded and benighted Syrian women." To her they were "like innocent children" whom she yearned to enlighten. As girls, they spent most of their time at home "helping their mothers keep house, cook, serve meals, take care of younger siblings and wait on male relatives." As Sarah well knew from growing up in Norwich where well-off families had both white and free black servants, and knowing of slavery in America, these native females

> were treated as servants with no future to look forward to other than being married off to a husband who would expect the same from her as a wife and would treat her accordingly. Whether Christian, Muslim or Druze, young women, either as daughters or wives, had to be fully veiled and accompanied by a male member of the family when outside her home. Learning to read and write was often out of the question since that was not necessary to do the "women's work."[19]

Joining his wife on the Mission House terrace one morning, Eli, who had developed a special interest in the education of girls while traveling through Turkey, Armenia, Georgia, and Persia before meeting Sarah, offered a sympathetic ear. Sarah longed to improve the situation of her Syrian "sisters" upon whom "not a ray of comfort would ever beam through the endless duration of their existence." The couple felt that somehow their "very existence should be identified with them." Realizing that it would require all her diligence, Sarah then and there resolved that her work "should hereafter be identified with them." She "hoped to live to a good old age among this people," working to improve the lives and save the souls of Arab girls and women. Eli saw a "wide door of usefulness opening before her, from which no other engagements would interfere or divert her energies."[20]

In March William and Eliza Thomson were reassigned to open a mission in Jerusalem. Most likely because of her previous teaching experience in Princeton and her fledgling class in Beirut, Eliza was to start a girls' school in the Holy City. Meanwhile in Beirut, Martha Dodge and Sarah, still with the assistance of Mrs. Wortabet, took turns carrying on the class of little girls on alternate weeks until early summer. Sarah took special note of one little girl who "was enough advanced to aid in teaching; and, knowing some English, could act as interpreter." With her smattering of Arabic, Sarah may have been able by then to teach some simple reading, writing, and prayers, and perhaps even some children's hymns in English.

Thinking ahead, she began to see how this small class could be expanded into an actual school like the one she had organized for the Mohegan children. She might have similar success instructing native children in Beirut, especially if she had a more experienced colleague to assist her. Sarah at once wrote to her friend, Rebecca Williams, to whom she had entrusted the Mohegan school, asking that she come and join her in missionary service. Miss Williams did not hesitate in accepting the invitation, but it would take her two years to make all the necessary arrangements and sail to Beirut to join Sarah.[21]

Since Sarah's educational efforts were directly connected in her mind "to the great [Calvinist] work of saving souls" from damnation and eternal torment in hell, she wished to "have God formally acknowledged in her class." To that end, she invited Isaac Bird to close the school day with prayer in Arabic. Eli recounted that the little children, who were accustomed to praying while standing up,

Fig. 10 – The early missionaries disapproved of Syrian women and girls dressing up in ornate native costumes and jewelry.

Sarah and Her Sisters | 39

"were so amused at the novelty of kneeling, that all were overcome with laughter." This grieved Sarah and made her weep. The children, "being already much attached to her; and perceiving, how their conduct had affected her, came forward and expressed their sorrow for what they had done. From then on, prayer was rarely, if ever, omitted for a single day." As word of the little school spread, more parents wanted to send their daughters, so they could receive the benefits being provided—and at no charge.[22]

KEEPING HOUSE

Overall, Sarah was in good spirits in her new surroundings. Other than the struggle to learn the language, the strangeness of the diverse culture, and the "unclean habits" of some of the natives, she was comfortable in their shared accommodations and "never for a moment wished herself in her native land." In late May, the Smiths moved from the Mission House into a rented apartment far enough away for her to ride a donkey to and from her class.[23]

To free herself from domestic responsibilities she thought "degrading to her calling" and used to having servants at home, Sarah hired and trained two women "fresh from the mountains and free from evil habits" to help keep her house perfectly neat. With no further explanation than "chiefly as a charity," she also took in "a poor, colored Abyssinian [Ethiopian] girl, emancipated from slavery." Being a good seamstress, Sarah provided "suitable and becoming apparel for herself and others." Apparently influenced strongly by the theories and teachings of the Rev. Sylvester Graham on how to lead a healthier, more wholesome life and to prevent cholera, she was a vegetarian who fasted on the first Monday of every month when the missionaries shared in scripture reading, preaching, prayer, and reflection on their work.[24] Meals in her household were reduced to breakfast at 7:00 a.m. and dinner at 5:00 p.m. so the rest of the day was free for work. As much as she objected to the custom, Sarah too kept her female servants as secluded as possible and veiled when they went out to "put a guard upon morals and keep the confidence of the natives."[25]

As noted, the ABCFM encouraged missionary couples to produce indigenous missionaries who were born into the local language and culture. While most other wives were able to give birth, some frequently, Sarah remained barren. Knowing of her desire for some other "object of attachment" in her home, Eli agreed to their informally "adopting" eight-year-old Raheel Atta, one of her most promising scholars and likely her little teaching assistant and translator, to live with them. With her dark eyes and thick, black hair, Raheel was strikingly pretty, as well as noticeably bright. With the blessing of her parents, Raheel assumed a role somewhere "between a daughter and a servant" in the Smith household, as Eli put it.

Raheel was taught needlework and how to assist with domestic chores, with the goal of constant occupation: she was never to sit down with nothing to do. She was kept in her native dress and was not to be "Europeanized so as to remain fit to live contentedly and usefully among her countrymen." She could practice her Greek Orthodox religion and visit her parents regularly, but it was hoped she would eventually become a Protestant. Raheel became increasingly attached to Sarah, who taught her to read the Bible and pray. Eli boasted that Raheel "acquired a knowledge of religion as good as an American child her age." Raheel, in turn, helped Sarah with her Arabic. This was the beginning of a loving and fruitful relationship of major importance, not only to the two of them, but for generations of Syrian girls and women to come.[26]

Unexpected Developments

Aside from a revolt among Muslim peasants who were being forcibly inducted into Ibrahim Pasha's army, Beirut remained calm throughout 1834. Intense early summer heat caused Martha Dodge and Sarah to discontinue their class, thus allowing the Smiths and Raheel to escape to the village of Bamdoon on Mount Lebanon in mid-July. There Sarah began teaching six little mountain girls as had Martha Dodge the previous summer. She hoped more would join her class, but her students replied that reading "was for boys, and not for them." Several village women acknowledged that "they knew no more than the donkeys," causing Sarah to write: "Alas, the curse rests emphatically upon our poor sisters!" When two unusually bright girls were absent, she was told that their Maronite priest had forbidden their attendance and that, if they came, he would not allow them in church. Why, she wondered, would those who "professed to be their spiritual guides, deny them the key of knowledge." Still, "a Greek priest sent his own daughter, a pretty, rosy-cheeked girl, to be taught."[27]

Sarah was shocked to learn in July of 1834 that the promising Eliza Thomson had died suddenly during a terrifying peasants' revolt in Jerusalem that May. She grieved for her dear and valuable friend whose "cultivated mind, warm heart and animated manner won the affection of all." Renewed and in vigorous health after her summer away, Sarah returned to her educational work only to find that Martha Dodge and her physician husband, Asa, had been sent to Jerusalem to replace the Thomsons. This left Sarah in sole charge of the weekday class of little girls. She further learned that the former Miss Gliddon, whom she had befriended in Egypt on her way to Beirut and with whom she had corresponded about her class, had married a wealthy British merchant. But what surprised and delighted her most was that the new Mrs. Tod had solicited her husband and other friends and raised $200 to build a schoolhouse for Sarah! Therefore, the mission was planning to erect a substantial stone schoolhouse adjacent to the Mission House that would be ready for occupancy in the spring of 1835.[28]

With a free hand to organize her own school for Syrian girls similar to her Mohegan school, Sarah consulted with Mr. Bird about the plans and hailed this development "as the dawn of a happy change in Syria." Yet, sensing the magnitude of the challenge and the limited impact she could have, she added, "I cannot but think that these feeble beginnings for this land are like the little stone that was cut out of the mountain."[29]

Sarah faced considerable obstacles. Far from home and the support of family and friends, she was trying to educate girls under primitive conditions in a foreign language in a male-dominated society that was indifferent, if not vehemently opposed, to her efforts. Although highly literate and knowledgeable, she had only a partial secondary education, no formal teacher training, and limited teaching experience. She had to create a curriculum from scratch and did not yet have a school building in which to teach.

On the other hand, Sarah loved her students. She had a strong sense of calling to enlighten those whom she believed lived in "intellectual and moral darkness." Looking back, this may seem a dated and simplistic view; Sarah was persuaded that her students were "benighted," or weighed down by darkness. However, American females in the 1830s, although confined primarily to homemaking and childrearing and with fewer opportunities for education and vocation than males, were still better treated, better educated, and freer to go about on their own than women in Syria. While the issue of "moral darkness" is debatable, there is no question that American girls and women were more educated and more liberated in many ways than their Syrian "sisters." The Syrian girls' desire for education and a better life was demonstrated by their attending and performing well in school. Proof of their mothers' desire for them to be more enlightened and treated more equally like the missionary wives was obvious in their decision to send their daughters to Sarah's school.

Sarah was well-organized and persistent. She knew how to lead a classroom, discipline her pupils, and model self-discipline and affection for her charges. Sarah was freed of many domestic responsibilities. Her husband encouraged her, as did the other wives and, increasingly, men of the Syria Mission and Mission Board. Drawing on her experience teaching in Sabbath School and the Mohegan school, and having the valuable assistance of Raheel in the classroom and in learning Arabic, Sarah could now hone her teaching skills in her own Beirut Female School.[30]

SCHOOLMISTRESS FOR SYRIA

When Sarah reopened the Mission House classroom on Tuesday, October 28, 1834, only four little girls came. But another six showed up on Wednesday for a total of ten. Confident the numbers would grow, she walked through the narrow streets of the walled city to her pleasant home at sunset, "with a quick step amid Egyptians, Turks and Arabs, Moslems and Jews, musing: 'Can it be that I am really a school-mistress, and the only one in all Syria? I sometimes indulge the thought that God has sent me to the females of Syria and to the little girls for their good.'" She warned her family, "My hours are now so systematically and fully appropriated that I can only steal short intervals for writing."[31]

Sarah knew enough Arabic to lead prayers in her Sabbath School. Eighteen of those Sunday pupils also came to her weekday school. They let her know they very much enjoyed both schools, although their attendance meant that they risked being excommunicated by their priests. Sarah was pleased they "showed marked improvement in learning and deportment." She was pleased too that their parents became more trusting and supportive of her efforts.

Yet the schedule was grueling. Teaching twenty little girls, now *every* weekday, plus her Sabbath School class, through the fall and into the winter months of penetrating dampness took a toll on Sarah. William Thomson forebodingly observed:

While her school prospers wonderfully, it is at the expense of her health. I fear her flame might go out and she ascend to heaven. May the Lord prolong her valuable life. We can hardly spare her; she is our only hope for a female school in Beirut at present.[32]

Sarah assured her blind stepmother, also Sarah, that she did watch her diet and tried to avoid exposure to cold, dampness, and fatigue. But she conceded that "unbraced by the cold [and dry] New England winters" she was used to, she was particularly susceptible to periods of weakness and a loss of vigor that prevented her from doing all she normally could. "I sometimes feel that God has sent me here to make an impression upon the female character in Syria," she wrote, but she worried, "I might be cut off quickly and my work cease. God forbid! Rather let me behold the fruits of my labors."[33]

A six-week tour of Palestine with Eli in April and May of 1835 fulfilled Sarah's lifelong dream to visit the Holy Land. Eli hoped the warmer clime would restore her heath. In Jerusalem they visited the Whitings and Martha Dodge, whose husband Asa had died of disease three months after she had arrived. Sarah surely discussed with Matilda her plans to open a school for a few girls in her Jerusalem home, as Sarah herself hoped to someday do in Beirut. Beyond that Matilda was trying to gain the trust of Muslim mothers to open a day school for their daughters. Tired but refreshed, Sarah returned to her teaching in Beirut with renewed energy and optimism and eager to begin teaching in her excellent new schoolhouse, which was then ready for occupancy. (This modest historic building is commemorated on a stone tablet in front of the National Evangelical Church in downtown Beirut near where stood "the first edifice built in the Turkish Empire for a girls' school, erected in 1835... for Mrs. Sarah L. Smith, its first teacher.")

Imagining the Schoolhouse

There are no known drawings or plans of the Beirut schoolhouse built for Sarah Smith. We can only assume it was similar in size and design to the one-room New England schoolhouses familiar to the missionaries. We know that it had stone walls and probably a flat, tiled terrace roof because Sarah later complained that the walls were porous and the terrace broke up in heavy rains. It would have been aligned so its glass pane windows, assuming glazed glass was available, could catch the morning sunlight. Glass or no glass, the windows surely had shutters that could be closed in cold and inclement weather. The interior walls were likely plastered and whitewashed with oil lamps or candleholders strategically placed for overcast days. The floor too was certainly tiled for easy sweeping and washing. If there was an internal source of heat, it must have been a small wood or charcoal burning iron stove, as a traditional charcoal brazier would have been hazardous and inefficient in so large a room.[34]

Individual student desks would have been expensive, so the schoolroom likely had rows of movable benches facing the teacher's desk used by Sarah. She wrote of having a blackboard up front. Perhaps each girl had a small slate and chalk as well for writing letters, numbers, and simple words in Arabic and English, working arithmetic problems, and drawing. Also likely were some traditional oriental carpets, perhaps in a corner with pillows for rest periods. Eli confirms that Sarah had a low sitting stool for storytelling and probably singing and simple games. Perhaps the girls had their own small stools to draw up around her. Water for washing and drinking from long-spouted earthenware pitchers (*ibrik*) would have been readily available from the Mission House cistern. The girls either had access to the ladies' "water-house" (*beit al-mayy*) next to the Mission House or to one specifically designed for them.[35]

Having no record to go on, we can only imagine further what the first morning was like. We can visualize girls brought by their curious mothers who peered through windows to see inside. Sarah assuredly greeted each of her thirty-three pupils ranging in age from four to nine at the door with a smile, while Raheel ushered them to their benches—youngest and smallest up front, older ones in back. They were mostly Greek Orthodox girls and a few Druze and Muslims, but still no Maronites as their priests continued to forbid them from attending. Once the door was closed and all were seated, Sarah would have allowed a minute or so for their excitement to subside before greeting the children in her fast-improving Arabic. Once she had their full attention, Syria's "only school-mistress" surely offered a simple prayer in Arabic giving thanks for their new school and asking God's blessing on the learning that then began. She may have provided a morning snack of perhaps fruit or yoghurt and bread, but since school was only in the morning the children could go home for their midday dinner.

Sarah and Eli moved their Sabbath School to her new schoolhouse. His touching account of his wife teaching one Sunday provides some reason for imagining the school as we have above.

> I found Mrs. Smith seated on a low stool, with six or eight bright little girls half-surrounding her, and in their eagerness to catch her instructions bending forward till their heads often formed a semicircle very near her own; while their lively faces, and animate inquiries showed the interest excited by the words that fell from her lips.[36]

Like the weekday school, the Sabbath school grew rapidly until two Americans and three native Syrians were needed to teach twenty to thirty children, mostly girls and chiefly from her weekday school. Sarah was able to translate a lesson from the *Union Questions* of the American Sunday School Union into Arabic during the week. The teachers then studied it around her dining table on Friday evenings in preparation for Sunday. She proudly affirmed that she "never had a more interesting and improving class than this one of untutored Arab girls." Echoing Eli's assessment of

Raheel, she found them easily a match for "those of the same age she had instructed in America." The Sabbath School was an educational bonus for Sarah's weekday pupils. They enjoyed reading and discussing in Arabic the histories and stories of the Old Testament that spurred on their learning to read. Girls who could read a little in English were committing up to forty verses of the Gospel of John to memory. They were more perseverant and exact than girls in Sarah's Norwich Sabbath School class.[37]

Despite her busy schedule, Sarah's health improved from what it had been in the winter. "Through the goodness of God," she wrote home, "my health continues perfect; and I am able to keep school every day from 8:00 to 11:00 a.m. My school interests me more and more every day, and I do not love to think of suspending it even for a few weeks, during the hot season."

Sarah's work was not confined to the classroom but extended outward as she sought to build relationships in the community. With Raheel's assistance, she began making afternoon visits to neighborhood women, especially the mothers of her pupils, for "religious conversation."[38] She won over many of her girls by providing clothes for the poorer children who otherwise could not attend. A wealthy Jewish mother begged Sarah to take her youngest daughter into the school provided she could skip religious exercises as "their prayers were of a different kind." The woman also asked that her older daughter be taught Italian, Arabic, and ornamental needlework. Sarah agreed even though it was an extra burden and very much enjoyed instructing these two sweet sisters. She was disturbed, however, to discover that a good deal of anti-Semitism had been instilled in her other pupils. In answer to her question in Sunday School, "Who was the first direct ancestor of the Jews," rather than answering "Adam," one little girl blurted out, "Satan!" Sarah surmised: "By general consent among young and old, this afflicted race seems to be condemned to ignominy here, and irretrievable destruction hereafter."

Except for the Christmas and Easter holidays, Sarah kept her school open five mornings a week. She complained about the other frequent religious festivals that pulled girls out of class and interrupted her teaching. She was always punctual whatever her commitments or her health—which was once again beginning to fray. She admitted that caring for the school took all that her strength would allow. Eli became increasingly concerned that his wife was overexerting herself. He frequently urged her to take another extended break, but she responded instead that once Rebecca Williams arrived, they could extend the school hours to a full day.[39]

The Summer of 1835

Despite the summer heat, Sarah kept both her weekday and Sunday schools operating through July. Finally, when it became just too hot and tiring for her, she gave in to Eli's pleas and closed the school on July 31, their second wedding anniversary. In her school's first-ever closing ceremony, she distributed rewards to thirty little girls. The audience included the American and English Consuls and a few "Arab" friends who "expressed much pleasure at seeing so many young natives in their clean dress." Sarah was especially pleased that a few of the more advanced scholars were able to read aloud some passages from the New Testament.

To accommodate a new printing press and simultaneously promote Sarah's health, Eli and Sarah moved once again. They took a ten-year lease on a large, airy, and comfortable two-story stone house further inland that was owned by "one of the wealthiest and most respected families in Beirut." Here Raheel had her own room. To Sarah's delight, the house was "back from the road" and "surrounded by gardens of mulberry trees."

Rebecca Williams had by August arrived in the Greek city of Smyrna (now Izmir, Turkey) on her way to Beirut. Sarah wrote to her there that during the last days of school "one head and a pair of hands were hardly sufficient for forty untutored Arabs." She warned Rebecca that the native people were "exceedingly social" and to expect "visits at all hours from persons of every rank and age. But we have reason to love them and do love them."[40]

August proved to be a busy month. The missionaries rejoiced in the marriage of the widower William Thomson to Maria Abbott, widow of the late British Consul, Peter Abbott. On the other hand, the Smiths were saddened by the departure of their closest friends, Isaac and Ann Bird, due to Ann's declining health. At the same time, they had to fire their Maltese servant, Ahmed, for not telling the truth, which they considered an intolerable breach by a trusted member of the household. Meanwhile, the Beirut populace was alarmed when some Christian youth were seized by the authorities and, instead of being conscripted into the all-Muslim army, were forced to work in Acre. Thirty frantic Christian refugees, mostly mothers and sisters begging protection for sons and brothers, gathered in and around the Smiths' home.[41]

Sarah and Eli escaped to the cooler mountain village of Alay for three weeks in September, but political unrest continued. When the Smiths returned home they were surprised to discover that the story of their offering sanctuary to fearful Christians had spread, as had their reputation for trustworthiness and treating people of all sects fairly. Fourteen Muslim refugees sat silently at the bottom of their stairs fearing that the Pasha would seize them and send them to the Bekaa Valley to join his soldiers. Their fear proved groundless, as the order applied only to those already enlisted. The following month a family from Mount Lebanon begged the Smiths "to take their valuables and best clothes for safe keeping," while some Druze sought sanctuary because other Druze had been seized and imprisoned following a slaying on the beach. Nine of them sought further protection by accompanying Sarah when she went aboard her donkey to reopen her new schoolhouse on September 28.[42]

The Beirut Female School opened the new school year with twenty girls, a good number for the first day. Yet, for some reason unbeknownst to Sarah, the Muslim girls did not return. Despite this momentary disappointment, Sarah was pleased to receive word that Matilda Whiting had launched her family school in her Jerusalem home with ten little Muslim girls. Sarah must have taken considerable satisfaction in the launch of this new school by her good friend. Meanwhile, William Thomson opened the all-male Beirut Seminary, a boarding school with six older boys that was a combination college and school of theology to prepare young men "to preach the gospel and explain and defend the Protestant faith."[43]

ASSISTED BY MISS WILLIAMS

Sarah was overjoyed and greatly relieved when her dear friend Rebecca Williams stepped ashore at last on November 19, 1835. After exchanging a warm embrace and sharing news of family and friends in Connecticut, Miss Williams cheerfully retired to the guest room. Sarah meanwhile dropped to her knees and prayed that she and Rebecca would "prove messengers of mercy to their degraded sisters." The next morning, Rebecca went to the school to begin sharing the workload. Sarah had already told Eli that she preferred that the school should benefit most from Rebecca's presence. Thus, instead of reducing her own hours, she kept the school open twice as many hours and continued to give to it nearly as much time as she had previously.[44]

Sarah and Rebecca both lacked formal teacher training, but there is strong evidence that they were acquainted with and used aspects of two educational methods developed in England and widely used in America in the early nineteenth century. The first was John Lancaster's "Lancastrian" or "Monitorial" system developed in England and then in vogue in the United States whereby older children tutored or "monitored" younger ones, freeing up the teacher to supervise them. This system had a multiplier effect and enabled Isaac Bird and William Goodell to quickly develop a network of thirteen indigenous "common schools" that served six hundred boys and one hundred girls on Mount Lebanon and in Beirut.

Evidence that the mission still employed this system is found in Isaac Bird's reporting that 325 pupils, mostly boys, were attending ten free common schools run by the Mission. With only one male Syrian teacher per common school, a school of eighty to ninety students could only have operated effectively with older "monitors" instructing younger children. In the same report Bird added that "about forty pupils, two of whom were Jewish, and many Mohammedans [sic] attended the highly prosperous female school originated and cherished by Mrs. Eli Smith." This brought the overall number of girls being taught by the missionaries in October 1835 to eighty-five. He also stated that there were then forty-six students, "mostly girls and a fourth of them Moslems," in the Sabbath School.[45]

Although the number of girls who were taught at one time or another in Sarah's female school was reported to be "nearly one hundred," average daily attendance was forty girls. Since she always had another full-time teacher plus maybe another volunteer and likely still had "one girl" (almost certainly Raheel) who was "far enough advanced to aid in teaching" in the Mission House classroom, the teacher/pupil ratio was much lower than in the (mostly male) common schools. Therefore, she had little need to resort to Lancaster's "monitor" system on a large scale, although she may have occasionally had a few older students assist in teaching younger girls. It is much more likely, however, that the two women made greater use of Samuel Wilderspin's system for educating poor young children.[46]

WILDERSPIN'S INFANT EDUCATION

There is direct and indirect evidence that Sarah Smith, and by inference, Rebecca Williams too, were both very familiar with Samuel

Wilderspin's treatise *On the Importance of Educating the Infant Poor*. Wilderspin's ultimate goal in educating poor children was likewise to save their souls as well as teach them the fundamentals. Published in London in 1820, the book was widely read in America, especially by pious Christians such as Sarah. She may well have applied Wilderspin's methods in teaching the Mohegan children, and if so, would have already passed them along to Rebecca.

Sarah's first direct reference to applying Wilderspin's methods in Syria is a December 14, 1835 letter, probably to her sister Faith, in which she writes of the difficulty of teaching *"infant school lessons"* without adequate children's literature in Arabic. (The italicization represents Sarah's use of underlining in her letters to accentuate a point.) In another letter that same month to her niece Mary, whom she hoped would follow in her footsteps, there is an even more direct reference: "I think that the *infant school system* is admirably adapted to the uninformed and undisciplined habits of this country, and I hope you will familiarize yourself with it, to a great extent," inferring that Wilderspin's book was readily available to Mary. The third reference is in a letter to Martha Temple, a missionary wife starting a school for forty Armenian girls in Smyrna, in which Sarah despairs of

> doing anything in the way of infant schools, because the Arabic language cannot be simplified under existing prejudices. If every hymn and little story must be dressed up in the august habiliments of [classical Arabic], what child of three and six years old will be wiser and better for them?[47]

In all three cases—Wilderspin's London Infant School and Sarah's Mohegan and Beirut schools—the pupils were needy and disadvantaged. Wilderspin taught 150 "poor" children ages eighteen months to seven years. Sarah taught "grossly neglected and much degraded" Indian children in her Mohegan School. In Syria, she found that Wilderspin's system could be "admirably adapted" to teach her "benighted" and "indigent" Syrian girls.[48]

There is also anecdotal evidence that Sarah adapted Wilderspin's methods in Beirut. For instance, he states that it is paramount to establish order in the classroom so the "children should have some idea of it," and stick to a strict schedule each day. Sarah agreed that order was essential for children "so ignorant and so unaccustomed to the restraints of a school; who had so little relish for study, and whose parents were ignorant of the value of education." To maintain order without instilling "a disgust for the place of instruction" that would keep them away, she established rules. These were enforced, not with a whip like her first teacher had used in Norwich, nor even by Wilderspin's "pat on the hand," but rather by positive reinforcement. Emulating the "Rewards of Merit" issued by her two young progressive teachers in Norwich, Sarah placed debit and credit marks on a blackboard and then rewarded obliging pupils with clothing items she had sewn herself. "Her girls soon learned to understand and regard this system and it made them love school the better," her husband Eli testified. "A more orderly collection of cheerful faces was not often found in a school-house in a Christian land."[49]

Sarah possessed the qualities Wilderspin called for in a teacher. "The mind of a child was like a blank sheet of paper," he wrote, but it took more than "a few printed lessons to give children ideas and lay a religious and virtuous foundation." It took a teacher who possessed—and displayed— "much patience, gentleness, perseverance, self-possession, energy, knowledge of human nature and, above all, piety, so the children see them shine forth in her conduct, character and patience." Wilderspin surely would have found Sarah "a fit and proper person to manage an infant school."[50]

At first Sarah taught only sewing and "a little reading from the New Testament," but soon her curriculum included "reading, spelling, geography, first lessons in arithmetic, Scripture questions, the

English language, and sacred music." Lacking children's literature in Arabic, she likely turned to Wilderspin's inventory of teaching methods and materials, which she could adopt or adapt for lessons in these basic subjects. For instance, Wilderspin printed each letter of the alphabet on a large sheet of paper, placed them against the wall, and had the children fetch a certain letter until each child had identified them all. To teach writing, the children were given slates with the letters "engraved" so they could trace them. He did the same with numbers. Sarah may well have used these same techniques plus needlework to teach reading, writing, spelling, and arithmetic—but she had the added challenge of teaching in *two* languages with very different letters and numbers.[51]

Wilderspin taught "arithmetic tables with one-inch cubes of wood." Pupils would say the number of cubes before them; then add to or subtract from them, saying the number remaining. For multiplication, the cubes were arranged in rows of ten so the children saw how eight rows of ten equaled eighty, etc. Sarah could have had native craftsmen make such aids. She, like Wilderspin, taught using pictures. To teach Scripture, she had illustrations of biblical stories published in London and America: "Joseph and his brethren; Christ raising Lazarus; the Nativity and flight to Egypt; Christ baptized by John; Jesus curing the blind and lame; the Last Supper, Crucifixion, Resurrection, etc."[52]

Growing Health Concerns

The 1835 rainy season came early, and November began with the second of two violent storms. Sarah found it "sublime and terrifying to watch the lightning's play over the deep blue sea; and during the long night listen to the thunder's roar reverberating through Mount Lebanon." However, as the rain continued, the days and nights became less awe-inspiring and more beset with a bone-chilling dampness. Sarah became fatigued and did not feel well. The

Sarah and Her Sisters | 55

...ission and the anniversary of her brother Peter's ... to her being uncharacteristically depressed by year's end. Her daily religious exercises failed to inspire her, and her prayers lacked fervor. This gloominess carried over into the New Year. On January 3, 1836, she wrote home that she shuddered to think that her parents might die while she was away and dwelt on the magnitude of her sins and her unworthiness to be a missionary. She feared she might never enter heaven. When Jabez Huntington expressed concern for his daughter's health in his next letter, Sarah replied that she did not believe she was "in danger at present; as I am almost uniformly calm and quiet." Still her "duties were arduous." When she completed the week, she felt as if she had to "take a long breath."[53]

By the second anniversary of her arrival in Syria, Sarah's spirits had somewhat improved. On January 28, 1836 she wrote to a childhood friend, also named Mary, that she was "entirely happy and felt blessed in her marriage relationship." She loved her "pleasant residence overlooking the illimitable sea towards the setting sun and friends left behind." Beirut was increasingly important and she would not exchange her mission station for any in America. Yet she lamented "the absence of God's Holy Spirit in our hearts and those of our neighbors and friends... (w)ithout which our planting and watering will be in vain." In February she wrote to her brother Edward that she was "grateful for a comfortable degree of bodily vigor and mental composure" and she welcomed "the mildness of spring, the time of the singing of birds." But she ominously confided to a cousin in Philadelphia that she was

> suffering from a severe cold upon my lungs from sitting within the cold, damp walls of our school-house. Our exposures of this kind in the winter are very great. I have had an incessant and somewhat painful cough for some days, but I think it is now breaking up. This urges

me to make some early provision against a simi[...] ter—if I should live.[54]

Sarah later provided more details of her difficult fall and win ter. "Soon after the rains commenced, the terrace [roof?] of our newly-made school house was broken up, and its walls soaked; and I there caught a severe cold, which produced a tight and violent cough." She took to bed for a few days, but her "cough continued through the whole winter, weakening my lungs." Still, "feeling no anxiety," she took no precautionary measures and continued her labors as usual.[55] Sarah kept to an incredibly busy schedule throughout the winter, rising at 4:30 a.m. and "communing with God in the stillness of the morning." After breakfast she taught school for three hours each weekday morning and, after a lunch recess, for a similar period in the afternoon. Every other day she studied Arabic and on alternate days translated a portion of her Arabic grammar into English. She took daily lessons in Italian and translated the weekly Sunday school lesson into Arabic. Each week, she attended a Mission meeting and two female prayer meetings and still managed to answer fifteen to twenty letters with every arrival of the mail by ship. Her Beirut family by then consisted of herself, Eli, Raheel, the still unnamed Abyssinian girl, three servants, four unnamed mission associates, and occasional guests. Eli marveled at how she accomplished all she did and could not have been prouder of her ability to "converse acceptably on most topics" in Arabic. Despite her distaste for language study, she mastered difficulties many foreigners never could.[56]

Keeping On

By February of 1836 Rebecca Williams had become familiar enough with the language that she could manage the school's afternoon sessions by herself. Sarah, somewhat recovered from her coughing and weakness, was then freed up to visit the mothers of her

Sarah and Her Sisters | 57

pupils to engage in "religious conversation" that would lay a foundation for their possible conversion to Protestantism. "But alas!" she complained:

> I cannot, as in America, go from house to house alone. Many are within the city walls. I must go upon my donkey, attended by a man servant, and can make only one, or two calls in one excursion. There is no dropping in unobserved here. Our presence attracts all the neighborhood, and I have often had quite a congregation when I went to see one only.[57]

It was still a challenge for Sarah to communicate in Arabic. Eli wrote that she had to be careful not to "excite the apprehensions and prejudices of her hosts, thus defeating her objective." Eli believed that by visiting the homes of her more indigent pupils and organizing other missionary wives to "enter the cellars and hovels of the needy with a little charity in hand," Sarah was establishing a valuable precedent for spreading the gospel. Rather than exciting jealousies, these missionaries were providing "bodily relief in a proper manner," thereby "winning women over, while gaining the confidence and applause of the community." Sarah admitted that it would be a long time before her effort bore fruit, but she was committed to trying it as long as she was able.[58]

That winter Sarah read the first edition of *A Memoir of Mrs. Harriet W. Winslow, Combining a Sketch of the Ceylon Mission* while in bed recuperating from her cough. She was struck by the parallels between Harriet's life and her own. Both women had grown up in Norwich in Congregational families. Both taught Sabbath school and both founded schools for poor children in Norwich. Each married a missionary who took her to live and work in Asia, where she had to learn a difficult language. Each began a girls' school despite opposition from indigenous religious leaders. Each suffered from chronic health problems. Harriet died in childbirth in Ceylon at the age of thirty-seven in 1833, the year Sarah met Eli. Would Sarah suffer a similar fate? Little did she imagine that within a decade the *Memoir of Mrs. Sarah L. Huntington Smith of the Mission in Syria* would also become a national best seller, but with an even more dramatic ending.[59]

Had Sarah been born a decade later she likely would have had a complete secondary education as the number of more advanced female schools, commonly called "seminaries," in the United States grew rapidly in the last three quarters of the nineteenth century. This development occurred even in her hometown of Norwich, where a new female academy opened in 1828. Before leaving for Beirut, she had taken "a deep interest" in the school and in a "young lady" who taught there who had been in her prayer circle.[60]

On February 26, 1836 she wrote a letter to the Norwich girls fortunate enough to attend the school "on the great subject of missions." Revealing her own privileged background and pietistic prejudices, Sarah contrasted their lives with those of Syrian girls. They as Americans, Sarah said, are "neatly dressed, and well supplied with books, paper and everything necessary for pursuing their studies." At home they are treated with "kindness, gentleness and respect" and "encouraged to improve themselves"; whereas girls there, although having "a fine form and beautiful face, take no delight in intellectual or moral improvement, nor are they attentive to personal cleanliness or neat and tasteful in their dress." They lack books and other "means of moral or intellectual improvement," because being able to read and write is "a serious obstacle to marriage, the main objective of their parents." Surprisingly, "abhorrence of learning is strongest among the higher classes," whereas, the girls sent to her school were almost all poor. Syrian females were loved within their families, but "the father and brothers sit and smoke in one room, showing little respect for the mother and sisters relegated to another room to gossip about some mode of dress, or something quite as foolish."

Sarah challenged the young ladies of Norwich to become "laborers to cultivate this field of unhappy females in Syria" or elsewhere abroad or even in America. But to do so they had to forget all romantic notions regarding missionary service. It was hard work that required serious spiritual preparation and intellectual study, especially of foreign languages. She wrote of the "inequality of condition and privileges" of girls in desolate places like "Jerusalem, Hebron, Nazareth, Sychar, Damascus, Tyre, Sidon, Yafa... and the villages of Mount Lebanon." She then asked: "Why cannot one missionary family and one female teacher be stationed at every one of these places? You, my dear young friends of the Norwich Female Academy," she concluded, "are called upon to answer this question."[61]

Certainly, missionary life was demanding, particularly the ongoing challenge of being far from family. Sarah was therefore heartened when the first steam packet ships began carrying mail from abroad in record time. One such state-of-the-art vessel, which had originated in England, made it to Beirut from Alexandria, Egypt, in "only forty-eight hours." She wrote of this historic event to her brother Edward saying: "It is the first of a line which is to visit Beirut once a month. We begin to feel a great deal nearer to you than formerly."

Despite missing her family and suffering ongoing health challenges, Sarah kept to her demanding schedule, which included a revolving door of houseguests. While "taking medicine for an uncomfortable cough," she was a week later hosting an Anglican clergyman "in feeble health." Arriving in good health a week after that were the Rev. John Lanneau of South Carolina, and the Rev. Story Hebard and Miss Betsey Tilden, both from New Hampshire. Working with William Thomson in his new Beirut Boys' Seminary, Hebard "excited much interest by giving lectures on electricity and pneumatics, accompanied by experiments." Many of "the first people in Beirut attended his classes," as did the male and female students. Both Hebard and Tilden would soon play important roles in the further education of youth in Syria.[62]

Story Hebard brought letters from Sarah's father, who was again inquiring about her health. Sarah responded that, while it had been excellent after her return from Jerusalem the previous spring, her severe cough was continuing as a "consequence of exposure within the damp walls of our school-house." Nevertheless, she was confined only a day or two. Besides, as her father well knew, her lungs were "not her weak part." She was eating only "a very little of almost any kind of food and was perfectly well and happy," but had to avoid too much exertion. Meanwhile, their "press, schools, preaching, conversation and other social intercourse" kept her and Eli busy from morning to night. They felt "that a broad foundation was being laid, upon which, at some future day—God knows when—a glorious superstructure will be raised." She asked her father, as a member of the American Board, to "send us as many more as you can to help us. The field is wide. There are no idlers here."[63]

Ebbing Strength

Sarah's comment about there being "no idlers" in the mission field applied to herself most of all. During the longer, sun-filled days of spring, the steady decline in her health and physical appearance became alarming. She was still, with Rebecca's assistance, instructing twenty to twenty-five of the forty girls then enrolled in their school. William Thomson again worried that while "she possessed an energy which urged her on, her labors were often too arduous for her feeble frame." She used every "fragment of time. Nothing was lost." Yet, "for several months she seemed to be doing her last work, and her thoughts and conversation were much on heavenly things."[64]

As Sarah's Arabic improved, she came to love the language. She even thought she could spend her whole time reading and studying it. Delighted to read of the successful start of Matilda Whiting's read. In another instance, Raheel went home to find her little sister, Keffa, giving their mother a reading lesson. "It was affecting," Sarah wrote, "to see the six-year-old standing at her mother's knee as her teacher. The whole family is under our influence!" Yet a major hindrance was the lack of books. Even Raheel, who was "advancing steadily in intelligence and knowledge, has no book but the Bible to read—not one." Sarah was translating for her excerpts from *The Child's Book on the Soul and the Memoir of Mary Lathrop* published by the American Tract Society. "Oral instruction is a slow process," she complained. She had to give "lessons in geography on the globe, but how much they forget for want of books in their hands. I never fully realized the great privileges of American youth." Sarah viewed her work as the start of a long chain of events with herself being "assigned only a few links." Still she was hopeful that others, eventually, would carry on the work.[66]

EXHAUSTION AND ALARM

As spring advanced, Sarah began to cough up large amounts of blood and suddenly became exhausted. When her pulse rose to 110 beats a minute, Eli, greatly alarmed, called in the English physician, Dr. Whitely. He "examined her lungs with the stethoscope and pronounced them diseased; though in what way, and to what extent, he did not positively determine." Whitely urged that she immediately relinquish all her work and rest. Sarah complied and improved slightly, but she grew more and more resigned to her fate. Even though she was consumed by fever, she showed an odd reluctance to seek divine healing; Eli knew of only one instance when "she prayed for recovery during the whole of her sickness."[67]

Sarah exhibited all the symptoms of pulmonary tuberculosis, a disease identified forty-six years later as being caused by a slow-growing bacterium that thrives in the lungs. In Sarah's day it was called "consumption," a communicable and usually fatal disease prevalent throughout the world at the time. As she often complained, her condition was made worse by the dampness of the Syrian winter. She may have become infected in Beirut, but more likely before. Perhaps she contracted it while working closely with members of the Mohegan tribe, which had been decimated by disease. If it was an earlier infection, then it might have surfaced the summer before she met Eli when she feared "my constitution was so injured by an illness that I almost relinquished the expectations of becoming a missionary."[68]

Near the close of the school year, Sarah set aside her prescribed rest and relaxation long enough to arrange an arduous day of examinations for her pupils. Wishing them to exhibit what they had accomplished, as well as develop self-confidence, Sarah and Rebecca administered exams to all forty girls in the presence of "members of the mission, several parents and other female friends" who filled the schoolroom. Eli recorded that the girls were examined in all the subjects taught: reading, spelling, geography, arithmetic, Scripture, English, and music. Following the examinations, Martha Dodge gave a brief address, after which the mothers came forward to thank the teachers for all they had done for their daughters.

The school exams left Sarah exhausted, but with a sense of satisfaction and closure. Physically and emotionally unable to continue teaching into late May, she turned her beloved Beirut Female School over to her trusted and capable friend, Rebecca Williams, and retired to her home. Her worsening condition only added to the gloom that swept through the mission community when a new outbreak of the Black Plague forced them to suspend all activities and flee to safety in the mountains.[69]

Meanwhile, Eli had come to an important juncture in his work. He had by then painstakingly gathered samples of Arabic calligraphy, letters, punctuation marks, and numerals that could be easily read by the Syrian populace. From these he set about creating a more complete and elegant font of Arabic type for the Mission Press that conformed to native taste. The next step was to take those samples to Smyrna to have them engraved onto copper plates. These, in turn, would be taken to Germany and cast as movable metal type in Arabic. Since Dr. Whitely believed that a sea voyage would be the best thing for Sarah's health and would remove her from all her cares and responsibilities, it was decided that she would accompany Eli to Smyrna and, if possible, continue on to Connecticut to recuperate.[70]

Fateful Voyage

Eli booked passage on a Prussian schooner bound for Smyrna. With aching hearts, he and Sarah, with the help of servants, packed their trunks with many more clothes and personal articles than they needed. Hoping to return in one or two years, they covered and stored their furniture. Sarah had become so strongly attached to Raheel that she had set her heart on taking her with them to America as a legally adopted daughter. Understandably, Raheel's parents were opposed to the idea. Therefore, one of Sarah's final acts before leaving was to entrust the ten-year-old girl to Rebecca's care. Sarah's separation from the young girl she now considered her only child was the most difficult aspect of her departure.

Because most of the missionaries had fled the city to avoid the plague, only a few native friends, neighbors, and servants gathered in the Smiths' empty parlor on Friday afternoon, June 10, for a sorrowful farewell. Their Druze neighbors came in and sat down. Eli made a short speech and prayed in Arabic. He later recalled: "Every heart seemed ready to burst with grief, and all wept together." It was especially hard on the Smiths' young translator and Sarah's Arabic teacher, Antonio, who, "inconsolable, seized their hands and sobbed violently." Sarah then went up to Rebecca's room where the two wept and prayed together. Unable to say one last goodbye, Sarah came downstairs and exited the house, only to have a Muslim servant burst into tears as he helped her on to her little donkey before leading them both down the hill to the waiting schooner. The fragile *Staffetta Prusiana* set sail for Smyrna the next day with five passengers, including several from England, the Prussian captain, and his crew of eight.

Once at sea, Sarah at first showed some improvement, but was very seasick. Strong westerly winds forced the captain to follow the same route charted by the Alexandrian captain taking the Apostle Paul to Rome eighteen centuries before, first sailing due north and then turning west under the lee of Cyprus. Unfortunately, this voyage would suffer a fate similar to Saint Paul's. On the evening of June 15, Sarah and Eli were awoken by a crash when the ship, fighting strong head winds, struck a reef. Eli ran up on deck leaving Sarah to pray for the lives of all on board. Subsequent violent crashes threatened to destroy the vessel. Amid much confusion, Eli called for Sarah to come up on deck as the crew attempted to lower its longboat while waves broke over the deck. When they finally succeeded, Eli helped Sarah into the boat as the badly damaged schooner took on water. The passengers, crew, and captain, fourteen in all, somehow managed to get into the boat too. Eli took command from the panicky captain and ordered the crew members to row toward the North Star.

Fortunately, the wind ceased and the waves subsided as they rowed through the darkness to a sandy cape extending eight to ten miles out to sea. Finding a break in the surf, they could beach the boat and step ashore on a desolate coastline, thankful to be alive. The drenched and feeble Sarah was made as comfortable as possible behind a makeshift windbreak on the damp sand. Meanwhile, crew members returned to the ship and retrieved, among other items, the Smiths' soaked mattresses and Eli's travelling bag, razors, and purse. Tragically, their writing desks and chests went to the bottom of the sea, containing all of Eli's valuable books, manuscripts, carefully collected Arabic fonts, a rare history of Syria, invaluable travel journals, and sermons. Sarah's detailed journals and letters, a sum of money, and their medicine chest were also lost.[71]

MAROONED

At dawn the party found itself on a deserted, treeless beach with only unpalatable sailors' hardtack to eat. Seeking shelter from the sun, they miraculously sighted and hailed an Egyptian cargo vessel that took them on board. The surly captain initially offered to take them to Cyprus, but instead sailed further west and anchored in a deserted harbor Eli later identified as Silifke (Turkey). The Egyptians gave them a few small fish fried in oil, which Sarah ate eagerly, before he extorted a large sum to take the stranded passengers to the nearest inhabited place. After two days on the Egyptian ship and two nights sleeping on shore under a large "*kharoob*" [sic] tree where they cooked a dinner of rice and oil, it became apparent that their host was trifling with them. He refused to give them more rice without being paid more, leading Eli and some of the sailors to set out in search of another ship.[72]

In the ensuing days, the Prussian captain, seeking to rescue himself as well as his crew and passengers, ventured to the nearby harbor to secure a firm contract for transport. Sarah, ever weakening, was helped to the ruins of a stone stable where she spent a sorrowful thirty-fourth birthday on her mattress spread on an earthen floor. Her birthday was made a little brighter by a sailor's gift of a few lumps of sugar and some tea that Mr. Stobart, an evangelical English passenger, had rescued from the wreck. Once on board a small Greek ship whose captain had agreed to take them westward on to the Greek island of Evia (Euboea) for a reasonable fee, Sarah, realizing that her days were numbered, spent the daylight hours on deck under a large umbrella salvaged from the schooner. At night she slept in a small cabin in the stern while Eli worried that the small ship with little ballast would founder in the strong winds.

Sarah's cough and seasickness worsened, leaving her so exhausted they both feared she would not see the next dawn. One of their fellow passengers, a young Englishman apparently ill with syphilis, did not make it through the first night and was buried at sea. To make matters worse, the ship was infested with fleas. Meals consisting mostly of dry bread, pounded wheat, oil, onions, and carobs were served in two bowls and eaten with spoons shared among the twenty-two people on board. Being poor navigators and unsure of their new craft's seaworthiness, the crew hugged the coast and put into harbors every night, thus lengthening the voyage.

On June 25 the ship at last anchored in the busy harbor of Karistos under *Castello Rosso*, the historic red Crusaders' castle. Here they booked passage with a kindly Greek captain and transferred to his ship to take them back eastward to Rhoades. That schooner was so filthy and their cabin so small that Sarah spent the two-day trip on deck despite strong, but apparently favorable winds. Finding no better vessel in Rhoades after a three-day stopover, Sarah, whose pulse had quickened and whose lungs continued to fail, was carried back to the same vessel in a chair and they continued north toward Smyrna.[73]

Conditions aboard ship had not improved. A fierce headwind beset them yet again. The perpetual motion and filth of the ship made this final leg of the interrupted journey indescribably tedious and wearisome for Sarah. Her condition worsened with nights of coughing and vomiting. Under an awning on deck during the day, she was seldom able to sit up, read, or converse, other than dictate to Eli her thoughts for her new journal. He wondered how she could endure such suffering. After ten more days at sea, the ship landed on the Greek island of Chios, still seventy miles west of Smyrna. Sarah was given her first blanket since the shipwreck twenty-seven days before. After crossing a narrow strait, the Smiths probably covered the last fifty miles overland by carriage, reaching Smyrna on July 13, 1836, thirty-three days after departing Beirut.

Fig. 14 – The schooner *Staffetta Prusiana* on which Eli and Sarah Smith
began their fateful voyage to Smyrna in June 1836
may have resembled the schooner *Henrietta* shown here.

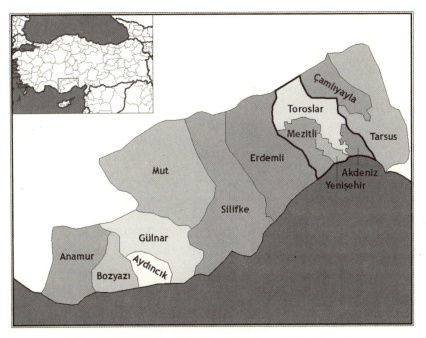

Fig. 15 – Map of Turkish coast showing Silifke (center)
where Eli, Sarah and their party were marooned.

"Forever with the Lord"

Upon their arrival the Smiths were joyfully received by their missionary colleagues Daniel and Martha Temple, who bestowed every care in settling Sarah comfortably in their home. They summoned the best physician available, who prescribed an appropriate regimen. It was hoped that by resting there she would revive enough to continue her journey home to Norwich. However, the treatment failed to alleviate her pulmonary distress. Sarah's depression deepened as her symptoms worsened. Eli worried about her "spiritual darkness," yet hoped she could rally and live through the winter.

To escape frequent visits by well-meaning friends, Eli hired a sedan chair and moved Sarah on August 7 to a summer home offered by English friends in the nearby village of Boojah. In these more restful surroundings her spirits improved momentarily. She read her Bible, prayed, dictated a few pages of her new journal, and wrote some letters. Grieving that after "laboring unremittingly" she would be called away from her mission work, Eli recorded Sarah's last days and hours in the melodramatic style of the times. He wrote that she soon became despondent, dwelling on all her sins since childhood until he counseled her to focus instead on God's forgiveness, thus bringing her some resolution. Believing that it would be a relief to get to heaven, she set about arranging her worldly affairs with renewed hope. Eli sometimes felt he "could not let her go," to which she replied that she had "given up all her friends except him."

Eli thought Sarah's physician was trying to spare her from the seriousness of her condition, but she was already well aware of it. In fact, when she learned that an unidentified American friend nearby was also dying of "consumption," she asked to see him privately to prepare him for his death. He later remarked she was the only person who had told him of his danger. Sarah's coughing continued, and her pulse grew more rapid. She became feverish and restless, at times lapsing into delirium. Eli remained at her bedside day and

Sarah and Her Sisters | 71

night, adjusting her pillow after each coughing spell. Awakening suddenly one midnight, she told him that her letters to her family ought to be made available to her friends. Then she said she "would rather be dying here on missionary ground, than be in health at home." Her wish was about to be fulfilled.

On Wednesday, September 21, the third anniversary of the Smiths' departure from Boston, Sarah started fading in and out of consciousness. She clung to life until the afternoon of September 30 when Eli, perceiving from the "death-like coldness" of her hand that "her hour was come," gathered the household, including her trusted Druze servant, at her bedside. They all wept openly. That evening Sarah opened her eyes and smiled at Eli with affection. Bending over, he kissed her lips and she returned his token of love for her. Gradually her heart ceased beating and, in Eli's words, "her soul took its final departure to be forever with the Lord."[74]

The next day, flags on American ships in the harbor were lowered to half-mast. Missionaries and many of the English residents "assembled at Mr. Adger's home" at 10:00 o'clock for a funeral service in which Mr. Temple, a fellow Congregationalist, "addressed them in a most appropriate and impressive manner and prayed." Then a large procession, including ladies who broke "with the immemorial custom in Smyrna of not attending funerals," followed Sarah's coffin to the quiet Anglican churchyard in Boojah. There, at Eli's request, the Anglican priest, the Rev. Mr. Lewis, read the solemn funeral service of the Church of England. Then, as those assembled sang: "Unveil thy bosom, faithful tomb/Take this new treasure to thy trust/And give these sacred relics room/To slumber in the silent dust," Sarah Lanman Huntington Smith's earthly remains were laid to rest.[75]

Sarah's life was cut short at age thirty-four, but her story and work lived on. In accordance with her dying wish, her letters to her family were assembled by the Rev. Edward Hooker, husband of her sister Faith, and published in 1839 as a popular missionary memoir. Moreover, the school she founded began a new chapter, which is where we turn next.

Fig. 16 – Memorial stone marking site of girls' school built in 1835 by Mrs. Tod for its first teacher, Sarah L. Smith.

Fig. 17 – Marker Eli placed on Sarah's grave in Bujah, Turkey reads: "Sarah Lanman Smith, Wife of The Rev. Eli Smith, who was born in Norwich, Conn. June 18, 1802. To Benevolent Efforts for the youth and the ignorant in her native city; for the neglected remnant of the its aboriginal inhabitants and for the benighted females of Syria, she devoted all her ardent expansive and untiring energies as a service of Christ until, sinking under her missionary labors at Beyroot, she was brought hither and died in triumphant faith, Sept. 30, 1836/ AE 34."

CHAPTER TWO

Sarah's Successors in Beirut (1836–1858)

We are doing a little in this work and perhaps, if faithful, we shall rest in heaven and others will come and take our places and our work.

Sarah L. Smith to Mrs. David Temple
Beirut, May 6, 1836

As noted in the prologue, Sarah Smith's Beirut Female School was not, as is commonly thought, the first school for girls in Ottoman Syria, but it *was* the first girls-only school housed in a one-room schoolhouse modeled on an American grammar school of the time.[1] Sarah was the first American to instruct indigenous girls in Arabic. She taught girls of different ages a variety of academic subjects and basic living skills that broadened their outlook on life, opening doors that had not been accessible to their mothers and grandmothers. Her school was orderly and became well established, operating on a regular weekday schedule, first for three hours and then for six hours a day from October through July except for religious festivals and holidays.

These were some of the unique features of Sarah's first-of-its-kind school. She elevated female education in Beirut to a whole new level and gave it greater importance. Mothers and fathers saw how their daughters benefited. Although Sarah's tenure was short, she lit a torch for female education in the Arabic-speaking world that was carried forward, as she had prayed it would be, by a "long chain" of missionary teachers and their students. That legacy began with the next "links," Rebecca Williams and Betsey Tilden, both assisted by Raheel Atta.

Rebecca Williams Hebard (1836–1840)

As Sarah's health declined, Rebecca Williams carried more of the teaching load in the school until, at Sarah's departure in June, she, for the second time, assumed full responsibility for a weekday school and Sunday school started by her colleague and mentor. Assisted by ten-year-old Raheel, Rebecca carried on six-and-a-half-hour days, broken only by a half-hour recess for the girls to play in the mission garden. Of her forty regular day students, a quarter also enrolled during the summer session that extended into August. Final exams were given in August, after which the school was closed until October. During that two-month break, Eli and Sarah's matchmaking bore fruit when, in October 1836 to the delight of the entire mission family, thirty-two-year-old Story Hebard from Lebanon, New Hampshire married in the shadow of Mount Lebanon twenty-seven-year-old Rebecca Williams of Lebanon, Connecticut.

There is no doubt that Story fell deeply in love with Rebecca, just as Eli had over time grown to love Sarah very deeply. That Rebecca was equally taken with him was evident in her ready acceptance of his proposal. They had a good deal in common. Both were New England Protestants, both were teachers, and both felt a strong calling to their work as missionaries. On their honeymoon, the Hebards returned to Mount Lebanon where they had once picnicked with the Smiths. From there they climbed to the renowned Cedars of Lebanon before descending into the Bekaa Valley to walk among the Roman ruins in Baalbek. When they returned to Beirut, the widow Martha Dodge, just returned from her summer school for illiterate Druze girls in Alay, invited the Hebards, Raheel, and another unnamed girl of six or seven (possibly the Abyssinian girl?) to move in with her and her two daughters for the winter.[2]

After Greek Orthodox clerics threatened parents with excommunication if they sent their daughters to the female school, only a few girls showed up when Rebecca, Martha, and Raheel reopened the school in late October. Mysteriously, only one Muslim student returned. Nonetheless, enrollment gradually increased to a record forty-five girls with an average of twenty-five attending daily. The girls remained very fond of their school and continued to work hard. The credit and debit system Sarah had introduced still functioned very well, so Rebecca never had to punish a girl for disobeying the rules. Religious instruction continued and most of the girls attended the Sabbath school and Arabic church service, but there were no religious conversions.

Outside school hours, Rebecca continued Sarah's practice of sewing with Raheel, who was by then very advanced in needlepoint. Two years after Sarah's death, Raheel stitched with red, green, and blue thread and sent to "the parents of her former beloved Teacher, Mrs. Sarah L. Smith" in Norwich a beautiful linen sampler "wrought in the Beyroot Female School." She dated and signed it "1838 — Raheel Atta" and stitched on it the entire English and Arabic alphabets (upper and lower case), the numbers 1 to 9 and 0, and two verses of a hymn. "Weep not for the saint that ascends to partake of the joys of the sky," it began, ending, "for she has found her reward and her refuge in heaven."[3]

Rebecca also taught English to another five girls and gave the two Jewish sisters Sarah had begun teaching Italian lessons using the Old Testament as the text, and Arabic using the New Testament. The Jewish girls enjoyed singing the Psalms of David with the other pupils. Rebecca also continued the native Sabbath School which had been merged with the English Sabbath School since some of her students were now strong enough in English that they could take their

Fig. 18 – Portraits of Rebecca Williams and Rev. Story Hebard reproduced in *Rebecca Williams Hebard of Lebanon, Connecticut: Missionary in Beirut, Syria and to the Druzes of Mount Lebanon – 1835-1840* by Samuel H. Williams.

Fig. 19 – Narrow Bab ed Dirkeh stone gate well known to Sarah and Rebecca.

Fig. 20 – Druze girls taught by Martha Dodge and Rebecca Williams in Alay might have worn on special occasions native costumes featuring an elaborate *"tantour"* headdress.

Sunday lessons alongside the American and English pupils. Others took their Sabbath School lessons separately in Arabic in a different room. In all, eighteen day students came on Sundays, twice the number of boys from the boys' seminary.[4]

Rebecca and Story supported one another's work, hers in the girls' school and his in the boys' seminary. They spent their weekdays teaching followed by language study when she was not making dresses, mending, instructing their two girls, or attending to other domestic duties. When Story succeeded William Thomson as principal of the boys' seminary early in 1837, the Hebards moved into the boys' school where Rebecca added matron duties to her teaching, studying and domestic chores.[5]

The Hebards spent the summer of 1837 in the mountain village of Alay with other missionaries. Rebecca assisted Martha Dodge who resumed her summer school teaching Druze peasant girls to read from the Bible, learn the Ten Commandments, and memorize the Westminster Shorter Catechism so they could recite the answers to a list of up to 104 religious questions.[6] Rebecca reported that the girls, who lived under oppressive rulers, appreciated receiving such instruction as there were "no schools for the children, no books, no religious teachers, and no means of enlightening their minds, improving their intellects or purifying their hearts."[7]

With limited medical knowledge and equipped with only two medical books and a medicine chest, Rebecca found herself cast in the role of school nurse as well as teacher. Her summer home was often filled with women and girls seeking treatment for their illnesses. She did what she could for her patients and took satisfaction in being "the means of relieving a great deal of suffering of mothers and children alike." By late September, when she and Martha turned instruction over to a Druze teacher, six or seven girls could read in the New Testament and answer basic questions on Protestant doctrine.[8]

Rebecca and Martha continued to share the teaching in the female school until February 1837 when Martha, at age twenty-seven a widow of two years, married the Rev. John Paxton, a recent widower. In December she gave birth to her third daughter, Martha Sarah Paxton. The Paxtons returned to America in May 1838 where John continued his ministry. Rebecca was grateful when Miss Roberta Badger, a British citizen hired by the Board in December 1837, took Martha's place. With Raheel's help, the two teachers kept the school operating normally.[9]

Hanover, New Hampshire native Betsey Tilden, the second unmarried female teacher after Rebecca to be sent to Syria, returned from teaching in Jerusalem in the spring of 1838 to assist Story Hebard in the Beirut Boys' Seminary.[10] In addition to teaching the boys mathematics and reading, she found time to teach basic arithmetic to girls in the female school. In comparison to the school in Jerusalem, she found the Beirut girls' school larger and more promising. Confirming that Rebecca had by then mastered a good deal of her new language, Betsey noted that while the male boarding students learned in both Arabic and English, instruction for the female day scholars was in Arabic only.[11]

Rebecca remained in good health until her third summer in the mountains, when she began to experience fatigue and pains on her left side. Upon resuming school in Beirut in October, she developed a chill. In November 1839, the fourth anniversary of her arrival in Beirut, her husband, Story, began journaling the daily progression of a serious but unnamed illness that Dr. Whitely could not adequately treat. After three months of intensifying pain and suffering, she summoned the native seminary boys to her bedside and urged them to "let their light shine by loving one another." Many tears were shed in a scene that was reminiscent of that around Sarah's deathbed. Firm in her faith, Rebecca Williams Hebard died on February 18, 1840 at the age of thirty-three and was laid to rest in the Mission Cemetery near her girls' school. Rebecca had taught in

Sarah's Beirut Female School for almost four years and, for three of those years, managed it on her own.[12]

Distraught over his young wife's death, Story Hebard suffered a mental and physical breakdown. He was given a furlough to recover but died in Malta on his way home to New England. Fourteen-year-old Raheel, now grieving the loss of two loving guardians, continued to assist Rebecca's replacements, thereby maintaining the school's tie to its founder.[13]

BETSEY TILDEN (1840–1843)

As Rebecca lay dying in January 1840, Betsey Tilden, Roberta Badger, and Raheel Atta took over the school teaching on average twenty-one of the forty pupils enrolled. After Story Hebard left, William Thomson resumed the headship of the struggling boys' seminary. Meanwhile, a peasants' revolt on Mount Lebanon was quelled by the Pasha's army and its Christian allies. That gave Britain and Austria an excuse to ally with the Turks, who then attempted to retake Syria. Daily life was so disrupted by the amassing of the Pasha's troops in the city that the female school was suspended. Some girls transferred to the mission's common schools beyond the city but longed to return to their all-female school with its higher standard of teaching. The situation became so dangerous that Miss Tilden returned to Jerusalem to wait out the crisis during which all the mission schools were suspended. After the Turks' failed attempt against the Egyptians, British and Austrian troops intervened on the side of the Ottomans with a naval blockade and bombardment of Beirut. Caught in the middle, the remaining missionaries retreated in mid-August to the American corvette *Cyane*, which was anchored in the harbor. From there they viewed the arrival of a large allied fleet and a fierce bombardment of the city followed by troop landings, at which point the *Cyane* evacuated the missionaries to the safety of Larnaca, Cyprus.[14]

Sarah and Her Sisters | 83

The Allies finally forced the Pasha to evacuate and took posses-
sion of the city on October 9, 1841. To their great relief, the returning
missionaries found little damage done to their property and posses-
sions. They quickly resumed their normal activities, except that it
took some time to get the disbanded schools, including the Beirut
Female School, back into operation. Betsey Tilden, assisted only by
Raheel as Roberta Badger had left, was able to reopen the school
in December. Enrollment recovered to twenty-five girls who were
taught Arabic, reading, and writing. Three or four girls had lessons
in geography and arithmetic, and all learned sewing and knitting
from the missionary wives.[15]

The girls' school begun by his first wife was in full swing when
Eli Smith returned in June 1841 with his new wife, Maria Ward
Chapin Smith of Rochester, New York, who was eighteen years his
junior. One of the first things he did was visit the school. His presence brought tears to the eyes of teachers and pupils alike, Raheel's
especially. As he stood watching the little girls doing their lessons, he
silently prayed that "the seed Sarah had sown would take root and
bear fruit so that she would someday welcome many of these dear
children, the objects of her great effort and affection, in heaven."[16]

Maria Smith assisted in the Beirut Female School and planned
to open her own girls' school. Regrettably, she died of dysentery
on May 27, 1842 at the age of twenty-three, just eleven months after
giving birth to a son, Charles Henry Smith, who became a distinguished professor at Yale College. When she was nearing the end
of her life, Maria said she "was not sorry she had come to Syria
even though she had come to die." She was buried in the Missionary
Cemetery "under a fig tree and cypress" and next to Rebecca
Williams Hebard.[17]

Peace did not last long in the region. The Turks and the British,
wanting to foment rebellion and drive out the Egyptians, fostered uneven socioeconomic development among the Druze and
Maronite peasants on Mount Lebanon. Their meddling fueled civil

strife and triggered the first of three major Christian-Druze civil conflicts during the next two decades after fierce fighting erupted in October 1841. Order was not restored until a year later when the Ottomans and British divided Mount Lebanon into a northern Christian district and a southern mixed district. This is where the story of the female school becomes murky because the only record thereafter is that Miss Tilden left Beirut in March 1843, long before the usual summer ending of the school year. For all intents and purposes, Sarah Smith's Beirut Female School and Sabbath School thus ceased to exist under missionary teachers. It would reopen, but only for three brief periods under three separate native teachers, one trained by Sarah (Raheel) and two taught by Sarah's friend and missionary "sister," Mrs. Matilda Whiting.[18]

Jerusalem Girls' School (1835–1843)

Matilda Whiting of Newark, New Jersey, who was the wife of the Rev. George Whiting, had started two other schools for girls, the first in Jerusalem and the second in Abeih. She and Sarah overlapped in Beirut from the Smiths' arrival in January until October 1834. Matilda was then sent to Jerusalem to replace the late Eliza Thomson and start up the school Eliza, who evidently had the most previous experience teaching, was slated to begin had she lived. During their nine months together, Sarah and Matilda developed a close friendship. Furthermore, Matilda would have had ample opportunity to observe, if not assist in, Sarah and Martha Dodge's weekday classes and in Sarah's Sabbath School for native girls. The two also spent a week together in and around Jerusalem when the Smiths visited the Whitings there in the spring of 1835. There would have been time for Sarah to share her schoolhouse plans and for Matilda to ask Sarah's advice about starting up the day school she had in mind for Muslim girls. Conversely, Sarah must have been intrigued by and envious of Matilda's plan to open a boarding school in her Jerusalem home.

Fig. 21 – The Holy City at time of Matilda Whiting's Jerusalem Girls School c. 1835.

In fact, it may have been this conversation that either gave Sarah the idea or further fostered her vision of doing the same in Beirut—a dream that, alas, she would never fulfill. Sarah mentored Matilda and, to a lesser degree, was mentored by her. To put it another way, in starting her own two schools, Matilda spread the flame for female education ignited by Sarah in Beirut.[19]

When Mrs. Whiting went to Jerusalem to carry on the work that was to have been done by the late Eliza Thomson, she took with her two Armenian Protestant children: Salome Carabet, age eight, and Hanna Wortabet, age six, who had lived with the Whitings in Beirut. She then added Salome's five-year-old sister Melita and younger brother Philip. George Whiting and the Rev. Charles and Martha Sherman had already moved into a very fine, spacious Mission House with marble floors and a large garden that George had rented in the Muslim Quarter for fifty dollars a year. Matilda saw immediately that it would serve nicely as a school for her girls. Once all were settled in, the Whitings brought from Beirut two orphaned Armenian sisters, Sada and Rufka Gregory, ages three and one.

When Muslim mothers were unwilling to allow their daughters to live with the Whitings and have Matilda teach them in her home, she forged ahead with a family school with her five Christian girl boarders. As word of Mrs. Whiting's school spread, three Muslim girls were brought during the day to be taught to read and sew. They enjoyed learning and made good progress. In what George Whiting termed "the Oriental style," the girls' parents considered their daughters "adopted" by the Whitings as long as they remained with them and learned what they considered proper. This modest breakthrough excited much talk in the city, particularly among mothers. Following her visit to Jerusalem, Sarah Smith was very pleased to read that by fall the number of Muslim girls in Matilda's school had increased to ten with the promise of more. Within a year the older of her five young boarders had learned enough in their family school to assist Matilda in teaching up to fifteen girls who came during the day.[20]

Relations with the Muslims continued to improve, as evidenced by two sheikhs from the Al-Aqsa Mosque one day asking to see what the girls were being taught to read and borrowing the little spelling book Matilda used. George also gave one sheikh a copy of the Psalms in Arabic, so he could compare it with his version of Psalms. In return the sheikh invited George, but not his wife, to visit him and meet his family. By spring more Muslim girls were coming.[21]

Further growth of the day school was hampered by the Whitings' limited resources and Matilda's waning health. It would have foundered badly had not Miss Betsey Tilden, soon after arriving in Beirut, been sent on to Jerusalem in October 1836 to help Mrs. Whiting. (As previously mentioned, Miss Tilden later assisted Rebecca Hebard and eventually took over Sarah's Beirut Female School.) Miss Tilden, apparently an experienced teacher, was able to build up the school in five months to fifteen or twenty girls a day and continue it for the following year. Even though local Christian girls did not normally mix with Muslims, some eventually started coming, probably for the free sewing and knitting lessons. Daily attendance fluctuated between ten and sixteen mostly Muslim girls. Meanwhile, Matilda used her limited energy to continue teaching her family of five Christians separately.[22]

Declining health made it increasingly difficult for Mrs. Whiting to give her five girls lessons in the Bible and Protestant beliefs, let alone teach her day students. She was able to keep up her Sabbath School for a dozen Christian and Muslim girls. She and Miss Tilden kept all three schools going through the spring of 1838 when Matilda was finally persuaded to return home to New Jersey to recuperate. All instruction ceased, and Betsey took the five boarders back to Beirut where she began helping Story and Rebecca Hebard in the boys' and girls' schools.[23]

Mrs. Whiting returned to Jerusalem in April 1840. Her five girls, Salome (by then fourteen), Melita (twelve), Hanna (eleven), Sada (nine) and little Rufka (seven), were all returned to live with the Whitings for another three years. Matilda resumed teaching them to read and write in Arabic and English, while Martha Sherman trained one (not identified) "to be industrious and develop useful domestic habits." With such disparity in ages, they learned at different rates and had varying dispositions, but all "made good progress in gaining useful knowledge, domestic industry, deportment and appearance." In other words, they were being groomed to become good wives, mothers and, hopefully, teachers of native girls whom they would also convert to Protestantism. Over time, the five would not disappoint them.[24]

Mrs. Whiting and Miss Tilden were reunited briefly in the summer of 1840 when the latter returned to escape the growing tension and danger in Beirut. By this time local prejudice against educating females had lessened greatly and more girls sought admission to both the boarding and day school—not only from Jerusalem, but from Bethlehem and other places as well. Sadly, Matilda, with her school reestablished and growing, again became ill and had to withdraw to America a second time in 1843. Betsey Tilden, then teaching in Beirut, was unavailable to carry on her work and the Jerusalem girls' school was disbanded for good. Meanwhile, the Whitings' five girls returned once more to Beirut to continue their education in other missionary homes.[25]

ABEIH GIRLS' SCHOOL (1844–1858)

Since the residents in the mixed Druze/Christian village of Abeih 2,500 feet above Beirut had been receptive to the girls' summer school run there by Martha Dodge and Rebecca Hebard, and since the missionaries could work there with less government interference, the Mission decided to open a mission station in Abeih.

Therefore, when George and Matilda Whiting returned to Syria once more in October 1844, they took up residence in the spacious new brownstone Abeih Mission House with beautiful views of the city and sea below.[26]

Matilda was to begin another school for younger girls, but those plans had to be postponed for a year because of another outbreak of bloody fighting between Christians and Druze. Abeih itself was attacked and many homes destroyed in April 1845. When peace was restored and the village was being rebuilt, Matilda could at last open her Abeih Girls' School in August 1846. She was aided by two of her former pupils. Now married, Mrs. Salome Wortabet and Mrs. Hanna Reichardt had both received secondary educations while living with missionaries in Beirut. The school got off to a strong start. A dozen day students quickly grew to twenty-five Druze, Maronite, Greek Catholic, and Greek Orthodox students. To accommodate them all, the Mission built a one-room schoolhouse next to the Mission House at a cost of $100. (It was probably like Sarah's in Beirut, but cost half as much.) Records of the school are sketchy, but we do know that all pupils were taught the Bible and Protestant doctrine (catechism) during the week. On Sundays some girls attended the Sabbath School.

Matilda remained healthy and continued the school for another decade during which two other former students, Sada and Rufka Gregory, replaced Salome and Hanna. By 1853 enrollment had reached a peak of sixty girls. We can assume that over time girls continued to attend as they grew older, thereby raising the average age of the pupils. The Abeih Girls' School would have continued under Mrs. Whiting had it not been for her husband's increasing illness and fatal attack of cholera in November 1855.

Unable to carry on alone, Matilda turned the school over to Sada Gregory and returned to Newark, New Jersey in March 1856, thereby ending the Whitings' twenty-five years in Syria. Sada, with her younger sister Rufka's help, finished the school year, after which Sada was transferred to the new Tripoli Girls' School. Rufka probably returned to Beirut for further education with a missionary family. In any event, the Abeih Girls' School closed for lack of a teacher and would remain so until it was reopened as a school for older girls early in 1858.[27]

CHAPTER THREE

First Boarding Schools
for Older Girls (1835–1862)

My mind is much upon a female boarding-school; and if I can get the promise of ten girls, we shall, God willing, remove the press from our house, and commence one in the fall.

Sarah Smith to her sister, Faith
Good Friday, April 1, 1836

Day schools were all very well for young children, but Sarah Smith soon came to believe that to have a lasting impact on her students' lives, they should in due time live at the school. She envisioned turning her day school over to Rebecca Williams and starting a boarding school in her Beirut home for older girls. Then attendance would be assured, and the girls shielded from what she viewed as superstitions, prejudices, and other bad outside influences. In addition to daily school lessons, she could teach her boarders basic living skills while modeling Protestant family values, including mutual respect between husband and wife.[1]

Sarah's dream did not die with her. Matilda Whiting was the first to try out the concept of a boarding school in her Jerusalem home, only it was with a select group of young girls, all Christians, whom she had "adopted" in a manner similar to Sarah's adoption of Raheel. These Matilda started to train as future mothers and teachers. Because of the continued success of Sarah's school under

Rebecca Williams and Betsey Tilden, there was a growing demand among Protestant parents in Beirut that their older daughters, like their sons attending the Beirut Mission Seminary, have their own boarding school. With this in mind, the Syria Mission recommended to the Foreign Mission Board in Boston in 1840 that one be established in Beirut for girls. They had first made their case at the Board's annual meeting in Troy, New York, in September 1839:

> Advances in our other departments make our deficiencies in female education painfully obvious and spur us to more vigorous efforts to start a girls' boarding school with the least possible delay because many of our Protestant girls are suffering irreparable loss for want to a school.[2]

Although the Board authorized the project and the Mission had found "suitable accommodations in a good location," Boston could neither appropriate the necessary funds nor send a teacher who was qualified to head the school. Sarah's dream was deferred until 1847, when it came to fruition through the pioneering efforts of Dr. Henry and Kitty De Forest, Anna Whittlesey, and Sarah Cheney. These labors were renewed in 1858 by Daniel and Abby Bliss with the invaluable help of Mrs. Whiting's student, young Rufka Gregory.

THE DE FORESTS' FEMALE SEMINARY: FIRST STUDENTS (1845–1855)

Henry De Forest and his wife Katherine ("Kitty") reached Beirut in March 1842. Like Eli and Sarah Smith, the De Forests were both from Connecticut. He too had attended Yale College and Andover Theological Seminary, but he was not ordained as a minister. Instead Henry earned a medical degree from the Yale Medical School and was, like the late Asa Dodge, assigned to Beirut initially as the mission's physician.[3] He would, however, become better known as an educator who, with his wife, founded and oversaw for a decade the first boarding school for girls ages twelve to eighteen. Today it would be considered part middle school and part high school.[4]

The De Forests may not have planned to start a girls' boarding school at the outset, because five years elapsed between their arrival and the time they officially opened one in 1847. Rather, their roles as educators seem to have evolved gradually as they were settling in, learning Arabic, and young Dr. Henry was starting as mission physician. The venture began with another connection to Sarah and Eli Smith—Raheel Atta. After Rebecca Williams Hebard died in 1840, Raheel was home-schooled successively by two missionary wives, Hannah Beadle and Julia Lanneau, until 1843, when at the age of seventeen she moved into the Mission House to live with the De Forests who took over her schooling, thus making her their first boarding student.

While under the De Forests' care, the beautiful Raheel caught the eye of the dashing twenty-four-year-old Butrus al-Bustani, who was assisting Eli Smith in translating the Bible into Arabic. With the blessing of both the De Forests and Eli, who still considered Raheel his adopted daughter (and who, like Henry, was anxious to promote the marriage of two native Protestant converts), Butrus and Raheel became engaged. Raheel's Greek Orthodox family, on the other hand, strongly objected to her marrying a Protestant. To prevent this eventuality, they kidnapped her and took her home. They might have succeeded in keeping her there had not Eli and Henry, accompanied by one of the Pasha's officers, gone to the Atta family home to obtain her release. When Raheel's brother-in-law grabbed her arm to keep her from leaving, the officer seized her other arm and a tug-of-war ensued. The official finally managed to free her and she left with the three Protestant men. Butrus and Raheel were married in the mission church in the summer of 1844 and became the first Syrian Protestants to wed one another.[5]

Having finished her secondary education with the De Forests, Raheel took up housekeeping for Butrus and soon had their first child,

Fig. 22 – Rev. Henry and Katherine De Forest c. 1841.

Fig. 23 – Raheel Atta married Butrus al-Bustani who became the famous Lebanese writer and scholar and was considered the first Syrian nationalist.

Fig. 24 – 1863 photo of Old Mission House (Burj Bird) built by Isaac Bird in 1833 and home of De Forest Female Seminary, 1843-1853.

a daughter whom they fittingly named Sarah Huntington Bustani in honor of Raheel's adoptive mother and "beloved teacher." (Sarah Bustani was the *second* Syrian child so named. Sarah and Eli's good friend and Arabic tutor, Tannoos al Haddad, had in 1838 named his new daughter Sarah Smith al Haddad.) In the fall of 1846, Raheel was very pleased to be asked to reopen the vacated Beirut Female School and happily began teaching thirty little girls on weekday mornings in Sarah's former schoolhouse. Unfortunately, funding soon ran out and it was again closed in the spring.[6]

Raheel was not the only native Syrian to live with American missionaries. "When quite a child," Khozma Ata Witwat was taken from her Druze family "still under the shadow of old superstitions," and lived first with Rev. Elias and Hanna Beadle for a year. She was then an invalid, not often able to leave her house even for church. When the Beadles left Beirut, young Khozma was passed on to live with Miss Betsey Tilden for six months, first in Aleppo and then in Jerusalem. She was finally settled with the De Forests and resided with them from 1843 until 1854. Building on their experience of further educating Raheel, Henry and Kitty entered Khozma and another girl, Lulu Shebly, into their "family boarding school for girls" in the fall of 1847 in the hope of grooming them to become, like Raheel, good Protestant wives and mothers and to perform missionary service. Khozma fulfilled the De Forests' expectations as a wife, mother, and teacher although she continued to be plagued by illness and hard times in adulthood, when her husband's business failed.

Lulu too was a "delicate child" born into a Greek Orthodox family and placed with a missionary family when she was eight. There she was "instructed in her own language and in the Holy Scriptures" as well as in sewing. She lived with the De Forests for eight years during which she assisted in both the Beirut day school and the fledgling boarding school. She bonded closely with Raheel and Khozma while they were living in the De Forest household, and "became truly pious in 1846 and tried to live according to the precepts of the gospel." Lulu was "almost like my own daughter" to Kitty De Forest, who was "very sorry to part with her but hoped she would yet be useful to her countrywomen" and become the head of an exemplary Protestant home. As will become clear in the next chapter, Lulu Shebly Araman would exceed her mentor's fondest dreams.[7]

The Academic and Religious Goals of the Female Seminary

When other girls enrolled, the boarding school started to be referred to loosely as the "female seminary." While "seminary" now refers to "a school or college to train Christian ministers or priests," nineteenth-century missionaries used the term for boarding schools "to educate native helpers for... missionary and evangelistic" work. In antebellum America, the term was commonly used to refer to girls' schools that offered education "beyond the rudimentary level." For both these reasons, and to differentiate the school from the mission's thirteen common schools that served 163 girls as well as 462 boys, the De Forests' family school loosely became known as the "female seminary." (It is important to distinguish this informal family school from the more structured, stand-alone Beirut Female Seminary that comes later in our history.)[8]

The girls in this school boarded and were taught in the De Forests' Mission House residence, the very same three-story "Burj Bird" where the early missionaries had lived and where the missionary wives' first class for little girls had met thirteen years before. A long flight of outside stairs led to the second-floor dining room, bedrooms, and classrooms. There was also a spacious, high-ceilinged salon with carved and tinted pine that was lined on three sides with cushions for social conversation. Eli Smith had a study in the third floor "attic" where he was translating the Bible.[9]

The De Forests' school year was divided into two five-month terms. The cooler winter months were spent in Beirut, while in the

Sarah and Her Sisters | 97

summer months the missionaries decamped, first to the mountainside village of Bamdoon and later to Abeih. The terms were separated by six-week spring and fall vacations for reasons soon to be made plain. The four years of study began with a two-year "junior" class taught only in Arabic followed by a two-year "senior" class for older girls taught in both Arabic and—in defiance of the Board's policy that all instruction should be only in Arabic—English. "Seniors" in the second two years studied more advanced reading, writing, mathematics, and geography. Dr. De Forest insisted upon the girls mastering English, so they could read and understand the Bible in English and have access to the richness of English literature.[10]

The introduction of science, or more specifically the basic elements of astronomy and physics, marked a major advancement in female education in the region. This is verified in the list of materials and scientific equipment Dr. De Forest assembled. In addition to many academic and religious books, numerous maps, and two globes for teaching geography, he utilized "astronomy maps and a center of gravity apparatus." To conduct experiments in electricity he acquired "a galvanic trough, a circular battery, electro, horseshoe and revolving magnets, a wire coil and hemispheric helices apparatus—and a shocking machine," the purpose and design of which is left to our imaginations. From other reports we know that physiology, an early form of biology, was introduced in the curriculum. Teaching science to boys was then considered very progressive, but to teach science to *girls* was revolutionary.[11]

Although the De Forests' emphasis on academics was impressive, Henry De Forest stated openly to his supporters at home that their primary goal was to convert girls to Protestantism and save their souls so they could in turn convert other girls and women. To this end their seminary students were being trained in mental discipline and given the intellectual tools to become knowledgeable, well-behaved, effective evangelists. The older girls were given special instruction in "the preached word." This was, however, only part of a grander plan to reconstruct Syrian society. Syrian men, despite their exposure to foreigners through commerce, were still thought to be hostage to superstition and prejudices that caused them, in De Forest's opinion, to act like children in their treatment of wives and daughters; many men did not allow women to read a book or expand their vocabularies. But "enlightened" females, no longer isolated from the outside world, could overcome long-held superstitions and play a key role in influencing their husbands while training their children properly.

De Forest believed that the best way to help females break this demeaning cycle of oppression and servitude was to educate them without "denationalizing" them. It was important that his students remain in steady contact with their society; hence, their long summer vacations at home as well as six-week breaks in the fall and spring. Although English was important for the older girls, the overall language of instruction remained Arabic. The girls maintained their Syrian dress and manners so they would not appear like foreigners. We can be sure that De Forest did not share his goals with his girls' parents or they may never have sent their daughters to the school.[12]

Records of the De Forests' female seminary were lost, but at least the names of twenty-three girls who attended between 1848 and 1852 are known. A few graduates twenty years later reconstructed a list of their schoolmates by both their maiden and married names. Of these, "twenty-one headed families, esteemed and honored by their communities," which were listed. Twelve had joined the native evangelical church and nine were teachers.[13]

Beyond this information and that regarding the first three students mentioned above, we have anecdotal information of only one other student. Sada Sabunjy, placed in the seminary in 1848 at the age of twelve, was at the outset by her own admission as an adult, "not clever in studies. My mind was more at play than at learning. I was clever at housework, dressing dolls, and the leader in all games. I was punished twice... for not being able to translate into Arabic

'The hen is in the yard.'" After two years she wanted to "become a real Christian like my dear teacher, Dr. De Forest." She struggled spiritually throughout her remaining years there, even reading *Pilgrim's Progress*, but did not join the church until 1856 while teaching in Sarah Smith's temporarily reopened day school. Yet, as we are about to see, Sada would be key to continuing the seminary beyond the De Forests' departure.

Anecdotally we know as well that in 1851 Mrs. De Forest organized the girls into a Missionary Sewing Society that did sewing and embroidering to raise funds for "women anxious to read" in Aintab, Syria. "The needles were briskly plied, and in due time, two hundred and fifty piastres were collected and forwarded to Aintab." In February 1852 Mrs. De Forest wrote to a Sabbath school class in Thetford, Vermont: "Our school has now nineteen pupils, most of whom are promising. Some we hope are true Christians. The girls opened their box the other day and found that they had forty dollars from their earnings. One half they sent to China, and the other half they gave to the Church here."[14]

FEMALE SEMINARY TEACHERS

Henry and Kitty De Forest, assisted by her parents who lived with them for some time, provided all the instruction at first in the new boarding school. As enrollment grew, the two oldest remaining students, Khozma and Lulu, were enlisted as assistant teachers. Kitty, however, did not enjoy teaching. Overseeing a household of some twenty-plus people was itself a full-time job. Given the success of their educational venture, Henry thought it time to turn the female seminary over to an experienced teacher and requested that the Mission Board send someone as soon as possible. Miss Anna Whittlesey of Rochester, New York, was recruited to take over the school in the spring of 1851. To Henry's delight, Anna was well received by the girls, especially those older ones who spoke some

English. She made rapid progress in learning Arabic, had industrious work habits, and demonstrated a strong sense of duty and selflessness. As the demand for female education grew and some girls had to be turned away, the mission was blamed for not making sufficient provisions for them. Some families even resorted to asking individual missionaries to take their girls in and homeschool them as some had done before. Henry De Forest looked forward to putting the entire enterprise in his successor's capable hands soon— but alas, it was not to be.

Just as Miss Whittlesey was to take over as principal, her cheek became infected with streptococcus, either from a scratch or an insect bite. She developed a high fever, chills, shaking, headaches, fatigue, and vomiting. Ugly lesions began growing on her face. For nine months, Dr. De Forest and another physician, distraught at her worsening condition, stood helplessly at her bedside. Anna Whittlesey died an excruciating death in her Burj Bird bedroom on May 1, 1852—exactly 365 days after arriving in Beirut.[15]

Dr. De Forest developed his own health issues. Used to taking long walks in New England without fear of the sun, he walked regularly about the city and on the deep sand dunes and beaches nearby, protected from the blazing sun by only a small black hat and no umbrella. After one walk he felt a strange sensation in the back of his head and realized that he had suffered a sunstroke, a life-threatening condition caused when the body's temperature rises beyond its ability to cool itself through perspiration. He never fully recovered from this episode, which was to greatly shorten his life.[16]

Yet he and Kitty, assisted by two recent graduates, had no choice but to go on teaching until another teacher could be sent. Meanwhile, applications kept increasing as more girls, in hope of admission to the secondary school, were attending the mission's twenty or so common schools and the former Beirut Female School, reopened again by Sada Sabunjy and another unidentified De Forest graduate.[17]

The Promising Sarah Cheney

Due to Dr. De Forest's illness, only three girls were admitted in the fall of 1852. Two transferred from Mrs. Whiting's Abeih school, and the other was Sarah Huntington Bustani, the nine-year-old daughter of Raheel and Butrus. Aware of the urgency of the teaching situation, the Board in a few months selected Sarah Cheney of Phillipston, Massachusetts, to replace Anna Whittlesey. To the De Forests' great relief, she arrived in April 1853 and, like her late predecessor, plunged into her language study. Miss Cheney was soon teaching the older girls English and to sing hymns.[18]

The De Forests added courses in Arabic in moral philosophy (ethics), history, church history with an emphasis on the Protestant Reformation, and geography using an atlas. After completing the Companions to the Bible in Arabic, the whole school engaged in daily study of the four gospels as well as other biblical and religious instruction. Hetty Smith of Northampton, Massachusetts, Eli Smith's newly arrived third wife, taught the rudiments of drawing. Three other missionary wives—Emily Calhoun, Hannah Eddy, and Sarah Bird—gave lessons in vocal music, for which some of the girls "had considerable taste." Within her first year, Sarah Cheney was able to stabilize the school of seventeen students just as Dr. De Forest's health declined rapidly, and he was forced to return to America in May of 1854. He died four years later at the age of forty.[19] The Syria Mission concluded:

> Dr. De Forest's Seminary proved that there is the same capacity in the native female mind as in the male, and that under proper instruction, there will be brought forward a class of intelligent, pious and efficient female helpers in the great work of evangelizing this community.[20]

The departure of the school's founders led to a period of uncertainty. Because it was considered only proper for a married couple to oversee a girls' boarding school, the seminary under

Fig. 25 – Rev. Eli Smith and his third wife,
Hetty Butler Smith of Northampton, MA, 1846.

Sarah Cheney's direction was moved into the home of the Rev. David and Emmeline Wilson. Annual tuition was 1,200 piasters, or about fifty dollars; eight more girls graduated in the summer of 1854. The school did well enough to employ Sada Sabunjy, the 1852 graduate then teaching in the reopened Beirut Female School, as a second teacher. Cheney and Sabunjy taught together in the Wilsons' home for only six months until the Wilsons were transferred to Homs early in 1855 and the female family school, having no "proper" home, was suspended. Sada married and went to Damascus to teach. Sarah Cheney remained in Beirut and began eight months of intensive Arabic study in preparation for her next assignment.

The De Forests' "Female Seminary" demonstrated the viability of a secondary boarding school for older girls. Rather than reopen the school in Beirut, the Mission decided to relocate it to the village of Abeih, near the all-male Abeih Seminary and Mrs. Whiting's day school for girls. Daughters of Protestant families concentrated in the area would be given priority for admission because they would make more suitable wives for ministers and teachers graduating from the male seminary. Miss Cheney was the obvious person to carry on the De Forests' school, now officially called the Female Seminary, in the village of Abeih. But in direct contradiction to Dr. De Forest's preference for teaching some in English, she was mandated by the Mission Board to henceforth teach exclusively in Arabic, which explains her intensive language study while awaiting the arrival of a new missionary couple.[21]

THE BLISSES' FEMALE SEMINARY: ABEIH AND SUQ EL-GHARB (1858–1860)

The Rev. Daniel and Abigail (Abby) Bliss arrived in Syria in February 1856. Even though Daniel, a graduate of Amherst College and Andover Theological Seminary, is best known as the founding president of the Syrian Protestant College (later renamed the American

Fig. 26 – New missionaries Rev. Daniel and Abigail Bliss c. 1855

Fig. 27 – American Poet Emily Dickinson was Abby Wood Bliss's close girlhood friend and neighbor.

University of Beirut), he was at first a pioneer in Arab female education. He first met his wife Abby in Amherst, where she grew up next door to the reclusive poet, Emily Dickinson, who was a girlhood friend. Once in Syria, the Blisses and Sarah Cheney climbed Mount Lebanon on horseback to the village of Abeih, where they were to restart the De Forests' relocated "female seminary" in the Mission House vacated by Mrs. Whiting after her husband's death.

The large house of native stone was otherwise simple and resembled those of the girls who would attend the school. It had the requisite number of classrooms and a larger recitation room, but still offered adequate living quarters for a missionary family, one or two teachers, and several boarding students. The plan was to reopen the female seminary straightaway, but just after they arrived, Sarah Cheney was sent to Homs to nurse Susan Aiken. (She was the wife of the Rev. Edward Aiken, whom Miss Cheney later married after Susan died.) This left the Blisses struggling to adapt to the culture and learn Arabic, meaning they were totally unprepared to open the school without an experienced teacher.[22]

To Daniel and Abby's great relief after an almost two-year delay, Rufka Gregory, now twenty-two, agreed to return to Abeih in January 1858 to open the relocated female seminary. Rufka had been homeschooled and trained by Matilda Whiting and Kitty De Forest, and also had experience assisting Mrs. Whiting and her sister, Sada, in the former Abeih school. While not as qualified as Sarah Cheney to teach older girls, she had enough experience and natural talent to take on the task at hand, and was soon teaching as many as thirty-four girls from ages five to fifteen. Most were day students with a handful of older boarders.

Daniel described the school as a source of "hope for the females of this dark land." But shortly after the birth of the Blisses' first child, Mary, the mission decided to move the school because of its proximity to the all-male Abeih Seminary; it was feared the boys could distract the girls and vice versa. For the safety and welfare of the girls, an alternative site was deemed prudent. Since Bamdoon was too high and too cold, the village on Suq el-Garb, five miles north and 1,000 feet below Abeih, was chosen as the new site.[23]

In October 1858 Daniel and Abby dutifully left for Suq and moved into a new house perched on a precipice overlooking Beirut and the sea. They would spend four satisfying years in the village, where he served as a preacher, pastor, lawyer, real estate agent, carpenter, physician, and diplomat. But his primary charge was to oversee the second reopening of the female boarding school, headed now by Amelia Temple, the newly arrived American teacher sent to replace Sarah Cheney, and her traveling companion and assistant, Jane Johnson, also an experienced teacher. This allowed Rufka Gregory to return to Beirut to take over (or perhaps resume) the teaching of sixty girls in the day school housed most likely in Sarah's old schoolhouse. At first the Suq villagers were polite but cool to the Americans or ignored them altogether. Unfazed, Abby, who had a passion for educating girls, soon attracted three daughters of a prominent leader in the Greek Orthodox Church to her home by playing her small reed melodeon (organ) and teaching them hymns. (Fifty years later Daniel wrote, "These three little girls... became the wives of three leading Protestants, one a preacher, another an assistant editor in the American Press and the most learned Arabic scholar in the East, and the youngest the wife of a most influential editor and proprietor in Egypt.") Gradually a few other parents allowed their girls to board with the missionaries. Misses Temple and Johnson could, with Abby's help, then begin instruction.

Abby Bliss balanced caring for her little family with managing all the meals and lodging for the "five Americans, including the two young ladies, five little pupils, one Syrian teacher and servants." (It is unclear whether the "Syrian teacher" referred to Rufka's replacement or to Rufka herself, since it is possible she stayed in Suq briefly before returning to Beirut.) Vowing to spend less than Kitty De Forest, whom she thought extravagant, Abby had her cook, Jirjius, whom

Fig. 28 – The village of Suq el-Gharb on Mount Lebanon, site of the Female Seminary from 1858 to 1860.

she paid $3.60 a month, prepare one meal for the Americans and a separate native dish for the Syrians. She bought eggs in the village for six cents a dozen and milk at two cents a quart. The biggest expense was for baking homemade bread in the village oven.

During the first winter in Suq, a now-familiar problem arose. Strong winter rains soaked through the masonry walls and multiple leaks required pans and tubs to be placed strategically throughout the house. Following a second even worse winter and a measles epidemic, Abby, sorely taxed and again pregnant, gladly turned over her household and matron duties to the American ladies and moved her family into a more substantial home where she bore a son, Frederick, in January 1859. She also took in and homeschooled two native "daughters." But her respite from seminary duties was cut short when Jane Johnson became the latest American woman to fall in the line of duty. Too ill to continue teaching, Jane was sent home in March of 1859.[24]

POLITICAL UNREST AND EVACUATION

With Abby once more managing meals and sleeping arrangements in the school, Amelia Temple carried on the teaching in the face of political unrest sweeping across the mountain. By one account it all started on August 30, 1859 when a Druze boy and a Christian boy got in an argument over a chicken. Yelling gave way to pushing, shoving, and rock throwing. Soon other youths and older adults joined in. By the end of the day, scores lay dead and vengeance was avowed by both sides. Suq el-Gharb was soon at the center of a murderous firestorm just as Jane Johnson's replacement, Adelaide Mason, arrived on horseback in April 1860. Only a month later she would find herself, along with the other Americans, fleeing back down to Beirut.[25]

As the fierce fighting, burning of entire villages, and horrific massacres closed in around them, the missionaries received instructions from Beirut to close the school and return to the city. Daniel Bliss was at first reluctant to do so as he felt that he, his family, and the school were protected by the local Druze chieftains. But as the violence grew worse and the women and girls became more frightened, he decided it was too dangerous for them to stay. He therefore made arrangements to have them escorted back down the mountain to the city. As they descended, bands of fighters rushing into battle passed by the party but left them unmolested. Looking behind them, the evacuees could see columns of thick smoke rising from burning villages. Once they reached the Plain of Beirut, the roads were clogged with refugees. When they finally entered the relative safety of the city five hours after leaving Suq, they discovered that Beirut was in turmoil. Homeless and hungry refugees were being threatened with violence. The fatigued and frightened group reached the mission compound and were taken in to wait out the Mount Lebanon Civil War of 1860.[26]

Beirut remained in chaos throughout that horrific year, overwhelmed by mostly Christian villagers fleeing the fighting and massacres on the mountainside. The missionaries were stretched to the limit providing food, clothing, and housing. It is little wonder that Amelia Temple and Adelaide Mason had to abandon a short-lived attempt to resume teaching the nine girls who had fled Suq with them and send them home. Temple and Mason instead joined in relief work for two years while improving their Arabic. The bloodshed and destruction continued. One estimate is that at least 5,000 people were killed, 200 villages burnt, and 100,000 people displaced during the conflict. The civil strife ended only when several European powers (Britain, France, Prussia, Russia, and Austria) pressured the Sultan to intervene on July 28 with 4,000 Turkish troops under Fuad Pasha. Two weeks later 6,000 French troops landed to join the Turks and bring the fighting to a halt. A European Commission oversaw punishments, reparations, and reconstruction, and devised a new social and political status for

Mount Lebanon. The French remained for one year as the new government for Greater Lebanon within Ottoman Syria took hold, order was restored, and most refugees returned to their homes. Daniel and Abby Bliss returned to Suq el-Gharb for a year to oversee the distribution of aid to some forty ravaged villages.[27]

The mission's extensive relief efforts brought thousands of Syrians in contact with the missionaries and their work, thus contributing to a growing demand for education and more mission schools in the freer, more stable Syria. When the mission decided to reopen the all-male Abeih Seminary, but not the girls' boarding school in Suq, Daniel Bliss and William Thomson began discussing how to meet the new demand for higher education for Arab men. The mission agreed that it was time to establish a men's college equal in worth to those in America. In January 1862 Bliss was named the first principal of the Syrian Protestant College, thus beginning his fifty-year presidency of what eventually became the American University of Beirut.[28]

Much to the distress of the Americans, just as the civil strife ended in Syria, a much greater and bloodier Civil War broke out between the northern and southern states in their homeland and gravely diminished their financial support. New England Congregationalists strongly backed the Union (northern) cause. Northern and Southern Presbyterians, however, were divided over the issue of slavery, with northerners favoring its abolition and southerners staunchly supporting it. The rift grew wider until the southerners withdrew from the denomination in 1861 to form the Presbyterian Church in the Confederate States of America. The schism worsened the war's negative impact on financial support for all foreign missions, including the Syria Mission.[29]

CHAPTER FOUR

Syrian Female Seminary (1862–1867)

Miss Rufka Gregory, who taught in the Beirut Syrian Girls' School for five years, was the ablest Syrian teacher of modern times.

Rev. Henry H. Jessup
Beirut, January 1, 1910

INCLUSIVE AND IN ENGLISH

Amelia Temple returned to Massachusetts in the spring of 1862. Adelaide Mason, on the other hand, was sent to Sidon by the American Board to reopen the Suq el-Gharb girls' boarding school there.[1] It was to be for Protestant girls only and taught in Arabic. The girls were *not* to adopt Western behavior but maintain their native customs in eating, sleeping, and dress so they would be accepted when they returned to their villages as evangelizing teachers. Miss Mason taught in Sidon for three years until the school was turned over, first to native instructors and finally to English missionaries.[2]

Two elementary schools for girls were opened in Beirut in 1862. Once Sarah Smith's former schoolhouse was emptied of 250 refugees, Rufka Gregory reopened it as a day school in March 1862. In a short time, she recruited two of her unnamed peers to help teach seventy girls. In examinations her pupils proved proficient in Arabic reading and grammar, geography, arithmetic, Bible lessons, English, and needlework. In the fall Sada el Halaby, another of

Dr. De Forest's students, started a school for seventy more girls in an upper room in the Rev. Henry and Caroline Jessup's house. This she continued until August 1864 when Elizabeth Bowen Thompson's British Syrian Schools Society took it over. Presumably both of these schools for young girls were, like Sarah's, taught primarily if not exclusively in Arabic.[3]

The Rev. Henry Jessup of Montrose, Pennsylvania was a Union (New York) Seminary graduate who had arrived in Syria with Daniel and Abby Bliss in 1856 and been stationed in Tripoli. After marrying and bringing his new bride, Caroline, from Branchport, New York to Tripoli in 1859, she became pregnant before the couple relocated to Abeih in the spring of 1860. There Henry was to work on an Arabic atlas and assist in the boys' seminary. When the fighting erupted around them, however, they fled down the mountain with the evacuees from Suq el-Gharb to Beirut. There Caroline gave birth to Anna Jessup, who, like Mary Bliss, would play an important role in later efforts toward female education in the region.[4]

The venerable William Thomson, DD, the distinguished Arabic linguist Cornelius Van Dyck, MD, DD, and young Henry Jessup were not satisfied with the Mission's directive that the female seminary opened in Beirut by the De Forests, which had been relocated to Abeih and then moved to Suq el-Gharb, now be reopened in Sidon by Adelaide Mason. Furthermore, they were strongly opposed to the Mission's Arabic-only policy, as well as the mandate to admit only Protestants. Rather they advocated for a school, like the De Forests', that would be open to girls of all religions and nationalities, taught primarily in English, and advancing Western ideals and culture. Therefore, acknowledging all that Rufka and Sada had accomplished in a short time in their two elementary day schools, the three missionaries sought to build upon the foundation they had laid and reopen the female boarding school in the more vibrant, multi-ethnic, multi-cultural city of Beirut.

Overcoming Challenges

The complexities were intimidating. First there was the divisive issue of language. With the British controlling Egypt and Cyprus and the French in charge of Syria, it seemed foolhardy not to educate future teachers for the region in English and French. Like Henry De Forest, Thomson, Van Dyke, and Jessup preferred to teach the Bible in English and introduce girls to English literature. Second, since support was diminished due to the American Civil War and the Board would not fund a school in English, other means had to be found to finance the new female seminary. Lastly, there were no qualified American female teachers left in Syria. Unprecedented steps were required to overcome these obstacles and provide an American-style education for "the daughters of the more advanced and refined families of Beirut." Willing to take the risks, the three men, plus the American consul, boldly constituted themselves as a Board of Managers to reopen a Beirut Female Seminary.[5]

As for finances, they devised a two-part formula. First, they would be charging tuition, which was a totally alien concept in Syrian society, especially since all the mission schools were free. If there was no charge for their sons' instruction, room, and board at the prestigious Abeih Academy, why must parents pay for their *daughters'* schooling? The second means was less radical but more labor-intensive: they would have to raise funds from outside sources.[6]

Raising funds for a girls' school in a region that had just gone through a civil war appeared daunting. Americans were at that time pouring their human and material resources into their respective sides in their own civil war, making a successful fundraising campaign seemingly impossible. Yet an interesting phenomenon was occurring in the disunited States. Ironically, Americans of wealth, some making even more money from the war, began vying with one another in giving to good causes. By 1864, donations to the

ABCFM had increased by fifty percent. However, due to the Board's "Arabic only" policy, none of those funds were available for a school in English.[7]

LEAD GIFTS

Interestingly, the first contributor to the renewed boarding school for girls was an Englishman, Col. A. S. Frazer, H.B.M. (His Britannic Majesty), head of the international Joint Commission on Syria. But he was an anomaly. This was an *American* mission project. Hence, Henry Jessup began his fundraising career by welcoming and cultivating American tourists. One of the first such visitors must have been Alexander van Rensselaer, a wealthy aristocrat from Albany, New York and likely a prominent Dutch Reformed churchman. After the death of his twenty-four-year-old wife and, four years later, both of their young children on the same day (apparently of the same disease), van Rensselaer made a generous lead gift, perhaps in their memory, to launch the female boarding school. Another lead gift came from Anna Whitman Farnum, wife of the wealthy railroad baron and Yale University benefactor, Henry Farnum. Mrs. Farnum had a strong interest in missions and as a girl had attended the Litchfield (Connecticut) Female Academy. With her generous lead gift plus those of Col. Frazer and van Rensselaer, the Board of Managers could begin organizing the school and hiring staff.[8]

Among other American visitors were passengers aboard the steamship *Quaker City* on a five-month cruise and pilgrimage to the Holy Land and Egypt. Jessup greeted the sponsor of the cruise, Moses S. Beach, publisher of the *New York Sun*, and thirty of his shipmates, including many clergymen and their wives, and invited them to visit the mission compound. Beach contributed $200 to the mission and Jessup gave all the visitors copies of Eli Smith's Arabic Bible with their names written in Arabic. Regrettably, one passenger was at the time elsewhere in the city arranging an overland trip to

Jerusalem. He would, however, receive his Bible later. That young gentleman was Samuel Clemens, whose account of the group's voyage would later be published as *Innocents Abroad* under his pen name, Mark Twain, who also wrote *Tom Sawyer, Huckleberry Finn*, and other American classics.[9]

ALL-SYRIAN STAFF

A trusted Protestant couple, Michaiel and Lulu (Shebly) Araman, were hired to administer the new boarding school for girls that would begin in their home. Michaiel had graduated from and taught at the Abeih Academy and would be the principal and teach Arabic. Lulu, one of the De Forests' first students, had taught other girls there and assisted Raheel in the briefly reopened Beirut girls' day school. As the school's matron, she would oversee the girls who were boarding with them. But with no American teachers available, who then would teach? Was there a missionary-trained native Syrian teacher qualified to teach older girls in English? Yes, and the choice was obvious. The mission once again turned to Rufka Gregory, who had learned English from infancy in the Whitings' care; attended and assisted in the De Forests' seminary; taught in the Abeih girls' school, first with Mrs. Whiting and then with her sister, Sada; taught older girls briefly in Abeih under the Blisses; and most recently re-opened the highly successful girls' primary school in Beirut. With these three native Syrians in place, the new boarding school was opened on October 1, 1862 with two paying students and four "charity" students added to the nucleus of day students Rufka was already teaching.[10]

The following October the school started with a total of twenty day and boarding students, all desiring a bilingual (Arabic and English) education with the option of instruction in French. By July there were twenty-five. In two years, the school had grown to sixty students, a mix of native Syrians, Egyptians, and a few Armenians

Fig. 29 – Passengers aboard the side wheel steamship *Quaker City* visited Rufka Gregory's Syrian Girls' School in 1867.

Fig. 30 – Quaker City passenger Samuel Clemens skipped visit to the mission girls' school. Under his pen name, Mark Twain, he wrote his bestselling *Innocents Abroad*, a humorous account of the Quaker City cruise. Later books included *Tom Sawyer* and *Huckleberry Finn*.

from ages ten to sixteen. The school's rapid growth in the absence of any American instructor demonstrated the validity of training native teachers to instruct Syrian girls. And by circumventing the "Arabic-only" policy, the school was training English-speaking students to teach in Egypt and Cyprus under the British plus a few French-speaking students to teach in Syria under French rule.[11]

Some families could afford to pay full tuition, others only part, and some none at all. Of the sixty pupils in 1865, half were charity students. Bright, deserving girls from poorer families were awarded partial or full scholarships. Since tuition covered only a part of the operating expenses, that meant the school had to be subsidized from outside. Furthermore, as enrollment outgrew the space in the Aramans' home, capital funds were needed for constructing, equipping, and furnishing a new building. One member of the Board of Managers would have to go to America to raise the funds in person.

Pioneer Fundraiser

The burden of soliciting contributions fell squarely on Henry Jessup, at thirty the youngest manager by far. With the mission's blessing he would go to the States as the North and South battled each other, and try to raise $10,000 for a new building. Though that was a substantial figure for the time (it would amount to $161,000 today), it was only one-tenth the amount sought to launch the Syrian Protestant College for men. For the next nine years Jessup would work tirelessly raising funds from American churches, Sunday schools, women's organizations, and wealthy individuals to pay for teacher salaries, student scholarships, and other capital needs of the Beirut Female Seminary.[12]

Daniel Bliss, who had a two-year head start raising funds for the college for men, but was still a strong advocate for female education, paved the way for Jessup to visit some of his biggest donors whom Bliss thought good candidates to support the female seminary as well. But before he could begin this task, Jessup was hit with a personal tragedy that rocked him to his core. His wife Caroline, the mother of their two children, had a mental breakdown that so affected her physical health that she died in Alexandria, Egypt, on the first leg of a desperate journey to get her treatment in America. Devastated by the sudden loss of his wife and in a daze, Jessup pushed on with his two children, Anna and William, through Liverpool and New York to his homestead in Montrose, Pennsylvania near Scranton. All the time he was asking himself: What was God's purpose in bringing him home under such tragic circumstances?

Jessup was convinced that Syria's future depended on the education of its girls and women. As he began to recover from the shock of Caroline's death, he became more certain that God had given his life new purpose by calling him to raise funds to erect a suitable building for Rufka Gregory's girls' boarding school that he affectionately called the "apple of my eye." With the school's future in his hands, he set out amidst the tumultuous last full year of the American Civil War, 1864, to do all in his power to raise $10,000.[13]

Jessup took the train to Jersey City and the ferry to Manhattan in September to meet with William Booth, a wealthy Presbyterian banker who had given Bliss a lead gift for the Syrian Protestant College and agreed to chair its Board of Trustees. Next, he visited William E. Dodge, another prominent Presbyterian and good friend of Booth who was the major shareholder in the Phelps-Dodge copper mining corporation. Mr. Dodge had been primed by his son and daughter-in-law, the Rev. Stuart and Ellen Phelps Dodge, who had visited Beirut three years before and seen the work of the mission first-hand. Henry did not leave Dodge's office disappointed. While the amounts of these gifts are unknown and undoubtedly much less than those for the men's college, they were certainly major contributions toward the $10,000 goal.

Jessup next journeyed to Philadelphia to solicit Matthias Baldwin, likely travelling aboard a train pulled by a steam engine built at Baldwin's Locomotive Works. His next Philadelphia visits were with John Brown, a banker, and Jay Cooke, who helped President Lincoln finance the Civil War. All three businessmen made substantial gifts. Jessup's itinerary then took him to other cities to call on various prospects until by early October he had raised the needed funds and had "awakened wide interest in missions and in the support of the school."

On November 26, 1864, three weeks after Lincoln was re-elected President, Henry Jessup reluctantly left his two children in the care of his extended family in Pennsylvania and sailed for Beirut via Liverpool. After visiting with Daniel and Abby Bliss in London, he took a steamship from Marseilles in late December and arrived in Beirut on January 11, 1865.[14]

Renovating Burj Bird

With construction funds in hand, the frugal missionaries figured out how to get two new buildings for the cost of one. Rather than erect a new school building, they decided instead to use $1,200 of the $10,000 for a new building for the mission press, thereby freeing up the old Mission House for the girls' school. The remaining funds could thus provide twice as much renovated space as newly constructed space. With the hope that the building would be ready for occupancy early in 1866, work began in June. But progress was impeded by a series of unforeseen problems that must have made Jessup, as project manager, feel like the sorely afflicted Job in the Old Testament.

A month into construction, the workmen fled to the mountains to avoid another cholera epidemic. Work was suspended until it was safe for them to return in October. Other woes included an outbreak of dengue fever, *sirocco* winds from the eastern desert that brought

Major Donors to Beirut Female Seminary

Fig. 31 – William E. Dodge, Phelps-Dodge & Co. and "Merchant Prince of Wall Street."

Fig. 32 – Matthias Baldwin, Founder, Baldwin Locomotive Works

Fig. 33 – John Crosby Brown, Brown Brothers & Co, investment bank

Fig. 34 – Jay Cooke, American financier

Fig. 35 – Henry Jessup, Beirut Female Seminary fundraiser.

Sarah and Her Sisters | 121

stifling heat, and a drought that lasted from May to September. This particular affliction meant that water had to be carried to the site in jars from nearby wells.

Jessup's workload was greatly increased due to several missionaries being away. He wrote 500 pages of correspondence and raised thirty annual scholarships at eighty dollars each. Just as construction of the lower story was finished in January, the building funds gave out. Partitioning the upper story was postponed. In March hurricane-force winds blew off the upper tier of stones, requiring more funds to reinforce all the walls and build additional partitions. Jessup sent out an emergency request to his major donors for more help. Henry Farnum, William Booth, and Robert Arthington, a British Christian philanthropist, together contributed £390 (about $3,000 then or $44,000 today) to complete the building. The missionaries were especially touched when Alexander Tod, in honor of his wife who had contributed the funds for Sarah Smith's schoolhouse in 1834, sent £100 (about $770) for the second girls' school building. An additional $800 came from a very generous "Mrs. Young in Massachusetts," who paid for a rainwater cistern with a capacity of 10,000 jars. That solved the water problem and saved $200 a year.[15]

While the renovations were underway, enrollment in Rufka Gregory's all-Syrian female seminary grew to sixty girls, testing the limits of the increasingly cramped Araman residence. Of the forty-two boarders, thirty paid their way. The remaining twelve were "charity" students who were housed, fed, clothed, supplied with books, and taught at no charge. All eighteen of the day scholars paid full tuition.[16]

BEIRUT FEMALE SEMINARY

The dramatic makeover of Burj Bird was completed in 1866 at a cost of $11,000, only ten percent over the original budget. An imposing building even by modern standards, its white sandstone walls incorporated remnants of the old Beirut Female School. Its interior wood and glass-paned windows were imported from New England; decorative roof tiles from Marseilles; windowed cupola and zinc roof from England; and additional glass from Vienna. Italian pavement with crescents of lighter tiles led to a handsome portico of Mount Lebanon stone given by a "lady from New York." Above the double front doors was a large fan window and atop the portico sat a small, covered balcony.

The interior had "spacious halls, marble floors and marvelous doors from Massachusetts." Inside, desks were arranged in classrooms illuminated by lamps fueled by oil from the northern coastal city of Batroun. Boarders slept in iron bedsteads from England. Residents enjoyed singing along to the accompaniment of a melodeon organ donated by church women in Washington, D.C., and a pump organ from donors in Rhode Island. An adjoining playground was shaded by Pride of India trees planted in 1839 by William Thomson and Story Hebard and now full grown. Thanks to Ellen Phelps Dodge, a handsome front porch was added to the building three years later.

When Rufka Gregory's still all-native female boarding school moved into its own beautiful building in the fall of 1866 and was dedicated as the Beirut Female Seminary (BFS), it claimed its rightful place as the successor to the De Forest Female Seminary begun nineteen years before in Beirut and moved temporarily to Abeih and Suq el-Gharb. By charging tuition, it was attempting to be the first self-supporting school in Syria. Michaiel Araman continued as principal, with Rufka Gregory as the "preceptress" or principal teacher. She and her native Protestant assistants—Luciyah Shekkur, Asin Haddad, and Sara Sarkis, all trained by missionaries—started the year with eighty girls. Fifty boarders paid $30 each for a total of $1,500 in gold. The upper school curriculum was taught almost entirely in English and French and included instruction in languages, arithmetic, algebra, astronomy, botany, biology, history,

Sarah and Her Sisters

and ethics, with electives in music and drawing for extra fees. Mr. Araman taught Arabic grammar. A regular academic course of study led to a diploma that prepared graduates to become teachers.

The school was thoroughly evangelical. All students had a daily Bible class and were urged to attend Sabbath School classes, worship in the Mission church, and participate in the family life of the boarding school. Regardless of religion or nationality, parents were willing to pay for the privilege of sending their daughters to a Protestant school since, as Jessup hypothesized, "Orientals did not believe in non-religious schools. Rather they thought everyone was bound to have a religion of some kind, and therefore they preferred to have their children taught one religion rather than none at all."

Once the new school building was open, Jessup could concentrate again on cultivating donors, which sometimes took him to great lengths. This was especially true in the case of Eleanor Williams Baker from Dorchester, Massachusetts. A devout church woman and the widow of Walter Baker, who owned the Baker Chocolate Company, Mrs. Baker arrived in Beirut in May 1867 after touring Palestine. She came to see the work of the Mission, but first invited widower Jessup to join her on an excursion to Damascus, Baalbek, and the Barouk Cedars. He gladly accepted and found her to be "a God sent messenger of joy and comfort." (Mrs. Baker found Jessup to be a savior too when he kept her horse from falling over backwards on a precipitous climb up the face of the Barouk mountain.) Once back in Beirut she became very interested in the female seminary and pledged a significant gift to the school, of which she would remain a benefactor.[17]

As was customary, Miss Gregory ended the school year in June with a public examination, this time in front of several hundred Greek Orthodox, Maronite, Muslim, Catholic, and Protestant parents and family members gathered in the American Mission Chapel. The students, divided into twenty-two different classes according to age and subject, were quizzed in three languages over the course

Fig. 36 – Totally renovated Mission House (Burj Bird) was first opened as Syrian Female Seminary in 1866.

Fig. 37 – Evangelical Church and Mission Press Buildings (left) with Female Seminary in background c. 1872.

of three days. Girls answered questions in Bible history, recited important dates from Adam to Christ, and listed the names of all the patriarchs, judges, kings, and prophets in order. Others read original compositions. It was obvious that all had made excellent progress due to the dedication and competence of Rufka Gregory and her staff. Beirut's official Turkish newspaper proclaimed the examinations "the most satisfactory that had ever taken place in Syria." An English clergyman surreptitiously refused to believe that they were Syrian girls, insisting, to everyone's delight, that they must have been English. The day culminated with the memorable and heartfelt words of the Greek Patriarch's representative, who told the assembled crowd:

> God in His Providence awakened the zeal of good men in distant America... to leave home, friends and country to spend their lives among us, yes even among such as I am. In the name of my Syrian countrymen, I thank them and those who sent them. They have given us the Arabic Bible, numerous good books, founded schools and seminaries, and trained our children and youth... I thank them, and Mr. Michaiel Araman, and Miss Rufka Gregory, a daughter of our own people, for the wonderful progress we have witnessed these three days among the daughters of our own city and country, in the best kind of knowledge. Allah grant prosperity to this Seminary and its teachers and pupils, peace and happiness to all present and long life of our Sultan Abdul Aziz.[18]

DIFFICULT LOSSES

From late December 1865 through early January 1866, Raheel and Butrus Bustani agonized at the bedside of their eldest daughter, twenty-three-year-old Sarah Huntington Bustani. Sarah, an alumna of the De Forests' seminary and, like her parents, an active member of the Protestant community, had been stricken with typhoid pneumonia. She declined rapidly and died on January 5. Raheel was distraught to lose her best friend and peer in education and ideology. Both women were independent and refined, and could discuss religion and culture within their home. Raheel mourned the loss of all the promise she saw in her Sarah.[19]

The rapid success of the reestablished Beirut Female Seminary was not due to an American missionary teacher, but to Rufka Gregory, the wonderfully capable thirty-year-old Syrian teacher who had been taught and trained by the Americans. But as her first year in her new school building progressed, it became obvious to those around her that this challenge had taken its toll on her, for by July 1867 she was, in Henry Jessup's words, "quite broken in health." In the hope that she would recover, Rufka was granted a six-month furlough to visit friends in Egypt. Soon the young woman Jessup called "the ablest Syrian teacher of modern times" departed Beirut for Alexandria—never to return again to her native land.

Surprisingly, Rufka had not by then professed the Protestant faith or joined the Beirut Evangelical Church. While in Egypt, however, she had a profound religious experience, perhaps the culmination of a physical and spiritual crisis that led to her sudden departure. In July 1868 she wrote to Matilda Whiting that, after a period of deep agonizing, she finally felt forgiveness for her sins and could say that her adoptive mother and teacher's "precious Savior" was now precious to her as well. Whatever the case, she made a full recovery and opened her own school for girls in Cairo until she met and married the Rev. Henry Muir, a Scottish clergyman, and accompanied him to Melbourne, Australia in 1869. There she conducted yet another thriving girls' school for many years. Following her husband's death, she returned to teaching among the British in Melbourne, again with great success. In his final tribute to Mrs. Rufka Gregory Muir, Henry Jessup wrote:

Sarah and Her Sisters | 127

As a teacher and a disciplinarian, she had no equal among the women of Syria, and under the joint management of this corps of teachers, aided by competent assistants in the various branches, the Seminary rose in public esteem, until it became one of the most attractive and prosperous institutions in Syria.[20]

Rufka, an adopted daughter of the Protestant Mission in Syria and a product of its teachers and schools, proved to be a vital link that connected the educational work of the missionary teachers before her with those who would succeed her. After her departure, the search began for the next teacher to head up the Beirut Female Seminary and carry female education forward in Syria. The burden of finding someone capable of replacing her fell, not unexpectedly, on the shoulders of her strongest backer, Henry Jessup.

CHAPTER FIVE

Eliza Everett's Beirut Female Seminary (1868–1895)

> *The Beirut Girls' School was carried on for six years with Syrian teachers, but when the principal broke down under the load, and as no available Syrian woman was qualified to take her place at that time, it became necessary to secure American teachers.*
>
> Henry H. Jessup
> Beirut, January 1, 1910[1]

REPLACING RUFKA GREGORY

A hired sleigh dropped Henry Jessup off in the deep snow in the small upstate New York village of Clinton around 8:00 p.m. on March 3, 1868. Standing in a drift above his knees in the dark of night, he faced a house he thought to be the Houghton Female Seminary. Jessup trudged up the walk and knocked on the door, only to be told that the school was down the street. Dragging his heavy satchel through the snow, he was at last welcomed into Dr. Marilla Gallup's commodious residence, which housed her prestigious school for young ladies.[2]

The Rev. Jessup's third return trip to America was for two reasons: he needed to recover from physical and nervous exhaustion and visit his children, and he was to conduct a search for Miss Gregory's replacement as principal of the Beirut Female

Seminary. His trip had begun well when, during a stopover in Paris, Mrs. Eleanor Baker had pledged to fund the new principal's salary. After spending a Thanksgiving respite with his children and family in northeastern Pennsylvania, Jessup set out to find an experienced female teacher, preferably single, who exhibited a strong evangelical Protestant faith and who would be interested in heading up a school for Arab girls nearly 6,000 miles away.

Jessup's quest took him to Yale University in New Haven, as well as to Boston, New York, Montreal, and Mount Holyoke Female Seminary in South Hadley, Massachusetts. As America's first women's college, Mount Holyoke was noted for its high standards, demanding liberal arts curriculum, and record of producing missionary wives and teachers. To his great disappointment, Jessup found no qualified candidate willing take the job. His further search was fruitless until late February when the Rev. Charles Bush in Rochester, New York suggested he interview a promising young teacher at the Houghton Female Seminary in Clinton, New York.[3]

We know little about Jessup's first meeting with the young woman destined to elevate his beloved female seminary to new heights of excellence, but we can imagine how, after she took his snow-covered hat, coat, and bag, Dr. Gallup ushered him into her parlor and introduced him to twenty-nine-year-old Eliza D. Everett. From a later photograph, we know Everett was a handsome, though not strikingly beautiful, woman of medium height who wore her wavy brown hair parted in the middle. She was likely neatly dressed in a high-collared, long-sleeved white blouse offset by a long dark skirt. She undoubtedly greeted the tall, distinguished Rev. Jessup with a warm handshake and a smile that reflected a curiosity as to the purpose of his visit.[4]

Jessup learned during the interview that Everett was a native of Painesville, Ohio and a member of its First Congregational Church, where she had professed her faith at the age of seventeen. She was almost certainly an early graduate of the Lake Erie Female Seminary in Painesville, the first female college in Ohio modeled on Mount Holyoke and taught by its graduates. Dr. Gallup, herself a Holyoke alumna, surely spoke highly of Everett, who already had upwards of ten years of teaching experience. Jessup, in turn, would have described the Beirut Seminary's history and growth under Rufka Gregory. He then popped the question. Would Miss Everett consider leaving her comfortable and promising situation at Houghton Seminary and move permanently to Beirut to become principal of the school for Arab girls? He was encouraged that she "received the proposition favorably," said she would give it serious consideration, and promised an answer once she had consulted with her parents in Ohio. Retiring for the night, Jessup was convinced that he had found the perfect teacher to "put new life into the Beirut school."[5]

Jessup pushed on through three more months of meetings while also becoming engaged to Harriet Dodge, the niece of donor William E. Dodge. When he returned to Clinton in June, he was thrilled to learn that Eliza Everett's parents had given their blessing and that she was ready to accompany him and his new wife to Beirut to take charge of the female seminary. When informed of Jessup's good fortune, Eleanor Baker convinced a twenty-two-year-old friend, Ellen Carruth, to accompany Eliza and help her in her new position. The two young women sailed from New York with Henry and Harriet Jessup and his daughter Anna, who was returning to Syria, on October 17. The five reached Beirut by way of Liverpool and Paris on November 22, 1868.[6]

GETTING ORIENTED

Eliza soon wrote home of attending the Arabic Sunday School with fifteen of her students who were separated from the males by a partition. The men and boys wore the red felt *tarboosh* (fez) with a tassel on their heads, while the women wore colored head scarves. Her girls, with their "beautiful dark complexions and eyes, were

Fig. 38 – Beirut quay and new harbor as it appeared in the 1860s when Eliza Everett and Ellen Carruth arrived.

bright and intelligent and quite bewitching in their white veils with scarlet dresses and sashes." Most were Greek Orthodox, although two were Muslims. All were well-versed in the Bible and Protestant doctrine, but most seemed just to parrot the religious concepts with little understanding.[7]

On another occasion Miss Everett dined with the family of a student in their village home. She was seated on a floor cushion at a bare, round table six inches high with no forks, knives, spoons, or napkins. After drinking an excellent soup from a bowl, she was shown how to use her bread to scoop up bits of lamb and tomato from a shared dish, and how to bite off a mouthful of boiled summer squash (*coosa*) stuffed with rice and meat before passing it on to the next person. Other meat dishes followed. The meal concluded with oranges and figs, after which water was poured on everyone's hands from a pitcher and wiped off with a coarse towel.

Eliza described her newly renovated school as a handsome structure surrounded by a large yard with rows of golden flowering "Pride of China" trees and the beginnings of a flower garden. In addition to classrooms and dormitory rooms, it contained a common dining room and kitchen, a laundry room, and a parlor for gatherings. She and Ellen Carruth had private, furnished bedrooms. The school's enclosed cupola afforded a magnificent view of the city, sea, and mountains. In warm weather, their accommodations were comfortable except for the mosquitoes.

Eliza found rainy winter days damp, dreary, and trying. Only their private sitting room had a fire to combat the chill. Otherwise, she wore heavy socks and shoes to contend with the cold stone floors, high ceilings, and open areas. The teachers supplied only their bedding, but she later advised newcomers to bring also "a writing table, study lamp, easy chair and mosquito netting as well as a personal knife, fork and spoon, table napkins and a good supply of U.S. postage stamps." Letters were addressed in care of the seminary or the American Mission. Copies of the *New York Tribune*,

Fig. 39 – 1871 photo of Mission Compound with Beirut Evangelical Church (left) and Female Seminary (center).

Fig. 40 – Breadmaking as Eliza Everett may have seen it while visiting the village home of a student.

New York Evangelist, American Presbyterian, Eclectic, Foreign Mission, and *Mission Herald* were received regularly.[8]

Eliza began her first year as principal of the Beirut Female Seminary with certain advantages. It was a period of political stability and economic growth in Syria. Her school had been well-established by Rufka Gregory and maintained by Michaiel and Lulu Araman, and then by Abby Bliss and twenty-eight-year-old Emilia Thomson who both stepped in to teach on short notice. Assisted by Miss Luciyah Shekkur, Mrs. Phoebe Carabet Salt, and six other native teachers, the two substitutes were able to keep the school operating at full capacity with thirty-five boarders and an equal number of day students.[9]

Despite these advantages, Eliza Everett's first two years were challenging. She had to master a difficult language, adjust to the culture, learn the ways of the school, and get to know her native assistants and students. Her rapid progress in overcoming these hurdles was due in large part to the invaluable assistance of Ellen Carruth.[10]

PRESBYTERIAN TAKEOVER

In 1870 the American Board of Commissioners for Foreign Missions decided to divest itself of its missions in the Near East except for Turkey. This left Palestine and Jordan to the care of the Anglican and Scottish Presbyterian Churches; and Syria, Iraq, and Persia (Iran) to the Presbyterian Church in the U.S.A. (Protestant missions in Egypt were the purview of the Anglicans and American *United* Presbyterian Church.)[11]

As adherents to John Calvin's "reformed theology," Congregationalists and Presbyterians were "Reformed Protestants," their main difference being one of church polity or governance. Congregational churches were "pure democracies," where every member had a vote and decisions were made by majority rule. (The voting included women, if they were members of the congregation.)

Presbyterians, on the other hand, elected representatives to terms on a governing board (session) that made decisions on behalf of the members. When the Presbyterian Board of Foreign Missions assumed responsibility for the Syria Mission, Eliza Everett requested that she, as a Congregationalist and "a stranger to the Presbyterian Church," be received as a Presbyterian missionary.

Everett further argued that it was "in the interests of the school and the cause of Christian female education in Syria" that the Presbyterian Board adopt and sustain the seminary in order that "the daughters of Syria would have an institution of a rank equal to that of the Syrian Protestant College for boys." In her view, the female seminary should be placed "on a permanent basis with a prescribed course of study and facilities as good as the College." She made such a strong case that the all-male board agreed thereafter to pay the teachers' salaries and subsidize the annual operation of the school. The Presbyterian Church's support for this school and the women's college that followed continued into the 1960s.[12]

FACULTY AND STAFF (1868–1895)

Over her almost three decades at the seminary, Eliza Everett had a total of ten other American women teaching alongside her: Ellen Carruth, Ellen Jackson, Sophie Loring, Helen Fisher, Eliza Van Dyck, Emilia Thomson, Alice Barber, Mary Bliss Dale, Anna Jessup, and Ellen Law. All were single when they taught except for Mary Bliss Dale. Other than Ellen Carruth who came at her own expense, each was an employee of the Presbyterian Board of Foreign Missions and paid an annual salary of $450 plus room, board, and travel expenses. Ellen Jackson, a former student of Eliza Everett, had a significant impact on the development of the seminary. Sophie Loring showed equal promise but severe eye strain (asthenopia) forced her early return home where she became a generous benefactor. Eliza

Van Dyck, Emilia Thomson, and Mary Bliss Dale were all daughters of missionaries and born in Syria.[13]

Each teacher participated in faculty meetings and had an equal vote in faculty decisions. Minutes were kept and votes on policy decisions recorded. The American teachers and the native assistants all answered to Miss Everett, who in turn answered to the school's Executive Committee in Beirut, which gave her strong backing. Initially made up of the Revs. Henry Jessup, William Thomson, and Cornelius Van Dyck, it was later expanded to include the Revs. William Bird, Daniel Bliss, and Simeon Calhoun (principal of the Abeih Boys' Seminary), as well as Dr. George Post, a medical professor at the college and the school's physician.[14]

The school could not have functioned without forty-some native Syrian teachers assisting the Americans. Most were former students hired directly after graduation. All but one was unmarried. All were bilingual, if not trilingual (Arabic, English, *and* French). They initially received a very modest salary of fifty to 125 piasters ($10 to $25) per month depending on their length of service. Their salaries were later raised to $330 annually, but still considerably less the $450 the Americans received. The difference reflected, on the one hand, the greater experience and responsibility of the Americans, but on the other, the subordinate status of indigenous teachers that continued into the early twentieth century. Some assistants boarded with the older girls, receiving free meals and lodging in return for helping supervise the residents. The rest of the assistants lived at home. A high percentage of the native teachers were, as preferred, Protestants.[15]

Sadly, little is known about these invaluable mostly young women beyond their names listed intermittently in irregular reports by Misses Everett, Jackson, and Thomson between 1871 and 1892. Mention is often omitted altogether. It is not always possible to decipher correct spellings. However, we can identify over thirty (see Appendix B) of these women who deserve individual recognition

Fig. 41 – Eliza D. Everett, Principal, Beirut Female Seminary 1865-1895.

Fig. 42 – Beirut Female Seminary students and teachers pose in school garden used as a playground. (Eliza Everett at left center?)

Sarah and Her Sisters | *139*

for the important role they played in furthering the education of their countrywomen. Of them, Farha Haddad bears special mention as the senior assistant who served the longest. Confirming that Haddad was one of the natives teaching with Rufka Gregory, she was awarded in 1890 a six-month furlough to recover from exhaustion after teaching for twenty-four years. Two others taught for twelve years: Asine Fuaz from 1873 to 1885 and Feridy Habaica from 1878 until her marriage in 1890.[16]

ENROLLMENT RECORDS

If they still exist, internal school records from this period have yet to be found. Nonetheless, certain facts and figures were included in occasional annual reports written by four different faculty members and in sporadic letters to the mission boards in Boston and New York. They follow no standard format, vary greatly in length and content, and are largely anecdotal. The reports that have survived cover only thirteen of Eliza Everett's twenty-seven years. Therefore, it is a challenge to construct a detailed picture of the school at any given time. This is especially true in trying to verify annual enrollments and in tracking trends. For example, the only seminary enrollment figures prior to 1873 are from an 1872 letter that states the seminary grew from thirty-seven pupils in 1869 to forty-three in 1872. The first of subsequent annual reports by Miss Everett was written in 1873, her fifth year as principal. Thereafter yearly reports exist through 1889 except for 1876, 1881, and 1886–88. After a gap of another five years, the last one is dated 1892.[17]

Even though the record is incomplete, we can extrapolate from these reports that between 1873 and 1892 enrollment in the seminary's Intermediate (middle school) and Academic (high school) Departments combined ranged from a low of thirty-seven students (1879) to a high of seventy-five (1885), and averaged fifty-three students. The number of boarders ranged from thirty-one to fifty-five and averaged forty. Day students (including Intermediate and some Academic students) dipped as low as six and rose as high as twenty-three, but averaged thirteen.[18]

The largest number of girls tended to be Greek Orthodox (average eighteen) followed by Protestants (sixteen), Greek Catholics (eight), and Maronites (five). Desiring even more diversity, Eliza Everett attracted and enrolled a small number of Druze, Roman Catholic, Armenian, Sunni Muslim, and Jewish girls, the latter most likely residing in Wadi Abou Jamil, the Jewish quarter in the center of Beirut. The partial records account for at least ten Druze, six Jews, five Muslims, and five Armenians attending during Everett's years. Alice Barber later observed that the "names (of the various sects) which form such insuperable barriers in Syrian social life were forgotten within the school, except on feast days."[19]

COURSES AND TEXTBOOKS

During Miss Everett's first four years as principal, the seminary remained divided into an Intermediate Department day school with three years of preparatory education for girls from ages ten or eleven to about fourteen, and an Academic Department, sometimes called the "Upper School," "Higher Department," or "High School," with four years of advanced courses for girls fourteen to eighteen or nineteen. Most advanced students were boarders. The school day was six and a half hours divided into periods with lunch and recess breaks.[20]

The new BFS principal did not immediately outline her "prescribed course of study." Rather, with the help of Misses Jackson and Loring and their assistants, she designed a curriculum of comprehensive and rigorous courses. Modestly understating the magnitude of all they accomplished, she reported in 1873 that they had made "steady progress in working out ideas and plans for higher education for girls and training teachers."[21]

Intermediate pupils were taught "simple and voweled" reading, mental and written arithmetic, and geography, all in Arabic. Arabic literature and Arabic grammar were added later. Reading the Bible in Arabic prepared the girls for biblical study in English, the main method by which they learned the language. Once proficient in English, they could advance to the Academic Department and over four years take classes in natural history, physiology (study of living organisms), natural philosophy (study of nature), and astronomy, plus Arabic grammar and rhetoric, algebra, and geometry. There were daily Bible classes, and all the boarders and some day students attended the mission Sabbath School. There was an extra charge for lessons in English, French, and piano but drawing instruction was free. In the fall of 1871 Miss Everett proclaimed her school "fully organized and much more to our satisfaction than in my previous years."[22]

With the help of Professors Van Dyck and John Wortabet, the seminary took a major leap forward in 1879 by adding a beginning course in chemistry with lectures and experiments given at the college by Dr. Edward Lewis. Miss Everett greatly appreciated "Seminary classes being allowed to visit the college observatory and other scientific rooms, use the telescope and study the astronomical instruments, botanical and anatomical models, and philosophical and chemical apparatus." The three professors also served on the seminary's examining committees.[23]

The lack of textbooks plagued the school. However, by 1876, a Mission Press was printing textbooks in elementary and advanced grammar (presumably English), elementary Arabic grammar, Arabic rhetoric, arithmetic, algebra, astronomy, logic, prosody (metrical structure of verse), geography, geometry, and natural history. Miss Everett translated *Steele's Fourteen Weeks in Astronomy* into Arabic and wrote an Arabic text titled *Mukhtasar 'Ilm al-Hay'a (Life Science)* and an arithmetic text, *Al-Hisab al-'Aqli (Pure Math)*. Ellen Jackson's contribution was *Al-Durus al-Awwaliyya fi al-Falasafa al-Tabi'iyya (Early Studies in Natural Philosophy)*. These were major steps forward in Arab female education in math and science. A modern Arab scholar wrote that the school was proving to be "one of the most attractive and efficient agencies in the land."[24]

New Initiatives

In 1871 Eliza Everett wanted to organize an English department for American and British daughters residing in Syria. With no local secondary schools in English, many were sent to schools in America, England, Egypt, or even Turkey for further education. Others were taught in French at the Prussian Deaconesses Girls' High School in Beirut. Since Everett was bringing her high school up to a higher standard for Syrian girls, adding classes in English would attract local American and British girls. It would raise the school in the eyes of wealthier Syrians who would conclude that if it was good enough for those girls, it was good enough for their daughters.[25]

With the strong backing of her executive committee, Everett proposed she start such a department. To her great disappointment the Mission Board rejected the idea for lack of funds for a fourth teacher and the extra classroom. The Syria Mission would instead establish girls' schools in Tripoli and Sidon, both in Arabic. Nevertheless, the indefatigable Miss Everett introduced other groundbreaking initiatives: in addition to the regular graduating course of study spelled out above, she set out to organize a separate primary department for younger day pupils, and develop a Normal (teachers') class for seniors.[26]

In describing the seminary in 1871, Sophie Loring wrote, "English is taught as a branch; much attention is paid to French as it is spoken very generally, but Arabic is the specialty, the object of the school being to train native teachers in their own language." English "as a branch" likely referred to the Intermediate Department where most instruction was still in Arabic. French was offered in the

Academic Department. In most primary schools in Syria, including the Mission's ninety-one common schools with a total of 4,000 students, children were taught in Arabic. A small minority of girls were introduced to English by former students of the De Forests, Rufka Gregory, and the American missionary teachers through the reading and retelling of Bible stories. Some might have qualified for the BFS Intermediate Department where some instruction was in English, but not enough for Eliza Everett who wanted to raise primary standards.

Her English department vetoed, Miss Everett opened her own primary department as a separate day school so the seminary could offer the best basic education possible and feed better-prepared pupils to the Intermediate Department. To entice more applicants and ensure a healthy enrollment, the new department was open to girls as young as five and six free of charge. Like all her predecessors, Everett's underlying goal was to convert Syrian girls to Protestantism and train them as teachers so they in turn could teach, proselytize, and train a new generation. Previous efforts to do so had been primitive and uneven compared to her ambitious plan. With the equivalent of a college degree in the liberal arts and many years of teaching at the prestigious Houghton Seminary, she was well-versed in the latest educational theories and teaching methods. She was thus eager to establish a teacher training track that would lead to a teaching diploma rather than a high school diploma.

Seniors wishing to become teachers could enroll in a "Normal" (a French term for teacher education) or teachers' class that included theory, methods and, most importantly, supervised practice teaching of primary pupils. The primary department within her seminary provided a controlled environment where would-be teachers could get "hands-on" classroom experience under the supervision of her faculty and senior assistants.[27]

Upgrading the Mission's female seminary was important if it was to keep ahead of the increasing number of other private and religious schools. Among Protestant schools alone there were by 1881, besides the seminary, the Mission's "high school" for girls in Tripoli and the girls' school in Sidon "to raise up female helpers." Then there were thirteen British Syrian schools with fifty-five teachers teaching 1,862 girls; two Church of Scotland schools teaching sixty-four girls; Miss Taylor's Muslim Girls' School with six teachers and eighty-eight pupils, and two German Deaconesses' schools with twenty-two teachers and 215 girls. Another 3,492 girls and 4,893 boys were enrolled in other schools. Seventeen of those were Roman Catholic, eleven Muslim, ten Greek Orthodox, nine Maronite, four Greek Catholic, four Jewish, one Italian, and one run by a "Madame Melhamy." Henry Jessup wrote:

> The success of (Protestant) Evangelical Schools so alarmed the Jesuits who, working with the Lazarists, Capuchins, Sisters of Charity and Sisters of Nazareth, (and with the financial backing of the French government) are opening schools alongside the American, English, German and Scotch Protestant Schools in every direction. The battle for Syria is to be fought to a great extent in these schools.[28]

EXPANSION AND IMPROVEMENTS

Attendance in all three departments in 1873 totaled one hundred girls. Many of the day students were in the new Primary Department, which, Miss Everett reported, "increased so rapidly" that the rooms used were "unable to accommodate the school comfortably." Because space within the seminary was at a premium, the children would have to be housed elsewhere. Fortunately, the adjacent residence of Tannoos and Warda al Haddad to the east of the school was available for rent. Within only three years, the Primary Department alone grew to over seventy children and eventually to as many as 110 with an average of eighty pupils per year. By 1875 it was necessary to either get a longer-term lease or purchase the property outright. Two years later Miss Everett urged the Mission Board to buy it while the al Haddad family seemed willing to sell at a "cheap" price. Luckily the Board either did buy it or received it as a gift from the al Haddads in 1882 instead of seeing it passed into "hands unsympathetic to the School." It was then named "Im Beshara House" (mother of Beshara House) in memory of Warda.[29]

Principal Everett was always looking for ways to improve and expand the school's facilities. Two second-story rooms were added to the west side of the main building in 1879. Named for its unspecified donor, the Dodge Wing made it possible to accommodate a total of fifty boarders comfortably. Another gift from former teacher Sophie Loring was used to extend and turn the ground floor parlor into a multipurpose room. The renovated Loring Wing was used for evening gatherings and as a music and sewing room. In the hope that the girls would become a little more enthusiastic about exercise, it became an exercise hall and playroom in stormy weather. These improvements enabled the teachers to train their charges in more aspects of domestic life so they could become "useful Christian women." There was enough of Miss Loring's money left over to raise the wall around the roof of the Lower School for use as a playground. Sophie Loring's benevolence continued after her marriage to W. W. Taylor. Aware from personal experience of the constant stress on the teachers, she raised funds in the late 1880s to construct a faculty retreat house in Suq el-Gharb. In gratitude, the teachers named this "haven of rest" perched on a rocky ledge overlooking the Mediterranean Beit Loring (Loring House), and referred to it as their "life-saving station."[30]

The estimated value of all four buildings within the Mission Compound (Female Seminary, Mission Press, Evangelical Church, and Sunday School Hall) in 1881 was $60,000 to $65,000, which would be about $1.5 to $1.6 million today. These buildings were subject to damage from seasonal rain and wind storms, periodic civil uprisings, and even military bombardment during times of invasion and war. The region was also prone to earthquakes, but the greatest threat of all was fire. Although all the buildings were primarily stone and masonry structures and had tile roofs, their finished interiors contained a good deal of wood and wooden furnishings, not to mention petroleum used for lamps. The coal-fired steam printing press was another hazard. It was no wonder that Henry Jessup was greatly alarmed when, on October 1, 1881, he spied from the mountain village of Shemlan a "vast column of flame" over the city. A major fire had erupted in a nearby lumber-yard and burned for four hours. Fortunately, it failed to reach the 30,000 boxes of refined oil stored next to the yard, and there was no wind to drive the flames toward the Mission Compound. Jessup's report of the fire to Dr. Ellinwood, the Mission Board's General Secretary in New York, began with the words: "And now a word about Insurance," for not one of the buildings was insured.[31]

Progress in Teacher Training

The three students who completed their Normal courses and student teaching satisfactorily in the spring of 1875 were the first graduates awarded the teaching diploma. Two stayed to teach at the seminary and the third went to the Tripoli Girls' School. They demonstrated the value of young women completing their secondary education to work outside the home as professional teachers. The following year, eight teaching diplomas were given out, and another five in 1877. Graduating sixteen teachers in three years convinced the missionaries that their school stood "at the head of the Female Schools of Syria, and in moral and religious advantages was second to none."[32]

Subsequent years were not always as productive. Four girls in the Teachers' Class of 1882 left the school; another four were dismissed for being so unpromising that it did not seem right to spend the church's money on them. Another young woman, who "was so conscientious and exemplary that her school mates irreverently called her 'Holy Spirit,'" left to marry a theology student. Happily, her sister took her place and two of the dismissed girls came back as day students, all at full cost. The following year all sixteen in the Teachers' Class "gave good promise of future usefulness."[33]

The teaching program took a major leap forward in December 1892 when Ellen Law arrived, bringing with her "special training in modern methods of teaching, particularly kindergarten work and elementary studies." She was an ideal person to head up the very important Normal Class, training girls for village and boarding schools throughout Syria and Egypt. Law made an immediate impact, giving several girls special lessons on methods of teaching, which took them considerably further than previous graduates. Her one senior passed her June examination in teaching methods quite satisfactorily and went to teach in Mardin in eastern Anatolia.[34]

Principal Everett lamented that even with Miss Law on staff, the education department's work remained below the desired standard for "want of any matter in Arabic on the science of teaching." Such materials could help the new teachers who were under constant pressure to prepare and give lessons to their pupils. It seemed "high time that Syrian teachers had the benefit of educational periodicals, teachers' institutes, etc., etc. in their own language that were such invaluable aids to teachers in America."[35]

RAS BEIRUT GIRLS' SCHOOL

The success of the Primary Department proved that Miss Everett had tapped into the growing demand for female primary education that dated back to 1834. To meet this demand and prepare more Arabic-speaking girls for admission to the seminary, the Mission assigned the Rev. James and Mary Dennis to open in the spring of 1882 the Ras Beirut Female School, a brand-new day school for girls, probably four or five to eight, located in West Beirut. They were assisted from the outset by seminary graduates. Emilia Thomson reported in 1881 that of the three BFS girls to receive diplomas in April, one was "to teach in the Girls' school opened at Ras Beirut by Dr. & Mrs. Dennis."[36]

With the advent of this new feeder school, the seminary's primary enrollment declined, perhaps because it was now charging tuition and the new school was cheaper if not free. If fees were charged, they were supplemented, as with a grant from the London-based Turkish Missions' Aid Society for the Promotion of Evangelical Missions in Bible Lands. Since half the girls were Muslims, the school's British supporters were pleased to learn from Jessup in 1892 that the "Western Asia Missions' ultimate object was the conversion of Mohammedans [sic] to the Christian faith." The Dennises' school for girls was so successful that the Syria Mission, at the request of families in the vicinity, opened a Ras Beirut *Boys'* School with thirty-five boys in the spring of 1892. It quickly grew to over sixty-five students. A free Sunday School conducted in the girls' school for both sexes attracted some 125 girls and boys.[37]

TEACHING PROPER MANNERS

Principal Everett felt strongly that her girls needed to be taught proper manners as well as academic subjects. Without making them "unfit to live happily in their homes," she insisted upon neatness and politeness, especially since her ideas of politeness differed widely from theirs. No longer could they wipe their mouths on the tablecloth, throw bread, or pass food from hand to hand during mealtime, but rather on a plate. Each dining table had a pile of blue-edged plates and each place was furnished with a glass and a fork. A pile of the flat round loaves or thinner oval slabs of bread, minus a plate, were placed in the middle just beyond the reach of those seated. Breakfast consisted of hot milk or coffee with bread, maybe with pickled olives, native molasses (*dibbs*), or strained yogurt, which Everett called "*lebing*" and described as "sour milk worked up to look like Philadelphia ice cream when frozen." Lunch was much the same with the addition of other dishes such as "eggs stained red and boiled very hard when the cook found it convenient," boiled potatoes, raw green peppers, and raw turnips pickled in vinegar with olive oil. With all the oil and raw vegetables, not to mention what she considered the rich and unwholesome sweetmeats in Syrian diets, Everett concluded that the girls either "had the digestive systems of camels or suffered constant indigestion."

One custom that the American principal was unable to change was the manner in which indigenous women washed clothes. Miss Everett lamented that the maids "sat flat on the floor of the wash room, rubbing clothes in their hands, knowing nothing of washboards, or pounders, much less washing machines." Yet she marveled that the clothes were always well washed. The "washtubs were like the brass or copper cooking vessels or bread-trays or dishbowls about the size of American washtubs, but only six inches deep. The clothes were boiled in a larger and deeper one." She observed that while the seminary had its own washroom and kitchen, women in the villages, with only two rooms and no kitchen, washed and cooked and baked bread outdoors.[38]

To learn stewardship, the girls were encouraged to contribute small amounts of money to foreign missionary causes at monthly "missionary meetings." In 1893, for instance, they dispensed with their weekly treats of candy and nuts and put their savings in a money jar. When broken at the end of the school year, the jar contained $9.62 ½, which they designated for work in South Africa.[39]

Putting on "the Screws"

The seminary's budget at the time of the Presbyterian takeover was very modest. Annual expenses totaled 77,000 piasters, which at 4.5 cents to the piaster, Henry Jessup estimated to equal only $3,500 in gold. Major expenses were the salaries of the three Americans and their Syrian assistants. The next greatest expense was room and board for the resident teachers and thirty-five boarders; third was building maintenance. The largest source of income was, of course, tuition, paid either in full or in part by the students' families. When Rufka Gregory had been principal, total income from paying students had grown to $1,500 in gold, but by 1871 it had fallen to only $500 and therefore had to be increased. Income from fees was barely worth mentioning.[40]

Early on Miss Everett told the Board she believed the school could attract "*paying* pupils from Beirut, Damascus, Tripoli, Aleppo, Latakia, Jerusalem and Alexandria and better families in mountain villages." But first she had to get current parents to pay the tuition in full and on time. Although it was her least favorite task, she was determined to improve the collection process by sending out invoices. She then considered ways to attract more girls from wealthier families, such as providing kosher meals "to attract more Jewish girls."[41]

When receipts still lagged behind, Everett joked that her efforts to "put on the screws to collect the funds nearly won her a martyr's grave." She resorted to "dark and mean" methods such as refusing admission to all not paying in full and charging new applicants to the otherwise free Teachers Class a 500-piaster entrance fee. She was delighted when some "well-to do businessmen, who preferred to keep their money earning interest in banks, writhed and twisted in the face of these tactics, but finally paid up." She decreed that "this victory compensated or all the slaughter in their combat and trials."[42]

Having learned this lesson the hard way, she was not about to let up. Her diligence paid off. By 1880, half of the thirty-two boarders paid full tuition and only one-fourth paid only some or none, with the shortfall covered by scholarships from U.S. Sunday Schools and church women. When the fathers of sixteen applicants "pretended they would pay only 1000 piasters yet were unwilling to have their daughters enrolled in the teachers' class," she stood her ground.

Sarah and Her Sisters | 151

Recognizing the value of the education provided, the men caved in and paid the full amount. By 1882, full paying students were three times greater than the previous fall, and receipts exceeded those of any previous year by 10,000 piasters.[43]

American donors were generous in providing scholarships and salaries. Ten individuals gave a combined total of $1,200 and several Sunday Schools gave a total of $1,300 to cover the $80 tuition of fifteen "charity pupils." The latter category included Eliza Everett's former Sunday School class in Painesville, Ohio, and the still faithful Norwich, Connecticut class Sarah Smith once taught. Other individuals, churches, and Bible classes contributed another $500 for a grand total of $3,500. Grants designated for each of the three teachers were important too. A "lady in New York" now provided all of Miss Everett's salary.[44] Sophie Loring's home church in Scranton paid her wages, and Ellen Jackson was the beneficiary of the new Women's Board of Missions.[45]

The school's executive committee (formerly the board of managers) was quick to endorse Everett's idea of establishing an endowment. Without it, the teachers would have to continue raising their own salaries as well as scholarships for their pupils. Both required an inordinate amount of correspondence that took away from teaching. The school operated in a perpetual state of uncertainty living from month to month and mail ship to mail ship, whereas, "securing a permanent endowment of $30,000 would relieve both the Board and the Mission of all future anxiety as to the stability and success of the School." Everett again suggested that the most likely source of an endowment was Presbyterian church women. Such women could have, she believed, "no more worthwhile and promising" cause than to put the school on a firm footing. Without it, she and the other teachers would be laboring in vain. The executive committee strongly seconded "enlisting the sympathies of mothers and daughters in America," though there is no indication that the Board presented this idea to church women at that time. It would

Diversions, Decisions, and Disease

be left to future generations of Presbyterian women to rally for the cause of Arab female higher education.[46]

Syria remained relatively peaceful until new turmoil within the Ottoman Empire in the mid-1870s caused outside powers to intervene in Turkish affairs once again. Even though Sultan Abdul Hamid II declared that all foreigners should be respected, the Americans were reassured only when the USS *Franklin* steamed into the harbor in June 1876 to show their nation's flag in the face of some hostility toward the missionaries. Ellen Jackson, Eliza Van Dyck, Henry Jessup, and fifty-four girls were entertained on the ship by a military band playing patriotic songs. (Miss Everett was ill and did not attend.) The girls reciprocated by singing Arabic hymns and songs for 500 appreciative sailors. The bandmaster arranged one Arabic tune, which the girls sang again with full band accompaniment. Aside from four girls getting seasick, the occasion was "most satisfactory" and the ship's visit left a "good impression (of America) on all classes of Syrian society." Nevertheless, Jessup still feared an outbreak of violence against Christians and informed New York that "every house was full of loaded fire arms and that Christians (with the exception of the non-violent Protestants, we assume) were ready to fight." He urged that an American naval vessel remain close at hand to offer protection on short notice.[47]

Other changes were afoot, including the power dynamics around gender in the mission. Missionary wives and "assistant missionary" teachers had always answered to the male missionaries in Syria. In Sarah Smith's time they were thrilled to be invited to sit in mission meetings, but only as observers. Much to the consternation of some older missionaries, however, the Mission Board in New York made a major change in that policy in 1890. The Syria Mission was informed that "the lady-workers were to be invited to

Fig. 43 – BFS girls and teachers were entertained aboard USS *Franklin* during its June 1876 visit to Beirut.

Fig. 44 – The missionaries "of middle and advanced age" in Syria were forced in 1890 to invite "lady workers as *participants*" to all mission meetings. (Henry Jessup, first row, far left/Daniel Bliss, second row, white hair.)

all mission meetings *as participants!*" There were a few loud objections, but soon full compliance. The women finally had their say, not only in how the school was run, but in the overall work of the Mission as well. In a region known for earthquakes, this marked a seismic shift in the operation of the Mission.[48]

Numerous diseases and periodic epidemics were still a threat and added to the stress on these "lady workers." Reports and letters home were interspersed with accounts of various afflictions striking down adults and children alike. In 1876 three children of the Rev. Samuel Jessup, Henry's younger brother, were fortunate to survive "a touch of Malaria." Two years later "a great deal of fever" and fatal cases of gastric disease and typhoid swept Beirut. In the first week of school the "Angel of Death took for his victim one of the most mature, healthy and loveliest" of Miss Everett's students. While on a summer vacation in Egypt in 1881, Everett herself barely escaped an outbreak of cholera. Then in the spring of 1882 Henry Jessup's second wife, Harriet, was caring for three of their children "ill with influenza and fever" when she was attacked with the same malady and died. In the meantime four of his children contracted, but recovered from, the measles. Henry subsequently charged that due to a "neglect of vaccination and an utter disregard of measures to isolate patients and protect the public," small pox scourged Syria in 1884. Thankfully, 1889 was "a year of health, and quiet, steady advancement."[49]

TROUBLE WITH THE TURKS

In 1885 Henry Jessup attributed the Turkish government's "hostile policies toward foreign and Christian Schools, Churches and Hospitals" to its "jealousy of foreigners." New schools were required to obtain a *firman* (government permit), and some existing schools were closed because they had no *rukhsa* (operating permit). While the new laws had no immediate impact on the female seminary, the Turks were proposing a system of universal education that, if carried out, would exclude all Christians who could be identified by name, physical appearance, manner of speech, dress, neighborhood, or village. The most serious threat to the seminary came in 1886 when the governor of Mount Lebanon, Wassa Pasha, announced that he had orders to close every school that had no *firman*. If he had executed these orders, he would have closed all the seminaries, boarding schools, and day schools run by all the American, English, Scottish, German, and Italian missionaries, be they Protestant or Catholic. The American Consul raised the issue in Washington as the Turks were violating their treaties that supposedly guaranteed protection to foreigners. Jessup argued that since the Mission and the church had "immense financial interests in buildings, apparatus, libraries and furniture," the U.S. government should protect missionary teachers just as it "protected American merchants in the petroleum, wool and licorice business."[50]

The Turkish issue with the schools was eventually resolved locally when, as required by the new law, the Mission sent to the Waly (governor) of Syria a complete set of the books used in its schools, the curriculum schedule, and a list of its ninety-nine teachers with their diplomas. The closed schools were then permitted to reopen, and further interference was ruled "manifestly illegal." Nonetheless, harassment continued through 1887 when the Ottoman Minister of Public Instruction in Constantinople proposed that foreign schools not give instruction "injurious to the interests of the country, state and public morals" or in the interests of a foreign power. Moreover, the language of instruction would be *Turkish*! The missionaries again met with Wassa Pasha, who assured them that "he understood perfectly that they had no object but one of pure benevolence and no ulterior political object whatever—as some others have." He could also assure the American government that he would do all within his power to protect the missionaries and their work. Subsequently the Waly of Syria telegraphed the Mission in April 1887 that the 290 books examined by the Academical [sic] Bureau in Damascus had been found non-subversive and were therefore sanctioned for use in Mission schools. Jessup "praised the Lord for this favorable result." Meanwhile, the female seminary had been operating without letup and with "encouraging prospects."[51]

"THREEFOLD CORD"

Preparing lessons and giving instruction in a classroom for six-plus hours a day for five days a week was a full-time job. Having also to supervise and care for the girls sharing their residence seven days a week added greatly to the teachers' stress. It took tremendous stamina to keep up the unrelenting pace. Working at first with only Ellen Carruth, Eliza Everett quickly confirmed the wisdom of a favorite verse in the book of Ecclesiastes: "A threefold cord is not quickly broken." The new principal concluded that from then on she needed at least *three* American teachers plus eight assistant teachers to run the school efficiently.[52]

This optimal scenario was, however, not always possible, which became evident at various times between 1875 and 1894. When Principal Everett, having worked nonstop for seven years, took a furlough in 1875, responsibility for the school fell on only Ellen Jackson and Eliza Van Dyck. When Everett returned, Jackson took her turn on furlough, leaving only Van Dyck to share the burden. But Van Dyck showed increasing signs of strain, causing Everett to worry that she might break down altogether. Sure enough, Van Dyck's "delicate health" forced her to withdraw in 1879. Only Emilia Thomson's stepping in again salvaged the situation. This episode convinced the principal she now needed either a fourth teacher or a full-time matron to manage the boarders so as to maintain a faculty of at least three teachers at all times.[53]

Misses Everett, Jackson, and Thomson made an especially strong team until Ellen Jackson left in 1883. Eliza Everett and Emilia

Thomson managed to keep the school going until Alice Barber came two years later to begin her record tenure at the school. She fit in well and was quickly able to assume major responsibilities, which was fortuitous as Everett, who had by 1887 gone another eleven years without a furlough, suddenly left for America "for much needed rest."

Any thought of rest ended quickly when Everett inexplicably accepted a matron position in a Working Woman's House in Denver. Hoping she would eventually return to her post in Syria, the Board wisely deferred acting on her hasty resignation. When her sister died suddenly, she had to rush to Illinois to care for her sister's children and bereaved husband. The Board then extended her leave with full pay, thus supporting her for another year while, this time, she cared for a brother who soon died from tuberculosis. Acknowledging at last that her heart was still with her girls and colleagues in Beirut, she agreed, much to the relief of the Board and Misses Thomson and Barber, to return in 1889—but only, she insisted, for three more years.[54]

Eliza Everett might have held to her three-year limit had not Emilia Thomson abruptly resigned in 1892 to care for her dying father in Denver. Luckily, Mary Bliss Dale and Henry Jessup's daughter, Anna Jessup, were readily available as substitutes. Everett pointed out in her annual report that that was "the fifth year out of the eight and a half since Miss Jackson left that the 'three–fold cord' has been only two-strands." Since Alice Barber had been sent to the States to look for an experienced teacher with special training in modern teaching methods, Everett had to run the school by herself for six months. Only the recovery of her senior assistant, Miss Farha Haddad, and the extra responsibility assumed by her loyal and capable band of native teachers saved her, as a single cord, from breaking.[55]

Leaving and Returning

These missionary educators were victims of their own success in that they inadvertently prepared young women and men to emigrate to more promising lands after graduation. The British takeover of Egypt in 1878 led to an exodus of enterprising and ambitious young people who left economically depressed Syria to seek well-paying jobs in Egypt. The men became "editors, merchants, clerks, government officers and interpreters in the British Army," while the women became teachers, the only profession then open to them. Jessup was especially worried that glittering inducements were tempting the mission's newest teachers to emigrate and that the brain drain would add to Syria's economic woes and reduce the number of paying pupils. By 1889 "the tide of emigration to America, Australia and South Africa was carrying away hundreds and only a small fraction returned to remain permanently." It was getting so bad that a new missionary questioned the viability of the Syria Mission itself, asking, "shall we set all the missionaries to teaching in Boarding Schools even if the graduates all go to America to become peddlers?" William Bird bemoaned the "stampede of native teachers going off to America" because it could "compel the mission to shut up some schools." Miss Everett deeply regretted losing her Arabic master of seven years, Mr. Jeboor Saad el Khuri, who resigned to go to the States, thus adding to the "dearth of teachers with any modern ideas."[56]

In 1883 the faculty made good its promise to the class of 1873, the first graduates to receive diplomas, by organizing a tenth-year reunion the day after graduation exercises. Of the twenty members invited, thirteen attended. Others sent letters that were read aloud. The first-ever alumnae meeting was a "pleasant occasion for all who participated." As a result, "a permanent *alumnae society* was organized in the hope of strengthening the school's bond with its graduates and stimulating more earnest cooperation in all that pertains to the elevation of women in Syria."[57]

The twenty-fifth anniversary of the Beirut Female Seminary in 1887 was a time for celebrating the success of Syria's first independent, self-supporting school for girls. Miss Everett reveled in the hundreds of mothers, teachers, and "even girls still under their fathers in every grade of society" across Syria, and "in Egypt and even across the Atlantic" who had studied in their school for up to six years. They were to her "living witnesses to the power of Christian education." The alumnae, husbands, and friends who crowded into the school's largest hall were interested to hear addresses marking the milestones in the school's history and enjoyed the social gatherings afterwards.[58]

END OF HER ERA

Just when the BFS faculty returned to full strength in 1894, two of the three teachers in Tripoli departed. As an interim measure, Tripoli principal Harriet La Grange requested that Ellen Law be sent to help her. Miss Everett objected vehemently to the transfer, saying such a move "would be a great hindrance in getting into the special work she is to do" and would "block the wheels in our Seminary for another year." With the strong backing of Dr. Van Dyck, who was "against weakening a second institution because one is weak," she won the argument and Miss Law stayed in Beirut.[59]

When Emilia Thomson returned in 1894 after her father's death, Miss Everett at last felt that, with Alice Barber back and Ellen Law then on board to reshape the teachers' class, her three colleagues were strong enough "strands" to carry the school forward without her. In a letter dated February 7, 1895, she informed the Board of Missions that she would relinquish her position at the end of the school year. After tying up some loose ends and preparing Alice Barber to take her place, she sailed home to America on June 25,

1895 after twenty-seven groundbreaking years as principal of the Beirut Female Seminary.[60]

Eliza Everett's heart still remained with her school in Beirut. She corresponded regularly with her former colleagues and some of their replacements. She remained a strong stateside advocate for the school and did what she could to promote its stability and further development. But during the last seven years of her life, Miss Everett must surely have agonized over the fate and future of her school as a series of crises befell her successors, one by one.

CHAPTER SIX

Testing Miss Everett's Heirs (1895–1904)

I can withdraw from my post feeling my associates need not be overburdened, and the school will in no way suffer. It will have in Miss Barber a wise and efficient executive head, ably sustained by Miss Thomson and Miss Law, each indispensable and each beautifully supplementing the others for the needs of the school.

Eliza D. Everett
Beirut, February 7, 1895

SEAMLESS TRANSITION

Eliza Everett had assured the Mission Board that her three colleagues (Alice Barber, Emilia Thomson, and Ellen Law) were well up to the task of taking over the school. With the ever-faithful Farha Haddad rounding out the faculty, "the school would in no way suffer."[1] All went well at first. The 1895–1896 school year began with 112 girls, of which fifty-eight were boarders and fifty-four day students. Twenty-six were Protestants, the same number Greek Orthodox, with six Greek Catholics and a few Maronites, Armenians, and Muslims. A significant milestone noted was that "sixty daughters of former students had by then attended the school and several had graduated." Attendance was good except during an outbreak of typhoid fever and flare-ups of political unrest that made parents anxious. When the seminary requested a small tuition fee for its primary day school, many families transferred their children to free Catholic and Muslim schools. The decline in enrollment was cause for moving the department back into the main building from Im Beshara House. Paradoxically, this made some parents willing to pay full tuition to have their daughters housed in the upper school.

Would-be teachers had no problem finding jobs. By 1897 all twenty-five diploma graduates were fully employed, fifteen in Syria and five each in Palestine and Egypt. The following year Martha Fiske, the childless widow of wealthy New York banker Josiah Fiske, visited the school. Perhaps inspired by the girls in the Missionary Society giving out of their own limited means to support mission work in Laos and Africa, while designating another $9.00 toward liquidating the Foreign Mission Board's debt, she sent an unsolicited gift of $1,000 "to be used for special needs not provided for in the regular appropriations." The faculty proposed that some of the money be used to purchase library books and science apparatus, with the rest kept aside "for various unforeseen insatiable items for which they have to beg travelers to pay out of their own pockets."[2]

Fraying and Unraveling

Despite Miss Everett's confidence, her successors soon began to show signs of being overburdened. Within two years the "three-fold cord" began to unravel. Ellen Law was the first to break when she literally collapsed in July 1897 while riding on horseback to Sidon in the hot sun. Appearing to recover from exhaustion after a few days, she continued to have "sensations in her head" that eventually required absolute rest under medical supervision. Reluctantly she returned to Brooklyn, New York in October to recuperate. She regained some strength but, after nine months, was still weak and forced to resign. The loss of her leadership was a major setback to the teachers' class that she had been developing. Henry Jessup's oldest daughter, Anna, then thirty-seven and living with him in Beirut, took Miss Law's place in return for only her board so Law could continue drawing her salary.[3]

The next cord to snap was Alice Barber. Burdened by much of Ellen Law's workload as well as her own duties as principal and teacher, she could barely drag herself around the school by February 1898. She struggled through the spring term before sailing home in July on the advice of her physician. Upon entering the Clifton Springs Sanitarium near Rochester, New York, she began a water cure treatment in the renowned sulphur springs while contributing half her pay toward a salary for Anna Jessup. Emilia Thomson contributed the remainder, believing that Anna ought not be paid less than $349.98 for her nine months of work.[4]

Henry Jessup wrote to the Mission Board's new Asia Field Secretary, Arthur Brown, in New York that the Board staff

> should not be surprised at these frequent failures in health because theirs is the most exacting and exhausting service in the mission field. They are confined without let up day and night, week after week with their pupils, in health and in sickness, teaching, disciplining, watching and advising. They need strong nerves and sound health to bear the strain. Unlike itinerant missionaries and wives, these 'sisters of faith, hope and charity' never have a change of scene or work and have few vacations.[5]

It was left to Emilia Thomson, Anna Jessup, and their assistants to reopen the seminary in October 1898 with forty-seven boarders and many older transfers from other schools who wanted the "advantages in English or advanced studies they could not get elsewhere." Anna's father reported that the "outlook for all the schools was good and the members of the Mission were in unusually good health." Regarding his own daughter, Jessup spoke prematurely. Anna's stress was compounded by a rumor that one of the seminary teachers was to be transferred to Tripoli, with her workload assumed by native assistants. Anna wrote Arthur Brown herself that that would be unwise because the American teachers' higher level of English gave them an advantage over the Greek, French, Prussian, and other schools for attracting paying students, and she and Emilia were always having to correct the errors of their native assistants trying to teach English. She added that they were "constantly on the jump" receiving visitors, visiting former students, and going up and down the stairs in the large building. It was all "terribly wearing." She warned that she and Emilia might both break. Furthermore, since they were sharing salaries, was it "fair to establish the precedent of having one full-salaried teacher and another receiving only $155? Pray pardon me," she added, "if I am too zealous for the welfare of this dear school, but we long to sustain its good name and go forward, not down."[6]

Just before Christmas 1898, Henry Jessup alerted Brown that something had to be done quickly to relieve the pressure on Misses Thomson, Jessup, and Haddad. Anna's health appeared most in danger. Jessup's concern for his daughter proved valid as Anna suddenly had to leave due to "nervous exhaustion."[7] It was recommended that Mary Bliss Dale, who had recently returned from the States to teach at the Tripoli girls' school, again be brought in to help. Returning to Beirut not only alleviated the teacher shortage but also gave Mary the opportunity to be near her mother, Abby Bliss, who was living in the president's home at the college in "uncertain health." Hence, in January 1899 Mary rejoined Emilia Thomson plus six Syrian teachers, five servants, and forty-seven boarders in the female seminary next to the house she had lived in as a little girl. Her days were "full and happy" when she saw "how easily they could touch and impress the girls and how readily they responded to human love and kindness." Thomson was delighted with this interim arrangement until Alice Barber could return. Henry Jessup reminded the Board that operating the seminary with less than three teachers was perilous. If Barber could not return, the school would need another "first rate lady teacher of strong physique from America" as they had already had more than enough invalids. Miss Barber could be asked "to look about for such a teacher."[8]

Harriet La Grange Raises the "Schools Question"

Some missionaries feared that the "secular work" of its press and schools would soon overshadow the mission's spiritual work. Others believed that had already happened. Veteran missionary William Eddy thought it "a sad day for Syria when Beirut became a great publishing center and a great educational center, crowding its spiritual work back into a corner." Worried by this debate, Henry Jessup was almost disabled by an outbreak of hives on his forehead. These concerns were, however, merely a prelude to inquiries that questioned—and threatened—the operations of the mission's schools.

It started with a blunt letter from Harriet La Grange, the petite but strong-willed and outspoken principal of the Tripoli School for Girls, to Arthur Brown in June 1899. Miss La Grange questioned the wisdom of operating five boarding schools—two boys' and three girls' schools, the most expensive of which was the Beirut Female Seminary—when funds were becoming limited. She thought Brown might be "more open to women's ideas than the missionaries regarding the girls' schools situation." Three girls' boarding schools within seventy miles of each other along the coast (in Tripoli, Beirut, and Sidon) seemed to her uneconomical. But as a woman with no voice on the matter she had previously remained silent. While on summer leave in upstate New York, however, the situation struck her with "a new force as radically and overwhelmingly wrong!" Could it be remedied? Her challenge triggered a serious review of the matter.

La Grange laid out the difficulty of maintaining all the properties involved. Since the British Syrian School was "doing good

Fig. 45 – Tripoli Girls' School where the visionary and feisty Harriet La Grange was principal.

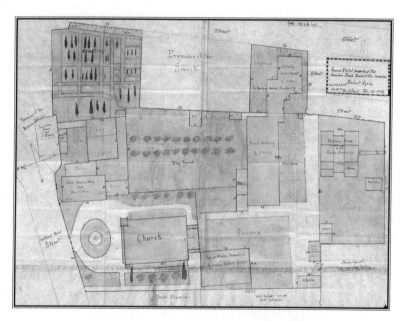

Fig. 46 – Henry Jessup's 1894 hand drawn map of the Syria Mission Compound is preserved at the Presbyterian Historical Society in Philadelphia.

Sarah and Her Sisters | 167

work providing a Protestant education to the higher class of girls" who could pay for it, why not close the Beirut Female Seminary and sell its valuable downtown property? Its building, "an old one with alterations and additions made from time to time," had a good deal of ground on two sides. Its entrance was "not convenient being midway up a steep ascent and at a sharp turn." The Sidon or Tripoli schools could teach village girls more economically. A less desirable alternative in her opinion would be to close those two schools and sell the properties, but the return would be less than the amount that had already been spent on the buildings. Besides, the "plainer, simpler and cheaper education" they provided seemed to her a higher priority.

Was Harriet La Grange jealous of the Beirut School? After all, she had struggled to keep her Tripoli school afloat for twenty-two years. Working thirty miles to the north, she was removed from the male decision makers to whom the Beirut teachers had ready access. Whenever she had requested assistance, she was told that Beirut teachers could not be spared. Most recently, Mary Dale had left her for Beirut. But what galled Harriet most were the missionary elders, especially Henry Jessup, who favored the Beirut school, and would no doubt be unwilling to give it up, let alone even consider that option. "Should an old missionary, however worthy, be allowed to block the course of the Mission to any considerable degree?" she asked pointedly.

Then the feisty La Grange put forth a revolutionary idea. Why not "raise the rank of the Beirut school to that of a College?" Granted, doing so would be quite expensive because the present building was not suitable for a college. Moreover, the present faculty and teachers were not qualified to staff a college, nor was any other woman then in the mission. Nevertheless, she ardently believed that two schools, with less money and effort, could do just as well what three schools were then doing and their precious resources could be better used. She ended her letter a bit disingenuously: "I have not written in the spirit of 'tattling'—or complaining, but with the hope that possibly something better may grow out of it.[9]

Harriet La Grange certainly got Arthur Brown's attention. In retrospect, she was a visionary on a par with Sarah Smith and Eliza Everett. Although her idea of a women's college was revolutionary, time would prove her prophetic. Still the logic in her arguments prodded Dr. Brown to write two letters to Jessup and the Syria Mission that initiated a flurry of transatlantic correspondence.

In his first letter of July 27, 1899 to Beirut in response to the Mission's request for funding for a new school in Zahleh, Dr. Brown from New York raised the delicate question of the schools with the missionary elder most invested in the Beirut school, Henry Jessup. "Before the Board votes another large school property," he wrote, "we wish your counsel on a larger educational question, namely whether it is expedient to maintain all the boarding schools we now have in Syria." (Miss La Grange's letter of the month before had indeed made an impression.) He listed the schools' costs, including salaries, furloughs, a house physician, and house rent. In all, annual expenditures for the three girls' schools were $10,000 and the two boys' schools $5,000. After pointing out that, compared to China and India and other mission fields, Syria was compact and its schools, in comparison, did not serve many students, Brown asked the general question: Were they "using the Lord's money to best advantage?" He then followed up with a barrage of specific questions that must have jolted Jessup. Could not larger boarding schools, one for boys and one for girls, be maintained for less money, thus freeing up funds for more missionaries? The number of schools could be reduced, Brown thought, without great harm to the educational work. Then Brown raised the matter of real estate, asking how much land and how many buildings were involved. He wondered aloud if these properties could be better used for other purposes, or if it would be wiser to sell all or some of them. Lastly, he gently challenged Jessup about the students being served when the geographical distribution of boarders covered no great distance. Although it was unlikely all current students would attend the one remaining school, yet if there were more funds to equip it better, might it be attractive to more students?

Sensing correctly that Jessup would be taken aback—if not stunned—by this outpouring of concerns, Brown, perhaps a bit late, implored him not to magnify the significance of his inquiries beyond his intent. No decisions had been made. He was simply asking Jessup's advice since Syria was, he wrote soothingly, "one of the most intelligent and able Missions and his judgment had great weight with the Board." Brown assured him that he too believed strongly in the educational work in Syria and had no intention to cripple their effort, but rather to increase its efficiency. So as not to lose sight of the main question, he concluded by asking once more, "Was it better to have five small and struggling schools, or two larger and stronger ones?"[10]

Jessup was most assuredly stunned to be asked these questions. Once over the shock, he rallied against this threat to the "apple of his eye" in which he was so deeply invested. He countered on two fronts. First, he preemptively circulated a "confidential detailed statement of the whole case for the *girls'* schools" (notably ignoring the boys' schools), as he supposedly saw it with a "fair, impartial, and judicial mind," and requested feedback. Admittedly, it was difficult for the missionaries to be both advocates for individual schools while judging what was best for the Mission overall. Nevertheless, as a good Presbyterian he laid out, "decently and in order" on five legal-sized, single-spaced, typed pages a detailed review of the alternatives regarding the three schools, listing the pros and cons of each. The possible actions were:

1. Leave the three schools as they were.

2. Suspend the Beirut school, and keep the Sidon and Tripoli schools.

3. Suspend the Tripoli and Sidon schools, and make the Beirut school a girls' college.

4. Establish Sidon and Tripoli as Preparatory Day Schools for a girls' college in Beirut.

5. Transport the Tripoli girls to Sidon and leave Beirut unchanged.

6. Suspend the Sidon School to save $2,500.

7. Abolish all three boarding schools.[11]

Once the internal discussion was underway, Jessup wrote several responses to Brown that added up to respectful but firm pushback. He assured Brown that the Mission was giving his questions "conscientious and deliberate consideration." He added: "The ladies of the Seminaries (including Miss La Grange) were preparing their views on the subject." But then, pursuing an entirely different tack, he suggested that a personal visit by Brown would be worth more than exchanging "a cartload of documents since the *raison d'être* of these schools was not so easily explained in writing." He then helpfully mapped out how Brown could reach Beirut in only thirteen days: New York to Southampton by steamship (six days); train to Constantinople (three days) and finally to Beirut by French steamer (four days). They could then spend twenty days together dealing with "this great Consolidation question."[12]

This exchange between the two men occurred against a backdrop of major changes to Protestant foreign missions in the 1890s. Inspired and motivated by the Second Great Awakening, the first Protestant missionaries sent to Syria beginning in 1825 were primarily to preach the gospel and convert the "heathen" natives to Christ. Any social concerns beyond that were, in the words of church historian Williston Walker, "expressed largely in individualistic terms, stressing charity and moral reform." But after expanding for fifty-five years, the missionaries' religious influence began to level off by 1880 and then started to shrink in 1889.

Sarah and Her Sisters | 171

Certainly, the zeal of the great awakening had long since dissipated in America and interest in and support of mission work was waning in American churches. While veteran missionary William Eddy faulted the mission itself for allowing its press and schools to eclipse its spiritual work, Henry Jessup cited the inroads made by the British Syrian Mission as a cause for the decline. He resorted to a battlefield analogy reminiscent of the American Revolutionary War by saying:

> So many Presbyterian Mission flags have been pulled down in Syria, and so many scattered tents struck down that if we vacate the headquarters camps, the enemy would begin to sound the note of triumph. And in the place of our deserted schools and outstations, the British will gain the heart of our hard fought and won Presbyterian field. They increase! We decrease!

Yet there was another reason for this shift in emphasis that transcended the mission in Syria and "was strongly felt throughout mission fields worldwide." The Social Gospel movement arose from "a deep social concern on the part of many progressive American Christians, especially Presbyterians, Congregationalists, Episcopalians and Northern Methodists and Baptists." Instead of viewing the gospel primarily in individualistic and moral terms, the proponents of the social gospel "focused attention on the corporate aspects of modern life and on the achievement of social justice" and expanded the emphasis on "agricultural, medical and educational mission." It could be argued that Jessup, knowingly or unknowingly, adhered to this new social gospel when he explained to Arthur Brown that "Syria was first and foremost an educational mission."[13]

Brown's schools question had stirred the Mission deeply. The three schools were well-rooted in the Syrian soil—and in the minds and hearts of Presbyterian church women. With increasing dramatic effect, he warned Brown that "the Women's Board at home might object to tearing them up, lest some other precious things be rooted up with them." It was becoming clear to Jessup that "the suspension of any one of them would be distressing and calamitous." Already, Brown's demands for answers on "the schools question had caused the ladies in Beirut to postpone building repairs lest they prejudge the question of suspension or consolidation." The teachers of all three seminaries felt "as if they had a halter around their necks!" Still, he coyly added, "they would reopen their schools in October 1899 with good hope and courage."[14]

Brown, apparently realizing he had stirred up a hornet's nest, replied in an open letter to the Mission that he was "perplexed to discern an apparent undertone of fear that the Board was disposed to sacrifice the educational work" in favor of evangelizing, or that its members failed to "adequately understand how necessary the educational work was." He worried that the missionaries in Syria had read between the lines and mistook his intention. Backpedaling, he now stated his view that Christian education was "more important in Syria than in most any other field." He only meant to question whether resources could be used to better advantage to increase the efficiency of the schools. If consolidation would do irremediable harm to their educational work, then the Board would not even consider it. The "schools question" was thereafter put on hold until he could assess the situation in person, which, it turned out, would not be for another eighteen months.[15]

Frustrated by this postponement of the issue, Harriet La Grange sent Brown her "minority report" following the December Mission meeting saying: "Consolidation had few advocates. The older missionaries were inclined to 'let well enough alone.'" For Henry Jessup, the Beirut seminary was not only "a pet child" but a vital hobby; as he was aging, it provided him a "field of work." Then too was his sentimental attachment to the old room in the seminary where Smith and Van Dyke had translated the Bible.

Miss La Grange took some satisfaction in knowing that a majority of those serving in the Mission seemed to agree that, "if any school were to be closed, it should be the Beirut school, which was doing charity work like Tripoli and Sidon, only on a more expensive scale." But Beirut was not the best place for such work. She reaffirmed her long-term vision. Since the Beirut seminary's land was far more valuable than that in Tripoli and Sidon, it should be sold and the proceeds "invested and kept until there should be a demand for higher education here in the East."[16]

College President Daniel Bliss felt the schools question was valid, but cautioned that those involved in this discussion had to be careful not to give Syrians the impression that the mission was backing off from any of its work. Attachments toward each school were strong. The Beirut school, in his opinion, "had a good plant and great promise and... it would be a serious matter to abandon it." Besides, with improvements in transportation, it was becoming more accessible to students from a wider area. Those in Tripoli could now reach Beirut by carriage and the new coastal railroad in as little as five or six hours. Or they could sail back and forth on three or four steamer lines. Since travel and communication were improving and reluctance to travel had virtually disappeared, he saw no reason why the Tripoli girls could not attend the Beirut Seminary.[17]

PROVIDENTIAL APPOINTMENT

Mary Dale had planned to stay until Alice Barber's return, so it was a shock to Emilia Thomson when in 1899 the Board, without consultation, reassigned Dale to work in Ras Baalbek. Still recovering stateside, Barber offered to search for a suitable replacement, but Thomson and Dale begged her not to proceed. They felt that a newcomer, who would have to spend a year in language study, would be of little assistance. All four women were then amazed to learn that Dr. Brown had, without consulting with any of them, already appointed Miss Rachel Tolles as Mrs. Dale's replacement. Had their advice been sought they would have made it clear to him that, aside from a true missionary spirit, the new teacher should have a knowledge and love of music. During Alice Barber's tenure she had been able to provide accompaniment on the piano, but no one was qualified to teach singing. Normal students needed to be able to sing and utilize music in their teaching and missionary work.

Alice Barber was "much dismayed" to learn upon meeting Tolles that, although she could play the piano some, "she did not sing." She informed Brown that the new teacher would *not* do, but, fortunately for the future of the school, it was too late. Tolles's passage to Beirut had been booked. Not wanting the new teacher to know of their unreceptive feelings, Barber wrote Tolles that the Lord seemed to have sent her to them. On behalf of herself and Emilia Thomson, she welcomed her most cordially and heartily to their school.[18]

Rachel Tolles sailed from New York to Liverpool in late August 1899 accompanied by Harriet La Grange, who was returning from her summer vacation. After spending time together in London, they sailed up the Rhine to Mainz and down the Danube to Vienna before crossing the Austrian frontier. The highlight of their train journey from Sophia to Constantinople was Serbian peasants with flickering torches having to push them on flatcars through the unsafe Belgrade Tunnel at midnight. From Constantinople the ladies cruised aboard a steamer by way of Smyrna to Tripoli, where La Grange disembarked to resume her duties at her girls' school. Continuing overnight along the coast, Rachel Tolles arose to a brilliant morning on October 2 to observe the busy scene in Beirut harbor:

> water craft lying all around, smoking steamers, great sailing vessels, and scores of gay little row-boats dodging here and there, the scene one of life and color. Brightly garbed watermen swarmed over the sides of our steamer, all so good-natured, so light-hearted, so quick-tongued.[19]

Fig. 47 – Rachel Tolles described Beirut's busy harbor on her arrival in 1899.

Beyond the harbor she saw for the first time the city's "mosaic of color amidst olive groves against the magnificent Lebanon." Warmly welcomed to the seminary by Miss Thomson and her assistants, Tolles began her Arabic study while assisting them as best she could. No one at the time could have suspected that her tenure in the school would last twenty-three years (nineteen as principal), and that she would bring it to the threshold of higher education for women.

The newest teacher settled in quickly and within a week wrote Brown that she was in love with Beirut, "the sea, mountains and whole atmosphere of the place!" The few natives she had met were "interesting," she reported. By coincidence, the school opened on her birthday. Enrollment was expected to be about the same. One student, who had been taught for several years by Catholic sisters, was placed in the seminary by her uncle, a graduate of the Syrian Protestant College. He paid her full tuition and board because he knew she would get a better education there even though the French Mother Superior warned that the girl was in danger of losing her soul by being placed with the Protestants.

Tolles gave Arabic study her best efforts and was glad to be helpful by teaching classes on Saint Paul and conversational English, rather than just "laying a foundation for the future." Never having dreamed of Syria, she was now sure that it was "God's place for her." She overlapped for a year with Mary Bliss Dale, who found her "capable, adaptive and brave—three foremost qualities necessary in a missionary." Tolles proved to be a "pleasant companion with an earnest desire for spiritual things—just what they wanted in a new teacher—and there was no Syrian dish that Miss Tolles could not eat or did not like."[20]

Her first winter passed quickly and happily. Studying Arabic was "enjoyable despite its difficulty." At first it seemed like a blank wall through which she had "only a few pin holes" like the words for "good morning" and "thank you." But gradually the pinholes became larger and provided "some pretty good glimpses of what lay on the other side." During the summer, however, her studies were interrupted when she developed a malaria-like fever. Alice Barber later attributed this to Miss Tolles overexerting herself by

> taking too long a journey in one day that should have been taken in two days. Newcomers cannot take the jaunts that those more accustomed to the country can perform with impunity, and those of us who do comparatively little riding during the year cannot do what those who ride constantly do.

Luckily, Tolles's summer fever lasted only ten days with no lasting harm other than the loss of two valuable months of language study.

Alice Barber returned to Beirut in time to spend the end of the summer at Beit Loring. With Mary Dale having left to take up her new responsibilities, Alice Barber, Emilia Thomson, and Rachel Tolles were all glad to return to their seminary home in the fall, finding that it had been cleaned and put in order to begin the first full school year of the twentieth century. With the faculty and enrollment back at full strength, the teachers wished that Dr. Brown were coming to inspect the school that year rather than the next. The senior class of ten was unusually large, although five or six other advanced students did not return for unspecified reasons.[21]

GROWTH IN BEIRUT

Swollen by tens of thousands of refugees fleeing the worsening poverty on Mount Lebanon, Beirut's population at the turn of the century was estimated to be 120,000, triple that of 1860. As part of Sultan Abdul Hamid II's bold efforts to modernize his empire, the municipal government tore down residences and the souks in the old city to make way for new shops, markets, four- to five-story office buildings, and a new City Hall. The city's first department store featured its first elevator. The city limits expanded well beyond the old city walls. Former villages and farmland gave way to wealthy residential suburbs such as Ras Beirut, Msaytbeh, and Ashrafiyyeh where newer homes, schools, hospitals, churches, and police stations were built among older mansions.

Beirut residents enjoyed new public squares and parks with fountains and widened streets accommodating horse-drawn carriages, omnibuses, new streetcars, and even the very first horseless carriage, which startled and scared inhabitants. A railroad line now linked the city to Damascus. People crowded the streets in daylight and strolled under gas streetlights at night as they visited the city's proliferating cafes, hotels, restaurants, and clubs (and brothels). A lighthouse showed ships the way to the new harbor, port facilities, and renovated Custom House. A seaside railroad station opened, and the new public pier was popular with strollers. The new public water system provided clean, dependable water to all. The Ras Beirut campus of the Syrian Protestant College, purchased in 1870 and larger than the original walled city, added a Preparatory Department building and a theological seminary.[22]

The girls' seminary was burgeoning too, with 1901 proving to be another record year. Ten seniors graduated in July, including one who was the daughter of an alumna of the class of 1876. Eighty-eight girls enrolled in October. Sixty boarders from Beirut, Mount Lebanon, Constantinople, Cyprus, Tartous (Syria), Damascus, Tiberius, Jaffa, and Alexandria crowded into quarters designed and furnished for only fifty-four. The faculty attributed the school's widening appeal to its growing prestige and were further motivated to sustain this lead in the higher education of young women just as the Syrian Protestant College was the region's leader in the higher education of young men.[23]

To strengthen its Primary Department, the Beirut Female Seminary took over the well-established Ras Beirut Day School that could also serve as a teaching laboratory. Miss Malory Jasmine, a well-qualified teacher trained in the Prussian Deaconesses School, was hired as the new primary head. She recruited Christian, Muslim, and Jewish children as young as four and five. Kindergarten exercises included motion songs, busy work, and first lessons in sewing. Her young pupils were taught to read and write in Arabic. "To connect them with the living thought of the times," they learned some English and beginning French as well.

The children loved their new teacher who taught them psalms and hymns, the stories of Abraham and Joseph and David, and even the New Testament, which for many was forbidden. A senior in the teachers' class did her practice teaching by assisting Miss Jasmine. Each year, a half dozen or so of the oldest children advanced to the Intermediate Department where each "took great pride in being assigned her own American desk with an ink well and place for her books and being subject to the rules of school life." If she was able to keep up her grades, a girl could graduate in seven more years. Miss Jasmine, who later became Mrs. Hashim, remained the head of her Ras Beirut School for the next twenty-five years.[24]

Arthur Brown's Visit

In the spring of 1901 Arthur and Jennie Brown began a tour of Presbyterian missions in Asia. Disregarding Jessup's suggested route via the Atlantic, they sailed west across the Pacific and visited missions in Japan, China, Korea, the Philippines, Siam (Thailand), and India before rounding the Arabian Peninsula and stopping in Cairo where they were greeted by fifty of Miss Everett's former students. When the travel-weary Browns finally reached their last stop, Beirut, on March 21, 1902, they were immediately rushed off on a five-week tour of mission sites throughout Syria with side visits to Jaffa, Jerusalem, and Damascus. Dr. Brown was then sequestered for a full week in meetings with the missionaries to discuss the issues that were most important to them. He asked questions, took copious notes, and stayed up until midnight writing reports. The missionaries appreciated his wide experience and found his "clear judicial and judicious view" beneficial and inspiring. They expressed their gratitude to the Board for sending Dr. and Mrs. Brown to Syria.[25]

In between three daily work sessions, Brown attended receptions, gave addresses in the church and at the college, and, on one somber occasion, joined the Mission community in a memorial service for Eliza Everett, who had died in Chicago in February. Henry Jessup's third wife, Theodosia, described how "American, English and German missionaries, professors and teachers from the College, Syrian preachers and teachers, business men and mothers with children" crowded into Dale Memorial Hall to mourn the loss and celebrate the life of Eliza Everett, with "the majority of the congregation composed of her former pupils."

Standing beside a large photograph of Miss Everett framed in palm branches, Henry Jessup led the service for the woman he had recruited thirty-four years before, pointing out that it was not easy to become a teacher in a strange land. She was remembered for her "attractive personal appearance and rare intellectual gifts" and eulogized as a person

> who cheerfully gave herself to work with the strong faith that female education, which was then an experiment, would justify all the effort and grow to be the power for good which it has become. As a teacher of science, history and kindergarten, she modeled character, truthfulness, purity and self-government and had a magnetic influence over her pupils whom she stamped with her own character as perhaps no other woman had. She exhibited a quick sympathy in joy or sorrow, but above all, had a simple, childlike religious faith. The fruits of her labor could be seen in teachers, mothers and loving women all over Syria, Palestine and Egypt.

Although they had never met Miss Everett, Dr. and Mrs. Brown recalled meeting fifty of her former pupils in Cairo who praised and mourned her. These former students were having her portrait painted for their alma mater that was carrying on her noble work. The service concluded with the reading of letters of condolence and the hymn, "For All the Saints Who from Their Labors Rest." A memorial tablet was placed on the wall of the school hall alongside one marking the translation of the Arabic Bible by Eli Smith and Cornelius Van Dyck.[26]

The Browns' thirty-six-day visit ended on April 25 when they and Anna Jessup departed for New York. During the voyage, Dr. Brown wrote up his notes on the visit and the various agreements reached on policy. After attending the Presbyterian General Assembly in New York, he spent a long period recuperating from an illness Jessup attributed to "overtaxing his physical strength during his year-long tour visiting too many missions and subjecting himself to mental and physical tension too great for ordinary human strength." Seeing as Jessup had lobbied Brown to come and caused much of the tension he experienced, this was a rather presumptuous and hypocritical diagnosis. Nonetheless, much to Jessup's relief, one "policy agreed upon" was that each of the three girls' schools in Syria would remain separate and independent. There would be no consolidation of schools.[27]

Fortieth Anniversary

Two weeks after the Browns' departure and only eighteen months since she returned from the "water cure" in Clifton Springs, Alice Barber abruptly resigned and returned home again, this time to care for an aged parent. The Board accepted her decision with "profound regret," although the seminary had not seen the last of her. The twentieth commencement and triennial alumnae meeting were moved up to take place before her departure.

Before Alice left she penned in her near-perfect hand an interesting and informative sixteen-page anniversary tribute later published in *Woman's Work for Woman*, the Presbyterian Women's Foreign Mission Society's monthly journal, as "Beirut Seminary after Forty Years." In it she endeavored to explain the history of the institution that had been founded as an independent, all-Syrian boarding school in 1862. It began: "Beirut Seminary, like the River Jordan has its source in more than one hidden spring. One of these sources may be traced to the (elementary) day-school opened in 1835 by Mrs. Eli Smith of Beirut Station." Although she mistakenly attributes it as being "the first school for girls in Syria," she confirms that "stones of that building were incorporated into our own when it was erected in '65–'66." Reflecting the still masculine bias of the times, she traces "the other two sources to the missionary homes of Rev. George Whiting" (making no mention of Matilda Whiting, the teacher) and Dr. De Forest (overlooking co-teacher and matron Kitty De Forest). But Barber does corroborate that "the future Preceptress [Rufka Gregory] and Matron [Lulu Shebly Araman] of the Seminary were taken in childhood and trained previous to their studying in Dr. De Forest's school," affirming that Rufka was brought up in part by the Whitings, and both she and Lulu by the De Forests.

In the tribute Barber touches on some of the highlights of the forty years. According to records that may not have been complete, since the boarding school's beginning in 1862 under Rufka Gregory, a total of 840 girls had received at least some instruction in the school. Seventy-eight had graduated, sixty as teachers. Another 102 non-graduates had gone on to become teachers. Twenty-three were teaching in Egypt, ten in Beirut, and another thirty-six in "Jaffa, Jerusalem, Nazareth, Hasbeiya, Sidon, Deir el Komr, Shweir, Shemlan, Wady Shahroor, Adana and Tartoos." Five had "entered the cloister" and one had become a Prussian deaconess. An additional "380 were known to have married... preachers, teachers, physicians, pharmacists, journalists, editors and businessmen" and were residing in "Syria, the United States, the West Indies, Brazil, Egypt and Sudan." As wives and homemakers, they "conducted women's meetings, sewing classes and clubs as well as taught their ignorant servants, and engaged in evangelistic work."[28]

Rachel Tolles and Ottora Horne

Although the missionary teachers hoped Miss Barber might return as principal, they found a capable leader already within their ranks. Rachel Tolles, with three years of on-the-job training and still mastering Arabic, stepped in as principal, a position she would hold for the next nineteen turbulent years. She and Miss Thomson were greatly relieved when Mary Dale and Mrs. Bertram Post, wife of the Mission physician, agreed to help until another new teacher could be found. They and the six Syrian teachers, all Protestants, taught ninety-two "studious and thoughtful" girls, twenty-three of whom were daughters of former students.[29]

Principal Tolles recommended that her best friend, Mary Elmore, be hired to replace Miss Barber. A graduate of Elmira College, Miss Elmore had taught for three years in a girl's preparatory school before doing post-graduate work at Bryn Mawr College. Despite this strong personal endorsement, the Board, again providentially, offered the job instead to Miss Ottora Horne who arrived on December 19, 1902 and began a strong partnership with Miss Tolles that would last for two decades.[30]

Now knowing the culture of the school and the girls well, Tolles was not about to resort to what she called "Jesuitical methods" to enforce the easily evaded mandate that they speak English among themselves, so she shrewdly created the Golden Key Society and the Laurel Society. These two English-speaking societies vied with each other in not permitting members to speak Arabic except during brief intervals. The competition was so infectious that the new girls who knew no English organized themselves into the Look-About Club. The faculty was amused "to see them on the outskirts of a group of girls speaking English trying to absorb the meaning with open ears, eyes and mouths." Because the Americans mistakenly thought Arabic literature to be meager, they believed learning English would open the girls to the wider world of English literature.[31]

Greater fluency in English facilitated the introduction of new and advanced textbooks in history, physiology, botany, chemistry, physics, and astronomy. Daily Bible study classes made good use of courses supplied by the Bible Study Union Company. In addition to taking educational theory and practicing their teaching skills in the Primary Department, future teachers of Syrian, Palestinian, and Egyptian girls could elect to take French. Nor was music neglected: though few students "had any decided talent in that direction," some took piano lessons for an additional fee.

Emilia Thomson reported that boarders were required to "do much of the housework and spend part of each day in the Serving Rooms" so that they did not have "many idle minutes." She hastened to add: "It was not a case of all work and no play as the playground often testifies at recess time and after school hours." (The "playground" was a broad, tree-lined garden in front of the school and beside the Syrian Evangelical Church. There was also a smaller garden behind the school the girls could use.) "Saturday afternoon sends them all off for a long walk and on Saturday evenings they spend lively times in the school room either about the English Literary Societies or in unorganized merry making."

Prevalent diseases remained a constant threat. Sadly, the only senior in 1903, Lulu Salisky, a sweet, dignified, and beloved girl of seventeen, died ten days after contracting typhoid fever. More worrisome than typhoid was the cholera creeping up the coast from Egypt. Rev. Franklin Hoskins, who, like Jessup, kept the Board in New York well-informed of local and regional events, wrote that although the Turkish government was aware of the threat, it did nothing to guard its frontier from cholera. Week by week, the residents of Beirut watched with alarm as the disease advanced steadily toward them and threatened the opening of the school. To make matters worse, the yellow flag was flown over the port to warn approaching ships of known cases of the Black Death in the city. One rumor traced the source to an inn catering to caravans to and from eastern Asia, where cameleers and muleteers had come down with a suspicious illness. Hoskins feared that local authorities were "not taking any radical measures to cleanse the place." Amidst all these worries, Mary Dale concluded her 1902–03 report with a brief poem:

> We are not here to play, to dream, to drift,
> We have hard work to do and loads to lift,
> Shun not the struggle, 'tis God's gift.

The burdens were about to get heavier and the struggle to keep operating more difficult as a new threat brought back nightmares from the past.

"The Troubles"

Coining a term Catholics and Protestants in Northern Ireland would use decades later, the missionaries referred to 1903 as the first year of "the Troubles." A revival of fanaticism during the rule of Waly Ramiz Bey in the 1890s ended decades of relative peace in which missionary enterprises had flourished. Hoskins recalled that intolerance toward all Christians had increased under Ramiz's successor, Waly Rashid Bey, who joined forces with "desperados and smugglers of tobacco, rifles and ammunition and engaged in various nefarious enterprises while condoning crimes including the swindling of his own government, thereby demoralizing every government department." By October 1902 increased harassment prompted the missionaries to send a delegation of prominent Presbyterians to call upon President Theodore Roosevelt and alert him to the deteriorating situation.

September 1903 began a tense and terrifying year for the residents of Beirut, especially Christians. It started with ten horrific days when, according to Hoskins, "all the forces of lawlessness and corruption were at work, [and] matters grew steadily and hopelessly worse with a maelstrom of destruction and robberies, stabbings and murders." News of an uprising against Turkish rule in Macedonia further enflamed "hatred of everything Christian." A report that the American Consul had been shot caused President Roosevelt, like Glover Cleveland before him, to resort to "gun boat diplomacy." It turned out that the report was erroneous; the consul had been *shot at* but escaped the incident unharmed. Not knowing this, the United States president swung into action. He dispatched the USS *San Francisco* and the USS *Brooklyn* to Beirut supposedly to retrieve the consul's body and protect the other Americans there. When both ships steamed into the harbor on September 4, the city became "electric." Hoskins, assuming the role of an ad hoc foreign correspondent as missionaries often did for the folks at home, thereafter gave a day-by-day account of events.

Much his surprise, Admiral Charles Cotton was greeted and briefed by the still very much alive consul and twenty-five Americans, mostly missionaries. But just because the consul had not been assassinated or even injured did not mean Beirut was not a dangerous place for the missionaries. In three days, there had been five murders in the city. There were rumors of nine to twelve more and threats of attacks on foreigners. When some twenty-three people were killed on Sunday, September 6 and the city's terrified residents started fleeing to the mountain, Cotton readied 500 Marines to land.

On Monday a Turkish soldier was killed and only two of ten newspapers appeared. On Tuesday Waly Rashid Bey falsely proclaimed that soldiers had put an end to the rioting and restored peace. Businesses were to reopen, and troublemakers would be punished severely. However, residents were afraid to return to their

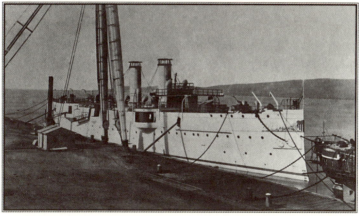

Fig. 48 & 49 – USS *San Francisco* and USS *Brooklyn* sent to Beirut in September 1903 by President Theodore Roosevelt to protect Americans during civil uprisings.

normal routines, as unruly individuals were still out of hand and arming themselves. The missionaries believed that only the presence of the American squadron had prevented a massacre. At the urging of Cotton and the U.S. government, Constantinople dismissed Waly Rashid Bey and sent in his place Waly Nazim Pasha, whom the Americans considered "one of the best men in the Empire" and well able to restore order.

The situation remained tense up to the October reopening of the seminary. The missionaries and teachers, along with thousands of refugees, returned from their mountain retreats skeptical that order could be maintained. All were glad for the continued presence of the American ships for they feared renewed chaos might lead to the massacring of Christians, which had happened in neighboring Turkey a few years before. The poor were suffering greatly and those responsible for the violence had yet to be apprehended.

Unrestful Calm

Rachel Tolles began her second year as principal hoping the worst was over. In early October she gathered her staff to prepare for the new academic year. The faculty consisted of herself, Emilia Thomson, Mary Dale (who was staying on for another year), and Ottora Horne, now with a full year of experience. With the addition of a competent team of both experienced and newer native teachers, the faculty was again at full strength. Owing to the preceding riots, the boarders dropped from fifty-eight to forty-seven because students from Egypt and Cyprus were afraid to return. This decline was, however, offset by an increase in day scholars, thereby keeping overall enrollment at an even hundred.

Thanks to the squadron remaining offshore, a quiet not seen for many years descended upon the city. Mission officials in New York were informed that despite competition from the Russians, the region's mission schools were full to overflowing with *almost*

Sarah and Her Sisters | *189*

the same number of boarders in the girls' and boys' boarding schools. The school's main stairway had been greatly improved, and two glass screens erected to shut off wind and noise. But, just as civil unrest was subsiding, cases of smallpox occurred aboard the *Brooklyn* and *San Francisco*. Equally distressing, cholera reappeared in Tripoli and caused that city's girls' school to close for the year. Then some "stupid official mixed up the English and American schools and reported to Constantinople that the Americans had *eleven* institutions or schools in Beirut!" It took the Mission six months to straighten out that misunderstanding. On the staffing front, Alice Barber wrote with a heavy heart from Joliet, Illinois in December that her "dear father reached the end of his earthly journey" and that her mother had "broken down so rapidly" that she had "often thought she might go before father." Barber's hands remained "full day and night."[32]

Beirut remained quiet at the start of 1904, but the governor did nothing to relieve the tension between Christians and Muslims. The missionaries agreed with the admiral that the presence of two ships had not been enough since the privileges of the Americans were curtailed more than those of the French, Russians, Germans, English, and other foreigners. This was because the United States had only a single minister in Constantinople with little access to the sultan due to his having a lower diplomatic standing than the ambassadors of the other nations. Those representatives could see the sultan at any time and get him to agree to their requests and demands on behalf of their countrymen living and doing business in Syria. In contrast, the American minister was too often stonewalled and "baffled" by the sultan.

There was another stabbing on January 19, yet, when there were no reprisals, it appeared safe for the *Brooklyn* to sail to Alexandria. Taking advantage of the extended calm, the school operated normally through the spring. Of note was one especially bright Muslim girl who ranked first in her class. Her father, who claimed to have been the first Muslim graduate of the Syrian Protestant College, declared his intention to have her "lead the rest of the school," to which Ottora Horne responded, "May she do so!"

With the onset of summer, simmering tensions broke out again. On June 20, just as classes were concluding and the school undertook final exams, graduation exercises, and another alumnae reunion, the city barely escaped a duplication of September's events. Waly Nazim Pasha was trying to remove the perpetrators of unrest and cut off the flow of rifles and ammunition flooding the city. Following an arms deal between Christian buyers and Muslim sellers, the buyers were relieved of their cartridges by some men Hoskins referred to as "ruffians," and one fugitive was shot dead in his tracks. Within a short time over 2,000 armed Christians and Muslims confronted one another. Only the intervention of hundreds of government troops averted bloodshed.

Another "ruffian" who was threatening Christians was shot and severely wounded by a soldier. As word spread that he had been shot by Christians, a stampede followed. Markets closed. Some people fled to their homes, but thousands rushed to where the soldiers stood between the Muslim and Christian quarters of the city. Waly Nazim Pasha declared that he would protect the people at any cost. The crisis seemed to pass, but the city was still troubled, and soldiers remained on guard. All told, four Muslims and one Christian were killed during the week. Even though shops reopened, people feared further violence. The Americans were greatly relieved to learn that three more ships—the *Olympia*, the *Cleveland*, and the *Baltimore*—were on the way and would remain "until the U.S. Government had completed matters hanging fire in Constantinople." These interventions by the U.S. Navy elevated America's profile in the region, as did the renaming of the Beirut Female Seminary.[33]

CHAPTER SEVEN

Decade of Progress and Promise (1904–1914)

We hope you like our new name as much as we do. By a resolution passed by the Mission at its last Annual Meeting, the old "Female Seminary" was changed to "American School."

Ottora M. Horne to Presbyterian Women,
December 1905

Thanks in large part to American intervention, the tension and unrest in Syria during the first years of the new century dissipated, and by 1904 that stability made possible a decade of remarkable progress and promise for the region and the renamed school for girls. The first hint of a name change in the records available to the author is at the end of a letter written by Rachel Tolles to Arthur Brown on April 23, 1900 from the "American Seminary." No further mention of this addition of "American" can be found until July 1904 in a draft of a mission report in Henry Jessup's handwriting. It has a section headed "American School for Girls" and begins: "The Beirut Female Seminary will hereafter be called the American School for Girls."[1]

No explanation was given for the change, but one possible reason was to distinguish the school from its British competitors since native Arabic and Turkish speakers easily confused the schools teaching in English with one another. Then too, parents may have preferred that their daughters be taught by Americans because of their increasing ties to, and familiarity with, America. As Rachel Tolles pointed out, "There was hardly a girl in the school without a brother in New York or Chicago or elsewhere in the States." The change would have made sense for recruitment purposes alone. Designating the former "seminary" as a "school" for girls most probably reflected the change in terminology in America. This may have been because of the emergence of more women's colleges and the new emphasis placed on preparing girls for college that made the role of female seminaries less clear; hence "female seminary" was fast giving way to the more contemporary girls' "school." For instance, the prestigious Troy Female Seminary in Troy, New York was renamed The Emma Willard School in 1898 in honor of its founder.[2]

There were probably political reasons too. Instability in the Turkish government abetted by the incompetence of the American ambassador to Constantinople prolonged concern for the security of the Mission's schools. The situation worsened dramatically in 1904 when local officials informed the missionaries that the Turkish government no longer recognized any American schools, which therefore had no legal rights. The only way to secure the schools on a permanent basis was to obtain a written Imperial *Iradi*, which the Sultan could issue in one day. It would bind the Sublime Porte (sultan's palace and seat of Ottoman government) and the government education department to recognize the schools' right to exist. But since an *Iradi* was not in the works, the Americans still had to rely on their own government for security. It may not, therefore, have been a coincidence that the name change occurred alongside the arrival of American battleships to protect American citizens, property, and interests. Identifying itself as the *American* Girls' School brought the former Beirut Female Seminary under the protective umbrella of the United States Navy.[3]

More Students Than Usual

After Alice Barber's father died, Rachel Tolles assumed Barber would be back soon and agreed to continue on temporarily as principal. By the fall of 1905, however, Barber was still having to care for her mother and would not be returning in the near future. Tolles, assisted by Emilia Thomson and Ottora Horne, would have to remain in full charge for at least another year. For a few months more, she could also count on the part-time assistance of Mary Bliss Dale, who was dividing her time between the school and her evangelism work among rural women and girls.[4]

Despite a rise in tuition to "fifteen pounds French," there were many more applicants than usual. The full complement of American and native teachers was needed to handle the 133 girls finally admitted, which was nine more students than in the previous year. Among the fifty-seven boarders were girls from Morocco, Egypt, and Cyprus, plus one or more from England. Yet for the first time the boarders were outnumbered by sixty-seven day students, thanks to the steady decade-long increase in Jewish girls who during this one school year outnumbered Protestants twenty-eight to twenty-five. Muslim enrollment grew to eight. Most of the students were from cities and larger villages thought to be "familiar with European customs." One exception was a girl from a distant mountain village who came down with a severe cold during her first days at school because, as she explained, the "blankets on her bedstead fell off every night," unlike at home where she slept on the floor. Regardless of origin, the girls quickly exhibited a marked increase in their use of English due to a system borrowed from the Sidon schools. Like the whole country, Miss Tolles found her girls "so full of modern ideas and customs that it was hard to find a typical Syrian anymore. If it were only the good they were getting we should be glad, but it isn't."

Temporary adjustments had to be made to provide enough beds for all the boarders. (Some from Cyprus and Egypt remained through the summer vacation, which added to the teachers' responsibilities but also provided more opportunities to instruct and train them.) A few girls had to sleep in the former guest room. As long as all stayed healthy, their former sick room could be the guest room. Larger and better bathing arrangements were a must. Renovations were also made in the teachers' quarters. To the staff's delight, the old kitchen that had been such a trial to everybody concerned was transformed into a bright new one. A new entrance to the grounds would require some changes in the front of the school building.

More importantly, instructional spaces had to be enlarged and increased as soon as possible. Because the large schoolroom was too small for the advanced and intermediate departments, the staff considered transferring the overcrowded Primary Department to its former quarters in the adjoining and now-vacant manse. Every available corner inside was being utilized for classes, and some even met outdoors on the playground.

Enrollment growth was offset to some degree by the steady pace of emigration. Five of the fifty-seven boarders left in 1904–1905 for South America. One went to the United States to study medicine. Four girls emigrated to the Americas the following year—three to New York and one to Brazil as a bride. An assistant teacher married a Sidon teacher and went to Australia. Her successor left to take the position of head teacher in a mission school in Assuit, Egypt, to join the host of graduates teaching there.

Nurses' Training

A heavier enrollment was not the only change afoot at the American School for Girls, which found itself adapting to the evolving educational and vocational needs of the area's residents in the early twentieth century. This included nurses' training. The chief medical center in Beirut was the Prussian (Lutheran) Johanniter Hospital, established in 1860 by the Knights of St. John of Berlin in response to the massacres on Mount Lebanon. It was originally staffed by Prussian physicians and Lutheran deaconess nurses. (The deaconesses also ran an orphanage and boarding school for girls.) Since the founding of the Syrian Protestant College in 1871, its medical professors had been recruited as the hospital's doctors. By 1900, "eight deaconesses, supported by local nursing staff, were responsible for the care of about 500 patients per year."[5]

Early in 1905 Mary Bliss Dale, eldest daughter of college president Daniel Bliss, was appointed Superintendent of the College Medical School's eighty-two-bed teaching hospital and Supervisor of Nurses. Far from being a simple case of nepotism, Dale was uniquely qualified for her position because "she had the administrative ability of her father and could speak and write Arabic, French, Turkish and German." She in turn recruited Jane Elizabeth Van Zandt from New York Postgraduate Hospital to be Head Nurse and Superintendent of a new Nurses' Training School that opened in May 1905 with two students. From the outset, Van Zandt found it extremely difficult to set up any respectable entrance requirements, which had to be "kept low to admit even the few girls who showed any inclination toward the profession."

It did not help that the school lacked proper housing for nursing students. Probationers had to sleep in hospital lofts or wherever room could be found. Nor were there private recreational facilities available for rest and relaxation. Nevertheless, a start was made in nursing education.[6]

A Woman's Pavilion and an Eye and Ear Pavilion were added to the hospital in 1908, and a Children's Pavilion in 1910. Together, the four facilities provided 200 beds for clinical instruction and created a demand for more nurses, but since nursing was regarded as menial labor, no training program existed. Hospital nurses were until then foreign-born and foreign-trained. It took Van Zandt several years to raise nursing education to a level where it, along with teaching, became a professional option for educated women.

These advances in health care were reassuring to all in a world where anyone could fall victim to disease at any moment. In a February 1904 harbinger of a pandemic still to come, many ASG girls were confined to their beds with influenza. Most recovered rapidly, but the epidemic that affected Syria, Palestine, and Egypt during an unusually harsh winter may have contributed to the deaths of three former students and two of the girls' fathers. Disease took a toll on the school's servants as well. In 1906 a careful quarantine of a case of measles appeared to have prevented its further spread until the school cook, Katrina, contracted the disease and died in the Prussian Hospital. Through much of 1908, an older unidentified servant was nursed through a long attack of erysipelas, a disease of the face or legs resulting in fever, chills, shaking, blisters, and painful lesions. She was extremely grateful for her employers' loving care that prevented septic shock and certain death.[7]

In 1909 a black slave woman of unknown origin infected with a strange disease entered the "French Hospital," meaning she was treated by the medical faculty at *Université Saint-Joseph* founded by French Jesuits. Six nuns who nursed her died from what might have been the plague or malignant typhus. Thankfully these outbreaks were either contained or they did not impact the school. But such was not the case when, that same year, the school was hit with an epidemic of dengue fever, spread by mosquitoes and commonly called *Abu Rikab* ("Father of the Knees") because it caused chills and shaking. In retrospect, Miss Tolles thought the previous school year one of "unusual leisure and remarkable freedom from sickness."[8]

With the strong backing of Mary Dale, Jane Van Zandt developed her nurses' training program to where it "demonstrated to a skeptical world the dignity and worth of the potential of native women" as nurses. "Among the skeptics were some American doctors and German sisters who had little faith in the School of Nursing until one probationer named Hosanna opened their eyes." One night on the surgical ward, she discovered blood dripping on the floor under an amputee's bed. Pulling off the covers and seeing that he was hemorrhaging, she quickly applied a tourniquet before a doctor could arrive, her rapid response saving the patient's life. "Thereafter the skepticism regarding the value of the Training Program diminished markedly." The School of Nursing grew steadily to where its graduates were at the center of healing service throughout the Near East in lands "where women were traditionally thought to be valueless except as bearers of children."[9]

ALONG THE NILE

Graduates of the teachers' class were highly prized as the demand grew. Some were even hired before graduation. Two of the eight teachers in the Class of 1905 dropped out early to take jobs, one in Kena, Egypt and the other in the Ras Beirut School, but she finished her teaching studies the following year. Another came from Mardin, Turkey for a year of advanced work. A missionary in Egypt wrote that they were "so pleased with the faithful and efficient work" of a graduate. "She is a real teacher. Can you not send us more like her!" The girl herself wrote, "I never feel tired, but am always happy in working hard. How can anyone be idle in this busy world which needs every body's work." Feedback like this was pleasing and encouraging to those training the young teachers. The only down side was that the school could not keep its own graduates, as evidenced by two younger teachers who "received advantageous calls to Egypt with largely increased salaries."

Several alumnae teaching in Egypt visited their former teachers in Suq el-Gharb during the summer of 1905. This may have started Misses Tolles and Horne dreaming of someday visiting them in Egypt to see for themselves all that their graduates were doing. The two women finally fulfilled their wish, boarding a French steamer to Port Said in September 1910 and taking a train trip along the Nile. They visited two women teaching at Presbyterian schools in the "uninviting Nile Delta town" of Zag-a-zig; toured "unique, stupendous, magnificent Cairo" and the massive pyramids; met a dozen former students teaching in Coptic Protestant schools and two missions; took in the Great Hall of Karnak in Luxor where they found two more graduates; and finally spent time with graduates in Kena and Assuit. All told, they visited with at least twenty-four former pupils, "some still in their fathers' homes, some in homes of their own, but most in responsible posts in American and English Mission Schools."

The two women enjoyed seeing the remnants of antiquity along the Nile, but their lasting memories were of visiting "their children" living together in their two and three-room homes and observing them teaching. The women gained new insight into the work the young teachers were doing. The principals of the schools they visited confirmed that their graduates were earnest, painstaking workers and fine examples to Egyptian girls; they could not do without them. Everywhere Tolles and Horne went, they were asked to send more graduates such as the two just then arriving to help begin the new boarding high school for girls in Cairo. The ASG leaders were inspired to continue "producing cultured Christian teachers with minds and hands trained for intelligent service wherever they may be called to spend their lives."[10]

Once back in Beirut, the two teachers thoroughly revised and strengthened the entire curriculum and most especially the teachers' courses of study. Since most girls in the teachers' class received financial aid, it was only fair that they provide service equal to their aid. So that both better and less able students could fulfill their practice teaching obligations, the Normal Course was extended over four years and required the service *before* graduation. In addition to the regular Junior and Senior year courses, they would study educational theory and apply those principles in practical work under the supervision of experienced teachers. Then they would devote a considerable amount of their time to actual teaching and assigned duties in return for their financial aid. An additional Normal Certificate would henceforth be awarded with a diploma upon completion of the course.[11]

ABSENT WITHOUT LEAVE

Mistakenly thinking that Rachel Tolles was on duty in Beirut, Arthur Brown was surprised in February 1907 to receive a letter from Attica, New York explaining her "sudden return without the Board's knowledge and consent." Her father Edward, a retired hardware merchant and wounded Civil War veteran, was in poor health from two strokes. Since Tolles was his only daughter whom he had "bravely given up to foreign mission service," she thought Brown would "not begrudge them the happiness" of being together one last time. She was sure she had sufficient reason to leave. Having completed plans for the next year, she left Ottora Horne, with the help of Daisy Mackie, the daughter of a newly arrived Scottish missionary, in charge.[12]

Tolles was still not able to return in the spring of 1907 as she had hoped. The constant care of her father until his death on November 19, followed by her having to break up her family home, took a heavy mental and physical toll on her. She, her remaining family members, and her physician all believed she should not return in March to begin another eight years without the recuperation a restful furlough was meant to provide. Besides, when able, she wanted to visit "her supporter, Mrs. Culbertson, in Louisville," and relatives in Milwaukee and Chicago. She thought the school was well provided for through the rest of the academic year and therefore asked permission to remain stateside until August 1908. Acknowledging her personal needs and her being "worth more in Syria during the coming years" if she could first rest and get things in order, the Board in January 1908 granted her the additional time. In return, she promised to use her extension wisely to be ready for work when she returned.[13]

Meanwhile, Acting Principal Ottora Horne, with the help of Miss Mackie (who assisted in teaching English and French "and taking full charge of the Sewing Department"), Miss Stella Ghoreyeb, a "Mr. March and several new, young and inexperienced Syrian teachers," had an unusually busy time teaching 129 students, fifty-four of whom were Greek Orthodox. Yet there was little change from the previous year because all but one of the native teachers were graduates, "full of zeal and goodwill and familiar with the school's methods." Most of the forty-seven boarders were prompt in paying their increased fees. The 2,285 piasters paid by twenty-eight primary children more than offset the 1,800-piaster rent for the former manse that housed their department. Of the seven girls receiving diplomas, two returned to ASG to teach, and another returned to her work in Egypt. Notably, another young graduate planned to study medicine either in Syria or America.[14]

ALL IN GOOD ORDER

Further refreshed by a voyage with perfect weather and quiet seas, Rachel Tolles returned in late September 1908 to a very hot Beirut. She retreated to the coolness of Beit Loring for a few weeks before returning to get things ready for the school opening on October 14. She was pleased to find that everything had been maintained in good order and that enrollment had increased slightly to 130. All of the teachers hailed her return with joy and relief, a testimony of how much she had been missed. She was especially pleased to hear the girls singing the new school song written by Dr. Mackie and most likely sung to a familiar hymn tune played by the new piano teacher, Miss Jessie Glockler. At the end of year she was sorry to lose Miss Stella Ghoreyeb, an assistant teacher who departed for America in July.

Giving back to the community remained an important emphasis at ASG. Henry Jessup taught a mission study class in 1905, and Bible classes contributed 671 piasters to the Board for Foreign Missions. The Junior Christian Endeavor Society raised tuition money for a needy primary student by making banners and flags for the Syrian Protestant College. The next year, 1906, an entire Foreign Missions Offering of $22.90 was sent to San Francisco for the rebuilding of the Home for Chinese Girls, which had been destroyed in the April 18 San Francisco earthquake. The Beirut girls, themselves living in a land subject to major quakes, were no doubt relieved to know that all fifty of the girls sleeping in the building at the time survived. In 1906–1907 the older ASG students contributed to the China Famine Fund, a boys' school in Homs, a Greek hospital in Beirut, a Catholic home for the elderly, and a Muslim day student. The younger girls supported an orphan boarder and made her a dainty dress for Commencement. In 1908 Home missionary societies raised $17 to support an orphan girl in school and the new tuberculosis sanatorium started by missionary Dr. Mary Pierson Eddy, the first female physician in the Ottoman Empire. Rachel Tolles believed they would long remember "what may be accomplished in a short time with systematic effort."[15]

Because her girls understood English so well, Tolles hesitated to write much about their religious experiences lest they find out they were being written about. She feared they would have considered that "as much a violation of confidence as any American girls would." Still she did report their increased interest in "things of the Spirit." Monday morning prayer meetings often went beyond the fifteen-minute bell. One Bible class became an hour-long prayer meeting, but still the girls did remarkably well in their final Bible exam. The King's Daughters, a Saturday morning prayer circle of nineteen girls, tried to make religion a part of everyday life. They were given little silver crosses to "remind them of the King's service." Many a girl inclined to shirk a disagreeable task did it promptly and cheerfully on being appealed to "in the King's Name." It made a great difference in the school.

At the end of the 1908 spring term, thirty girls signed a pledge to take an Arabic Bible home and teach someone to read during the summer. Only three failed to keep the pledge. Many taught servants. Others opened Sunday Schools in their homes and gathered children in the streets to teach them Psalms and Bible verses. One little girl read the Bible regularly to her bedridden grandmother. Another taught a servant to read and had a King's Daughters-like meeting every Saturday. Longing for the girls to become Home Missionaries, their teachers' "hearts overflowed with joy and gratitude over the summer's work." The practice continued through 1911.

STUDENT PROTESTS

ASG faculty members and students alike were shocked when, on January 8, 1909, Muslim students at the Syrian Protestant College refused to attend daily chapel and Bible classes but stayed on campus day and night for fear of being expelled. Eighty-eight Jewish students joined the strike. Another 128 students signed a petition supporting the strikers. Given the diverse makeup of the student body and Syrian society at large, the college faculty felt that acceding to these demands could be explosive. It therefore stood firm, saying that religion was a necessary ingredient in the development of the students, as was respect for the religion of others. Since SPC was a Christian school founded and supported by Christians, it therefore exercised the right to teach the Bible and Christianity without disparaging other religions.

The deadlock continued through February. Hearing nothing more from the faculty, the rebels started looking for a way out of their perilous position. A temporary settlement was finally reached when the college agreed that Muslim students would be excused for missing chapel and offered a study in the science of religion in addition to their Bible study. Furthermore, the faculty and college trustees would consider their requests. The students in turn had to submit to the authority of the faculty, obey the regulations of the college, and resume attending Bible classes as of March 8. Eight students withdrew, but the rest agreed to the terms and the crisis was resolved.[16]

The boldness of the strikers seems to have prompted a few impressionable and strong-willed ASG girls to test the rules and will of their faculty. We do not know what the infraction was or the nature and extent of their protest. Undoubtedly it was minor in comparison to those of the college boys, but it was enough to cause immediate and effective pushback from their equally strong-willed principal who wrote:

> The mistaken notion of "liberty," which manifested itself in so many quarters last year, was the cause of our most serious case of discipline. In May five of the older day-scholars were suspended; nor were the offenders allowed to return this Fall until they signed an agreement to conform cheerfully and heartily to all the regulations of the school. The effect upon the students has been good, and the five are now among our most exemplary pupils.[17]

Thus, the first student protest in the school's history ended quickly.

There were many outstanding students in the early twentieth century, but one unnamed Muslim girl was exceptional in the eyes of her principal. Her father, the first Muslim to receive a medical diploma from the college, had enrolled her in the primary department in 1900 with the expectation that she would finish high school. When he died in 1906, her brother consented that she could complete her studies, but only if she finished in two more years rather than three. This she did, omitting no courses while adding French and music, earning the school's coveted Certificate of Merit for scholarship four years in a row and graduating first in the class of 1909. Her teachers regarded this as an amazing achievement under the circumstances and were very moved when her relatives consented for her to appear "in full public view" in Memorial Hall to receive her diploma with the other five graduates, provided she was covered with her veil and gloves.

IMPROVEMENTS NEEDED

In December 1908 Ottora Horne made a list of building improvements needed and their expected costs. These included a larger kindergarten and school assembly room ($3,800), bathrooms and sanitary fittings ($1,000), and a new front, including roadway and grading ($1,400). She elaborated on these needs in July 1909. The Primary Department could take in new students from Aleppo, Latakia, Batroun, Deir al Camar, Abeih, Kafa Acarb, and Jaffa, but other new applicants had to be refused even if parents could pay in full because the Academic (Secondary) and Preparatory (Intermediate) Departments were enrolled at full capacity. All fifty-four beds were filled due to new boarders coming from American schools in Cairo, Alexandria, Jerusalem, and Sidon.

The resourceful Principal Tolles knew exactly what to do to accommodate so many children. She and the equally far-sighted Miss Horne had for five years repeatedly raised the need for a new assembly room since the present one seated only two-thirds of those enrolled. That room could instead be divided into classrooms, while a large, modern, well-lighted study hall could be built above the Primary Department. The original back of the building, which had in practice become the front, needed to be upgraded to provide a more dignified appearance. They further recommended that the kitchen be moved to the other end of the house. Last but not least, they repeated that the bathing arrangements demanded improvement.

Sarah and Her Sisters | 205

Since money so spent "would extend God's Kingdom," they begged the Mission to budget not less than $10,000 for these improvements. Unbeknownst to them at the time, the sudden demise of a wealthy Presbyterian gentleman in the States would provide an answer to their prayers within five years.[18]

"YOUNG TURKS" REVOLUTION

In July 1908 a cadre of young, educated Turkish military officers instigated a revolution against the Pan Islamist Regime of Abdul Hamid II. These "Young Turks" forced the sultan to restore the Turkish Constitution of 1876 and establish a secular government. As Ottoman subjects, Christians were promised a role in governing the empire. In support of the new Turkish government, President Theodore Roosevelt sent the battleships *Ohio* and *Missouri* to Smyrna in January 1909 in the hope that this move would free American Mission work from government interference. A counter-revolution within the military in April 1909 eventually failed, but not before reactionary forces and radical nationalist Young Turks instigated the massacre of an estimated 30,000 Armenian Christians in and around Adana in southern Turkey. In response to this second wave of Armenian genocide, the girls at ASG made "thirty-five pieces of underclothing" that the Red Cross shipped to Adana "where 4,437 homes were torched and half the town was razed." When Mehmed V replaced Abdül Hamid II, the constitution was amended, and power transferred to the Parliament.[19]

Although Beirut remained calm, the rest of Syria was in turmoil. Christians feared that, as in Adana, they too would be massacred. However, the reinstated secular government restored order through martial law and troublemakers were "hung by the hundreds." A Druze rebellion in the Hauran region was put down by better-equipped Turkish soldiers with heavy casualties on both sides. The missionaries had no choice but to wait it out and hope for the best. Since the old regime had drained the empire of its wealth, Turkey and Syria were left impoverished. There was no money to pay government officials who were suddenly prohibited from taking bribes to supplement their income. Earnest reform had to come quickly or the new nation was, the Americans believed, doomed. Yet surprisingly, the financial prospects of the schools were bright despite the economic depression. Payments were above average, but still not equal to the mission's increased expenses.[20]

The missionaries were perplexed by a contradiction in the government's new policies. On the one hand, there was to be universal religious liberty and perfect freedom for all, but on the other hand all schools were to be under the surveillance of the state. New college president Howard Bliss, third child of Daniel and Abby Bliss, worried that the schools and college were now in some danger. His fears were borne out when a new school law in 1910 proved to be anti-foreign and anti-Christian. Within 300 sections of the law were bound to be pitfalls and presumably harmless weapons that adversaries could use to thwart the operation of the mission schools. One new order was that "all foreign teachers in Ottoman schools be replaced by those of Ottoman nationality," but Franklin Hoskins interpreted "Ottoman" to mean *government* schools and therefore "could hardly be applied to foreign schools. Evidently the government hopes to force the Christians to follow their lead." But then the Ministry of Education stipulated that in the following school year no foreigners would be allowed to teach in non-Muslim communities. In spite of this specificity, Hoskins believed that this order "was a serious mistake on the part of the present Regime because it can never be enforced." It appears he was correct as the American missionary teachers continued to teach in the mission schools without interruption.[21]

Passages

There were, of course, a number of "native Ottoman" assistant teachers at ASG. In her 1906 annual report Principal Tolles made special mention of the retirement of one in particular, the beloved Farha Haddad. This most senior native teacher, hired as an assistant by Eliza Everett in 1876, had faithfully served the school for thirty years. In 1907 Jessie Glockler replaced another native assistant, the beloved Madame Josef Churi, who had taught piano and French "through storms and sunshine, heat and cold, good report and evil" since Eliza Everett's arrival forty years earlier. (This native teacher therefore served one year longer than Alice Barber would.) In tribute to their dear and valued friend, Ottora Horne wrote:

> As her step became feebler, she was none the less punctual. Her body weakened, but her iron will kept her at her post until the close of school last July. In September we were profoundly grieved to learn of her death from apoplexy [cerebral hemorrhage]. We place on record our appreciation of her conscientious, faithful work and of its value to the school.[22]

In addition to the loss of these two native teachers, Miss Horne took the unusual step of expressing her sorrow at the death in 1908 of a very special native parent, Rev. Yacob Junishian, presumably a pastor in the Armenian Evangelical Church that was closely allied with the mission's Beirut Evangelical Church. Pastor Yacob had an especially close relationship to ASG since three of his daughters were then in the school, one as a native teacher and two as pupils.[23]

Another death struck deep in the heart of the Mission. Soon after the death of his third wife, Theodosia, in December 1907, Henry Jessup, whose thick white hair and flowing beard accentuated his revered status as an elder statesman of the Syria Mission, developed a "serious digestive problem" that left him uncharacteristically feeble and confined to bed. On January 24, 1910, the

Fig. 50 – Rev. Henry H. Jessup DD, long time champion of the Beirut girl's school, died in 1910 at the age of seventy eight.

fifty-fourth anniversary of his arrival in Beirut, thirty-nine girls from the school that remained the "apple of his eye" stood outside his sickroom door and sang to him. He lingered another three months before dying of heart failure on April 28 at the age of seventy-eight. At the close of the school year the teachers and students gathered at the entrance of the Mission cemetery and sang a parting hymn to this revered champion of their school.

TWENTIETH-CENTURY PROGRESS

The Rev. James Nicol, who succeeded Henry Jessup as foremost male champion for ASG and higher education for females, arrived in Beirut with his wife Rebecca in January 1905. He was a graduate of the University of Minnesota and New York's Auburn Theological Seminary. Although young and healthy, Nicol needed to complete two years of language study and orientation before he could become an effective addition to the mission.[24]

Mission records provide glimpses of progress in transportation and communication in Syria. Railroads were revolutionizing travel as new lines were being put into operation. James Nicol was thrilled to ride the eighty-five-mile-long Beirut–Damascus railroad as far as Zahle in 1905. The first thirty miles were on the cog railroad that took five hours to cross Mount Lebanon at 4,875 feet. The train's slow speed gave him "some idea of the height" and time to absorb the "the grandeur of the Syrian scenery" from both sides of the passenger car. Train service was soon running regularly to Haifa and the south shore of the Sea of Galilee, and Dr. Ira Harris reported in 1910 that Tripoli was becoming a key railroad hub. The Germans were building a line to Aleppo that would "complete a direct line to Constantinople" and the French another to Homs that, while "only 104 kilometers long, would provide the port a quick means for transit into the interior and be the first link to the chain to the Persian Gulf." By June 1913 it was possible to make a round-trip excursion

Fig. 51 – Beirut, Lebanon around 1900.

Fig. 52 – Beirut train station alongside port c. 1900.

between Tripoli and Homs in one day "with far greater comfort than by the old methods of transportation." In addition to the train lines, the advent of the automobile and improvements in the coastal road enabled Rev. Samuel Jessup in 1909 to utilize an automobile service between Tripoli and Beirut to visit his older brother, Henry, before Henry's death. Such improvements in transportation made the American School in Beirut more accessible to girls from far away.

Sultan Abdül Hamid II viewed all printing machines as "diabolical" and banned them within his realm. Nevertheless, James Nicol managed to sneak a typewriter and a mimeograph machine into Beirut. He could then send home detailed typewritten reports and introduce the mission elders to these modern communication aids. Emilia Thomson wrote the first typewritten ASG annual report in December 1910. It is likely she had learned to type herself, because Nicol was then stationed in Tripoli. By 1906 Rev. George Doolittle was taking black-and-white photographs with his Kodak Brownie box camera. One snapshot shows Daniel Bliss, Franklin Hoskins, and numerous Jessups waving to Board president George Alexander's departing steamer. (George Kodak's popular cameras would soon become valuable tools in documenting the work of the Mission's teachers.[25])

The missionaries were not far behind the folks at home in "telephonic communication." In 1914 the Mission obtained a precious government permit to install a private telephone system connecting twelve scattered missionary homes and schools in Sidon. George Doolittle bragged that this "unique western touch cannot perhaps be duplicated elsewhere in the Turkish Empire!" The system evidently was not necessary in Beirut, as the Americans all lived in or near the compound and therefore had less need for telephones.[26]

An Otherwise Favorable Year

Another cholera outbreak occurred in September 1910. Mission physician Ira Harris reported that in two days 6,000 people left their homes in the cities for the country. Clinics were overwhelmed by throngs of sufferers. Yet, owing to the energetic efforts of the local government and precautions taken by the people themselves, there were far fewer deaths than in epidemics over the past thirty years. The epidemic was followed by a winter of excessive cold and deep snow that Harris called "the father of snows that added greatly to the suffering of man and beast."

Classes were delayed for six weeks in the fall of 1910 when several girls left due to dengue fever and other causes, but their places were quickly filled, and enrollment held steady at 130. Within a week of the late start they had to refuse new applications for lack of room. Once underway, the school year was "very favorable financially, healthfully and numerically." The Home Missionary Society gave funds to Dr. Mary Eddy's Tuberculosis Hospital, Mr. Schneller's School in Jerusalem (an orphanage for boys and girls, including blind children, run by a German Lutheran missionary), and the Foreign Mission Board. Miss Amy March, daughter of Rev. Frederick and Jennie March, filled in for Ottora Horne, who left during the winter on furlough through the following July, and Daisy Mackie, who resigned after three and a half years.

Many of the new girls who did enroll were advanced in their studies and did good work. Two sisters, among the oldest and reportedly the nicest girls in the school, had transferred from a convent school and spoke French fluently, but no English. The father soon wrote to Miss Thomson:

> Allow me to thank you and all the teachers for the great improvement
> my two daughters obtained last year under your kind attention and
> care. I found a great difference in their education and manners and
> am quite pleased and astonished at their progress in their English and

pronunciation. I beg you therefore to accept from me and their mother our profound thanks.

An interesting absence was that of the daughter of the head of the Bahá'í Faith. 'Abdu'l-Bahá, also known as "The Bab of Haifa," had just been released from a lifetime prison sentence by the Young Turks. He was very much impressed by the quality of education offered at ASG, and had applied in July for a place for his daughter. He even paid an advance in her tuition. But, to her would-be teachers' regret, she did not come in the fall. She and her father, however, wrote to assure them that she would certainly come the next year as the first of several of her faith to subsequently enroll.

Completing the review of this "favorable year" for enrollment was the news that among the five graduates was the second Jewish girl in her family to receive the school diploma. Another Jewish girl was granted an English-French certificate. At the annual alumnae meeting the classes of 1874, 1901, and 1904 were represented by a mother and her two daughters!

ASSISTING MUSLIM SCHOOLS

A predominately Muslim village requested in 1911 that the Mission establish a school in their town. Given the cultural preference for educating males over females, the Mission sent a well-prepared male teacher to open a boys' school, which was successful from the start. Three-fourths of the pupils were Muslim, and all paid some tuition. Enrollment grew so large that an assistant had to be appointed. This scenario was repeated numerous times in the life the mission.

A similar but much more unusual request came two years later from a group of "reputable Muslim *women*" organized as a society for "uplifting and teaching young Muslim *girls*." Under the banner Awakening Syrians, their long-term goal was to establish an advanced school to prepare their own girls to become teachers. With the assistance of a Muslim ASG graduate, they created a Student Aid Society to help Muslim girls attend the American School. Desiring to advance female education in any way possible, the ASG faculty met with the women and agreed to accept several of their candidates at a reduced rate.

The Muslim women next sought the faculty's advice on how to organize a female school that would teach girls who would later teach in their Muslim schools to uplift other Syrian females. Feeling it a privilege to be so asked, Rachel Tolles and her colleagues readily provided their advice along with a great deal of encouragement, for they and the entire Mission believed this society would prove to be an inspiration and blessing to the country. They therefore prayed, "May God take them by the hand!"

Regrettably, all aspects of the plan could not yet be implemented owing to a panic caused by another conscription of males into the Turkish army. Husbands and fathers either had to purchase an exemption from military service for thirty Turkish pounds or be drafted. Even if the fine for non-compliance was paid, it could be levied two or three times. Poor Muslims, as well as Jews and Christians who were accepted into the military under the new government, could not pay as much as seventy pounds, either in cash (about $312) or in horses and household effects. These men were taken immediately, leaving their wives and children to fend for themselves. Still the women persisted in the face of many hardships and much uncertainty.

Changes and Clouds of War

In the early twentieth century, ASG was affected by changes both familiar (staffing transitions) and new (political realignments in the lead-up to World War I). The Italo-Turkish War began in 1911 when Italy set out to establish colonies in North Africa at the expense of Turkey. Although the conflict lasted only a year, it was long enough to damage Beirut. Claiming infringement on Italian interests, the

Italian navy occupied the coastal towns of present-day Libya, Rhodes, and other Turkish islands. While sinking two small Turkish warships in Beirut Harbor on February 24, 1912, an Italian naval squadron also shelled the city, causing many civilian casualties and extensive damage to buildings. Fortunately, the Presbyterian Mission yet again suffered no loss of life or property, which included ASG and the Mission Press that also served as a bank, clearing house, express office, post office, bookstore, and storage warehouse for missionaries.[27]

The 1913–1914 school year marked the fiftieth "Jubilee Year" of the Beirut Female Seminary (now ASG) started by Rufka Gregory in 1864. The year-long celebration culminated in July with commencement exercises. A special gladness (jubilee) was expressed in the words of the speakers and the singing of the girls, filling the hearts of all—teachers, missionaries, friends, graduates, and students. The Alumnae Society initiated a Jubilee Fund that raised $200 to be used to furnish either the library or a science classroom in the new building that was being contemplated. Their generosity was much appreciated since war and cholera had made times difficult for alumnae, whether married or single. The students conducted their own Jubilee subscription, contributing small amounts from their limited means to help pay for ten-pound allotments of flour distributed by faithful "Bible Women" to families made destitute by the ongoing conscription. Mrs. Harriette Eddy Hoskins, whose daughter taught English and gymnastics at ASG, reflected on how ninety years before "not a woman could read until the Americans began taking two or three girls into their homes and teaching them," and how "from among these early Syrian pupils came a long line of most excellent women, children and grandchildren."[28]

Yet as the school continued to carry out its mission and legacy, staffing changes were inevitable. Having faithfully served the school in various capacities for thirty-five of the previous forty-six years, the venerable Emilia Thomson, then seventy-five, went on furlough in 1913 to live with relatives in Beirut. As a young woman, she had helped keep the seminary operating after Rufka Gregory's sudden departure in 1867. Beirut-born, she was uniquely qualified to help orient Eliza Everett during her first two years as principal. No wonder Everett was very pleased when Miss Thomson became a regular member of the faculty in 1876 with only her room and board as remuneration. Emilia stepped in as interim principal when needed and was there to help both Rachel Tolles and Ottora Horne get established in the school.

Miss Horne was greatly saddened when Miss Thomson decided not to return from her furlough. The "'old girls' school," she wrote, "would not be the same without her cordial greeting and her familiar friendly presence. Her rare personality, wide knowledge of the former students, their families and associates could not be duplicated." Her colleagues were glad she would remain in Beirut where they could stay in touch with her and maintain "the sweet familiarity of old." Miss Thomson's place was taken by Miss Jessie M. Curtis of Whiting, Indiana, a graduate of Western College in Ohio, who proved to be a valuable teacher and delightful companion to her colleagues. Miss Glockler, assisted by two former pupils, spent her sixth year in charge of the piano department until she married Rev. Robert Byerly and left. The faculty therefore remained strong with three missionary and six resident teachers."[29]

Their mission was aided by generous funding. Emma Baker Kennedy (no relation to Mrs. Walter Baker) sailed into Beirut harbor aboard her yacht *Albert* on April 24, 1914. Mrs. Kennedy was the widow of John Stewart Kennedy, a multi-millionaire who had arranged the financing of the Great Northern Railway among other projects and who later gave away much of his fortune to charities. She was accompanied by Rev. Dr. and Mrs. Jewett of the Fifth Avenue Presbyterian Church in New York and President McLaughlin of the International College in Smyrna.

Sarah and Her Sisters | 217

Already a good friend of ASG, Mrs. Kennedy and her entourage toured the school and saw for themselves the obvious need for a larger facility. Miss Horne pointed out how it had been hard enough to accommodate 130 girls the previous year in facilities designed for a maximum of sixty-four girls. Now there were 162. Mrs. Kennedy got the message. Before she left, she pledged $15,000 to erect and equip the long-desired second school building next to the existing one. Everyone in the Mission was extremely grateful and expressed their thanks for her generosity. Previous contributors to the project were delighted to read in *Woman's Work* magazine that, as a result this major gift, all the money needed was now in hand.

Despite this excellent news, the school's position was precarious because of the uncertainty of the times. Elizabeth Eddy, widow of the Rev. William Eddy and absent from Beirut for six years, observed many changes upon her return in July 1914. Families of young people seeking their fortunes abroad were building modern houses with money earned by their children and sent home. Railroads, carriages, and tramcars were gradually supplanting camels and other beasts of burden. Yet mountain paths to destinations beyond the reach of these modern conveyances were still just as rough and stony, and the glare of the Syrian sun just as intense as ever. When visiting churches, she found that, because so many men had emigrated or been conscripted, most worshipers were women. It used to be the reverse. As for the overall status of women, "apart from the education of girls in the mission's schools, very little organized work for women had been done."

But Mrs. Eddy had one overriding and ominous impression:

All over the country the people are under a cloud of anxiety and fear. War is the all-absorbing topic. Men have been drafted for the army, and one assessment after another made for clothing and feeding the soldiers. Great distress threatens, for there is very little money in circulation and people are not able to lay in their usual supplies for the winter.[30]

The clouds of war fast gathering in northwestern Europe would soon not only obscure "the glory of Lebanon," but destroy much of it. At the close of the 1913–1914 school year Misses Tolles and Horne prayed for "God's care and guidance in this day when panic and evil are all about us as never before."[31]

CHAPTER EIGHT

Surrounded by Suffering
(1914–1920)

People come daily bringing all sorts of things to sell to buy food... I have been in homes where floor mats and bed covers have been sold. One mother of three sold her cooking utensils for bread. We have bought lace, house plants, orange flower water and a hundred other things to help the poor keep soul and body together.

Ottora Horne, Beirut, to Presbyterian
Women, September 1915

COSTLY ALLIANCE

A dizzying series of events following the assassination of Archduke Franz Ferdinand in Sarajevo on June 28, 1914 dragged Syria into a world war that pitted Germany, Austria, and Italy against Britain, France, and Russia.[1] Convinced Germany would be victorious and hoping to regain adjacent territories in Europe, Enver Pasha signed an alliance with Kaiser Wilhelm II, and the Ottoman Empire declared war on the European Allies on November 5. As a result, the Syrian civilian population would pay an unimaginable price over the next several years, beginning with another round of compulsory military service that could be avoided only by paying an exemption tax of forty-four gold pounds per head. A British Navy blockade forced Ottoman authorities to expropriate wheat and livestock for the army "and revealed the economic insufficiency of autonomous Mount Lebanon, which depended on overseas trade and cereals and livestock from the *Bekaa* and the Syrian interior." The destruction and social disorder caused by the Italian bombardment of Beirut in 1912 was "nothing compared to the desolation that descended upon the city after the outbreak of the war."

Banks were closed and business all but suspended. Many a poor man lost his means of livelihood as his mule or camel was led away by a soldier. Grain, sugar, rice, cloth, and clothing were seized. Shopkeepers were compelled to pay large sums of money to support the Turkish army. Although Turkey was not yet at war, the missionaries' treasury "melted like the morning dew" as they were besieged by destitute Syrians for help. As many charitable and educational institutions of other nations suspended their work in Syria, the Presbyterian Mission's hope to continue working and paying all salaries until the end of the summer heartened people of all classes of the community—preachers, teachers, parents, pupils, servants, tradespersons, and friends.[2]

The situation grew steadily worse through the summer of 1914. The government demanded that each conscript bring to his training camp at least eight days' rations and a certain amount of money. Gold could be obtained only in small loans at very high interest. The mission's treasurer had to seek a loan from the United Presbyterian mission in Egypt to pay mission helpers. Most other English-speaking missionaries were recalled, leaving the Americans bearing a greater burden than ever, but at the same time offering them greater opportunities for outreach. Thankfully, all remained well and able to resume their work in September, feeling it their clear duty to keep all services intact as much as possible. This included reopening all boarding schools with the expectation that tuition income would furnish about the same amount of support as usual.[3]

FAMINE AND CHAOS

Despite the chaos raging outside, the school attempted to make progress on its goal to upgrade its facilities to accommodate a growing enrollment. To make way for the new Kennedy Hall, demolition of the former Kikano House was begun on July 1, 1914 as the girls left for summer vacation. The new academic building designed by a local architect, Mr. Joseph Aftimus, would include a large assembly hall and modern classrooms. The Rev. O. J. Harden oversaw the construction carried out by a Mr. Hacho, also of Beirut, and his workers. All went well until August 10, which started with about sixty men and boys busily digging and laying the foundations but ended with only the head mason on the job. Untying his donkey to ride home, he explained that more conscription orders had caused the workers to flee and hide. Other than a bit more labor on the foundations, work was abandoned in November. Miss Horne conceded:

> We were obliged to accept the fortunes of war. But even with work at a standstill, and the grounds looking as if we had already undergone a bombardment, it is easier to go on in the old quarters now that the foundations for the new are actually laid. In the meantime, we think many grateful thoughts of Mrs. Kennedy.[4]

Under these new conditions, enrollment dropped from 161 in the spring to 120 in the fall. Only forty-two were boarders. Despite its reduced size, the school awarded nine diplomas in July 1915, one of the largest graduating classes on record. With no replacement yet found for Emilia Thomson, Rachel Tolles and Ottora Horne had to fill the void. Thankfully, Horne's students showed "a marked increase in thoughtfulness, a readiness to assume responsibility, and an awakened interest in spiritual things." As evidence of this growth, she wrote:

> Realizing the need of doing all that was possible for the relief of the poor of the city, the girls showed a fine spirit of self-denial when, of

their own accord, the boarders gave up for a whole week, their noon meal fruit in order that the money (450 piasters) might be used for charity. The whole school omitted their usual Christmas treat to buy flour for needy people of the *Moseitbeh* district... The girls also assisted in the weekly distribution of bread and liked to read the stories of Jesus' life to the waiting crowd who listened quietly and attentively.[5]

Amid rumors of a possible massacre of Christians in Beirut, the Mission's American residents were reassured in January 1915 that, while the missionaries were to be extremely careful, they could continue their teaching and evangelistic work without opposition. They earnestly desired, even at the risk of danger, to stand by those who had learned to trust them and looked to them for guidance and protection. Still, there was growing anxiety about the danger to Syrian Christians and to mission work and property. The government had cancelled agreements regarding the protection of foreigners, including their religious, educational, and commercial enterprises and the postal system that connected them to the outside world.

Food shortages due to the blockade, confiscation of food for the army, and speculation by usurers and governors resulted in widespread starvation. Beirut and Mount Lebanon were among the provinces hit hardest by famine. Miss Horne and her staff kept the school operating despite the deteriorating circumstances and frequent distractions.

> People come to us daily with pitiful stories of want and hunger. To-day there were three applications for places as servants, and many more for food. I dread the winter, for how are we to help all the poor and starving who are sure to come to us? One man, an accomplished linguist in French and Italian, could find nothing to do, and was glad to pump the water out of our cistern at thirty-five cents a day. We could have a hundred servants. Many women who have never worked away from home are begging for work. They bring all sorts of things to sell that they may buy food. Supplies are high in price—flour, sugar,

rice — indeed we can hardly get rice, our staple food, at any price. But we are so glad to be here, so thankful we have not been ordered home as our British sister missionaries were.[6]

The situation became even more dire in the summer of 1915 when a locust invasion of biblical proportions fell upon the populace. A missionary high up in the Hammana sanitarium wrote:

Our vegetable garden, which supplied all our needs last summer, was destroyed by locusts. They were like the flies in the Egyptian plagues. They entered the house and ate the curtains, the artificial flowers off one of the patient's hats and even got under the nurses' caps and up their sleeves. For six weeks they made life very hard and in addition left not a green leaf.[7]

New waves of refugees increased the demand for the necessities of life in Beirut where some weeks as many as two hundred deaths were recorded. A Maronite priest wrote painfully of

the ravages of locust, the epidemics of typhus, cholera and leprosy, prostitution and famine. People devoured the meat of dead dogs, camels, and, in extreme cases, human flesh... Victims of the famine stacked in the streets were collected by municipal carts and dumped into collective graves on the city's outskirts. Many were taken for dead and buried alive. Rich Lebanese have become devoid of any feeling of tenderness and pity toward their kin. Beirut usurers introduced the most cynical methods of robbing people of their properties and by lending money at interest rates of 25 to 50% and eventually 70 to 150%.[8]

Anxiety about surrounding chaos permeated the ASG student body. One distraught Muslim girl, Rohanguise, came to Ottora Horne in despair just before Christmas. A telegram had directed her and two cousins to come home, but they did not want to go. Her brother at the college urged that they be allowed to stay, but the reply was to send them by the first train. The girl who was "not very friendly to Christian teaching" came again crying, "I can't go. You must pray that they won't make us go." Miss Horne drew Rohanguise close and prayed aloud as simply and as naturally as she knew how that God would, if possible, let the girls stay or make them willing to go if they must. The girl was quieted and apparently comforted. The next morning another telegram announced the girls could remain in school. Miss Horne and her pupil were sure that God answered their prayers.[9]

Kennedy Hall

Perhaps because the Turks were still conscripting only Muslims, there were enough stonemasons, carpenters, and other workmen available to resume the Kennedy Hall project. They managed to keep it on schedule and within its $10,000 budget until March of 1915, when difficulties regarding drainage, a wall, and grading roads threatened to push the cost possibly beyond the $13,700 in the Mission treasury. Mission Treasurer Franklin Hoskins did not want to proceed until more money was in hand and threatened to resign if anyone wished to push ahead.[10]

By May imported material such as ironware, lumber, cement, marble, glass, and locks had risen in price. The increases were, however, offset by a favorable contract for all sorts of labor. Work continued through the summer with only one visit from the government authorities, who did not interfere. All of the workers engaged in the project, from the contractors to the boys who carried mortar, worked with no quarrels, little swearing, and but one minor accident. Mr. Aftimus gave careful attention to details and secured the necessary building permit. He even put marble brackets along the galleries at his own expense of $177.78. Standing adjacent to ASG's Jessup Hall, Emma B. Kennedy Hall was completed in time for the opening of school on October 11, 1915. The total cost of $13,164.48 was well within Mrs. Kennedy's $15,000 gift. American supporters

Fig. 53 – Emma Baker Kennedy Hall,
American School for Girls, opened in 1915.

of ASG were informed that the beautiful new building named for its major benefactor had been successfully completed despite the wartime conditions. Misses Tolles and Horne were indeed grateful for the careful planning and efficient management of the project. If they had to do it over again, they would want it exactly as it was.[11]

BUFFERED ENVIRONS

Supported by the church at home and staffed by native servants, the Americans could buffer themselves from, but not escape, the growing poverty, starvation, and indescribable conditions outside. For the most part, they worked, worshipped, and lived relatively comfortably within the confines of the Mission Compound, a beautifully landscaped, peaceful island with well-kept gardens and palm-shaded walkways amid the increasingly crowded and chaotic city. Since 1833 the compound had grown to include the Syrian Protestant Church, Church Assembly Hall, Mission Press, Theological Seminary, and Girls' School. The Girls' School now consisted of the new Kennedy Hall building and Henry H. Jessup Hall, formerly called Burj Bird, which was used as the teachers' residence and student dormitory with a main kitchen, common dining room, and shared living rooms.[12]

The closure of so many other mission schools dramatically increased the demand for admission to ASG. But finding enough food for sixty or more active and growing girls for two school terms under worsening conditions was a daunting prospect for missionaries who were barely able to feed themselves. As it turned out, it became impractical, if not impossible, for girls to board anyway. Few parents could afford the extra cost, and transport to and from the school, if available, was difficult and dangerous. ASG had to revert to being a day school only.[13]

The absence of boarders had no negative effect on enrollment. Quite to the contrary, an avalanche of day students flowed into the school on October 13 for the new school year. With no additional help, the two Americans and their five native assistants had to cope with a hundred more students than the previous year. However, not having to supervise and care for fifty-plus boarders twenty-four hours a day, seven days a week, eased their burden considerably and allowed the seven teachers to grow especially close. Attendance hit an astounding record high of 214 girls. Were it not for the readiness of Kennedy Hall and Miss Tolles receiving the keys to her new building just two days before opening, the school could not have accepted this number. As it was, it had to refuse at least fifty applicants admittance.[14]

Except for visits to students' homes and occasional forays into the city, the American teachers taught, ate, and slept within the self-contained Girls' School. Being protected from the turmoil around them enabled them to reestablish their routines and conduct an otherwise normal school year despite the overload of students.

Illuminated throughout by electric lights, the new academic building was a great improvement and had a very positive impact on students and teachers alike. Miss Tolles extolled its beauty and functionality, believing it "second to none in the Empire or America." She greatly enjoyed sitting on the front platform during study hall, observing the girls walking between the adjacent classrooms or filing out the wide doorways and through the pillared corridor in a long line. Following a recreation period on the playground behind Jessup Hall, the girls would wind their way back in single file through the palm-shaped garden and mount the steps leading to study hall. On rainy days, they made their way through halls and corridors back to their studies, chattering as they went.[15]

Misses Tolles and Horne and their staff pushed on through the seasons to the first commencement held in Kennedy Hall, where the singing was "unusually fine" and Mr. Bayard Dodge gave the commencement address. Little did the two teachers anticipate that they, and all in Beirut, were about to be cut off from the rest of the world and that Miss Horne, almost singlehandedly, would soon be improvising to keep ASG alive through a most trying three years.[16]

DETERIORATION AND ISOLATION

Despite the relative peace that reigned within the mission compound and girls' school, the war unleashed even more chaos outside. Conscription continued, and ordinary horses were commandeered. Those animals not taken died on their feet and dropped in the streets. Lawful business came to a standstill. Only U.S. Navy steamships entered or left the port. The cost of the necessities of life rose from 100 percent to 1,500 percent. All flour was held by the government and crowds of poor people at the distribution center became mad, howling mobs. Street dogs were skin and bones. People faced with famine aged ten years in one. Distress would have been even greater had it not been for the local government hiring 1,500 men to tear down the old quarters of the city to widen and lay out new streets.[17]

The Americans felt increasingly isolated because, due to the British naval blockade, all mail came and went overland via Constantinople, slowing communication. It did not help that all incoming and outgoing mail was also censored by the government. It felt very strange being "of the world and yet knowing nothing of what is going on in the world." Still the work went on as usual. Miss Horne was able to get a brief message to a friend in Washington, D.C. that they were "all well and all right!"[18]

Because the missionaries were judged trustworthy, Syrian immigrants in America began sending large sums to the Mission Board in New York, requesting that the money be sent on to the Mission in Beirut and given to relatives in Syria. The Board and Mission agreed to help and were somehow able to set up a secure system whereby the funds could be transmitted. The Mission Press, hardly functioning for lack of paper and transportation, became a temporary banking house for the distribution of the money to family members throughout Syria. The Board and the Mission, in view of the calamitous circumstances, absorbed the cost of providing this unique service. In the first year over $600,000 was transmitted, with the missionaries even rendering help to those who could not write. By December 1916 over $1,250,000 had been transferred, and by the end of the war immigrants in America had sent about two million dollars to starving relatives in their homeland, thereby establishing a relationship of trust that would enhance future missionary work. A grateful Syrian prophesied that "out of this horribly murderous conflict the American missionaries will emerge victorious beyond imagination."[19]

Yet victory did not happen immediately, to be sure. The Americans were horrified when, in May 1916, Jamal Pasha earned the name "Butcher" because he tried and hanged thirty-three Lebanese and Arab nationalist activists in Beirut and Damascus. May 6 was thereafter commemorated as Martyrs' Day. *The Evening Standard* in London condemned the executions as "a deliberate policy of destruction of Arabs, having apparently for its object their extermination." Within a month, Sharif Husayn of Mecca launched the Arab Revolt against the Turks.[20]

Without warning, the Turkish government suddenly moved to close the mission schools and the Syrian Protestant College and confiscate all mission property. American property north and south of Beirut was appropriated. The English, French, Scotch, Irish, and Danish missions, which were deprived of their accustomed support and which had already sent their expatriate teachers home, shuttered and closed all their schools. Of the Presbyterian schools, the Sidon School for Girls had to be closed because it lacked an imperial permit. It was only through the strenuous efforts of U.S. Ambassador Henry Morgenthau, aided by SPC President Howard Bliss and Rev. Franklin Hoskins, that the government was dissuaded from closing the Mission's other schools. Taxes were, however, greatly

230 | *Robert D. Stoddard, Jr.*

increased on them and they were required to teach Turkish to first-year students.[21]

Separated from the outside world, Rachel Tolles and Ottora Horne were unable to send annual school reports until mail services were restored three years later. Only then could Horne, with almost no data to fall back on except attendance records and her own memory, compile a lengthy, handwritten "Biennial Report." From this report and some information Miss Tolles was able to share in 1917, we can piece together what actually happened at ASG during those three blackout years.

Tolles and her trusted colleagues opened the school as usual in the fall of 1916. They still could not accept boarders because of the unsettled conditions and the difficulty and expense of securing supplies. There were fewer day pupils because many applicants lacked a sufficient knowledge of English for entrance to the Preparatory Department. As mandated by the government, Turkish was added to the curriculum in February 1916 and would be required until the end of the war in 1918. Otherwise, the year unfolded much like the year before—until April 1917.[22]

The United States had remained neutral during the first three years of the European war and maintained diplomatic relations with the Ottoman Empire so as to be able to intercede on behalf of the hundreds of thousands of Armenians being massacred and deported by the Turks. When the U.S. finally did declare war on Germany in April 1917, its Turkish allies severed diplomatic relations, leaving the Swedish ambassador to oversee American interests in the Empire. The Syrian Protestant College was abruptly forced to close and not allowed to reopen until Cleveland H. Dodge, a good friend of both the college and U.S. President Woodrow Wilson, helped convince Wilson not to declare war on the Turkish Empire. Otherwise Beirut remained totally cut off, causing church women in the U.S. to grow increasingly anxious about the girls' school and the safety and welfare of its teachers.[23]

Circumstances grew progressively uncertain for ASG. Miss Horne later described how: Guards were placed outside all Mission Compound gates and the teachers did not know for a time whether the school could continue or not. It all depended on the guard who happened to be on duty. One would not permit the girls to come in or go out, though his predecessor and successor accorded them the privileges, sometimes without, sometimes with their books. But within a few days, we grew quite accustomed to seeing a Turk on guard every time we passed in or out of the Compound, and the girls came and went without any hindrance.[24]

At one point the Swedish ambassador cabled the Board: "Just heard from Bliss all friends well and occupied in collegiate work. Keep you advised news of interest." Board General Secretary Stanley White assumed the ambassador was referring to all Americans in Beirut, for "had there been any serious trouble or illness," the cable would have said so. Despite this reassurance, the Board, working with the State Department, developed a contingency plan to send the American collier (coal supply ship) *Caesar* to Beirut should any missionaries and College personnel wish to leave. Realizing that some would doubtless remain, even under Turkish rule, the Board made it clear they were "permitted, but not ordered, to leave the field for home."[25]

Conditions spiraled downward. The missionaries were "pressed beyond words by the suffering around them," perpetually nervous and stressed. Cognizant of how some of her predecessors had collapsed under less trying circumstances, Rachel Tolles, on the faculty for eighteen years, eleven as principal, and not having had a furlough for a decade, was very much in need of a respite. Thus, when Board permission to leave coincided with the Turkish government granting "Americans not of military age" safe passage, she boarded the Navy ship taking other Americans who wished to leave.

RELUCTANT EVACUEE

It could not have been an easy decision to leave Miss Horne again in charge of the school since she too needed an overdue furlough. Nonetheless, Tolles, succumbing to exhaustion rather than fear, was the only adult missionary among the thirty-five mostly American children evacuated aboard the USS *Caesar* in mid-May 1917. Departing the desolate harbor, she compared it to the "busy scene of life and color" that had greeted her on a brilliant October morning eighteen years before. Two years into the blockade, the harbor was empty of vessels except for an occasional fishing boat that ventured out against the law, only to be overhauled by a French patrol launch.[26]

The evacuees were taken to Constantinople where Tolles, at exactly five o'clock on June 26, imagined the commencement exercises then happening in Kennedy Hall. It took over a month for the Turks to permit the American evacuees to move on from Constantinople. Sea travel being unsafe, Tolles traveled overland by way of neutral Switzerland, south of the fighting. There she received word that the school year had ended just as she had imagined it. From Switzerland, she managed to find and board a ship. It likely sailed directly to America from southwestern Europe, possibly from the port at Marseilles, for we next learn of her arrival in New York in August among a party of missionaries from Syria and Turkey, three and a half months after leaving Beirut. American Presbyterians were greatly relieved to hear from her that all in the Mission were safe and continuing their work under such trying conditions, and that "their faith remained firm; their courage unabated, and they would stand with the needy and carry on the Church's great work in Syria."[27]

Happy to be among friends in Elmira, New York, Rachel Tolles began her rest and recuperation. Yet, she felt a heavy responsibility to speak on behalf of the Mission and her ASG colleagues

Sarah and Her Sisters | 233

who remained completely cut off from their American church. Putting pen to paper, she described for her church readers in graphic detail what it was like to be "surrounded by suffering that beggared description."

CARRYING ON

Meanwhile, Ottora Horne and her assistants carried on bravely. What little news received of Rachel Tolles during her long journey home was of great interest to teachers and pupils alike. All was well within the compound except for one severe case of typhus and the death of the Revered Daniel Bliss at the age of ninety-three. Otherwise, the major problem remained the difficulty of obtaining food supplies, yet no one in the compound or school was in want.[28]

At the second graduation in Kennedy Hall so accurately imagined by Miss Tolles, happy and admiring relatives and friends craned their necks from the balconies to see the seven graduates marching in behind the other students. They sang as well as ever and listened attentively to a fine address by Rev. Henry Riggs, a missionary who had witnessed the Armenian genocide in Harpoot, Turkey.[29]

Three girls stayed with Miss Horne through the summer helping with the Vacation Bible School. There was no shortage of Bibles because, prior to censorship, the blockade, and the lack of coal for its steam press, the Mission Press had printed thousands of the Arabic Bibles translated by Eli Smith and Cornelius Van Dyck. These were distributed to mission schools where the youngest children memorized texts, while graduates left with an excellent knowledge of Bible incidents and many passages learned by heart.

COMPELLED TO CLOSE

Miss Horne reopened the school on October 10, 1917. Considering the conditions, she was encouraged by the prospect of an enrollment that had rebounded to 129 students, one third of whom were Muslim. The outlook darkened five days later when a friendly source warned her that unless the school was closed voluntarily, a government official would shut it down. Not wanting to lose the renewed momentum, Miss Horne was determined to remain open unless compelled to close.

But that was exactly what occurred at 4 p.m. on October 17 when two policemen appeared with orders to close the school and seal its doors. Having no choice but to submit to the order, Miss Horne called all the classes—primary, preparatory, and academic—to the Study Hall and announced the action of the government. The news was greeted with wails and sobs. Reluctantly, teachers and students cleared the building of all books and movable appliances—even the electric light fixtures—before the policemen affixed seals to two of the five outside doors. One policeman asked Miss Horne for the keys, but the other was doubtful that was necessary as she was firm about retaining them.

Miss Horne feared that one or both school buildings would be seized for a military hospital or barracks. Twice she, her assistants, and the three seniors still residing with them were almost evicted from Jessup Hall. They were saved both times by the timely and judicious intervention of an unidentified friend. This allowed Miss Horne on November 1 to begin giving lessons to all three seniors in Jessup for the duration, so they could at least graduate on time. Miss Horne worried too about the teachers who remained while the school was suspended, for all but one depended on teaching for their livelihood.

One upside to the forced closure was the new respect and trust Miss Horne gained from her girls' parents when she refunded all fees in full. One Turkish woman refused reimbursement for a month and a half in the hope that the school would be allowed to reopen. Though Turkish schools were opened in nearly every vacated French and English school, she wanted her daughter in the *American* school and nowhere else.

Freed of her normal teaching and administrative duties, Ottora Horne had time to receive visits from patrons and various other people, some previously unknown. She and her teachers returned the visits and called on other families as well. They were received cordially everywhere and widened their circle of appreciative friends, decidedly a silver lining in a dark cloud.

While the other teachers were doing relief work and making garments for the Brumana Orphanage, telegrams were sent to Djamal Pasha, the Swedish Embassy, and the Department of Public Instruction in Constantinople entreating that the school be reopened, but to no avail. Ottora Horne and William Jessup (Henry's grown son) then met with the Pasha when he visited Beirut at the beginning of December. He was courteous and grudgingly agreed to write to the Minister of Education to see what could be done. They never knew if he actually interceded on their behalf, but on December 31 Horne received unofficial word that the Department of Education in Beirut had been ordered to issue a permit and remove the seals as soon as the school complied with certain regulations.

SCRAMBLING TO OPEN

Early on New Year's Day Miss Horne started a mad scramble to fulfill all the protocols and reopen as soon as possible. She first sent off messengers in a pouring rain to her teachers for them to get the necessary statements from their village sheikhs so that the government would issue them citizenship papers. Each teacher, from the principal down, had to have on file a certificate of nationality, a diploma or its equivalent, and a certificate of good character. The sole surviving teacher at the Brumana Friends School, a lone Englishman, kindly forwarded to Miss Horne a diploma for one teacher. Every paper filed had first to be copied one to three times on expensive government paper with many stamps affixed.

By January 11 nothing more needed to be done except to have the seals removed. Miss Horne was riled that "it took *twelve* days to cut through two bits of fragile cloth!" Some friends had suggested "oiling the seals," which entailed bribing the officials, but the acting principal insisted that "not a *para* be used in this way!" Finally, after a three-and-a-half-month interruption, the school reopened on January 28, 1918 with fifty girls. Within a week ninety were back in class, and in another week 105. Students above primary age who had not been previously enrolled were refused admission because the focus had to be on making up as much of the year's work as possible with existing students. Accommodating new pupils would only slow down the process.

The previous training of the returning girls enabled them to make good progress. They were orderly and studious so there was little need for discipline. The three seniors, having continued their regular work with Miss Horne, were able to graduate in June. An Armenian girl earned an English-French certificate and the two others regular diplomas. One who took the extended course in pedagogy received the special Normal certificate. Each read a graduation essay: one in Arabic, one in English, and one in French. All three became Protestants.

After graduation, Ottora Horne sent her three boarders to the mountains for the summer as she supposedly rested in Beirut while running the Vacation Bible School, teaching a Bible class, making and receiving calls from pupils and patrons, enrolling pupils for the coming year, and listening to the too familiar stories of privation and poverty. Her commitment and ability to reopen the school quickly, combined with the compassion and trustworthiness the missionaries had demonstrated in their relief work, won them new admiration, which resulted in increased demand for admission to ASG.

Liberation and Reconnection

In the fall of 1918, Arab troops assisting the British drove Turkish forces out of Palestine and Syria. On October 7, cheering crowds greeted the French fleet as it arrived in Beirut harbor, and hailed the French and British troops as they liberated the city, once and for all, from Ottoman domination. As welcome as the troops were, they brought with them a very unwelcome, invisible stowaway — the H1N1 virus.

A month before this, the "Spanish flu" virus, which originated in America, had reached Jaffa via Europe and Alexandria. The second and most virulent of three waves of the global Spanish flu pandemic spread quickly throughout greater Syria due primarily to the massive movement of allied troops in the area after the war. Both civilians and soldiers alike succumbed to the pandemic, and mortality rates in and around Beirut were especially high. Many people who were succumbing to starvation-related diseases were surely victims of the influenza.[30]

The pandemic could not have struck at a worse time in terms of staffing the school, since attendance exploded after the war. Before the girls' school reopened in October, seventy girls had enrolled. At least twenty-five had to be turned away once again because they lacked the English required for the lowest Preparatory class. By December the lone American teacher and her handful of assistants would be struggling to teach 215 girls — another record! Seventy-five more were refused admission. Among the mostly day students admitted were 105 Christians, ninety-seven Muslims, and thirteen Jews.

How inopportune then, with record enrollment and increased demand, that some of Miss Horne's five regular teachers became ill at various times within the first two months of the school year. She needed from one to three substitute teachers at a time to keep going. Although she does not make the connection in her reporting, it is almost certain that this high and concentrated number of teacher illnesses was a result of the flu epidemic. Fortunately, none of them died, which may be because they were better nourished and had remained healthier throughout the war and were therefore better able to recover.

As was often the case, the school could first call upon its own graduates who were available and then on graduates from other mission schools to fill in. Ottora Horne praised their willing spirit as they eagerly did their work well and helped in every way possible. They were loyal, earnest, and unselfish. Some even refused remuneration. Never had Miss Horne felt so unable to cope with the work and never had she believed so strongly in God's ability and willingness to see them through it all.[31]

Most of the Muslim students attended the voluntary Bible class, joined in morning prayers, and went to meetings in the new YWCA. Horne saw boundless possibilities for making new friends, and hopefully, Protestant converts. It was especially frustrating then that she had no time left to accept the urgent invitations to visit in students' homes and the homes of girls who had been refused admission. When both Christian and Muslim parents entrusted their daughters to the school's care, they told Horne, "Yes, we want English, but we want more than the language, we want American manners and spirit instilled into our daughters." She, on the other hand, wanted to share with them her Protestant faith and was grateful that her assistants (listed in Appendix B) also felt a responsibility to minister day by day to these girls. She further desired to have more workers while so many hands were stretched out to them for help.

Many Syrians hoped the end of the war and their liberation from Turkish control would mark the beginning of Arab self-rule. But alas, a nascent government of Arab elites was immediately quashed by the French, who took control of the city on October 10. Arab independence would have to wait.[32] Not surprisingly, the

American missionaries preferred working under a military administration of their French allies to a fledgling and untried Arab government. Without hesitation, they welcomed their fellow Christians as occupiers. Their compatriots back home enthused: "With what a thrill did the Christian world hear of General Allenby, bareheaded and on foot, entering the Holy City, and of French warships in the harbor of Beirut!"[33]

The first Presbyterians to disembark in French-ruled Beirut were Board Secretary Stanley White and his wife on an inspection tour for the Board of Foreign Missions and the Commission for Armenian and Syrian Relief. If they remained for the commencement on July 7, they heard 170 young girls sing their school song to a familiar strain:

> Let some look back on days gone by forever,
> Or castles built for the days yet to come;
> We girls have no such vain emotion, --
> With present joys content we are,
> We love our school with strong devotion,
> Hip! Hip! Hurrah! For A. S. G.![34]

Others at home cheered the resiliency of the missionaries and the continuation of their work. President Woodrow Wilson, a lifelong Presbyterian and son of a minister, surely had the missionaries in Syria in mind when he said:

> It would be a real misfortune if the Missionary Program for the world should be interrupted. That that work should be continued as far as possible at full force seems to me a capital necessity, and I, for one, hope that there may be no slackening or recession of any sort.[35]

It took some time for the mission to reconnect to church officials and their stateside benefactors, who were anxiously awaiting word from Beirut. All were relieved when regular mail service was restored, and voices long silent began to be heard again across the Atlantic. With the war over, Miss Horne had reasons to be hopeful.

> Syria is freed at last from the Turk and the relief is immeasurably great. NOW we hear the whistle of the steamers bringing supplies for the troops, aeroplanes [sic] fly over our heads, automobiles thunder past our gates, and men in khaki are to be seen everywhere. We are one collective Rip Van Winkle for we have had only German and Turkish papers, and no new magazines or books for nearly four years.

Refreshed and anxious to relieve her war-weary colleague, Rachel Tolles returned to French-controlled Beirut for the start of the 1919–1920 school year. The arrival shortly thereafter of Alice Barber, recovered from her long illness and willing to resume teaching, was another major boost to the school's effort to get back up and running. When eighty-year-old Emilia Thomson offered to come out of retirement temporarily and teach, the vaunted "three-cord" faculty was restored, thereby enabling Miss Horne to return to her Columbus, Ohio home for a long-overdue and well-deserved furlough.

NORMALCY

Free of Turkish interference, the American School for Girls resumed more normal operations amidst the socio-economic devastation of five years of war, naval blockade, famine, and isolation. The school's very survival was a testament to the tenacity and ingenuity of Rachel Tolles, Ottora Horne, and their mostly Syrian assistants who remained at their posts and saw ASG through "the worst of times."

Tolles got the school got off to a strong start after the war, despite considerable turnover among the Syrian teachers. Of the five who had stayed on from 1916–1919 and worked so closely with her and Horne, one married and went to Egypt; another married and went to Baghdad; a third went to America; a fourth resigned for personal reasons; and only one remained at her post. Miss Tolles felt fortunate, however, to secure teachers of a high grade to fill these vacancies along with Mrs. Stoudt of the college part-time. She anticipated the additional help of a short-term worker being arranged in the States by Miss Horne. These extra hands proved especially helpful when Alice Barber was sidelined with pneumonia during the winter. Grateful for her rapid and full recovery, Tolles recognized "the good hand of God in the gift of health and strength which has been granted to those in charge."[36]

The reopened boarding department had fewer than the forty-two students who had resided in Jessup Hall in 1914–1915. Five girls previously enrolled had left for America, and two Muslim girls had gone to Constantinople. There was no resistance to an increase in boarding fees of four Egyptian pounds. The daughter of the *Kaimakam* (Ottoman deputy governor) showed great promise. Miss Tolles found her to be "intellectually keen" and said she showed "an unusual desire to 'find out just what you Protestant Christians believe.' Her talks with an older teacher were frequent, frank, and open," so it was disappointing when she soon left. Another disappointment was that two little girls awarded American Red Cross scholarships were withdrawn after only four months for an unexplained reason. While the narrative report did not provide enrollment figures, it did mention "a steady increase in Muslim girls among whom were a few older ones who stayed in school even though betrothed."[37]

The goodly number of registrations despite increases in fees indicated that money was available to the girls' families. Another indication was that deposits for their personal expenses were so liberal that the girls had to be urged to restrain themselves so as not to make unwise and disproportionate gifts to charities. There was also an extraordinary demand for music lessons even though those fees were higher. Only resident pupils had the privilege of using the pianos, and many had to be put on waiting list.

Academic work was generally satisfactory, with fewer failures than the previous year. The faculty was especially pleased that the most enthusiastic and useful member of the Student Council, a Jewish girl, attacked some of the school's most difficult problems regarding order and discipline. The student body raised thirty Egyptian pounds and paid two pounds a month to support a young girl who was ill and confined in the Lebanon Sanatorium. They sent her letters and little luxuries as well. Miss Tolles was indebted to the Near East Foundation for supplying rice and flour at greatly reduced rates and overjoyed when the Mission Press wiped out most of the school's debt. The year's most upsetting incident was a break-in one spring night and the theft of some twenty heavy wraps and sweaters from a coat closet, each worth many pounds. Fortunately, the parents of the girls involved did not hold the school management responsible.

The teachers marveled at the endurance of the Muslim girls who, during the long, hot days of Ramadan in June 1920, were fasting while reviewing the year's work in preparation for their final examinations. Happily, this severe test of their earnestness came to an end just before exams. Professor Laurens Seelye of the College was the commencement speaker.

Looking ahead, Miss Tolles lamented the shortage of American staff to administer the Mission's reconstruction efforts in Syria. With or without that extra support, she and her faculty and staff would need considerable strength and endurance to contend with the major transitions immediately ahead.[38]

CHAPTER NINE

Higher Education at Last (1920–1927)

> *Building a college out of a secondary school required a leader and a faculty with a persistence of purpose. It therefore depended on young women assisted by qualified part-timers and a staff from the College itself and the University.*
>
> Attributed to Daniel Roberts,
> Beirut College for Women, 1958

CHANGING TIMES

After their victory over the Ottomans, Britain and France partitioned the Arab Near East in April 1920.[1] The British took control of Palestine, Jordan, and Iraq, while the French ruled Syria. After snuffing out any possibility of establishing an Arab kingdom in Syria, the French carved out Mount Lebanon and the coastal cities and their provinces to form Greater Lebanon under a French governor and an administrative commission that had little concern for the will of the people, most of whom wanted unity and independence. Rather the French wanted to divide and control Syria by playing minorities against one another and making Lebanon part of the Third French Republic.

The French did invigorate economic development. Food supplies were mobilized, health clinics established, and rubble removed.

New construction transformed Beirut into a modern business center. Land prices doubled and tripled as new hotels, restaurants, cafes, and cinemas catering to locals and tourists were built. The port was reopened to international trade and as commerce grew, so did a new professional class. Public works projects included a sewage system, electrical grid, and street lighting. Mechanized vehicles replaced horses and mules. An influx of rural peasants and refugees helped double the population and Beirut became a metropolis. Since the city already had many foreign and local schools, the French introduced only primary schools and normal schools for teachers. Public secondary and higher education were practically nonexistent, but there were two private universities, the American University of Beirut and the Université Saint-Joseph.[2]

Under the French protectorate, the missionaries faced new challenges. Changes in moral standards resulted from the "reshuffling and reshaping of Syrian society." A missionary wife cited some examples. A woman who had formerly taken in washing became a professional beggar when her husband died, living in the streets with her children. Four years later she remained shiftless and untrustworthy. A naturally honest man stole vegetables from a neighbor's garden to feed his dying children. A girl of a reputable family in a village where German, Austrian, and Turkish troops were quartered voluntarily became a prostitute to avoid starvation. Shocked and horrified by these conditions, the Americans viewed their role as combating a shattered morality by promoting the benefits of literacy, social relations, and religion.

A cultural shift that worked to the missionaries' advantage was in attitudes toward menial labor. Because girls and boys had to earn their own living to stay alive during the war, it was easier to counter students' predisposition against physical work and insist they have jobs in return for scholarship aid. To demonstrate that menial labor was not dishonorable, the teachers themselves did household chores in the school. Older girls overcame their prejudice against working by becoming trained nurses and office assistants. New fields were gradually opening to girls with sufficient education.[3]

TIME OF OPPORTUNITY

Board General Secretary Arthur Brown noted from afar that Syrian females were suddenly "freed from their old inhibitions and might look forward to opportunities for service, rather than to sit about waiting for their parents to arrange a marriage." He was pleased that the Mission was quick to discern its new opportunities. Increased tolerance and the heightened status of females, to which the mission schools had been contributing, presented an opening for a daring new educational endeavor—female higher education.[4]

When the Mission decided to extend its educational outreach by providing college-level instruction for young women, it took time to research the best way forward. A new Education Committee was organized in 1920 to explore the issue and discuss the subject with its regional partners at an interdenominational Mission Conference convened in Beirut that spring. There "the development of the (German Lutheran) Girls High School at Jerusalem into a much-needed college for the women of Southern Syria was discussed, while the question of a second college in northern Syria was raised."[5]

The American University of Beirut (previously the Syrian Protestant College) had been admitting females into its School of Nursing since 1905. In 1920, it started admitting a few pioneering women to its graduate programs in pharmacy and dentistry. But there was still no institution anywhere in Syria that provided undergraduate courses for women. The increasing desirability of having one prompted the Syria Mission to consider expanding the educational program at ASG "to do for girls what the American University (AUB) did for boys."[6]

On the advice of its Education Committee, the Mission in December 1919 directed Rachel Tolles and her faculty to "raise their standards to a level that would lead to College grade work." They were to introduce an additional preparatory year that would provide stronger foundations in mathematics and language before students were promoted to the Academic (Secondary) Department. Tolles complained that "practically the whole of Prep. III will be kept back in this new class." Students required to do the extra year were not happy. What seemed good in theory was, in her opinion, unacceptable in practice. Although keen to see instruction advance beyond the twelfth grade, she and Ottora Horne, back from her furlough, were focused on starting the new school year. Amidst "all the upheavals of mandates, Syrian king, Zionists and Nationalists that have come with kaleidoscopic rapidity," they began ASG's fifty-ninth year in October 1920. Rounding out the faculty were Alice Barber and a dozen Syrian teachers.[7] (See Appendix B.)

Setting aside any reluctance to add a preparatory year, Tolles and Horne met the challenge head-on and introduced more advanced math and language courses. These proved successful, strengthened the Academic Department, and better prepared girls for college-level work. Only three girls failed to make the passing grade of 70 percent. Sixteen achieved a grade average of 90 percent or above, and a Druze girl averaged 95 percent. It helped that the lights in the school buildings were "improved to the point of excellence." Chronic problems with service from the "City electric plant" prompted James Nicol to "buy at a low price and install at a high price, a Delco light plant that was, on the whole, satisfactory."

The French did not interfere with the Mission's educational and religious work. Nevertheless only 176 girls registered at ASG in 1919 compared to a high of 215 two years before. More disappointing was the decrease in Muslim girls from 45 percent to 32 percent. Things did get slightly better: total enrollment between 1919 to 1924 averaged 180, with Christians making up more than half of the student body followed by Muslims (37 percent), Druze (6 percent), and Jews (4 percent). High school students fluctuated from twenty-three to thirty-six, while boarders ranged from forty-five to fifty-four.

Ottora Horne attributed these swings to rampant inflation and immigration. Fewer families could afford the modest tuition. Many were leaving to better their fortunes in Britain, Egypt, Brazil, Argentina, or New York. Another cause was the lingering impact of the worldwide influenza epidemic. One student died of tuberculosis made worse by an attack of the Spanish Flu and "almost literal starvation during the War." On the plus side, war conditions and relief work helped break down prejudices and religious antagonism, especially between Islam and Christianity, and "greatly facilitated the Americans' work, especially among females." More Muslim parents were willing, despite higher fees, to send their daughters to American schools to be exposed to Christian beliefs and standards.

Ottora Horne Leads Again

After twenty-three increasingly difficult years as teacher and principal, Rachel Tolles felt the time was the right to resign. She had steered the school through rapid and momentous transitions and most of the war; that was enough. Looking ahead, she felt she lacked the preparation and necessary degrees to lead the Mission into female higher education. Therefore, she disqualified herself and gave her successors a free hand going forward. No one was more distraught with her decision than Miss Horne, who, with a sense of "well-nigh irreparable loss," credited her close friend and colleague with having "rare gifts as an administrator and teacher combined with high missionary ideals that had rendered inestimable service to the school and the Syria Mission." Horne wished her "years of useful service in the home land to which she returns." Signifying that further administrative changes would be made,

Horne was named Acting Principal *pro-tem* (for the time being) of ASG in the fall of 1921.

A second deeply felt loss occurred in 1921. Diagnosed in April as being in an advanced stage of cancer, Emilia Thomson died in the American Hospital on July 3. Ottora Horne wrote, "She held a unique place in the hearts of her associates, her pupils and her friends. A rare personality has vanished. We shall not look upon her likes again. We thank God for her long, useful life filled with deeds of self-denial, generosity and gracious kindness."[8] Alice Barber added that this "'daughter of the land' could converse in French, Arabic and English as if each were her mother tongue. Her repartee and knowledge of Arabic proverbs gave her a strong and sympathetic hold upon the Syrian heart."[9] Literally a child of the Syria Mission, Miss Thomson, like many of her sister teachers, never married and remained childless—unless, as with Sarah Smith, we count the girls she taught as her daughters. Miss Thomson was eighty-two.

Succeeding Rachel Tolles as principal once more, Ottora Horne began the 1921–1922 school year with a faculty consisting of Alice Barber and a second-year teacher, Edith Hazlett. Lois Wilson came after Christmas to teach physical education. In response to the new political reality, French, under Mademoiselle Flendrich, was taught at all class levels. The girls made good progress speaking only French outside class two days a week. Science, particularly astronomy, was prioritized in the curriculum. Seniors taking astronomy at the theological seminary and a group of ASG day students had a "star party." They stayed at the school for an entire night and went to the roof four times to see the little moon near Spica and the four glorious morning stars. Three AUB professors provided "special demonstrations" to augment other science courses.[10]

The faculty was very pleased when the "honorable and reputable" Muslim women who had sought their assistance in 1914 in establishing their own school renewed the contact. With stability reestablished, they had started a private school to prepare Muslim girls as teachers. They again requested that some of their girls be admitted to ASG as previously agreed to. Unfortunately, only a few applicants qualified for admission.

Meanwhile, the Mission assigned Miss Horne the daunting task of developing "a year of study beyond the 12th grade," that is, a first year of *college* study. This was a major challenge for someone who was a Normal School graduate at best, trained only in the "norms" of elementary and secondary teaching. Nevertheless, she valiantly set about laying the groundwork for a freshman year while the Mission requested more personnel to begin the new program.[11]

In 1922 Acting Principal Horne, Margaret Doolittle of the Tripoli girls' school, and Rev. James Nicol were asked to explore with the British Syrian Schools and AUB the possibility of working together to start a college for women. They found the British unwilling to collaborate as it might give the impression that their Syrian Training College was lowering its standards. But AUB administrators and faculty members were willing to cooperate and pursue the matter further. Discussions with the British were put on hold for another three years.

Alice Barber in 1922 saluted the school's sixtieth anniversary. Referring to the opening of Rufka Gregory's all-native Beirut Female Seminary in 1862, she wrote: "Beginning with three boarding pupils, it has increased its scope and field of labor, and a long line of faithful teachers, American and Syrian, has gone before us. Leaning on their promises we gain strength and courage to go forward."[12]

AUB ADMITS SOPHOMORES

In the first year of Bayard Dodge's presidency, 1922–1923, the AUB faculty voted to take the "extremely radical step of admitting women students to all classes of the School of Arts and Sciences above Freshman year." Even though women had been admitted to the School of Nursing since 1905, the move was thought "radical" because, as AUB President Stephen Penrose, Jr. later explained in a history of the university, things had not changed all that much since the first missionaries landed. College for women was revolutionary for the times because:

> Muslim women still wore the veil in Syria despite its abolition in Turkey. The idea of education for women was almost totally new to the southern Near East. Woman's place was only in the home. She could talk only with other women or her husband, and her sole duties were to keep him comfortable and provide him with a family. Why should she be educated? It might give her ideas!

This decision precipitated a demand for the admission of women, but "there was serious doubt that Muslim girls would be permitted to enter classes with men and there was much hesitation about taking such a momentous step." It was feared that it "would be too much for the boys to be in a classroom with bare-faced women. It might place a terrible strain on their self-control and give them bad ideas, especially if they had never talked to or seen the faces of any women but those of their mothers or sisters."

Nevertheless, university administrators believed it was time to further emancipate Syrian women. But rather than open AUB up completely to female students, they instead encouraged the American Presbyterian Mission to establish its own junior college solely for females either in organic union with AUB or in affiliation with the university. Believing it unwise for women to attend a men's college because the extracurricular life of the men and women would be "utterly divergent," the Mission preferred an "affiliation." It therefore agreed to establish a women's residential junior college where young women could receive preparation for professional life rather than knowledge for its own sake, and where those who wished to "could prolong their days of freedom and postpone restraint and seclusion." The university, in turn, agreed in May 1924 that it would withdraw from the field of women's education, but announced publicly that, beginning in October of that year, it would admit females to the School of Arts and Sciences *sophomore* class and all classes above. Furthermore, the Mission's new junior college could provide accommodations for women attending AUB as well its own students.

In June 1924, the university proudly awarded its first degree in Pharmacy to a woman, Sara Levy, a Jewish student from Palestine. That fall seven women enrolled in AUB's School of Arts and Sciences. The experiment in female higher education was beginning well, but the admission of females at the freshman and sophomore level was only temporary and would continue only until a junior college for women was established.

COMMITMENT TO A COLLEGE

The Mission voted in December 1924 that it would provide a freshman year of college for women in 1925–1926. Miss Horne and her faculty therefore had to raise ASG's standard of instruction as rapidly as possible. The envisioned college was to provide freshman and sophomore years for women who could, if they wished, transfer to AUB as juniors to pursue a four-year degree. The Foreign Missions Board in New York approved the plan, provided funds were raised for two additional short-term teachers, one permanent teacher to be added in 1925, and a permanent fund for the maintenance and development of the college.[13]

While sympathetic to the idea, the Mission Board felt it could only sanction James Nicol and Ottora Horne while on furlough in the United States to secure from friends of ASG support, over and above the school's regular budget, for the three teachers. Beyond that it could not then pledge anything more. The Mission's plans would have to be kept within its share of the Board's annual distribution to ASG. Horne and Nicol began their fundraising for the teachers and permanent fund in the U.S. in the summer of 1925.[14]

Beyond developing an additional year of courses, Ottora Horne did not feel herself up to the task of starting a college as she too, like Rachel Tolles, lacked the necessary educational background. Nor was Alice Barber, in her thirty-ninth year with the school, a candidate given her age and lack of credentials. Therefore, anticipating the need for someone more qualified to launch the new venture in Beirut, the Mission Board by 1921 or 1922 began to search for a woman with the education, ability, and passion to take on the challenge.

The Board's search for a well-qualified woman to launch the first women's college in the Arab world was fruitful. Twenty-seven-year-old Frances Pryor Irwin somehow learned of the opportunity for a female college graduate, preferably Presbyterian with a master's degree, to start a women's college in Beirut. Frances was born in Virginia in 1895. She and her two sisters grew up in a staunch Scottish Presbyterian family in Minneapolis, Minnesota. After high school she earned a BA degree from the University of Minnesota in 1917. Probably with a goal of teaching at the college level, she continued her studies at the university and was awarded an MA in history and political science in 1922.[15]

Irwin corresponded with the Board of Missions and, perhaps after being interviewed by field staff in Minneapolis, she was offered the job. Since this was an opportunity to not only teach, she must have had a strong sense of calling to suddenly head for a foreign land and take on this challenge of starting the first college for women in the Near East from scratch. Bidding her parents, two sisters and friends farewell, she likely traveled by train to New York for her orientation at the Mission Board's headquarters at 156 Broadway. There she was given her travel documents and passage by steamer via Liverpool to Beirut, where she landed on November 5. In her first letter to her parents, Irwin wrote that "Beirut, the American School for Girls and the Mission Compound are so much more beautiful than I expected." She went immediately up the mountain to the Mission's Training School in Suq el-Gharb, where she spent most of her first year learning Arabic.

FRESHMAN STUDIES

1922–1923 was a year of disruptions, changes, and celebrations at ASG. A total of three months of instruction was lost due to severe illnesses among the teachers. Yet staff and students were spared the effects of an unspecified epidemic. There was also an epidemic of weddings, as three assistants married. One who stayed on until the very last day of school appeared a bit absentminded, giving rise to good-natured teasing by her fellow assistants, all of whom were still single. (See Appendix B.)

The success and benefits of Lois Wilson's physical education program were demonstrated in exercise drills, games, and a tennis match with girls at the American Community School. The class of 1923, whose motto was "Having torches, we share them with others," had a senior grade average of 84 percent, with seven girls at 90 percent or above. The fourteen diplomas set another record. Over half the members returned after Commencement to help with the examinations of the lower classes. On Alumnae Day, a record eighty-two graduates voted to continue the Alumnae Scholarship and meet monthly to study how they could have an even more positive impact on the region.

The school year had marked a major advance forward. Despite the ups and downs, Miss Horne had offered for the first time ever freshman studies beyond the twelfth grade. The faculty was especially impressed by one Muslim freshman who, when frequently absent due to illness, sent her younger sister for her Bible assignment. Influencing Muslim girls remained a priority. Alice Barber visited homes one day a week, calling on the mothers, sisters, and aunts of thirty-nine girls, thirty-two of whom were Muslims.[16]

One of the first graduates to have successfully completed her freshman year studies at ASG "considered entering the Sophomore class of the American University." Since the Mission did not formally approve a freshman year of college for women until two years later (1924–1925), it seems Miss Horne's new curriculum had been successful. Having pulled off this coup, Horne wryly wrote in her 1923 Annual Report:

> It may be of interest to mention that the Dean of the School of Arts and Sciences of the University assured me that our graduates are prepared to enter the Freshman class of the University. Of course, women are not admitted to this class, but his statement would seem to answer the question whether graduates of ASG are prepared to enter College.

MELDING IN MISS IRWIN

Frances Irwin mastered enough Arabic at the Suq Language School to return to the city in the fall of 1923 and immerse herself in ASG under Miss Horne's supervision. Most classes were full by the October 3 opening. Altogether, 186 students were enrolled. One older Druze girl was so anxious to come that she applied the previous spring. At first, she was horrified when a man entered the Study Hall, and she scuttled out as fast as possible. But before the end of the year, she sat through a Friday morning talk by Mr. March and cheerfully paid the deposit for the following fall."[17]

Miss Horne appreciated Frances Irwin's presence and was grateful for her helping teach through the first term. The twenty-nine-year-old newcomer's keen and intelligent interest in all aspects of the school made it easier for her to take the reins from Horne at mid-term in February 1924 as ASG's new principal to facilitate the addition of the new freshman and sophomore years. With their roles reversed, the older and more experienced Miss Horne graciously acknowledged her new young colleague to be efficient and tactful in winning over the hearts of teachers and pupils alike. She wished Miss Irwin "a long life of increasing usefulness and blessing" in taking ASG to the next level.

The major academic development in 1923–24 was raising senior year work to a college freshman level and strengthening the curriculum to support this advancement. Two assistants were replaced by recent graduates, Henriette Hekimiah ('23) and Kareemeh Khouri ('22). Otherwise it was a typical year. Scholastic achievement remained high with sixteen girls, led again by the same Druze girl, averaging 90 percent in all their courses. Enthusiasm for athletics, which now included basketball, grew steadily under Lois Wilson. A Girl Guides program was begun. The YMCA Social Service Committee made and sold articles. Speakers were from the Near East YWCA, Near East Relief and mission schools in Tehran, China, and Cairo.

The addition of a freshman year eliminated the need for the annual Class Day and Commencement Exercises in June 1924. A "drill exhibition" was held instead that included a Maypole dance, a basketball game, an Arabic Literary Society program, and entertainment by primary children. The brilliant Najla Azzeddin, now identified by name, had a 95 percent grade average. Another ten girls, who averaged 90 percent or above in all subjects and were in good standing in school spirit and conduct, earned certificates of merit. Most importantly, two ASG graduates would start their studies in medicine at the university in the fall. The Alumnae Society created an associate membership for former students who did not receive a diploma.[18]

1924–1926: A Series of "Firsts"

Frances Irwin and Ottora Horne were glad to welcome Alice Barber back in the fall of 1924 after her one-year leave. Sadie Woods arrived in October, the first of the short-term American college teachers paid $500 (BA degree) or $600 (MA) annually with full board that included a single room with maid and laundry service. Each also received railroad fare to New York and steamship passage to and from Beirut. Another welcome addition was Ida Manley, R.N., who also served as school treasurer. With renewed purpose and energy, they and their native assistants taught 183 students. Among fifty-five boarders were two daughters of the Prime Minister of Iraq, a girl from Busra, and another from Tehran, all there for an American education not available in their own countries. Primary enrollment was down, but the Upper School increased to the point where twenty girls lacked proper desks.[19]

With the reliable help of her faculty and staff, Frances Irwin could now focus more on creating a college for women by providing more advanced freshman college work while planning sophomore college courses for the following year. Eight young women enrolled in the first college freshman class, including five ASG graduates and three from other schools. One girl dropped out, but it was just as well that there were only seven because of their proximity to the crowded high school classrooms and lack of proper equipment. Irwin proudly stated that "for the first time, girls born in this country... may have college work in a woman's school." So began two years of precedent-breaking "firsts" in female education in the Near East.

In December 1924 Frances Irwin was given the added title of principal of the American Junior College for Girls as well as of ASG. Ottora Horne graciously wrote that her replacement worked with "a dignity and grace of spirit which embodied the purpose of the undertaking in her own personality." Irwin was especially glad when Winifred Shannon from Iola, Kansas, a 1921 Phi Beta Kappa graduate of the University of Kansas with a BA in French, arrived in the spring of 1925 to teach and serve as her vice principal, close confidante, and friend.[20]

Fig. 54 – University of Minnesota BA graduate Frances Pryor Irwin in The Gopher yearbook, 1917.

Fig. 55 – University of Kansas BA graduate Winifred Shannon in The Jayhawker Yearbook, 1921.

258 | *Robert D. Stoddard, Jr.*

The faculty of the junior college itself consisted of only Frances Irwin (history), Winifred Shannon (Bible and sociology), and Sadie Wood (mathematics and English). Mme. Olga Holenkoff taught French part-time. Otherwise volunteers filled in teaching Bible, Arabic, and whatever else was needed. All resident teachers took turns supervising the dormitory, playground, and study hall; they chaperoned the girls on walks to and from concerts at AUB and religious events. When some subsequent teachers objected to these extra duties, Miss Irwin explicitly listed them in their contracts from then on. Short termers, like the resident teachers, were to "give their full time and strength to furthering the ends of schools."[21]

Frances Irwin's first full year as principal began with another epidemic of influenza that "enrolled teachers and half the boarders." The girls seemed to want to keep the school nurse, Ida Manley, very busy, for the first case occurred just five days after the opening of school, and for the next six weeks "new cases appeared as soon as there was an empty bed in the sick room." Except for classes in Arabic and French, all college instruction was in English, a special challenge for the girls from French schools. The college women were, like their high school counterparts, permitted to speak Arabic among themselves on Sundays, but French on Mondays and Thursdays. English was mandated for the rest of the week. Winifred Shannon, soon well-liked for her sparkling personality, introduced her students to life outside the classroom and beyond the curriculum, including field trips. At the outset her first sociology class did not want to venture out and visit a furniture factory, but once there, they found it interesting.

As "special students" the freshmen joined university women in a weekly chemistry class taught by Professor Edward Nickoley in his AUB laboratory. Two ASG classes visited the observatory between star-gazing parties, and many girls enjoyed afternoon concerts at the university. Miss Irwin was very grateful for the cooperation and valuable assistance of the university, especially AUB's extending to

Fig. 56 – ASG Girl Guides on outing at *Beit Loring*.

Fig. 57 – New ASG Principal Frances Irwin with students
listening to records played on donated Victrola
in November 1924.

her freshmen and future sophomores the unique privilege of admission into its sophomore and junior classes "without examination."[22]

At Commencement in June 1925, all seven freshmen received the "old" ASG high school diploma before 300 guests. The four freshmen who would not continue were awarded the first "freshman certificates." The number of ASG graduates since 1862 thereby rose to 208, seventy of whom attended the alumnae reunion. All who had known Mrs. Ellen Foote, *née* Ellen Jackson, as a member of the faculty for fourteen years were saddened to learn of her death at age eighty-five.[23]

Female education advanced further in 1925–1926. Sixteen of ASG's seniors in the class of 1925 chose to continue as freshmen. Three of the first seven freshmen stayed on as the first AJCG sophomores even though they could have transferred to AUB. ASG's enrollment, now 211, was subject only to the limitations of the size of the faculty, the building capacity, and the number of beds in Jessup Hall. In contrast, the junior college's enrollment was constrained by the number of mostly ASG graduates wanting a higher education. Still the three-member college faculty was encouraged that, though small in number, these nineteen young women comprised the student body of the first institution for female higher education in the Arab world.[24]

AUB enrolled two women in dentistry, another in pharmacy, and thirteen in Arts and Science. Two Muslim females "attended classes without embarrassment." One of them apparently was Sunneyeh, a junior college sophomore who aspired to study medicine in America before returning to Syria to care for Muslim girls and women. Sunneyeh regularly walked more than a mile to and from Ras Beirut for her premedical study at the university, always wearing her veil and entering and leaving the laboratory with her professor. No other man on the campus spoke to her, though some apparently wondered why a woman wanted to be a doctor.

Sarah and Her Sisters | *261*

The other female student may have been junior college sophomore Munira Berbir.[25]

The 1926 ASG/AJCG Commencement speaker, AUB President Dodge, called attention to an ASG graduate who was the first female to receive a BA degree from the university. A dozen of the thirty-one ASG graduates received high school diplomas and the three sophomores (Munira Berbir, Sunneyeh Habboub, and Armenouhi Mugreditchian) were awarded the first "American Junior College for Girls, Syria" diplomas, signed by Misses Irwin, Horne, and Barber and dated June 18, 1926. Since the sixteen freshmen had not received high school diplomas, they too were awarded special freshman certificates. Thereafter diplomas would be granted only for members of the high school senior and college sophomore classes.

These first sophomore graduates were the pioneer students in female higher education in the Near East. They did exceptionally well academically and professionally and were a credit to their pioneer teachers and fledgling women's college. Sanneyeh Habboub studied medicine at Western Female Seminary in Oxford, Ohio before returning to practice in Beirut. Armenouhi Mugreditchian became an AUB bacteriology laboratory assistant before going to medical school and practicing medicine in Homs. Munira Berbir married and lived in Milan. Meanwhile, freshman Najla Azzeddin had the highest academic standing and was the first annual recipient of a silver cup that remains in Lebanese American University today. She went on to study in Paris and at Vassar before earning the first PhD of any AJCG graduate at the University of Chicago. One "certified" freshman became a teacher in the Tripoli girls' school. Two others taught in government schools in Baghdad.[26]

A good friend of Miss Irwin, Ellen Goodrich, came to help at the school. Among other things, she led the girls in calisthenics on the playground. She wrote Irwin's mother in Minneapolis that her daughter "had not found any males in Beirut that interested her." Nor had Goodrich "seen anyone good enough for Frances. There were some nice young 'staffies' [male helpers], but they were all just young boys." She worried that Frances was very thin and weighed only 110 pounds.[27]

EVOLUTIONARY TIMES

The American Junior College for Girls came into being during interesting times. In Lebanon in 1924–1925 the French High Commissioner attempted to appoint a Lebanese governor, establish public education, and subdivide Greater Lebanon into eleven mixed regions. His efforts were thwarted, and the various religious communities turned against the Mandate, triggering the Syrian Revolt that was put down harshly by the French military in 1927. The French still maintained control by playing minorities off one another. Lebanon and Syria were then each granted constitutions. On May 23, 1926, Greater Lebanon became the Lebanese Republic with French and Arabic as the official languages. The various sects and regions were represented in the cabinet of Lebanon's first president, Charles Dabbas, as well as in a Chamber of Deputies and a Senate. Article 10 of the new Lebanese Constitution "summoned the state to defend private religious education on condition it did not conflict with public education."[28]

With Ottora Horne back in October 1926, overall ASG standards were improved with more advanced mathematics in high school and more use of French in the lower classes. Meanwhile, Frances Irwin fretted that her ten new freshmen and four returning sophomores were still intermingled in the same building with the ASG girls. So too they participated in the same outside activities.

Besides the three full-time college teachers, Miss Horne taught the college students Bible; Miss Flendrich, French; and Mr. Gabriel, Arabic. A new full-timer, Lillian Donaldson, taught hygiene and chemistry. Her hygiene classes organized a Health Week during which her students weighed and measured everyone in the school.

Fig. 58 – Miss Irwin's friend, Ellen Goodrich, leading ASG girls in calisthenics during her visit in June 1925.

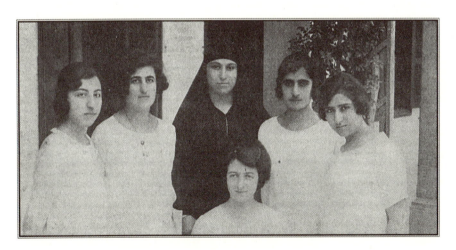

Fig. 59 – Miss Irwin (seated) with first American Junior College for Girls freshman class in 1925.

A study of the school menu prompted an increase in fresh fruit, milk, and better-balanced meals resulting in fewer visits to the sickroom. Her chemistry students were still allowed to use the AUB laboratory, but she and Irwin agreed that if the college were to accommodate the majority of girls who wanted professional training, it would need its own chemistry lab. However, furnishing one would exhaust the $1,000 available for improvements. Besides, if the college was eventually to have its own building, why spend money on a basic lab within ASG and then duplicate it elsewhere?

Irwin was heartened by the "growing spirit of friendliness" and positive relationships within the diverse student body. Armenian refugees living in nearby camps were not generally liked in Syria, but in school they were close friends with Syrian Muslims. A Syrian and a Kurd, both from wealthy families, organized a class picnic to promote friendships between rich and poor girls who were "not as friendly as they should be." Girls started games and engaged in "rollicking activity on the playground instead of strolling in groups or sitting listlessly under the trees." Eager to prove their prowess, "third Middles" formed a basketball team. A Damascus girl organized a "Laughing Hearts Society" to spread joy through entertainment.[29]

Winifred Shannon organized the First Annual School Girls' Conference in the spring of 1926. More than 140 students, teachers, and staff from a dozen girls' schools were housed at ASG and the British Syrian School for three days of prayer, hymn singing, good food, and fellowship. Talks on *A Girl's Love, Home Life, Service to Others, Need for Nurses, Co-operation, Fellowship*, and *Uplift* stimulated much discussion. Time was allotted for sports, rest, reading, and field trips to the University Museum, nurses' residence, and the Dog River. Conferees formed new friendships and discovered there were nice girls in other schools as well as their own. A second girls' conference in April 1927 on the theme of "Gift-Bringers"

 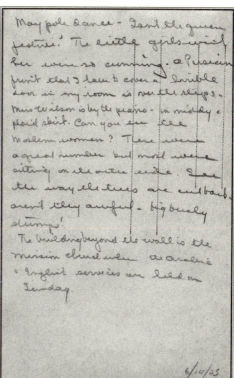

Fig. 60 – Miss Irwin snapped this photo of ASG girls dancing around Maypole in school garden next to Evangelical Church.

Fig. 61 – Miss Irwin's inscription on back of Maypole photo describes the scene.

was "marked by a spirit of fellowship and a deepening sense of spirituality."

Extracurricular activities rounded out the education of both the high school and college students. YWCA volunteers taught Arabic, French, and English to girls in an Armenian camp, worked with poorer children, and presented a pageant on Japan. A Brownie troop was formed for younger girls. Big Sisters looked after new girls, while Girl Guides taught first aid and sportsmanship in organized games. Support for the Mission's work with lepers grew. "Daily Dozen Exercises" set to music from records played on a donated Victrola were opened up to mothers and friends. The Arabic Literary Society offered a prize in Arabic composition. Three notable visitors in 1925–26 were the famous New York preacher Harry Emerson Fosdick, the Dean of the University of Missouri Graduate School, and University of Chicago Dean Quincy Wright. Wright had been Frances Irwin's former professor at Minnesota, and likely lectured on the role of the League of Nations in peacemaking.[30]

The Class Day theme was the value of the modern girl. Girls planted ivy and their senior class gift was a eucalyptus tree. At the outdoor Commencement, 700 guests witnessed girls in "all degrees of dress from ultra-modern; to the modish black silk coats with close-fitting black turbans worn by girls who delivered essays without veils; to the ultra-conservative girls who appeared as masked figures and spoke through their veils." As a sign of Mustafa Kemal Ataturk's giving Turkish women equal rights and putting female higher education on an equal footing with men's education, the Turkish consul's daughter wore a white dress and no veil or cover. (On the street she did wear a hat.) Another girl had a white commencement dress made and wore it to several class parties although she could never wear it in public. Thanks to his "dear old Chevrolet," James Nicol made it in time from an earlier graduation on Mount Lebanon to give the commencement address. Twenty girls, including two college freshmen and all four sophomores,

Fig. 62, 63 & 64 – Principal Irwin took these photos of ASG primary children (top), students in their native costumes (middle) and the high school freshman class on an outing (bottom) in 1926.

received diplomas. One sophomore was going on to dental school, another to evangelistic work, and two to teach.[31]

The faculty had their own transitions. At the end of the school year, Ellen Goodrich left to marry a minister; Sadie Woods returned to America; and dear Alice Barber, who asked to be relieved of the strain of schoolwork, was transferred to the Tripoli station. Among AJCG alumnae, the president of her AUB class took a BA with honors; another became Head Nurse at Pittsburgh General Hospital; another graduated from Teachers' College, Columbia; and Sunneyeh Habboub entered the Woman's Medical College of Pennsylvania.[32]

Since the Presbyterian Board was committed to establishing a junior college for women in Beirut, the university agreed to *not* admit women until the beginning of the junior year in order to steer those seeking professional training to AJCG for their freshman and sophomore years. Meanwhile, AJCG students still had access to AUB's library, laboratories, and Professor Nickoley's chemistry class in return for some compensation and AJCG housing AUB's female students in its original building, Jessup Hall.[33]

"Leap of Faith"

ASG could not provide enough college-bound graduates to sustain and grow the junior college. In fact, Frances Irwin had in 1926–1927 nine *fewer* college students than the previous year. She had to attract students from the few other schools in Syria and Palestine that prepared girls for college work in English. But AJCG's lack of a "real college atmosphere" was a hindrance. Prospective students were reluctant to attend college classes alongside elementary and high school students. And would the sending schools appear to be lowering their standards by sending graduates to a college housed in ASG? As mentioned earlier, this was a special concern of the British Syrian Training College, which could be a major source of applicants.

When the Mission again raised the possibility of collaborating with the British Mission in developing a junior college for girls, the university rejected any such arrangement because administrators feared it might look like the Americans and the British were teaming up against the French. The British then countered by proposing that, since AUB was already cooperating with AJCG, the university extend the same privileges to their teachers' college, which was also contemplating adding a freshman year. Once Frances Irwin caught wind of this, she quickly visited her British counterparts. She convinced them that such a move could cause friction between the two missions and would be uneconomical since the Presbyterians were already planning to open a separate women's junior college. When so informed, the British agreed that it would be much easier and cheaper for them to send their girls to such a college, provided it was *not* connected with the preparatory school and located in a different place.[34]

But there was a *quid pro quo*. If the American junior college would prepare young women for further study at the university, then the British—and only the British—would train native teachers in English. The Presbyterians reluctantly agreed to discontinue their longstanding teacher training program, and would urge their would-be teachers to enroll in BSTC. The British preoccupation with their teachers' college not being connected to ASG played into Miss Irwin's hands. She had long desired a separate site for her college. Competitors could only be expected to send their graduates to a separate, stand-alone college in Beirut. These British conditions only reinforced Irwin's case for "separating the college and moving it to its own building. This is the time, if not past time, to push hard for a real plan for future development."[35]

Although James Nicol and Ottora Horne had yet to raise all the $5,000 in the U.S, Irwin proposed taking a "leap of faith" and immediately move forward with a "real plan," beginning with finding and securing the best location for the new college. Nicol suggested it be close to the university so it could continue to house AUB's female boarders. Irwin also thought it desirable to have it near AUB's new nurses' residence "since young women were waking up to the need of a more solid education than just language and a dabbling in music or painting." Besides, if the university could find the funds for such an impressive building to house nurses, then surely money could be raised from wealthy Americans who wanted to help advance female education in the Near East.

Another reason for taking the "leap" was the surprising number of Muslim high school girls showing an interest in further education. Frances Irwin cited a freshman returning from Baghdad for her sophomore year, and a few others seriously considering a full college degree. Asma, an Iraqi, was so determined to continue her education that she passed her ASG entrance examinations while recovering from an auto accident that had occurred on her way to Beirut. She returned to ASG twice across the desert during the Druze Rebellion. Afraid of being stuck at home during the Iraqi revolt against the British, she stayed in Beirut for two years of English review and entered as a freshman in 1926. Miss Irwin declared Asma "indefatigable in her study and activities" and implored that she "should have every opportunity to develop her leadership qualities."[36]

When it became clear that AJCG had to be split off from ASG, the Mission formally voted to relocate the college in Ras Beirut no later than the fall of 1927, even if space had to be rented. The separation was in the interest of ASG as well because, with another record enrollment of 232, it was outgrowing its quarters and all beds were filled with boarders. Thus, it was time for a new chapter for both institutions.

Fig. 65 – Frances Irwin (center) with
1927-28 AJCG students.

Fig. 66 – AUB School of Nursing
First Year Class – 1928.

Fig. 67 – AUB's 1928 School of Arts and Science
Senior Class included one female student
(second row center).

CHAPTER TEN

Sarrafian House Women's College
(1927–1933)

> *Like the self-asserting and more independent younger generation of females, AJCW, though only an infant daughter of ASG, demanded a separate existence and untrammeled freedom to pursue her own life. We congratulate this young but growing daughter on the ability to walk alone and on the bright prospects for the future.*
>
> Ottora Horne, Principal,
> American School for Girls, July 1928

SEPARATION FROM ASG

By the late 1920s, Frances Irwin's fast-growing junior college for girls was ready to step out on its own as the American Junior College for *Women* (AJCW).[1] The first order of business was finding a new facility in a suitable location. When a large private home in fast-developing Ras Beirut became available for rent in the spring of 1927, Frances saw that, with certain alterations, its three stories would accommodate her fledgling women's college very nicely. Its large yard had a garden and areas for basketball, volleyball, and tennis courts. Inside was a room for games. It provided ready access to AUB's laboratories and special events, and could also house the university's female boarders. On Frances Irwin's recommendation, the Mission rented the house from its builder, Mr. Samuel Sarrafian, who first asked for $1,190 annually, but settled for a three-year lease at $1,000 a year.[2]

The second challenge was getting chartered by the Board of Regents of the University of the State of New York, since the college was founded by the Presbyterian Board of Foreign Missions based there. The charter would recognize the college as meeting American academic standards and therefore able to confer degrees transferable to colleges and universities in the United States. To help facilitate this process, AUB President Bayard Dodge in the fall of 1927 briefed the regents on the formation of the junior college. It was agreed that, if AUB's faculty of Arts and Science would act as a go-between, AJCW would not, for the time being, need to register separately with the regents. As principal of the junior college, Frances Irwin would be an honorary member of the university faculty, and AUB Professor Nickoley would be an honorary member of the junior college faculty.

AUB, not yet up to speed on the college's name change, then announced in Arabic and English that, because the American Junior College for Girls was to open in Ras Beirut in the fall, "no women would thereafter be enrolled in the University until they had *completed* the Sophomore Year." Female students wishing to register as freshmen and sophomores were instead referred to the junior college that was offering full academic courses with access to certain university courses required for admission to the professional schools. AJCW's entrance requirements were the same as for corresponding classes in the university.

Public interest in the school was suddenly heightened. The fact that graduates of seven different institutions in Syria and "Mesopotamia" (Iraq and parts of Persia and Turkey) applied for admission in 1927 and made deposits for 1928 confirmed that "(t)he hesitation of students of other preparatory schools to enroll in a department of another secondary school was entirely removed."

Tuition was fourteen pounds in Turkish gold, plus twenty-four pounds for board and an extra twelve pounds for those wanting music. Laboratory fees were eighty piasters for chemistry and sixty for zoology. A one-pound deposit was required with the application. All students were required to attend some course of religious instruction and worship services "for moral and spiritual development," though non-Christians could arrange to take "alternative courses and services." Interested girls could write to Miss Irwin directly for a catalogue and further information.[3]

In July 1927 Irwin informed her church women supporters that, in addition to a well-rounded, two-year college course taught in English, after which young women could go on to finish a bachelor's degree and even complete professional training, the renamed junior college had some other unique aspects. Regardless of what its graduates did beyond the two years, they received in that time practical training relating to challenges they would face later in life. The college also offered social and philanthropic activities that provided a wide variety of experiences within the friendly atmosphere of a Christian home where each student was in direct contact with the resident faculty. No other schools would do so much for them.[4]

ROUGH START

Moving the college to Sarrafian House and preparing for its October opening took a heavy toll on Frances Irwin. James Nicol, who was supposed to be overseeing the considerable alterations to the building, was preoccupied in his new role as Executive Secretary of the Mission. When Frances toured the building in July, she got "worked up a bit at the way the work was dragging along." The contractor was using only one or two men for each phase of the work. She hoped Nicol could speed things up, because, at that rate, the building would not be finished before September 15. She thought he could do a lot more since she was left "to do so much disagreeable squabbling with the contractor and workers." Exasperated, she confided in a letter to her parents that she was "disgusted with everything out here." Fortunately, having served five years in the field, she was granted a one-year furlough, starting in December, to resume her graduate work at the University of Minnesota. But there was still much to accomplish to get her college open before then.[5]

A late summer attack of dengue fever confined the harried principal to her bed feeling tired and discouraged. She spent "two horrid days" under the care of a head nurse and physician from the AUB hospital. Fortunately, she had a mild case and recuperated taking breakfast in bed and afternoon naps. Within a week she was back in the harness. Meanwhile, Ottora Horne came down with a very severe case. Pushing herself too soon, she relapsed and was not able to open ASG. On top of that, Winifred Shannon and Lillian Donaldson, returned from vacationing in Italy, were both laid up for a month with glandular fever. Not only did Frances have to contend with opening her new building, but she was the only American still upright to open the girls' school, which was further crippled by three more staff illnesses. Miss Irwin, not fully recovered herself, came to Miss Horne's aid. As she explained in two more letters home:

> Wild eyed about getting my school open, I now, at the 11th hour had to go to ASG from early morning until late to engage teachers, order texts and deal with the school correspondence. Exhausted and blue about running so far behind in my work, this week really did me up. It won't take much more for me to throw up the whole thing and resign from the Mission.[6]

After writing that she was "disgusted" with everything, Frances Irwin's very next sentence was: "The College opened (on October 6) very nicely." Somehow, she had managed to open *both* ASG and the junior college—on the same day. Luckily, Winifred Shannon had recovered enough to be put "in charge of the fireworks," as she

Fig. 68 – AJCG reopened in the Sarrafian House in Ras Beirut as the American Junior College for Women in October 1927.

Fig. 69 – Second floor addition and improvements to Sarrafian House grounds were completed by 1928.

described the chaos in Sarrafian House, as electricians, carpenters, and gardeners rushed to finish in time.

The first school day in Sarrafian House began with a chapel service led by Miss Shannon. The eleven freshmen and ten sophomores (sixteen Christians and five Muslims) then met with their teachers for abbreviated class periods. An early dismissal to buy books allowed the enthusiastic students time to tell girls at ASG and the British Teachers College how much finer their new junior college was than their former schools.[7]

New members of the college faculty were: Eva Beck (mathematics and social science), Laurence White (Bible), Frances Downing (English), and George Kafouri (Arabic). Esther Lecerf taught advanced French, which was useful because under the Mandate French had been made an official language. Frances Irwin continued to teach history; Winifred Shannon, history of religion; and Lillian Donaldson, science and hygiene. The new history of religion course prompted much discussion, while the new three-hour hygiene class included child care and community hygiene.[8]

Most of the classrooms, Miss Irwin's office, and a kitchen and dining room that could also be used for classes were on the first (ground) floor of the Sarrafian House. The second floor had been made into dormitory space where the boarders slept two and three to a room. Misses Irwin, Shannon, and Donaldson each had a private bedroom. The Trade School of Near East Relief made the simple furniture found throughout the building. As envisioned, tennis courts and a basketball court were laid out on the grounds. AUB provided some adjoining land for an athletic field. With periodic alterations and additions, Mr. Sarrafian's house would accommodate the junior college during its first eight years.[9]

On November 2, only three weeks after getting her new junior college up and running, Frances Irwin boarded the steamship *Patrice* to Marseilles en route to New York. The day before she left, she talked over a few last-minute concerns with Miss Shannon and

Sarah and Her Sisters | 279

attended a farewell party at which many girls wept. She was sorry for the timing of her furlough, but very much in need of rest. Miss Shannon observed that her colleague's face was quite drawn and white, and she looked very tired. "My, but she was happy to go!" The girls shot off fireworks from the roof as the *Patrice* left the harbor. Once in America, Frances traveled by rail to Minneapolis in time to spend Christmas with her family and start additional graduate classes at the University of Minnesota.[10]

MISS SHANNON MANAGES

Acting Principal Shannon had her hands full. In addition to teaching every day, leading prayers, and banging out tunes on the piano for Miss Donaldson's exercise class, she spent "every extra moment on the college books" and overseeing housekeeping matters. She worried whether there was enough food for everyone. When the cook came down with dengue fever, Shannon had to rehire a woman who had just been fired. All this while studying Arabic twice a week. There were also tensions within the faculty. Miss Donaldson was at first "scornful" of what she deemed "a feeble attempt at a college." Nevertheless, she was thought to be "a good and thorough teacher" and, because the girls liked her, she mellowed, made adjustments, and extended her contract for another year.[11]

Sarrafian House presented some challenges. Although it was a very fine building, after several days of heavy rain, the roof around the cupola leaked badly, proving the folly of Sarrafian's refusal to refinish the roof unless it became necessary. Well, now it was necessary. Water ran down the stairs in great sheets and collected in six-inch-deep puddles on the landings. Like the Blisses in Suq el-Gharb seventy years before, the teachers ran around placing pans under leaks in several rooms. "Now he knows!" wrote Miss Shannon. The tightfisted landlord had to replaster the ceilings as well as repair the roof. Once the rains stopped and the repairs were made, students and faculty settled into a new normal routine despite the lack of carpets, curtains, and lampshades.[12]

To ease her administrative burden, Miss Shannon gave the girls new responsibilities and privileges. To minimize expenses, they shared household duties. Some did extra work to earn part of their tuition, the hope being that this experiment would attract more girls of limited or no means and afford them the opportunity for higher education. But it was not all work and no fun. In March, the faculty took the girls up to Aley to play in the snow. On the way home in cars, they pelted passers-by with snowballs. "You can imagine," Miss Shannon mused, "the astonishment of some nice pompous gentleman to get a snowball right in the middle of his neatly buttoned front!" But she was *not* amused when some unruly girls pulled off typical dormitory stunts, causing her to confine them to the house and yard for a week. A storm of protest ensued, with the girls calling the discipline "imprisonment." They were sure "no other college girls had ever been so disgraced."

Miss Shannon's students also initiated service projects, as did college students in America. One group began a small neighborhood school for older, illiterate female servants. Pairs of students taught for an hour each afternoon and kept notebooks, so the next student tutors could pick up where they left off. Hygiene students helped in a baby clinic and an Armenian camp, weighed and measured city schoolchildren, and made health charts for the school. At Christmas, they decorated a tree, made presents, and entertained neighborhood children.

Miss Shannon predicted that six of the graduating class would be juniors the following year, but at the first commencement held at Sarrafian House garden, only five of her ten sophomores received diplomas, attesting to the high academic standards established in AJCW's first year (Appendix C). Three graduates continued at AUB, while the two best students continued at Park College in Missouri.

Many high school seniors showed interest in enrolling the following year, so hopes were high for growth.

GROWTH AND RIGOR: 1928–1929

Indeed, there were more applications than expected for admission in the fall of 1928. Forty-one young women were accepted, a 100 percent increase over the previous year. One quarter of the freshmen were non-Christians. To accommodate twenty-six boarders, including one Russian and one Swiss student, the top floor was finished as a dormitory and a nearby apartment rented for the faculty. With Miss Irwin still away, it fell on Miss Shannon and Mr. Nicol to "poke, poke, poke" to get the work done as soon as possible. That included poking the city to extend its water main to provide enough water for the college.[13]

Once again, things were in a mess on opening day. Workmen were still installing flooring, plumbing, and windows, while others were whitewashing walls. Miss Shannon complained that the "interminable delay in finishing" that lasted through December was "ruining the spirit of the school." In addition to teaching and administering the college during this initial period of rapid growth, she still had to keep construction accounts. Others pitched in to help deal with the unexpected crush. Katherine Nickoley taught zoology and gave athletic instruction; Mrs. Ward offered Near East history, and Mrs. Church conducted a glee club. Habib Hitti taught Arabic and James Nicol, George Scherer, and W. G. Greenslade divided up the Bible classes. Olga Holenkoff and Esther Lecerf tutored in French. Miss Donaldson carried on in chemistry, physics, and biology so students could enroll in pre-medical, pre-pharmacy, and pre-dental work. Eva Beck added a second mathematics course. Miss Shannon continued to teach the history of religion, Miss Irwin's history course, and a popular hygiene class that featured nutrition experiments with a blind white rat.[14]

Friendships among girls of different nationalities and religions were more evident than ever. An Armenian Christian, a Russian Jew, and a Syrian Muslim sharing a triple made up an especially friendly group. In only one room did roommates choose to be from the same country and of the same religion. Chapel attendance and either a Bible or history of religion class were still required, but Sunday evening meetings were optional. The religious diversity made for wholesome discussions of the Bible and various religious beliefs. One student said, "We must still outwardly maintain the religion into which we were born, even though we find better things in another religion which we inwardly believe and try to practice."

The junior college became known for its community service. Students created a little Sunday School in the garden for neighborhood children and a Christmas tree entertainment for poorer children. New extracurricular projects included organizing health clubs and giving health talks in primary and secondary schools, as well as holding discussions with girls and young women who worked in factories. Student Activity Club members supervised playgrounds and organized clubs for working girls. One AJCW student taught in a nearby orphanage, while another spearheaded local villagers in making oriental rugs. Another organized a health school for anemic children, instructing them to wash their hands and faces and drink milk. AJCW was already producing trained, effective female leaders as students took on problems around them.[15]

Winifred Shannon was greatly relieved when Frances Irwin returned in January to resume her role as principal of the college. Fresh from her graduate studies, Irwin's unsigned memo to the faculty in the spring of 1929 outlined stringent academic standards. Final exams, to be given from 2:00 p.m. on June 7 to 4:00 p.m. on June 12, would cover the year's work except for courses completed in one semester. Instructors were advised to begin a thorough review of the year's material as early as May 27. Sophomores who were expecting to graduate but did not make a passing grade could take a re-examination only if they had failed just one course. Yet students rose to the occasion, meeting the more rigorous standards. The graduation rate for the class of 1929 was 90 percent as compared with the previous year's 50 percent. Nine of the ten sophomores passed their exams and graduated on June 14, we assume once again in the Sarrafian garden.

New Students and Courses

Another surge in applications for the fall of 1929 pushed enrollment up to fifty-six. Misses Irwin and Shannon and two new full-time instructors, Elizabeth Markle and Martha Booth, had to move into a nearby house to make room for thirty-four boarders who, supervised by new matron Agnes Gaskell, filled every bed in Sarrafian House. Botany, political science, dietetics, and mechanical drawing were added to the curriculum. Expatriate Kate Seelye, the first faculty member with a PhD, taught child psychology.[16]

Dietetics students weighed and measured each other. Some were "condemned" for being either underweight or overweight. Others discussed calorie intake at meals until one student led a revolt and made such talk taboo in the dining room. Discussions of child psychology triggered good-natured ribbing that some classmates were spoiled as children since they did not eat all their food. An annual "Health Week" and a "Posture Week" were instituted. Students of various nationalities and religions organized an English Forum and a student magazine was well received.[17]

Sophomores taking social science, who were previously unaware of actual social problems in Lebanon, visited a Near East Relief rug factory; an Armenian refugee camp; a women's prison; a home for the elderly; American University Hospital clinics; and cigarette, box, and silk factories that employed women and children for long hours and low wages. The students were ashamed to find that most relief and charitable institutions were run by outsiders.

Political science students visiting the Lebanese Parliament had their ideals of parliamentary government shattered. They thought their own behavior in student meetings was far better than what they observed in government. One student asked, "Why aren't they more interested in doing good for their country?"

Irwin and Shannon were greatly relieved that, despite the troubles in Palestine, no such unpleasantness occurred between Palestinian Jews and Arabs within Sarrafian House. One young woman, speaking for students from both sects, asked: "Why should we be bitter toward girls who have done nothing and are not to blame for what has happened." They all felt the college was a place for trust and peace and friendship. Miss Irwin optimistically hoped these contacts and feelings would, in time, overcome the old hatreds and rivalries.[18]

SECURING A FUTURE

In the late 1920s Miss Irene Sheppard, Board Secretary for Syria, took a strong personal interest in the women's college and would henceforth provide invaluable assistance in securing the college's future. She first received and screened many inquiries regarding employment in the college. She then helped recruit short-term teachers with the qualifications and temperament to teach in Beirut. To promote AJCW and cultivate supporters, Sheppard's office mailed a campaign brochure called "Future Home Builders of the Near East" to names and addresses provided by Misses Irwin and Shannon. Illustrated with a group photo of the student body, the brochure presented the life and future needs of the college and suggested that crowds of girls wanted to be admitted. Coupled with progress reports, articles in Presbyterian publications, letters home, and speaking engagements by the teachers themselves during furloughs, the brochure boosted fundraising as well as faculty recruitment.[19]

Sarah and Her Sisters | 285

Such efforts were timely. As 1930 marked the beginning of the Great Depression in America, so began a decade of economic, social, and political troubles in Lebanon. Living standards remained low as unemployment and the cost of living rose. Economic disparity caused strikes and protests, and French High Commissioners continued to exploit political rivalries. These factors made it that much more challenging to launch the new women's college that was fast outgrowing Sarrafian House. The college, already having rented the house across the road as an overflow dormitory, could not expand in any direction. Serious consideration was being given to purchasing a major piece of property on which to build, so the Mission alerted the Board that at any time it might need to raise $50,000 to $80,000 for the women's college.[20]

Frances Irwin and Roy Creighton, the architect who had designed the Mission's schools in Tripoli and Sidon and AUB's nurses' residence, sketched out a future college administration building for a new campus, wherever that might be. Her essential needs were five classrooms, three laboratories, a library, an auditorium and lecture room, two offices, two storerooms, a reception room, a teachers' room, and a students' restroom. She wished also to have a chapel, gymnasium, dressing room with showers, two more classrooms, an extra office, and a book room. Creighton estimated a building with just the essential items would cost $34,420. The wished-for items would cost another $13,300, while a separate dormitory for fifty girls would add on another $24,500.[21]

In April 1930, one of the Mission's retired Syrian teachers alerted James Nicol to land suddenly made available a short walk from AUB. Nicol immediately sent a cable to the Board:

> There is a suitable site comprising 6 acres – Girls' College, the price will be about $60,000 Amer. Gold. Price of the land is rising rapidly. Executive Committee, Property Committee approve. Do you advise proceeding? Nicol.

Mr. Nicol followed up with a letter providing more detail.

A French camp occupying a very attractive piece of land estimated at about 25,000 square meters broke up and removed its temporary buildings. It is ample for the development of the College for a number of years and is not too large. The property extends from Rue Madame Curie down to some gardens below and lies on high ground about ten minutes' walk from the University gate. It has a ravishing view of the purple Lebanon mountains eastward, the blue sky above, and the bluer Mediterranean northward and westward... All who have seen the site are enthusiastic about it. Home building in Ras Beirut is escalating land prices. The College must have more permanent and adequate quarters soon. If the Mission can get the land, then we could provide for the gradual development of the essential buildings.[22]

Based on the information James Nicol, and later Winifred Shannon, provided, the Board voted on June 9, 1930 to recommend that the Board's Woman's Committee attempt to secure $30,000 for the administration building and $10,000 for the land, if it could be bought for $40,000. The Woman's Committee, encouraged by Miss Sheppard and other female staff members, made the junior college project their major property item for 1931–32.

But then the Mission encountered an unforeseen complication. First believing the land had only three owners—a Muslim, a Druze, and a Christian—and that the sale could be concluded quickly, Nicol discovered that the three parcels were subdivided into 2,400 parts distributed among *eleven* owners, most of whom had acquired their shares through partnerships and inheritance. Iskandar Araman, a practical builder of long experience with the Mission and a generous friend of the college, volunteered to bargain with the owners and carried the complex transition through from first to last with no increase of the purchase price. Furthermore, he never asked for a commission or fee. Once all the parties were in agreement, each owner—if a man—signed the necessary documents. If a woman, she would, Nicol recorded, "put forth a timid hand from the folds of her robe and press her thumb against the ink pad and then to the document as her signature." By December 2, 1931, a total of 1,925 shares (80 percent) had been secured at a cost of $39,168.30. But it would take another three years to acquire the remaining 20 percent.[23]

Architect Creighton considered the site splendid. It had a commanding view, cool clean breezes off the sea, and political security, all factors that were responsible for the boom in Ras Beirut real estate. It would need little grading. He advised against selling off any part of it, pointing out that some American colleges were going skyward with high-rise construction because they were stingy in acquiring more land initially.[24]

Going over the plans with Creighton again, Frances Irwin wanted her building to be no more than two stories to accommodate at least 100 students. There would need to be a separate dormitory to accommodate at least eighty boarders. The auditorium was to seat 300 to 400, and the lecture room sixty to seventy-five. She wanted to increase the number of classrooms from eight to ten and add a conference room and bookstore. The three separate laboratories were for zoology, chemistry, and general science, each to hold twenty students. If possible, individual teachers' offices should be fitted in. The half-basement was not desirable for classrooms. She envisioned future buildings for a library, chapel, gymnasium, auditorium, faculty residences, and more dormitories. There was to be a place for outdoor commencements, two tennis courts, a basketball court, and a baseball diamond. Gates would lead to the upper and lower roads and a small gate at the extreme east, nearest the university, would be necessary as a time saver." (Reviewing this list today, one is struck by how much of Irwin's vision for the campus became a reality.[25])

IMMEDIATE CONCERNS: 1930–1931

As another academic year approached, Irwin had to turn her attention to more immediate concerns. She wrote Nicol that she was relieved to get electricity, light fixtures, and study lamps installed in each room of the newly rented hostel. Already housing the teachers, this additional residence accommodated the overflow of boarders and featured a "big court on the girls' floor" where they could study together. Yet the AJCW principal had a serious concern about her students' safety and the security of the second building. She had observed "neighbors passing through the yard, beggars at the door and, worst of all, little boys [she supposed] tampering with the faucet in the garden," so she wanted "permission to build a wall around the new house." She also wanted "the night watchmen of our district watching our quarter a little more" because girls were being spoken to or followed home by men at night. "Men being fresh when the girls are alone is to be expected in this country, but it is a nuisance and frightens the girls." Having thirty-eight boarders residing outside the grounds increased the desire for a real campus. Staff and students alike were therefore enthusiastic about the purchase of land and longed for their dream of adequate housing and classrooms to materialize.[26]

Within the largest-yet sophomore class of twenty-six were three honor students, a young Muslim woman from Beirut, an Armenian from Baghdad, and a Syrian from Lebanon. The English and Arabic societies provided money to buy books to add to the 800 in the college's start-up library. AJCW placed a special emphasis on physical education, as ASG had ever since Professor Fulton taught the girls "Basket Ball" in 1910. An extra hour was added to the college day for supervised sports that helped develop a sense of fair play and team spirit. After basketball, the next American sport to catch on was baseball, which quickly became the favorite. A game pitting the freshmen against the sophomores caused much excitement among

Sarah and Her Sisters | 289

those not familiar with the sport as it was played in the United States. The victorious freshmen, in the spirit of good sportsmanship, gave a party afterwards for the losers. Tennis tournaments provided inter-school athletic competition. Swimming in the sea, supervised by university instructors, was available to students who had their parents' permission. An English lady taught "quaint old steps" of country dances on the basketball court on May Day. But all these sports and activities were held outdoors on the school grounds or the nearby AUB field, and therefore contingent on weather and seasonal temperatures. Not having a gymnasium available for indoor activities during the winter was a handicap.[27]

Discussions in the new comparative religion class produced a tense moment or two, but in the end, everyone felt better for having talked out some delicate interfaith issues and relations. One girl afterwards said:

> I never knew any Jewish girls before I came to college and thought I hated Jews. But in the discussion, I suddenly realized that I liked some Jewish girls best in the whole college. When we are all together here, we don't think about these things. I'm sure I can never feel so much against the Jews again.

The school continued to grow. Twenty-four sophomores—another record—graduated in June 1931. At least ten were expected to go to AUB, eight directly into teaching, and a few to study French. Miss Irwin was proud that almost every graduate used her college education in some concrete way. She hoped this same spirit would continue to animate them as they went into their own homes and that the ideals and training they had world not be lost but would help them serve others in their communities for the rest of their lives.[28]

Fig. 70 – Vice Principal Winifred Shannon was AJCW's acting principal, November 1927 to January 1929.

Fig. 71 – Nearby house rented for teachers in 1929 as well as for overflow boarders in 1930.

Fig. 72 – 1930-1931 AJCW student body photo.

Taking up the Challenge

Working from an aerial photograph and other photos and a topographical survey of the chosen building site, Roy Creighton produced a layout of the campus that showed the future locations of the administration/classroom building and two dormitories. Equipped with his plan, the New York staff took the case for raising funds for land and the administration building to the Women's Societies in the Presbyterian Church in the U.S.A. The church women, with little hesitation, accepted the challenge to raise $40,000 by April 1, 1932. The Board's promotion department then printed a ten-panel fundraising brochure, *Training Christian Womanhood in Bible Lands*, that explained how the new junior college had grown and how it was "influencing the new states of Syria, Iraq, Palestine and Transjordania [sic] by drawing women from Aleppo, Mosul, Baghdad, Basra, Jerusalem and Cairo." It contained photos of the view from the site; the entire student body, girls engaging in college activities; and the plan for first floor of the administration building. It also touched on plans for future growth.

The brochure emphasized that this was the first time that women's organizations could focus their foreign apportionment on one great project. "What an inspiration it will be," it read, "to realize that the first building of the new Junior College plant will rise as a gift from Presbyterian women in America to their young daughters in the Near East!" It included the school's anthem: "We greet thee, O College Fair/ In the shadow of Lebanon/ Where the mystic haze doth meet/The blue of the Syrian sea," sung to the tune of a favorite hymn of the women, "Follow the Gleam." Finally, to provide focus for fundraising, the brochure listed various parts of the building and their specific costs: auditorium [$5,800]; library [$3,300]; lecture room [$1,600]; three laboratories [$740 to $1,760]; nine classrooms [$580 to $1,700]; students' restroom [$1,600]; teachers' restroom

[$700]; four administrative offices [$170 to $520]; and a bookstore/post office [$460].[29]

With her chief assistant Winifred Shannon on study leave, Frances Irwin was simultaneously overseeing the day-to-day operation of the college and the planning of the new building and campus while assisting with the fundraising. As evidence of the growing reputation of the college and the fact that the Near East was awakening to the need to educate young women, an unusually large number of applications were received in 1930. The administrative burden Miss Irwin had shared with Miss Shannon the preceding year grew heavier and more demanding. She had to orient new teachers and supervise a larger faculty by herself; introduce new courses; and deal with sympathetic, but nevertheless sexist, male administrators in the Mission and the university. With faculty and student boarders now housed in two separate locations, security became a greater concern.

AJCW's third year as an independent institution began with her giving entrance exams that revealed that half the applicants were insufficiently prepared and therefore denied entrance. Still, those who passed brought the total enrollment to sixty-three, triple that of two years earlier. The new students were from sixteen schools in Syria, Palestine, and Egypt. Some were older and already teachers or in business, but wished to further their education.

Beyond her administrative duties, Miss Irwin, in conjunction with Mr. Creighton, Mr. Nicol, Miss Sheppard in New York, and Miss Shannon, first in Chicago and then Baltimore, took the lead in planning *her* new campus. All these aspects of the Ras Beirut project required the time-consuming exchange of transatlantic correspondence. In short, Frances Irwin was beginning another intense period in which, at an ever-quickening pace, she was tending to daily matters while making important decisions about the future. Although only thirty-five years old, she was still experiencing the lingering effects of her previous exhaustion and dengue fever without Miss Shannon at her side.[30]

Construction, which she hoped could begin in 1931, could not proceed until the funds from the women's campaign were in hand. This weighed heavily on Miss Irwin. Meanwhile, Miss Sheppard and the New York staff would request a special grant from the Sage Fund to be paid for three consecutive years beginning in August 1931, to cover the rent on the present properties.[31]

The 1929 stock market crash on Wall Street would soon have a negative impact on fundraising in America. It also ended the flow of remittances from Syrians living in the States, yet there was an upside to this latter development in that building prices in Lebanon fell. While local businesses took a hit, labor was cheap. Roy Creighton was therefore confident that inflation was unlikely, and that the administration building could be built for $30,000. Increases in material costs could be offset by substituting alternatives. He had added 10 percent in contingency funds to the budget to accommodate changes in prices and plans. The perimeter wall should cost $3,500, with another $500 allocated for a main gate, lower gate, and gate house. They hoped to save money by quarrying stone on the site and leaving more level ground for the dormitories and athletic areas. The bulk of the funds would be paid to the general contractor, Ilias Murr, who had built the Tripoli Girls' School and AUB buildings.

VICTORIES AND SETBACKS

The long, drawn-out negotiations to complete the purchase of the Ras Beirut property did not help Miss Irwin's stress level. By May the Mission had purchased seven-eighths of the property and was willing to pay a little more than intended for the last eighth. Without it, Creighton felt the whole axis of the campus would need to be shifted. Thus, no plan could be finalized until the ultimate purchase. Still, Mr. Nicol gave New York the green light to begin publicizing the campaign throughout the denomination.[32]

Miss Shannon, while at Johns Hopkins University in Baltimore, balanced her studies with being an excellent stateside advocate, promoting the college and helping raise funds. Miss Sheppard arranged for her to go to Pittsburgh twice to attend first the Presbyterian Women's Biennial meeting in May and then the Presbyterian Church's 142nd General Assembly in June. At both national gatherings, she managed the Syria Mission booth and spoke with women about AJCW's need for construction funds, making good use of Mr. Creighton's model, enlarged photographs depicting the activities of the students, and brochures advertising the junior college. Ignoring her Baltimore physician's recommendation that she stop going to conferences for a while, she continued to meet with women's groups right up until her September 18 sailing from New York.[33]

The Presbyterian Women's focus on just this project, the promotional efforts of the New York staff, and Miss Shannon's personal advocacy paid off quickly and handsomely. By November thirteen of the Presbyterian Women's Synodicals (state or regional bodies) had pledged to pay for all but three of the rooms in the building. Several Presbyterials (city or area bodies) pledged the funds for the lecture room and a classroom, bookstore, and post office, leaving only one classroom and one laboratory unsubscribed. Miss Sheppard attributed much of this success to Miss Shannon's effective presentation to many women's society officers at the Assembly booth.[34]

Based on this splendid response, the Board staff fully expected to raise the entire $40,000 goal and hoped for an excess for equipment and furnishings, if not for the dormitory. This amount, plus the $40,000 previously transferred from the Board's Harkness Legacy Fund to endow the college, would cover the $80,000 estimated cost of the land plus the building. But alas, the Great Depression took a toll on donations. By Christmas 1931, it became evident that the women's societies would not meet the full $60,000 for property needs. Prospective donors who had once been thought able to offer large gifts were now impoverished. By March 31, 1932, despite their Herculean efforts, the women fell short of their $40,000 goal by more than $7,600, causing the staff to adjust its promotional work and postpone mention of a dormitory for four or five months.[35]

The campaign pushed on despite the Depression. Donors were assured that the equipment and furnishings already in hand would be reused wherever possible, and that all new items would be simple and in line with the economic conditions of Syria. For fundraising purposes, Nicol listed the new items to be purchased and their costs. Larger donors could furnish and equip entire rooms ranging from $1,400 (auditorium) to $250 (chemistry lab) to $50 (student restroom). Other donations could be designated for individual items from chemistry tables ($250) down to a staff room couch ($25) and double bureaus ($12). He hoped some generous ladies would donate carpets and pictures to hang. Also needed but not listed were two pianos, one for the auditorium and the other for the dormitory living room.[36]

Two former missionaries stepped forward at this critical time. Alice Barber advanced the $500 she had designated in her will for the college, and Frances Irwin suggested the sum go toward furnishing the chapel or the library in Barber's name. Margaret Doolittle, formerly a missionary in Tripoli, directed that $6,000 from her cousin's estate, for which she was executrix, go to the AJCW. Miss Irwin requested that it be used to endow either a scholarship or a library fund.

ENCOURAGING YEAR

Miss Irwin breathed a sigh of relief when Winifred Shannon returned in time to welcome an attractive lot of forty freshmen, followed a week later by thirty-two returning sophomores making for another record enrollment of seventy-two. Even with the addition of a newly rented apartment, they were somewhat jammed in again. The boarders and their new matron, Miss Julia Heitman, had to make the best of cramped sleeping arrangements as former Sarrafian bedrooms were converted into classrooms nicely suited for eighteen students, but rather ridiculous for classes of twenty-four to twenty-six. The small dining room was simply mobbed at noon. Another room served as library-chapel-study hall. No wonder everyone was so enthusiastic about the building plans.

The well-qualified faculty members on staff in the fall of 1931 who had actual experience teaching their subjects included the five returning full-timers and three new part-timers: Mrs. De Forest, almost certainly related to Henry and Kitty De Forest by marriage, who taught physiology; Mme. Helene Fehmy, French; and the Rev. Labib Jureidini, Arabic. Fresh from her graduate studies in hygiene and public health, Winifred Shannon expanded her freshman course in personal and community hygiene to include field work in baby clinics and elementary schools. Mrs. De Forest offered her physiology course to sophomores and Mrs. Seelye taught child training. The rest of the curriculum remained unchanged. Due to the crowding, freshman classes in English, zoology, and chemistry had to be divided.

Given the college's rather meager resources, collaboration with and assistance from the university were of great help in maintaining the academic standards of the New York Regents, which made it possible for AUB to accept AJCW graduates as juniors without examination. In addition to AUB's allowing college teachers and students to use its labs, university faculty members gave occasional lectures at the college. Some departments loaned AJCW instructors' slides, charts, and other teaching aids. The university library loaned books and extended full library privileges to junior college students who could also attend lectures, concerts, and other university events.

In keeping with the mantra of the year ("To keep my health! To do my work! To live! To see to it that I grow and gain and give"), students began taking more initiative. They managed the Arabic society, English forum, activity clubs, house meetings, and the boarding committee efficiently. Instead of criticizing the food and asking for "fish and caviar" as in the past, they dealt with problems and complaints themselves. Students designed a little silver ring with a Phoenician ship carved on a green background that was symbolic of each young woman's adventure on the sea of knowledge. Almost all students could be seen wearing it. Outside of class, many became involved in art, glee club, country dancing, recreational leadership, special games, and parties. A student operetta sold out and marked the first time that women were allowed to appear in public on the AUB auditorium stage.

Thirty-three students attended the first conference for college and university women held in Baalbek during spring vacation. Perhaps inspired by Dr. Quincy Wright's earlier visit and lectures on international peacemaking, they discussed the barriers that prevented good will and proposed solutions. Students later testified to a new vision of what each individual could do in her own community.

Among an unusual number of good students were some of the best the college had ever had. Four completed the year with averages above eighty-five, and three above ninety. A Syrian student wrote: "I learned to widen my horizon in ways never heard of in high school where we studied only what was in our little text books. A student is not measured by the knowledge she shows in exams, but by the way she can meet problems in the future." And from a young Palestinian: "I find college a life of wealth abounding in beauty, health, knowledge, sympathy and friendship. It is not confined to books and papers, but is wide where one, in sympathy and thought, comes in contact with the different circles of humanity." Summing up the year, Miss Shannon maintained: "We have tried to give the widest opportunities to get our students in touch with the best and to learn to live a more abundant life graciously."

Encouraged by their enthusiastic response to her enhanced hygiene classes and field experiences, Miss Shannon proposed that students accept an invitation to conduct a summer school for girls in the village of Bint Jebeil in southern Syria. They jumped at the idea, contributed money and material, and conducted a successful summer-long camp. The experiment was written up in a pamphlet, "Veils Up," and widely distributed among American church women. From this modest beginning grew an ambitious and well-established Village Welfare Program.

Fundraising and Ongoing Expansion

Frances Irwin was thrilled to finalize the campus and building plans, but provoked that the Mission had yet to acquire the last bit of land. It had therefore not started the grading, planting of trees, and building of the wall for which the women of Immanuel Presbyterian Church in Los Angeles had promised $2,500, thanks to Miss Irwin's good friend, Ellen Goodrich Bushwell, who was married to the assistant pastor. Frances hoped the protracted affair would be resolved as soon as possible.[37]

Irwin was most appreciative of the interest her colleagues in New York took in the college and amazed they had raised as much money as they had. When the church women raised less than $33,000 of their $40,000 pledge by the March 31, 1932, deadline, the staff again turned to the Sage Fund generously bequeathed to the Board of Foreign Missions by Mrs. Russell Sage upon her death in 1918. The Sage Committee agreed to make the unmet balance of $7,646 available as soon as construction started. Because more funds were needed for equipment and any additional cost for the land, the Fund Committee also provided another $2,000 a year for three years

Sarah and Her Sisters | 299

in lieu of interest lost when the Harkness Endowment Fund was exhausted for the land purchase.[38]

The New York staff thought it unwise to ask the Presbyterian Women to commit to another $10,000 for the dormitory right away. Therefore, Miss Irwin proposed that they instead ask the Sage Fund for another $10,000 to build at least one floor of the dormitory, which might enable the college to get along for a while. The campus site was too far from their present quarters and the area around the site had no suitable housing to accommodate the school's swelling enrollment. They were expecting new students in the second semester and students were already enrolling for the following year. As well, the college was committed to housing females attending the university. Even though she made a strong case, Dr. Speer decided that the Mission's request for another $10,000 to complete the Deir ez Zor Hospital already under construction took precedence over the college. Whether one floor or more, a dormitory was still a way off. As of June 1932, there was only one contribution of $50 from a relative of Miss Irwin designated for building the dormitory. Irwin started preparing a pamphlet emphasizing this urgent need, while Irene Sheppard targeted the next fiscal year as "open season" for the dormitory.[39]

The need for the dormitory was especially critical given the growing presence of international students. First the American School for Girls and then the AJCG developed a special relationship with the new government of Iraq. It began in the fall of 1924 when King Faisal I's prime minister enrolled his two daughters and two other Iraqi girls in ASG. The following summer, two of the first freshman graduates of AJCG were hired to teach in a Baghdad girls' school. They did well and were rehired in 1926. By 1927 there were three AJCG teachers in Baghdad schools and more going for the following year. Miss Irwin hoped to continue this trend, but worried about keeping up with the increasing demand. Her concern was eased considerably when, in 1930, the Iraqi government began paying the full tuition for the girls it sent.[40]

After Miss Irwin judged the first few students to be "from good families" and found they "proved promising enough in intellect or character" for college work, she and the Iraqi consul agreed that ten girls were to be chosen for a special two-year course at ASG and that the government would pay for special teachers to instruct them if necessary. They could then go on to the junior college and ultimately for a BA degree. Thus, Iraq could raise the standards of its schools and ASG and the junior college could count on a steady stream of Iraqi students. The Iraqi director general's visit to the college in 1932 to engage more students as teachers made quite a stir. Since the four most recent college graduates were doing so well in Iraq, the government continued to turn to the college for new teachers, sending three more Iraqi girls at government expense for higher education. (No mention is made, however, of how this special relationship affected the Mission's agreement with the British Syrian Teachers' College.[41])

Despite the demand for girls' and women's education, the advancement of girls and women in Syrian society was still a work in progress hampered by narrow-mindedness and outright opposition. Just after the Lebanese state had instituted the French *baccalaureate* secondary school examination in 1931, the Mission reported that "the majority of girls were not yet allowed to attend schools with boys or men."[42] Nevertheless, 130 determined young women had by then received two-year associate degrees from the five-year-old junior college. Of these, twenty-four were teaching in Syria, Iraq, Egypt, and Cyprus; twenty were studying for their bachelor of arts degree in the university; two were preparing for YWCA work; and others for special service.

Yet some graduates still ran into strong resistance. Widad, a determined student from a very wealthy, conservative family, was allowed to finish her course and graduate in 1931. Tremendously interested in hygiene and welfare work, she wished to go to England to specialize in it. But her father refused to let her go. Grieved and disappointed, she arranged to take a course at AUB, only to have him stop her. Undeterred, she studied child welfare with a private teacher and began helping in the baby clinics. She would not give up her desire to serve others. "Do you wonder," Miss Irwin asked, "that we want a college of girls with such a spirit? Without an education, she would have lived in idleness; we wanted to help her live up to her ideals."[43]

THE INDOMITABLE MISS DAOUD

So it was with another exceptional and memorable young Syrian woman. At the urging of her teachers and with the help of friends of Miss Shannon in Kansas City, Lateefeh Daoud, after gaining her junior college certificate, enrolled in Park College in Missouri in the fall of 1928. Two years later, the intelligent Miss Daoud graduated with a bachelors degree in chemistry and went on for an MA at Rice Institute in Houston, where she had to take outside work to earn tuition and book money. When a summer job fell through, she proposed that she speak in Texas churches on the problems and plans of the junior college to earn money for herself and raise funds for the new administration building. Although Daoud undoubtedly wished to help, Miss Shannon was cool to the idea, presumably because of the difficulty in accounting for the funds raised and how they were divided between herself and AJCW. However, she left it to the Board staff to respond to Daoud's offer. The staff, while interested, agreed that it was inadvisable to accept it.[44]

Miss Irwin urged New York to find other ways to help Daoud remain in America to get her master's degree so she could teach chemistry and mathematics at AJCW the following year. The degree was essential because, as she explained, "When anything goes wrong, or students of our short-term teachers do not do well in the University, we were reminded that we ought to have better trained teachers. If a girl fails, it is because her teachers had only B.A. degrees." As much as the principal wanted her to finish her studies in the U.S., the plucky Miss Daoud refused a scholarship to do so because the economic conditions were so bad during the Depression. She instead returned to Beirut to complete her graduate work in chemistry at AUB.[45]

Just before AJCW reopened in 1932, an excited Miss Daoud, having just completed her oral comprehensive exam, made a breezy and joyful entrance into Miss Shannon's office. "Oh! Oh! I passed and am so happy," she announced. "After they quizzed me for an hour and twenty minutes, I thought they would never stop and I had nothing left in me—and I came out second!" Her former teachers hired her on the spot as the first Syrian woman with enough education to teach full-time as a staff member at her alma mater.[46]

SARRAFIAN OUTGROWN

The 1932–1933 AJCW Catalogue confidently announced: "In the fall of 1933, the Junior College will be located on the beautifully situated new campus on rue Mme. Curie in Ras Beirut with a splendid view of the Lebanon mountains and the sea." The dream of a new campus at last seemed poised to become a reality. The conclusion of the lengthy property negotiations came down to the members of one family who jointly owned 300 (one-eighth) of the 2,400 shares. In June 1932, they and the Mission finally agreed on the price, but the family members could not decide how the money would be divided among them, so it had to be settled in court.[47]

The expansion would be most welcome given the school's crowded conditions. Julia Heitman oversaw fifty-five college and fourteen university students boarding in two separate buildings and five scattered apartments. Sarrafian House became so crowded that, with ten or more girls wedged around each dining table, diners

Fig. 73 – Sarrafian House chapel was filled to capacity each morning (1933).

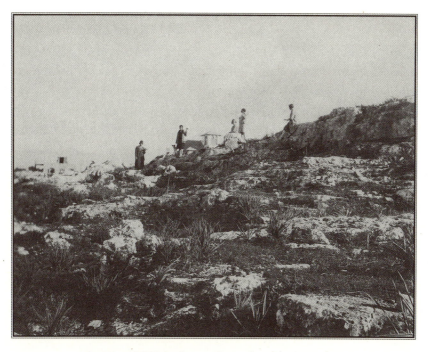

Fig. 74 – AJCW students take in the view from their future campus on rocky Ras Beirut hillside.

requested a second eating group. That was difficult to add because the kitchen, pantry, and service room were all so small and inadequate. Even those willing to pay extra for single dormitory rooms had to double up. Seventy girls squeezed into a chapel that fit only thirty comfortably and also performed double duty as a classroom. "We are so crowded," complained Miss Irwin, "We seem to be at the last stage. There is no more room!"[48]

Students were assigned a teacher as a guardian and advisor in personal and academic matters, and each resident had to have a guardian in the city to oversee her finances and "in case of difficulty." Visitors had to be listed and students needed permission to leave the grounds—with a chaperone. Boarders provided their own table napkins, towels, pillows, bed linens, mattresses, rugs, wall decorations, and laundry bags as well as "an athletic costume consisting of a plain, white blouse; full, dark bloomers; and white tennis shoes." Tuition was 7.50 Turkish gold lira per semester, with board an additional eleven lira. Single rooms, if they could be had, cost between four and six lira extra, depending on their size. Lunches for non-residents were eight lira per term and it cost a lira to have access to the piano. A limited number of work scholarships were available.[49]

Sarrafian House was about to be taxed in another way. In the fall of 1932 Miss Shannon, a strong advocate for early childhood education, fulfilled a long-held dream by transforming a downstairs bedroom in Sarrafian House into a nursery school for very poor two-and three-year-olds from the neighborhood. Supervised by Mable Erdman and Vivian Greenslade, the half-day school served as a laboratory where students in Shannon's child hygiene class could have practical training in the care of children.

Upon arrival, "eleven little waifs were bathed and dressed in little green dresses, sweaters and sandals" before a half hour of free play. After helping set the table, they had a mid-morning lunch of milk, biscuits, and cod-liver oil. Alumna Sanneyeh Habboub,

Fig. 75 – Workmen prepare former French Army camp site for construction of AJCW campus and first buildings.

Fig. 76 – Miss Irwin (left) Rev. James Nicol and Miss Shannon with contractors at long awaited campus groundbreaking in January 1933.

who had obtained an MD from the Woman's Medical College of Pennsylvania and then cared for neglected Muslim women, examined each child on Wednesday mornings and gave their mothers special help once a month. Miss Shannon described how Dr. Habboub was "now wearing a hat talking to the mothers with all the idioms and proverbs of the country, so that they take her advice eagerly." The college students also visited the children's homes to relay the doctor's advice. "Sleepy hour" followed lunch, which was followed by supervised play in the garden for those not still sleeping. The day ended with "rhythm work, a good story and some games" before the children were "dressed in their dirty clothes and sent home." The children showed marked physical improvement and learned to play amicably with their peers.[50]

DORMITORY DELAYED

The new administration and dormitory buildings could not come soon enough. If the college moved onto the new campus *without* the dormitory, then classes would be far away from the students' housing. Getting back and forth would probably require a truck or bus, especially in bad weather. Rented accommodations near the new campus would be difficult to find and very expensive. "One wonders," Miss Irwin questioned, "if we ought to continue to expand unless we can provide more adequately for housing next year."

Miss Irwin suggested that, if $15,000 could be advanced for the first wing of the dormitory, then most of the loan could be paid off in six years by the annual $2,000 savings in rents and student rental fees. With the Board facing a $426,737 operating deficit, its members, plus the Women's Committee and Sage Fund, at first all deemed this option too drawn-out and hazardous. However, at Miss Sheppard's suggestion, the women *did* put a $15,000 offering for the dorm into their 1934 budget. Construction was at least imminent.[51]

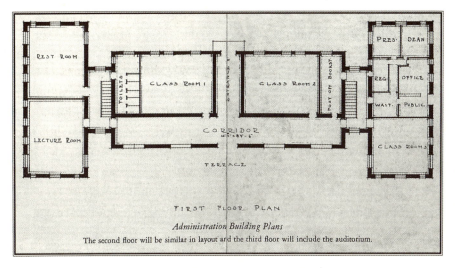

Fig. 77 – First floor plan for new AJCW administration and classroom building.

Fig. 78 – AJCW students took chemistry classes from Professor Edward Nickoley in AUB's George E. Post Science Hall until they had their own chem lab in 1933.

That was good news, since all foreign mission programs were being cut 20 percent because of the Board's large deficit in the context of the Depression. Fortunately, the Sage Fund did not suffer a large decrease in returns. The annual grants for rent would remain at $2,000, thus allowing the $40,000 endowment to be used to buy the campus property. Further actions on the dorm were postponed for a year or two until the women could raise the full amount for its construction. Meanwhile, Miss Elliott of the Board staff completed a field report in which she noted that $3,500 could be saved and the project accelerated if certain rooms were left unfurnished and equipment on hand, such as auditorium chairs and library tables, reused.[52]

For Frances Irwin, who was still teaching three courses while managing overcrowded facilities and planning new ones, the stress continued to weigh heavily. Negotiations on the land purchase had taken longer than anyone expected, the dormitory had again been postponed, and she was not always treated as an equal by male colleagues. Almost to the breaking point and longing for her next scheduled furlough still more than a year away, Frances had written to her parents in February 1933: "I'd come home in a minute to try to get a job if I thought I could. I don't believe I'll stick around much longer here."[53]

CHAPTER ELEVEN

AJCW's Ras Beirut Campus (1933–1937)

> *It was a proud day when the Junior College, after six years in rented quarters, opened this fall session in its new Administration building on its own beautiful campus. That the school could begin at all was a wonder as the corner stone was laid scarcely seven months before.*
>
> Winifred Shannon,
> AJCW 1933–34 Annual Report

LAYING THE CORNERSTONE

Once the last remaining owner, "a widow of considerable strength of character," saw the campus site being marked out for a building in January 1933, she finally decided to sell her small portion of the property.[1] Yusef Bek Artimus, a local builder, was then given the building contract and put in charge of construction. No longer as young as he used to be, he slipped on a banana peel and was confined to bed with a broken ankle for a month before work was to begin. Once recovered, however, the sounds of shovels and hammers were heard as he took the project to heart as his *magnum opus*, lavishing upon it all his skill and devotion until it was finished.[2]

The foundation and the building's two wings were well underway when the cornerstone laying ceremony for AJCW's administration and classroom building was held on March 2, 1933. Mr. Nicol borrowed a "movie machine" to record the event, but Miss Shannon worried that "the pictures wouldn't be good because of the gray, rainy day." Mr. Artimus had built a platform for the participants, and a wooden table was thoughtfully covered with a "bright pink bedspread, flowers and sweets" for the crowd, although Miss Shannon thought the cover "a bit too much and the red and yellow flowers atrocious." (Nicol had warned Artimus beforehand, "Ladies always want something different—don't be hurt if they want to change this."[3])

James Nicol welcomed the assembled graduates, students, and friends of the college, including the American Consul General, Herbert Goold. After this Rev. Mufid Abd el Karim, pastor of the Beirut Evangelical (Protestant) Church, read scripture and Dr. William Greenslade, president of the Near East School of Theology, gave the dedicatory prayer. They then placed inside the cornerstone a Bible, a newspaper of the day, various signatures of those present, a photo of the student body and faculty, the 1932–1933 college catalogue, coins from Syria and surrounding countries, and the college publication, "Veils Up." Misses Irwin and Shannon then troweled mortar onto the foundation wall and workmen lifted the large stone into place just outside the south doorway of the new building. The ceremony concluded with students and alumnae singing their Alma Mater:

> To thy portals, O College fair,
> We thy daughters have come from far;
> We have answered thy call to dare
> To adventure beneath thy star.
> Alma Mater, hail to thee;
> Receive our pledge of constancy.
> Alma Mater, hail to thee;
> Deep loyalty we vow.[4]

Fig. 79 – Laying the cornerstone for AJCW's first building, March 2. 1933. Borrowed "movie machine" in lower right records the ceremony.

Fig. 80 – Participants were, left to right, William Greenslade, Frances Irwin, Winifred Shannon, James Nicol and Rev. Mufid Abd el Karim.

Fig. 81 – Miss Irwin applied mortar to cornerstone as Miss Shannon and excited students watch.

The Mission hailed the event as "a third step in Women's education," but failed to clarify if this was a general reference to the successive and historic steps of education for females, or to the college recently having started as a part of ASG, then moving to Sarrafian House and at last having its own campus. The newspaper *Al-Kulliya* reported: "The Near Eastern woman has entered the field of enlightened action to help her brother in trying to solve the social problems of these lands. There are many fields of action for uplifting society in the East, where women are better fitted to serve than men." Miss Irwin rightfully acknowledged the building as a "sacrificial gift from the American women to those in the Near East."[5]

Miss Irwin was at first pleased by the pace of the work. The outer walls of handsome cream-colored Lebanese limestone were nearly completed by June. These walls excited many admiring comments, particularly because of the chiseled Gothic-shaped windows. Miss Irwin's sensitivity and intellect were evident in every detail: the floor tiles, the woodwork, the stairways, and the chapel that she regarded as the heart of the college. The architect promised the detailed interior would be finished in time to start the fall term.[6]

That spring the Mission Board sent three staff members, "Miss (Ruth) Elliot, Miss Miller and Mrs. Scott," to observe its work in the Near East. "Unfortunately," Winifred Shannon wrote home, "they had a car accident in Northern Syria in which their driver was killed and they were thrown out and rather badly injured." Somewhat recovered, they arrived in Beirut with only a few bandages visible and Ruth Elliot with a broken finger. They were able to visit the college when it was under construction before completing their report to New York, which undoubtedly spoke well of their much-favored project.[7]

Not Happy in Her Job

Although the construction work proceeded apace and the college was growing, not everyone associated with it was content. For an unspecified reason Miss Irwin was worried about her mother's health. In July she wrote to her, "You better inquire about a job for me and let me come home and care for you." But then, showing another sign of the accumulating stress, she added:

> I'm really thinking about it. I'm not happy in my job—I've always known I shouldn't be in charge and don't think I want to come back after my next furlough, if I ever get another. But the problem will be to find a job (in Minneapolis). I don't want any more teaching—something quiet with not too many people around me. You'll probably say "Frances is tired at the end of the year"—but I think there's more to it than that.[8]

Irwin had her own health concerns. On visiting Winifred Shannon's Bint Jebeil summer welfare camp where the students conducted hygiene work, she developed a fever that left her weak and shaky. She recovered quickly but then feared she had trachoma only to find that her eye problem was due to an abscessed tooth.[9]

Adding to Irwin's stress, construction that was estimated to cost $31,075 was already $800 over budget. By September the overrun exceeded a thousand dollars but was covered by Alice Barber's gift for the chapel and interest on deposits. Overage on the perimeter wall and gatehouse and the removal of heavy stones in the athletic field then added another $1,799 in cost. The extra expenditures paled in comparison to the steady drop in the dollar that by mid-1933 had added $7,000 to $8,000 to the total cost. Six months later the loss on the exchange for gold had risen to $10,500. Mr. Nicol lamented that they had not drawn $30,000 from the Board in advance and bought gold, which would have offset the loss in exchange. By September the exchange loss surpassed $16,000, a cost

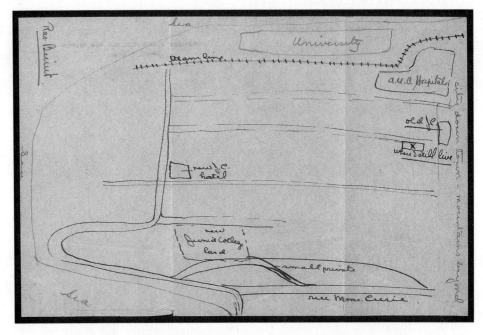

Fig. 82 – Frances Irwin's map for her parents showing (bottom to top) "new Junior College land," "new J.C. hostel," "where I still live," "old J.C.," AUB Hospitals," "University" and "Sea."

that, along with litigation fees, had to be absorbed by the Board. To address the Mission's immediate needs, the Board added funds from the Sunday School Easter Offering to those appropriated for the dormitory, so Beirut had more than $13,000 available for at least one dormitory wing. Inspired by Winifred Shannon's first photos showing the beautiful building and the glorious view over the city and the sea, the New York staff set to work to overcome the project's financial challenges. Keeping track of all these funds kept in numerous accounts in New York and Beirut was often left to poor Miss Sheppard.[10]

Supervising stonemasons, carpenters, plumbers, electricians, and other workers, Mr. Artimus did his best to keep construction on schedule throughout the spring and summer. As the multi-purpose building neared its October completion date, Miss Shannon admitted that she and Miss Irwin were not very rested or ready to start what promised to be a very tiring semester. Many interior details were still incomplete, and, while their boarders' house was ready for occupancy, she and Irwin were living in the university women's hostel twenty minutes away, making their chaperoning duties a "grand nuisance."

When a young English woman decided at the last minute to marry instead of coming to teach and be the college librarian, Miss Shannon wrote her sister, Margaret, and urged her to drop everything and come immediately as a substitute librarian. Intrigued by the opportunity, Margaret cabled back "yes" and signed a contract to serve *pro bono* as librarian, receiving only $250 for her passage and $50 for incidental expenses. Winifred was thrilled to receive this confirmation. In her reply addressed to "Dearest Little Bear" and headed by two dancing stick figures, she wrote that she wished Margaret could only have seen her and Olga (her maid) "capering around last night" when they opened the cable. "It's going to be a happy, happy year and I can't wait until October 19." Thanking Irene Sheppard for helping Margaret sail from New York, Winifred wrote that not only was the help badly needed, but having her younger sister there would mean a great deal to her. She added that "all the stew over the auditorium and Child Welfare lab on the third floor" had been resolved to everyone's satisfaction. The whole third floor was turned into an auditorium and the nursery school moved to "a tiny little house all by itself, built on one of the foundations left by the French military hospital that was there." To her it looked, appropriately, "like a little cub to the big building, but as cute as can be." In closing, she hoped that the year ahead would be less wearing on their faithful colleagues in New York.[11]

It could not have been easy for these two dynamic and intelligent women in their early thirties to keep up the stressful pace without the support of a spouse or significant other. There is no indication that the more introspective Miss Irwin, who seemed to be "married" to her college project, had anyone waiting for her at home other than family members. The more outgoing Miss Shannon had, on the other hand, an admirer in Kansas with whom she was greatly annoyed. Too stingy to pay the ten cents overseas postage, he sent a card addressed to her for her parents to forward to Beirut. Incensed, she instructed her father to return it to him. "This cheapness appalls me, but fits into his past performances, and is why my name is still Shannon—a very nice name, why should I want to change it?"[12]

In September Frances Irwin was meeting with Mr. Artimus twice a week. Her busy days included overseeing details such as the design of library table lamps and pots for ferns, laying out the lavatories with carpenters and plumbers, all while meeting with teachers, visiting with students, hosting guests in her off-campus apartment, and seeing a dentist daily for her abscessed tooth. "I get so tired," she wrote, "all I want to do is to sleep and yet I'm perfectly all right—the doctor said it's just my lazy character plus the warm climate." She did manage occasional weekend visits with friends and a "trip to the beach for a swim and tea" while telling herself, "No use hurrying the East." Despite all the workers hadn't yet finished at the college, she believed the building "really was going to be awfully nice."[13]

Nevertheless, Frances later in September renewed her request for her mother's help in finding her a job at home. Because some "holier than thou" mission society was cutting into the Board's giving, staff might be cut.

> We think, talk and sleep money because of our financial straits, college debt and the fall of the dollar. I'd like a year or so in the new building—but I can't see myself continuing this job. I feel like a square peg in a round hole most of the time and dislike having to struggle on. I'm getting about $50 a month, must feed myself on that and can't pay my insurance. I may ask next summer off.[14]

James Nicol ignored her pleas that he "scream and yell" at Mr. Artimus to hurry up because the contractor had assured Nicol the building would be ready in time. She had to admit: "As one by one we finish a room (by dint of following a white washer around—or a carpenter, etc.) we realize how very nice it all is going to be. We are in a mad swirl of cleaning, arranging rooms, interviewing new students all week—only a worse swirl ahead." With three days to go, Irwin's "handsome, well-built and nicely finished building" seemed nearly ready for classes. "We'll have to anyway," she declared, while admitting, "The dear, old architect has done well, though he has seemed eternally slow." She was weary of operating in three scattered buildings (the not-quite-finished freshman-sophomore hostel, the apartment she and the other Americans shared with the university boarders, and the new college) and having to arrange a jitney taxi service for Christian young women uneasy about walking through the Muslim quarter. Through all of this Irwin could only "hope for the best."[15]

GRAND OPENING

Frances Irwin and Winifred Shannon were too busy to write much about the first day in the new administration building. We know, however, that early on the morning of October 11, 1933, upwards of seventy young women streamed through the gates of the new campus. Those coming up the terraced walkway bisecting the barren hillside surely were impressed by the handsome Mediterranean-style edifice before them. Built of cream-colored native stone, the three-story main section featured a high central archway set off by two rows of paired, arched windows on either side, and an upper row of smaller windows. This was flanked on the east and west by two-story wings, also with arched windows. A low-peaked tile roof covered the entire building.

After funneling through the archway and solid double doors, the students would have found themselves in a spacious corridor leading left and right. There they were likely greeted warmly by Misses Irwin and Shannon and the rest of the staff who then directed them to the simple chapel on the main floor that accommodated them all comfortably. Once the faculty was seated up front, morning prayers began, only to be "interrupted," as Miss Shannon later reported, "by a quarrel among carpenters on the second floor and the clanging hammers of ironworkers completing the fence outside." After chapel students would have made their way to classes in the spacious east wing classrooms and well-equipped laboratories that replaced the cramped bedrooms, parlor, and dining room of Sarrafian House. The principal, vice principal, and staff must have reveled in having their own offices and faculty lounge in the west wing. All this, Shannon marveled, had been accomplished "scarcely seven months since the cornerstone had been laid."

That weekend Frances Irwin wrote home that there were "workmen all over the place the first few days of school," with "sudden hammering on the stairs." Stonemasons, she said, were "chipping busily on stones for our gate and gate house just under the chapel window. Although several things happened not as we wished, they can't spoil a thing—the building is lovely, and the girls are thrilled with it." She was especially pleased with "an awfully nice freshman class—very attractive girls better prepared for college work." They included for the first time "one Christian and one Muslim from Amman; a Muslim graduate of the Sidon School and two daughters of the Minister of Finance of Iraq. The Iraqi Muslims," she noted, "wear veils in Iraq but hats here with their parents' permission. They are 'very nouveau riche' but nice kids—don't act it too much. Overall everyone seems happy and things are starting off well." She expected "successful years scholastically" and had "stopped worrying about our debts since they are so big anyway.[16]

Principal Irwin was driven to the college every morning in time for 7:30 prayers but preferred at the end of each day to make the twenty-minute walk back down to her familiar and pleasant apartment next to Sarrafian House. The chapel lacked proper chairs, as did the auditorium, but she loved the woodwork around the platform. Sunday noontime prayers had to compete with the local muezzin's call to prayer. Because he was at the same level as the third-floor chapel, it sounded "like he was next door." Anxious "to get the grounds fixed up," she asked her mother to send her seeds, "asters and cosmos especially—perhaps larkspur, and I never thought I would ask for petunias, but they look quite pretty here in the gardens." She pushed to get the two entrances finished "so people won't fall down at the end of the steps where there is no walk."[17]

Preparing for a public open house the week of November 20, Irwin and her staff hand-wrote 500 to 600 invitations and had thirty day-laborers clean up the rock and dirt piles by the tennis courts, cart off trash, and lay out flowerbeds until everything was "polished and gleaming." Many invitees sent flowers and presents, including books for the library. Hundreds of guests toured the impressive building designed for 200 students and extolled its fine climate with

Fig. 83 – Near completion in September 1933, the handsome main building with its two wings was later named Sage Hall.

Fig. 84 – Margaret Olivia Slocum Sage, a Presbyterian and America's first female philanthropist, was a strong supporter of female education. She gave the Presbyterian Board of Foreign Missions an endowment that funded much of AJCW's campus and first building later named for her.

Sarah and Her Sisters

cool breezes in summer, and southern exposure and wooden floors that warmed it in winter. Irwin was surprised at how they raved about the building. "We've gotten so used to it and have worried so over it's not being finished that we've forgotten how really wonderful it is. The library is lovely, the laboratories are well-done, and the building is very handsome. We are very lucky." There was only one major slip-up during the event.

> The wife of the President of the Republic was not recognized until after a mere student had shown her around the whole building while the lady who was supposed to be watching for her was upstairs guzzling punch. I really was provoked for I had several people assigned to take care of officials whom we don't know well or at all and (who would) expect personal attention. But Mme. Debbas was very nice and didn't seem to mind particularly.

Otherwise, the open house was a grand success.[18]

SMOOTH START

Besides the librarian Margaret Shannon, who with her MA degree was also able to teach Bible, sociology, and political science, new faculty members included Mlle. Zwilling (French), Mr. Shakir Nassar (Arabic), and Mrs. Glockler (nursery school assistant). Typing and stenography were added to the curriculum as non-credit electives. Shortly after school opened, students and faculty went on a weekend retreat to Baalbek to weld together the diverse nationalities and religions represented. The students sang a popular pep song with several verses, each about a "little freshman" from a different country followed by the refrain: "For a mixture strange is the Junior College/So full of beauty and so full of knowledge/Yet we're glad we're here so we all acknowledge/The Sophomores and the jolly little Freshmen."

A new student council handled some difficult discipline problems and organized a tennis tournament, an all-day excursion, and several parties. To further free up the faculty, the service committee began organizing the social work projects. There were no further requests for an alternative service to chapel. Plays were given in the third-floor auditorium with a good stage and splendid acoustics to raise funds for the village welfare program and to help students who were struggling to pay their tuition in the poor economy. Religious plays were performed at Christmas and Easter. Beirut alumnae put on a fund-raising play in English and organized their own tennis tournament, gathered for discussions, and held reunions. Each class since 1925 planted a special tree and gathered funds for a stone bench to beautify the campus.

Relegating the nursery school to its own building (Miss Shannon's "tiny house") prevented "sudden tantrums from ringing through the whole school." That was not the only change. No reason is given why, instead of serving poorer children as it first had, the preschool admitted only children of the "better class Syrian and American families." The children learned rhythms and how to set a table and enjoyed lemonade and biscuits. College students fed and weighed them and taught them according to modern educational and psychological principles. Mothers often attended child psychology classes. A local Arabic newspaper saw the little school as the "best argument against those who say higher education directs women away from motherhood."

In 1934, half of the twenty graduating sophomores planned to continue their higher education. Many hoped that the junior college would someday be a full four-year college. Despite widespread unemployment, nearly all the rest found work, many as teachers. One preferred to teach in a village girls' school even though she was poorly paid. Another who was teaching in Iraq formed a Social Activity Club, dividing her sixty girls into three committees that were responsible for the cleanliness of the school, helping poor children get recreation and food weekly, and encouraging undereducated women to read and write more. Frances Irwin was especially proud of her two graduates studying at Columbia University in New York. Lily Trabulsi, after teaching in Baghdad for a year, decided to pursue a BA in physical education. She shared a room with another Lebanese alumna, Emma Saleeby, a 1928 graduate who had also taught in Iraq before completing her BA at Greensboro College in North Carolina. Miss Shannon believed that "the place and need for higher education and college trained women with ideals of service is being realized in the Near East."

The welfare camp was invited to return to the primitive and feudalistic Nasiriyeh villages in the north of Syria where almost 100 percent of the people were illiterate. Two graduate nurses and student volunteers conducted health schools, mothers' clubs, and evening programs using a "picture machine" (projector). The older people insisted that the children listen to the "learned teachers," while they themselves crouched nearby hoping to gather a few crumbs of information. A 1934 graduate later remarked, "Miss Shannon was a pioneer, putting her whole heart and spirit into the College. Her laboratory projects made students aware of the significance of hygiene, home improvement, and social responsibility, while increasing their self-confidence and spirit of adventure."[19]

"SORRY TO LEAVE"

When the American Junior College for Women began its second decade of existence and second year on the new campus, enrollment remained at seventy. A notable addition to the faculty was alumna Najla Azzeddin with a PhD in Oriental History from the University of Chicago, who was hired to teach history. Another was bookkeeper and treasurer Miss Eramian, an AUB graduate who tutored a few students in commerce. Madame Rignault took charge of French. Otherwise, no new courses or faculty were added.

Fig. 85 – 1934 photo of first graduates of American Junior College for Girls. Inscription: "Two are now doctors."

Fig. 86 – Miss Shannon's "Little Cub" nursery school.

Fig. 87 – Miss Irwin's photo of AJCW faculty and staff members in 1934. Miss Shannon is on the left.

Sarah and Her Sisters | 325

The constant stress of supervising an ever-changing college faculty and staff in three different facilities—one shared, one renovated, and one built from scratch—over ten years caught up with Frances Irwin again. Miss Shannon grew alarmed when she observed that the accumulated strain was imperiling her colleague's health, and others in the Mission and in New York agreed. The founding principal of the college was, after only fifteen months in her new building on her new campus, given a special furlough in the hope that she could regain her strength once more and continue heading up the school. With great reluctance but considerable relief, Irwin took up the offer and made arrangements to return to Minneapolis. In her last letter home, she told her parents: "I am sorry to leave the College in the middle of the year and not see this sophomore class through, but one would always be sorry to leave any class, so I think I don't feel too badly!"[20]

There were important loose ends to tie up before departing. With over $7,000 already set aside for the dormitory, the Mission hired Howell Taylor, a school architect teaching at the American Community School, to plan the first unit of the residence hall and supervise its construction. Irwin met with him to review his plans. To take better advantage of the site while retaining the building's orientation, Taylor suggested re-arranging the interior plan. By excluding servants' rooms, he increased the capacity of the overall building by twenty-three students and three teachers. This projected total of 101 residents exceeded the eighty-eight in Roy Creighton's plan. Paradoxically, Taylor reduced the floor area by 10 percent and lowered ceiling heights, thereby reducing the cubic meters by 25 percent while still keeping the cost within the original estimate. The first phase would actually be more than half the whole structure because it would include the dining room, kitchen, laundry, storerooms, and other areas. The Mission Committee eagerly awaited word from the Board regarding the prospects of proceeding within the year.[21]

Another last-minute item for Irwin to attend to was the purchase of trees and shrubs for the grounds. So too, she had to arrange to bus the whole college to a meeting of 600 mostly women at a downtown cinema to hear speakers for the international feminist movement and Federation of Women's Clubs. On the social front, Frances felt obligated to attend, as was the custom, a series of private farewell dinners, and to be feted as the guest of honor at a reception in the college. More exhausted than ever from the hectic pace of these final days, she boarded a ship in Beirut Harbor and sailed for Naples on February 4, 1934, not yet having had the satisfaction of running a college on a campus with a residence hall. Understating the impact of her sudden departure, Miss Shannon, who worried that her colleague's health was "imperiled," wrote: "Her experienced guidance of the College will be greatly missed."

The founding principal's abrupt exit was somewhat easier for her by her finally being able to take a long-postponed tour of Italy, visiting Naples, Rome, and Florence on her way home. To avoid winter weather in the North Atlantic, she embarked from Genoa on February 17 aboard the USS *Rex*, which, for a one-way fare of $160, landed her in New York on February 25. After a brief stopover, she once again made her way by train to Minneapolis where she would try to regain her strength and—as all her colleagues and students hoped—one day return to her college in Beirut.[22]

DORMITORY URGENT

After Irwin left, Winifred Shannon reported an incident that highlighted the pressing need for housing on campus. During a spring vespers service held outdoors in the moonlight, a familiar voice chanted from behind the college wall. He was soon "joined by several others in ribald singing interspersed with coarse laughter." The students felt safe behind the strong walls, but when a group walked down Rue Saadat to their off-campus hostels, "a car filled with a dozen merrymakers raced its engine near them and stopped in front of the main entrance, frightening many." This confrontation was an urgent reminder to the college staff of the vital necessity of building an on-campus dormitory sooner rather than later.

Those connected with the college were greatly relieved when the Board wrote off all the overage on the land purchase, equipment, wall, and grading. Now more attention could be paid to the badly needed dormitory—not just for comfort and convenience, but because the absence of one had become a security issue that could damage enrollment and tuition income. This prompted Irene Sheppard to suggest using money in the Sage Fund, set aside for a future women's college in Iran, for the women's dormitory in Beirut. Acting Principal Shannon and James Nicol picked up on this idea of advancing those funds that could be repaid from students' room fees in time for their use in Iran. After all, AUB was paying off a loan to build Fisk Hall from the fees paid by Fisk residents. It seemed to Nicol "a pity to have money lying idle when a going institution was in such urgent need of a dormitory." In view of the high rents being paid, the depreciated dollar, and the difficulties with the present arrangements, the Mission Executive Committee endorsed Miss Sheppard's idea, with the hope that the Sage Committee and Board could authorize the project by May 15 so it could be ready for occupancy in October. Otherwise a $4,000 advance was due to rent two more houses for two years.[23]

Having proven his worth on the administration/classroom project, Mr. Iskander Araman was retained to build the dormitory. He estimated the cost of the first half of the building at $14,250, which was $2,000 more than the original estimate of $25,000 for the entire project. The first construction bids were too high. Three new bids, although still high, were thought to be the lowest possible. Mr. Taylor thus modified the plan yet again for a "skeletonized" dormitory for forty students and teachers, matron, and servants at a cost of just over $13,000. It called for removing the west wing altogether, but included instead a second floor over the service wing. He omitted much of the interior finish and plaster, but the living rooms and studies would be finished so little comfort would be sacrificed. Miss Shannon worried that advance registrations indicated there could be as many as fifty boarders in the fall and the minimum plan would not be adequate. Probably, she estimated, $20,000 to $22,000 would be needed to complete the entire building.[24]

Predicting the number of boarders was difficult due to external political turbulence. Alumnae in Jerusalem convinced twelve Palestinian girls to apply for junior college admission, but the expected increase in enrollment evaporated because of a war scare in Palestine just as the school opened in the fall of 1936. Annual Jewish immigration to the region had increased sharply from 4,000 to 62,000. The Palestinian Arab population demanded that the British stop the influx, prohibit land transfers, and introduce democratic institutions. A legislative council proposed by the British was rejected by both the Arabs and the Jews. Many Palestinians were deterred from coming to Beirut because they feared England would intervene. Their fears were validated when a general strike in 1936 led to armed resistance and a violent Arab revolt against the British Mandate that was brutally suppressed by the British Army.

Another reason for the drop off had to do with campus security. Two Palestinian fathers refused to send their daughters because they had heard tales that the young women were not sufficiently protected in the scattered apartments. Still a third reason for the lower numbers was that the Ministry of Education in Iraq prevented a sizable delegation the Iraqis had promised from coming. To offset these disappointments, Miss Shannon admitted more local students, so the final enrollment held steady at seventy-four, the same as the previous year.[25]

Lebanon itself was not without political and sectarian tensions. Emboldened by growing nationalism and independence movements in Egypt, Palestine, and Syria itself, Lebanese President

Emile Iddi negotiated a Treaty of Friendship and Alliance with France in 1936 by which the French recognized Lebanon as an independent state. In return, Lebanon pledged to remain an ally in the event of war and allow the French military to remain in the region for twenty-five years. France, too, would aid Lebanon if it was attacked. A simultaneous Franco-Syrian treaty ended Syria's demands to annex Lebanon and recognized Lebanon's "internal independence." The different sects were guaranteed equal civil and political rights and equitable representation in government posts. This gave rise to the sectarian parties that would define Lebanese politics for decades to come.[26]

YEAR OF GROWTH AND ENLIGHTENMENT

Frances Irwin, still caring for her mother and not fully recovered herself, was unable to resume her position in October 1935 as all had hoped. Wishing to make the best use of her limited free time and energy, she reenrolled in the University of Minnesota to resume her graduate studies toward her PhD in history. This left it up to Acting Principal Winifred Shannon to open AJCW's third year on the Ras Beirut campus. Irwin's absence and the resignation of Miss Daoud required hiring Mildred Mitchell to teach history and Frances Weisbecker to offer instruction in science. The new Dean of Women, Mary E. Lee, was a great help to the acting principal given that forty-five boarders plus Miss Shannon, six teachers, and five servants lived in "three houses scattered all over." Accommodations in each were adequate for the time being, especially since they all could look forward to living in a new dormitory soon. The fully equipped kitchen (presumably in the newly refurbished Rue Sadat hostel) with its three-burner oil stove could feed up to fifty-five. The bathrooms lacked only a tank for heating bath water, but the furniture in the students' rooms was on its last legs. Nearly all of the rent for the three buildings was covered by boarding fees.

Dean Lee's genial guidance lessened problems in the school and its two off-campus hostels. Led by its able president, "Georgette," the student council planned social life, managed the general order, and handled disciplinary problems. She advised her fellow students to bring their problems to the council rather than complaining to the principal and teachers. Trips to the principal's office were cut in half. Student dissatisfaction centered on the issue of Arab nationalism. Some ardent nationalists wanted all Arabic-speaking students to join in sympathy with a strike in Damascus, but others felt this helped no one and would only cut into their valued instruction time. Some did cut classes one afternoon. When AUB men wanted the female students to strike in sympathy with the Palestinians, the women instead collected funds for those suffering. Money was also raised for the Poor Boys' Club, a library clock, and furnishing the new dormitory living room.

Just for fun Mildred Mitchell, the new history teacher, organized the first "Sophomore Sneak," a secret all-day trip in the spring of 1936. If any freshman could learn and inform her classmates of the sophomores' plans, then the freshmen were entitled to take the trip instead. But the sophomores kept their plans secret each year. Despite whispering campaigns, no freshman class ever discovered them. The "Sophomore Sneak" became a junior college tradition.

Once the twenty-six members of the Class of 1936 completed their final exams, they presented the traditional outdoor pageant, "Youth," written and directed by Margaret Shannon. The performance was a tableau of modern youth seeking a "satisfying philosophy of life amidst the clashes of tradition and evolution, religion and science, idealism and present-day conditions." Sadly, it rained but only two people out of an audience of 800 left. University President Bayard Dodge spoke at the baccalaureate service and the graduates received their AJCW certificates in the closing ceremonies. Looking back, Miss Shannon viewed 1935–1936 as a year of "growth, rich experience and enlightenment that was worth the price."[27]

Sarah and Her Sisters | 331

Miss Mitchell also organized twenty students and alumnae—including three Jews, two Muslims and one Baháʼí—in a village welfare camp in Deir Mama. Other faculty members helped for short periods. Children were given cod liver oil, sunsuits, milk, and daily baths. After surveying local health needs, camp volunteers implemented a preventive program against rickets, tuberculosis, trachoma, malaria, and dysentery. A twelve-year-old girl was trained in personal habits, scholastic advancement, and social activities, so that she could work in her village year-round. A second camp operated for a third year in the Nasiriyeh villages, where villagers had greater confidence than ever in the program. One camper at the close of summer said, "I think the perfect world will be when EVERY-BODY is interested in doing something for other people."[28]

Iran Fund Loan

Still in Minnesota on "special" furlough, Frances Irwin remained in touch with Winifred Shannon and Irene Sheppard by mail. Miss Sheppard consulted with her regarding her idea, previously rejected as being too risky, to have the Sage Fund Committee in New York loan money that had been earmarked for a future women's college in Iran to erect AJCW's dorm. Miss Irwin had previously tried to convince the Board that the college could build the residence hall, funnel annual student rents into a building fund, and pay back the entire loan in ten years. They were already applying student rent payments to reimburse the advances for the rent of the off-campus houses. She and Miss Shannon were convinced that having their own dorm on campus would not only alleviate rental costs but also increase enrollment and tuition income. They had fifty-five boarders as of March 1936 and if it were not for the war scare and economic depression of the last two years, they could count on an increase in the near future. The loan would not be a millstone, but rather a *relief*.

Being in their own building would more than compensate for any financial strain.

Irwin had made such a strong argument for the scheme that the Sage Fund Committee did not this time think it all that risky, especially given the "lack of unanimity" within the Board of Managers in Tehran "on the objectives and program for their fledgling women's college in Iran." Before drawing on its earmarked funds, the committee recommended "continuing the status quo until May 1937" to allow for "more consultation and modification of the proposed college plan." Then on April 6, 1936, it authorized that $16,000 be advanced from the Iran account to the Beirut college for its dormitory. Construction began on June 12. And there was more good news. The Fund was releasing another $4,000 for dormitory equipment as well as nearly $700 to cover the remaining balance on the exchange rate loss. The loan of their funds to AJCW was particularly upsetting to Sage College's managers and the Iran Mission, but they would soon have good reason to feel more warmly toward AJCW and its leadership.[29]

A More Difficult Year

After an "insufferably hot" summer visiting her family in Kansas, Acting Principal Winifred Shannon began her second year facing more difficulties than usual. A series of local strikes were triggered by a devaluation of the franc and dissatisfaction with the new Syrian constitution. Nevertheless, enrollment rebounded to eighty-eight, just two short of the 1932–33 high, thereby compounding the housing problem. The two rented off-campus houses were full and dormitory construction had just begun. Forty students ended up sleeping in the auditorium, including the stage, in the hygiene laboratory, and in one classroom. Plumbing never intended for living quarters gave way under the strain. During entrance exams, meals were served in the nursery school. Then heavy autumn rains slowed construction and caused the exterior plaster to ooze down the side of the dormitory building. Interior plaster was too damp to paint. The third-floor auditorium roof leaked, contributing to bad colds and influenza among the students sleeping there, some having to contend with the leaking roof until Christmas when they were finally able to occupy bedrooms on the second and third floors of the unfinished dorm. Things would have been worse had the young women not been such good sports. On the first day of school in October, the boarders had been dismissed early to clean, furnish, and decorate the windowless dining room area in the unfinished dorm so they could have supper there throughout the year.

Because the political unrest was expected to decrease enrollment, too few faculty members had been engaged. They included Miss Eileen Hersey (BA), an unnamed English woman who covered European history and political science, and Miss Viola Petitt (BA), formerly with ASG, teaching religion and child psychology. Mrs. Charles Fisher volunteered as a nursery assistant. However, the faculty had, in Miss Shannon's words, "bad sledding." Once past the November "Get Acquainted" weekend in Shweir, there was hardly a day when one or two, or even three or four, teachers were not ill. The constant substitutions and fatigue this caused prompted Acting Principal Shannon to hire Pettit full time. She turned out to be quite versatile and did not mind teaching math and chemistry one day, English and history the next, and religion the third. When a nursery teacher got sick, she even ran the nursery school. "This is certainly a wild way to run a college," Shannon wrote, "but who would ever have guessed there could have been so much illness."

Another difficulty had to do with required attendance at morning chapel. These joint worship services were a source of pride for Misses Irwin and Shannon, so the acting principal was quite upset when Muslim students went on a weeks-long "non-participation strike." They were joined by the few Jewish students who did not normally participate, leading to a "strained atmosphere."

The dissidents were finally called together to air their grievances "only to find that they did not exist." Rather, to Shannon's relief and delight, "diverse spirits welded together to form a warm fellowship as they planned chapel services involving students from every sect." Meanwhile, renewed nationalistic stirrings prompted greater interest in Lebanon's gaining political independence from France. Miss Shannon was very glad that the new campus was far enough away from the demonstrations and excitement downtown that the students heard about them only after they were over. The college suspended classes for only one hour during the strikes, whereas other schools were closed for days.

Options for Designation

As a sign of good faith, the junior college refunded $1,000 of the $4,000 advance to cover the rents to Sage's Iran account, presumably from boarding fees and as proof that the scheme was doable. The remaining $3,000 was used to buy iron bedsteads, wardrobes, chairs, eating utensils, and some internal finishing. Purchases for the administration building included sixty benches, Druze chests, eight palm trees, two pianos, typewriters, a Victrola, an umbrella stand, and two silver cups for athletics and scholarship.[30]

In the spirit of the late Henry Jessup, Miss Shannon took on the task of fundraising with considerable enthusiasm and wrote a well-crafted 1937 New Year's Day fundraising letter to AJCW alumnae. Below a drawing of the dormitory she began: "Something has happened to YOUR JUNIOR COLLEGE! We have become a CAMPUS. Towering up on the rocky slope at the east of the Administration building are the first sections of the long-awaited dormitory!" She described the "big bay windows opening to the sea and mountains—sun parlor—dining hall with fireplaces—balconies—big windows—long corridors—small studies—big dormitory bedrooms—private dressing rooms and guest room." She asked her

Sarah and Her Sisters | 335

former students to envision "boarders and teachers living under one roof on the CAMPUS!"[31]

The top floor and west wing, she explained, were still to be built, so AUB women and some teachers still lived in rented apartments. Where, then, were they going to put all the students attracted to the new campus? This prompted *the 'ask:'*

> Would you like to help erect the west wing this spring? Would you like to read your name on a door plaque reading: "Given by..." (your name) or "in honor of..." (name) just like plaques in the administration building honor our American friends? Already one sophomore has given her own room.

Construction was costing three pounds sterling a square meter. Rooms were ten to fifty square meters. And finally, the *challenge*: "If the educated women of the Near East WANT to do this thing, they can, from their own gifts." Donors could go in together and pay for a room. Then the *coup de grace*: "How many meters are YOU interested in building to make higher education permanent for the women of the Near East?" What loyal alumna could resist this challenge?

The almost finished east wing and connecting section were costing $15,000. Thanks to the constant attention and close supervision of Nicol, Taylor, and Araman, rapid progress was made in their construction so that by February, boarding students and teachers, including the now Dean Mildred Mitchell, finally gained full access to their new dormitory. The college was now — at long last — fully established on its own campus. Work then began on Units II and III, the west wing and top floor that would cost $6,000 each and would complete the H-shaped dormitory complex.[32]

Opportunity in Iran

During the delay the Sage Fund imposed on planning the Sage College for Women in Tehran, the fund's directors further recommended "cooperation in higher education for women among the missions of Iraq, Syria and Iran." Specifically, this meant that "the Syria and Iran Missions arrange for an exchange of visits of Miss Winifred Shannon to Iran and Miss Doolittle to Syria" to familiarize each other with their schools and needs. Miss Shannon was therefore pleased to welcome to AJCW in January 1937 Jane Doolittle, the principal of the Nurbakhsh School for Girls in Tehran. Nurbakhsh was founded by Presbyterian missionaries in 1874 as the Bethel School for Girls, a sister school to the Beirut Female Seminary. When Reza Shaw Pahlavi liberalized conventions for women in Iran after World War I, there was a demand for female higher education, but few Farsi-speaking young women from Nurbakhsh, though taught in English, wanted to go to Arabic-speaking Beirut and study at AJCW. Therefore, just as ASG had done, the Nurbakhsh School added a freshman year to launch the Sage College for Women in conjunction with the Mission's four-year Alborz College for men.[33]

Miss Doolittle spent a week in Beirut observing and sharing in the operation and life of AJCW. The following month Miss Shannon was Miss Doolittle's guest at Sage College in Tehran, still housed in the Nurbakhsh School. They agreed from their observations that the two schools were on an academic par except that the Tehran school still needed to add a sophomore year before being spun off as a separate junior college for women. Who then could organize it? Doolittle could not be spared from the high school and no one else on her staff was qualified. Snowed in for a week in the mountains above Tehran, the two women discussed all sides of the problem and came up with the revolutionary plan that Winifred Shannon be released by the Syrian Mission that fall for at least three years to organize and head the new Sage College. In return, the Iran mission would send personnel to Beirut to help in the junior college there. When Shannon readily agreed to take on the challenge of starting her own college, the Mission Board agreed to their joint recommendation and she was released to transfer to Tehran once she completed the academic year at AJCW.[34]

ACTIVE SPRING

The spirited Miss Shannon's final spring in Beirut (1937) began, appropriately, with the entire college going on an all-day picnic and swimming in the sea followed by an ambitious hike up the Nahr el Kalb (Dog River) to its source. For their Spring Sneak, the sophomores quietly slipped out for a day at the beach while the freshmen were concentrating on a test. Unfortunately, it was a hot *sirocco* day and some returned with sunburned faces and arms that lasted the next few days, but "without undue complaint." Fifteen students and faculty members spent Easter vacation in Egypt "seeing the sights and attending games between AUB and the Egyptian University (American University of Cairo?) teams." In late spring, the university offered AJCW graduates a combined Nursing-University course leading to the Nurse's diploma and the BS or BA degree. Miss Shannon hailed this as a real advance for young women studying nursing.

The baccalaureate service theme was the college motto: "To strive, to seek, to find." The student body president said the Trireme, an ancient ship, symbolized the passing on of college traditions to incoming students. Catherine Nicol's commencement pageant, "Web of Athena," highlighted the contributions of women in various fields through the ages and was a perfect note on which to award twenty-two junior college certificates. They brought the total number of alumnae in AJCW's first decade to 185.

Not able to return to the Nasiriyeh villages, the sixth annual Welfare Camp moved to a Shiite village of 1,500 in South Lebanon.

Student and faculty gifts from a Village Welfare night paid for the usual health schools, medical clinic, and a home school to teach older girls and young women sewing, cooking, and home decoration. Using Professor Shahla's revision of the Laubach method, illiterate adults were taught to read more rapidly.

With Regret and Sadness

As always, there were some losses and leavings noted at the end of the academic year. After the death of Dean Edward Nickoley, who had taken a warm interest in the college since its beginning and served on its Board of Managers, Mrs. Nickoley and her daughter Kathryn, who had generated much interest in home economics, returned to America. Catherine Nicol got married and Eileen Hersey returned to England. But the most serious losses to the college in 1937 were the two pioneers in higher education for women in the Near East, the invaluable Winifred Shannon and the principal whom she served so well, Frances Irwin.

With her last commencement behind her and many of her students and graduates who had majored in sociology at AUB off to their summer welfare camp, Shannon prepared to leave for her new post in Tehran. Toward the end of her twelfth (and final) annual report, with regret and personal sadness, she wrote in the third person:

> The Acting Principal has been transferred to the Iran Mission for three years to help in establishing a sister college for women in Tehran; hence a new principal will greet the large group which is expected this fall. Through our difficulties, [Miss Irwin and I] feel an increasing assurance that the value of college work for Near Eastern women is increasingly recognized and has become firmly established.[35]

In her final letter to "all Junior College students, past and present," Winifred Shannon told them that the first wing of the

Fig. 88 – "Teacher and village girls" at Miss Shannon's Village Welfare Camp in Bint Jebeil, Summer, 1932.

Fig. 89 – Village Welfare Camp girls learning to read using the Laubach method.

dormitory was full and construction of the west wing underway. Given the "present rate of registration," another floor could be built over the summer for $1,000, so, true to form, she urged individual contributions of $5.00 (one dinar, or one Palestinian pound, or one English pound) sent by the next mail. She then reported that the Village Welfare Camp in Tayyebat was going splendidly and the Beg (provincial governor) was cooperating fully. Saving the most significant news for last, she informed her audience that in October the junior college would have a "real principal."

> Perhaps he will be called "President" as many of the best women's colleges in America have men presidents and so the Junior College will be in the "latest fashion." Some of you know William Stoltzfus from the Aleppo College and his wife, Ethel, from the 1933 Older Girls' Conference. They have two sons, Bill and Jim, in the Community School and daughter Lorna who will be in the Nursery School. Trained in Junior College administration, Mr. Stoltzfus has brought back from America a very modern automobile—that will be more dignified than riding on a bicycle! I know you will give the Stoltzfus family a cordial welcome.

With the new principal on the way to take over AJCW, Miss Shannon was free to commence her new adventure. She began the 1937–1938 academic year as principal of Sage College, the new junior college for Iranian women. She found that it was about where AJCG had been when she first joined Frances Irwin in Beirut in March 1925, ready to add its first sophomore class. Shannon headed the Iranian school for three years until the government closed all foreign schools in 1941. From there she went to China to teach at the University of Nanking until 1944 when she moved on Lucknow, India, and taught for a year at the Isabella Thoburn College. After this dedicated and varied career in teaching and administration, Winifred Shannon finally retired from her work with the Presbyterian Church in 1952.

Fig. 90 – East wing of AJCW dormitory (Nicol Hall) completed in 1937.

Fig. 91 – Frances Pryor Irwin (seated in center) became an assistant professor of history at Macalester College in St. Paul, MN. This photo appeared in 1938 college yearbook, shortly before her death.

FRANCES PRYOR IRWIN: 1895–1939

Frances Irwin returned home to Minneapolis to regain her health and stamina, only to have to oversee the care of her seriously ill mother, Anna White Irwin. Nevertheless, she was able to teach classes in American history at the University of Minnesota while presumably continuing part-time study toward her PhD degree. In her limited spare time, she arranged chronologically from 1922 to 1935 all her letters to her parents from Beirut, occasionally clarifying or correcting names and dates. These she donated to the Presbyterian Historical Society in Philadelphia, making them accessible to anyone interested in her personal perspective on the startup and early development of the first college for women in the Arabic-speaking world. Up to this time, she had not definitely closed the door to returning to Beirut, nor had the mission board.

Hoping to learn more of Miss Irwin's situation and the prospects of her returning to the field, Irene Sheppard wrote her in November 1936. Given her increasing concern for her mother's health, her reluctance to resume her stressful duties at the college and the resumption of her own academic pursuits, the prospects were not good. Nor were they any better the following February when she finally informed Miss Sheppard that it was time to "present her resignation to the Board." Sheppard and others in New York and Beirut still held out hope that, as was the case with Eliza Everett in 1887, Irwin would someday resume her post. But it was not to be. Miss Shannon confirmed in her annual report, "In February, Miss Frances Irwin, who had been principal of the college since the first class opened in 1924, resigned, and the college will miss her leadership."[36]

Anna Irwin died at age seventy-seven in October 1937 just as her daughter was appointed an assistant professor in history at Macalester College, a Presbyterian college in St. Paul, Minnesota. Frances quickly became a popular teacher, inviting outside speakers

Sarah and Her Sisters | 343

into her classes and participating in a Student Peace Conference. Sadly, her stamina began to wane again until she was forced to resign her new post in the spring of 1939. Shortly thereafter she admitted herself to the Glen Lake Sanatorium with an undiagnosed illness. Over the summer her health declined rapidly and she died on October 12, 1939 at the age of forty-four. Frances Pryor Irwin was buried next to her mother in the Lakewood Cemetery in Minneapolis. At her request, memorial gifts were sent to the American Junior College for Women in Beirut.[37]

Epilogue
(1937 to the present)

Respecting our success, I would say,
that with our press, schools, preaching,
conversation, and other social intercourse...
we feel that a broad foundation is being
laid, upon which, at some future day, God
knows when, a glorious superstructure will
be raised.

Sarah Smith to Jabez Huntington,
March 17, 1836

The Syria Mission quickly selected Rev. William Stoltzfus to succeed Misses Irwin and Shannon as principal of the American Junior College for Women in the fall of 1937. With the exception of Henry De Forest, this ended the long line of women principals and teachers heading up the successive female schools since Sarah Smith in 1834.[1] Bill and Ethel Stoltzfus, who had first been stationed in Aleppo, had been good friends of the Irwins in Minneapolis, which was also Ethel's hometown. Frances, during her infrequent off-hours, enjoyed visiting Bill and Ethel in their home after they moved to Beirut. (Might they or University of Minnesota graduate James Nicol have recommended her for the college position in 1924?). She must have been pleased with his appointment.

Under President Stoltzfus, AJCW grew into the four-year Beirut College for Women in 1950 with majors in home economics, child development, education, and psychology. President Frances Gray

(1958–1965), an especially good fundraiser as well as academician, added a fine arts building and dormitory to the campus. Her successor, Dr. Salwa Nassar, was an AJCW alumna and renowned nuclear physicist. Sadly, Nassar died within two years of leukemia caused by radiation exposure. Dean Cornelios Houk was named acting president, followed by Acting President Marie Sabri who served until Dr. William Schechter was named president in 1969. He added a community college that accepted the first men and turned BCW to Beirut University College for women and men. Dr. Albert Badre and his dean and later president, Dr. Riyad Nassar, skillfully guided BUC through the worst years of the 1975–1990 Lebanese civil war. They not only preserved the college but expanded its outreach. President Riyad Nassar, assisted by Dean Nabil Haidar, added a campus in Byblos and transformed BUC into Lebanese American University in 1994. Since 2004, the institution has been under the dynamic leadership of President Joseph Jabbra and has become second to none in the Middle East. No one could have foreseen that this important institution of higher education would develop from Sarah Smith's Beirut Female School with forty little girls founded in 1834!

Author's Note

It will now be clear to the reader that Sarah Smith and the other missionary teachers who followed her were tainted by a classism that fostered certain prejudices. Born in the nineteenth century into upper- and middle-class Protestant families in New England, the Mid-Atlantic states and the Midwest, they lived in homogeneous and insular communities. I think it is fair to say they viewed themselves as socially above those who were less well-off, less educated, and less influential. Except for Sarah and the Mohegans, it is unlikely they had any contact with and therefore had prejudices against Native Americans. The same would be true with African Americans, who mostly lived in the South as slaves and later more widely dispersed as free blacks. Descended largely from the early English, Scottish, Welsh, and Scotch-Irish Calvinist settlers of North America, they surely looked down on and developed clear biases against the increasing influx of poor Irish, Italian, Polish, German, Eastern European, and Jewish immigrants who were poorly educated and certainly not Protestant. In a word, these women tended to view American society in terms of "haves" and "have nots," aligning themselves more with the "haves."

As missionaries, they applied their classism to Ottoman Syria where they found themselves in the unusual position of living and working between the ruling Egyptian, Turkish, British, and French "haves," and the native Syrian "have nots." The Americans saw themselves as superior to these occupiers and developed prejudices against them as one succeeded another. Meanwhile, they nurtured and never really overcame certain prejudices vis-à-vis their indigenous subjects. Viewed as members of a poor, uneducated underclass long ruled by superstition, clerical hierarchies, and outside powers, most Syrians seemed to have little to offer in return for the missionaries' labors and largess.

As mentioned in the preface, the American teachers even treated the young women they themselves had educated and whom they recruited as their assistants in an inferior manner. Beyond paying them less, they segregated them in their living arrangements. While the teachers had private rooms and maid service in the school, which was protected within the mission compound, their native assistants either lived nearby with families or roomed with the student boarders. The Americans ate at their own table and in the female seminary on a raised platform and may even have been favored with a more American menu, while their assistants shared tables and ate native fare with the students. In these and other ways, the Americans kept a certain distance between themselves and those they came to serve. Therein lies the dilemma, if not a tragedy.

Having now read the stories of these American teachers, the reader would do well to keep in mind three different views of their impact as outlined by former BUC faculty member Jean Said Makdisi in her memoir *Teta, Mother, and Me*. On the one hand, a "powerful mythology (based primarily on American sources) credits the girls' missionary schools especially with unilaterally modernizing an ancient and decadent society; as liberating, enlightening, freeing and bringing truth to Eastern women." The opposing postcolonialist view is that the missionary teachers "had imperial motives and imposed Westernization on females especially, turning them away from their own cultural tradition." Both of these views, Makdisi points out,

> emphasize missionary attitudes, motives, lives and work and rely on their writings... that eclipsed the less-documented role "natives" played in their own destiny. Rarely are the students' or their parents' attitudes, motives and lives considered or discussed in the missionary

writings. Had they no motives, no independent will to change, no need to participate in the modern world? Had their parents no mission of their own? Were they mere collaborators with the missionaries? Were there no Arab teachers eager to influence them? Had the Americans not learned anything from Arab culture that changed their own cultures and world views?

Makdisi agrees that the missionaries indeed "had an enormous influence on the education of women in particular." But she offers a third hybrid view that modernity came about by

> an interaction with them, rather than an imposition by them on a people without a will of their own; a synthesis of cultural resources rather than a unilateral initiative by one culture acting on another. It was a complex process involving local people in all sectors of the society who (after all) steered their children to the missionaries' classrooms. Otherwise the Americans might have remained irrelevant and extraneous to any significant change or progress.[1]

Enough said for now, but much still to think about.

Acknowledgments

This book would not have been possible without the previous histories of the Reverends Edward Hooker and Henry Jessup. After his sister-in-law lost all her journals at sea and died tragically abroad, Hooker collected her letters home and produced the best-selling 1840s *Memoir of Mrs. Sarah L. Huntington Smith* that preserved her story and inspired the early missionary movement. Without this work, I never would have known Sarah's story, nor been inspired to retell it. Realizing the historical and inspirational value of such memoirs, Jessup completed in 1910 his own sweeping, two volume *Fifty Three Years in Syria* that provides an invaluable outline and much rich material for half the period covered herein. I am greatly indebted to both men as well as to those whose memoirs are referenced in my prologue and early chapters, and to the more recent historian, Frances Irwin, who preserved and made available to future writers her own letters home.

Early in this project, I became indebted to citizens of Norwich, Connecticut, who introduced me to Sarah Huntington Smith's hometown and brought her much more to life for me. They include the late Bill Stanley, members of the Norwich Historical Society, the Mohegan Tribal Council, and fellow participants in the city's 350th anniversary celebration in 2009. I owe early thanks as well to the readers of my first chapter on Sarah: my late college classmate and noted historian, Albert Klyberg, seminary classmate and close friends Rod and Anne Hunter, and former newspaper editor, Bill Tudor. They validated the worthiness of retelling her story and encouraged me to push on.

I am much indebted to Dr. Christine Beth Lindner who shares my passion for the stories of the women who went to Syria as missionaries. A gifted historian whose knowledge of the Syria Mission far exceeds mine, Christine has been an invaluable colleague, researcher, advisor, and early editor. Without her scholarly assistance, encouragement and nudging this work would still be in progress.

Doing research at the Presbyterian Historical Society in Philadelphia was a pleasure, thanks to its welcoming and helpful research services staff directed by Nancy Taylor. Senior Reference Archivist Lisa Jacobson and her reference assistants delved time and again into the basement archives to locate the records requested. Special thanks also to Allison Davis for cheerfully and promptly providing digitized versions of illustrations requested from the archives.

A special shout out is due to my long distance editor at Hachette-Antoine, Pascale Kahwagi, with whom I have developed a warm working relationship via Skype. She has persevered through more troubling times in Lebanon and been instrumental in producing a book of which we can be proud. I look forward to someday thanking her and her colleagues at H-A in person.

I am beholden to my first readers of the manuscript who gave days of their valuable time to read and provide honest feedback. This is certainly true of my first reader, my wife Judy, whose careful reading, copious markings, and scores of post-it notes throughout made the next draft more presentable for subsequent readers. Those in Lebanon, including LAU President Joseph Jabbra and Dr. Nancy Jabbra, Professor Samira Aghacy, and Dr. Julinda Abu Nasr, corrected numerous errors and made valuable suggestions that have been incorporated in the final manuscript. Stateside readers such as BCW junior year abroad alumna Dr. Pauline Coffman, Presbyterian editor David Maxwell, and my sister-in-law Sharon Lynch, herself a teacher, were all most encouraging and offered additional ideas and practical suggestions to make the book more interesting and comprehensible.

Finding a good editor is important. Finding the *right* editor is critical to achieving the goal for the book and making the author look like a better writer than he otherwise is. Jana Riess has proven to be the *right* editor for *Sarah and Her Sisters*. Jana is the whole package. She coached me on a book proposal that was accepted by two major publishers. She helped shape the text into a narrative that was better organized, more concise, and easier to read. Her mastery of English grammar, punctuation, style, and attention to detail is awesome. She is a tough taskmistress who asks for frequent rewrites but has a sense of humor that adds fun to the editing process. Jana became genuinely interested in Sarah and her sisters as she got to know them. I cannot imagine having found a better partner in telling their stories.

My very special thanks, of course, to President Joe Jabbra who believes we cannot fully appreciate the present and prepare for the future without knowing what came before. He shares my curiosity about the evolution of female education in the Near East and has placed a high value on rediscovering the history and celebrating rich legacy of Lebanese American University. I very much appreciate his unflagging support and personal encouragement, not to mention patience, from my first lectures on Sarah in 2009 to the publication of this book, which he and the university so generously made possible. And I would be remiss if I failed to acknowledge also the roles his predecessors played in bringing this volume about: former president Bill Schechter, who graciously recommended me to President Albert Badre who hired me in 1979 to help him raise funds on many enjoyable and productive trips together throughout the U.S.; and President Riyad Nassar, with whom I developed a strong friendship working in tandem through the worst days of the Lebanese civil war and who brought me back in peacetime as an LAU vice president. It was a privilege to know, work with, and learn from these four educational leaders who successfully guided the institution through times of significant change, great peril, and impressive growth.

It was reassuring that I could always call upon the LAU New York staff for help. My immediate successors as vice president, Rich Rumsey and Marla Rice Evans, were genuinely interested in and supportive of this project. Ed Shiner made it one of his "special projects" and was my valued and prompt "go-to guy" in New York. The efficient and ever-pleasant director of operations, Marge Pfleiderer, competently oversaw all related administrative matters and expense reimbursements. Nada Torby, LAU's Director of Media and Public Relations in Beirut, has served well as my liaison with Hachette Antoine; and my former colleague, Abdallah Al-Khal in alumni affairs, remains my "go-to" contact in Lebanon. I look forward to sharing with everyone at LAU the early history of their university and to thanking them in person for their roles in helping make it happen.

My best friend and kindred spirit for over five decades, Judith Lynch Stoddard (Judy), has supported me day in and day out since my retirement in 2005 as I researched and wrote this book. Granted, she was happy I had a project that kept me "out from underfoot," but I was spending time with *Sarah and Her Sisters* that we might otherwise have spent together. Given her many contributions to and sacrifices for this project since its inception, I gratefully dedicate this book to my wife, as well to our very dear friend, Julinda Abu Nasr, who as a daughter of Beirut College for Women and pioneer in the early education of Arab children and Arab women's studies has furthered the work of these pioneering sisters. Judy and Julinda would also want me to mention here Baden, Evelyn, Ella, and Ian, who, one by one and at times all together, spent time playing under my desk and in my office as I worked on "Grampa's book."

APPENDIX A

American Elementary & Secondary Teachers in Syria/Lebanon

Teacher	Birthplace	DOB	Arrival	Departure	Death
Ann Parker Bird	Bradford, MA	1799	Oct. 1823	Aug. 1835	1877
Abigail Davis Goodell	Holden, MA	1800	Oct. 1823	May 1828	1871
Elisa Nelson Thomson	Baltimore, MD	1800	Apr. 1833	-	1834
Martha Dodge Paxton	Portland, ME	1810	Sep. 1833	May 1838	1855
Sarah L. H. Smith	Norwich, CT	1802	Jan. 1834	June 1836	1836
Rebecca Williams Hebard	Lebanon, CT	1807	Nov. 1835	-*	1840
Matilda Ward Whiting	Bloomfield, NJ	1805	Nov. 1830	Mar. 1856	1873
Betsey Tilden	Lebanon, NH	1811	June 1836	Mar. 1843	1891
Maria Ward Smith	Rochester, NY	1819	June 1841	-	1842
Henry A. De Forest, M.D.	Watertown, CT	1814	Mar. 1842	May 1854	1859
Katherine S. De Forest	Stockbridge, MA	1817	Mar. 1842	May 1854	1896
Henrietta Butler Smith	Northampton, MA	1816	Jan. 1847	May 1857	1893
Anna Louisa Whittlesey	Ogden, NY	1828	May 1851	-	1852
Sarah Cheney Aiken	Phillipston, MA	1825	Apr. 1853	May 1858	1913
Abby Wood Bliss	Amherst, MA	1830	Feb. 1856	-	1915

Teacher	Birthplace	DOB	Arrival	Departure	Death
Amelia C. Temple	Worcester, MA	1834	Aug. 1858	Apr. 1862	1873
Jane E. Johnson	Utica, NY	1837	Aug. 1858	Mar. 1859	-
Adelaide L. Mason	New York, NY	1832	Apr. 1860	June 1865	-
Emilia Thomson	Beirut, Syria	1839	-	-	1921
Eliza D. Everett	Painsville, OH	1839	Nov. 1865	June 1895	1902
Ellen A. Carruth	Dorchester, MA	1846	Nov. 1865	May 1870	-
Ellen Jackson Foote	Philadelphia, PA	-	Nov. 1870	Dec. 1883	-
Sophie Loring Wood	Scranton, PA	-	Dec. 1870	May 1873	-
Helen Fisher	-	-	Nov. 1873	Mar. 1875	-
Eliza Van Dyck	Beirut, Syria	-	Oct. 1875	1879	-
Harriet La Grange	Union, NY	-	Jan. 1876	1909	-
Alice Barber	Joliet, IL	-	Oct. 1885	1926	-
Mary Bliss Dale	Beirut, Syria	1858	Oct. 1892	1905	-
Ellen Law	Brooklyn, NY	-	Nov. 1892	1897	-
Anna Jessup	Beirut, Syria	1860	Oct. 1897	1898	-
Rachel Tolles	Attica, NY	-	Oct. 1899	1921	-
Ottora Horne	Columbus, OH	-	Dec. 1902	1930	-
Jessie Glockler Byerly	Whiting, IN	-	Oct. 1907	1909	-
Jessie Curtis	-	-	Oct. 1913	-	-
Edith Hazlett	-	-	Oct. 1921	-	-
Lois Wilson			Oct. 1921	1924	-

* A hyphen in a column indicates unknown or missing information.

Syrian Teacher	Birthplace	Birth Year	Departure	Death
Raheel Atta Bustani	Beyroot, Syria	1826	-	1894
Rufka Gregory	Beyroot, Syria	1834	July 1866	-

APPENDIX B

Native Teachers in Syria/Lebanon
(named in intermittent and incomplete records)

BEIRUT FEMALE SEMINARY (1868–1892)

Miss Everett's earliest known assistants were Katie Araman, Katiebeh Araman, Mirta Aramoony, Asine Fuaz, Miriam El Haj, Feridy Habaica, Marium Habib, Farha Haddad, Mirium Hashim, Libiby Khummar, Rufka Khottan, Marium Massod, Marium Nijjar, Marium Massod, and Luciya Zazooah.

Others included Laia Antoon, Fakoot Barakat, Hamduman Fleihusa, Miriam el Haj, Hanny Haddad, Melia Haddad, Mirium Hashim, Libiby Khummar, Rosa Manassa, Saada Saba, Layah Saheen, Rosa Sefateer, Layah Selino, Selma Tannoos, Katrine Trad, Hafiza Abd el Noor, and Marta Bender. Mrs. Khuri taught piano. Michaiel Araman, Ibrahim Hourani, and Jebboor Saad el Khuri taught Arabic. Regrettably, the records omit names of native servants such as cooks, maids, custodians, and groundskeepers.[1]

AMERICAN SCHOOL FOR GIRLS

1919–1921: Preparatory/academic departments: Fareedeh Aakle, Shafica Daud, Katrine Saad, Christine Sand, Haseebeh Shaib, Shafica Wakim, Mme. La Favre (French), Mr. Nicola Ghubril (Arabic), and Mlle de Souza (piano). Primary teachers: Barjute Cannan, Camra Dowli, and Isobel Tabet.[2]

1922–1925: Vergine Alianak, Berjout Canaan, Berjute Danaan, Shafica Daoud, Lulu Dumit, Labibeh Kourani, Rose Kourani, Kareemeh Khouri, Mme. Kougell (music), Nellie Kurban, Afeefeh Malouf, Camri Pauli,

Nelainie Shahin (Class of '22), Hasibeh Shiab, and Isabel Tabet. Zarouhi Shadarevian (piano), Mlle. Elise Flendrich (French), Mme. Olga Holenkoff (French), and Mr. Nicola Ghobril (Arabic).[3]

APPENDIX C

American Junior College
for Women 1924–1937

COMMITTEE OF MANAGEMENT, 1927–1937

James Nicol, W. G. Greenslade, Ottora Horne, E. F. Nickoley, Paul Erdman, and Mrs. G. H. Scherer. *Ex officio*: Frances Pryor Irwin and Winifred Shannon.[1]

ADMINISTRATION

Frances Pryor Irwin, Principal 1927–1935

Winifred Shannon, Assistant Principal 1927-1935/Acting Principal 1935–1937

Agnes Gaskin, Matron 1929–1931

Julia Heitman, Matron 1931–1935

Mary E. Lee, Dean of Women 1935–1936

Mildred Mitchell, Dean of Women 1936–?

FACULTY

(Full time and part-time): Eva Beck (mathematics & social science), Martha Booth, Mrs. Church (glee club), Lateefeh Daoud, (chemistry & mathematics), Lillian Donaldson (science & hygiene), Mary Dorman (English), Frances Downing (English), W. G. Greenslade (Bible), Olga Holenkoff

(French), Alma Hortleder (biology & athletics), Frances Irwin (history), George Kafouri (Arabic), Esther Lecerf (French), Elizabeth Markle (science), Mildred Mitchell (history), Edward F. Nickoley (chemistry), Kathryn Nickoley (zoology & home economics), James Nicol (religion), Kate Seeley (psychology), Margaret Shannon (librarian & social science), Winifred Shannon (sociology, hygiene & history of religions), George Scherer (Bible), Mrs. Ward (Near East history), Frances Weisbecker (science), F. Lawrence White (religion), and Sadie Wood.[2]

NURSERY SCHOOL

Winifred Shannon, Vivian Greenslade, Mable Erdman, Mrs. Charles Fisher.

DIVERSITY OF STUDENTS, 1926–1935

(Estimated from incomplete statistics)

Religions: Protestant (34%), Sunni Muslim (21%), Greek Orthodox (16%), Jewish (13%), Armenian Orthodox (5%), Roman Catholic (4%), Druze (3%), Bahá'í (3%), Maronite (1%), Greek Catholic, Syrian Orthodox, and Shia Muslim (less than 1%).[3]

Nationalities: The largest number of students were classified as Syrians or Lebanese. Among other groups, the largest in order were Palestinians (including Jewish settlers who identified as Palestinian), Iraqis, and Armenians. Beyond those were small numbers of students who identified themselves as American, Alawite, Cypriote, Egyptian, Greek, Italian, Swiss, Kurdish, Persian, Russian, and Turkish.[4]

Number of Students to Graduate, 1928–1937

	Enrolled	Graduated
1927–28	21	5
1928–29	42	9
1929–30	56	15
1930–31	63	24
1931–32	68	13

	Enrolled	Graduated
1932–33	88	28
1933–34	72	20
1934–35	68	26
1935–36	74	23
1936–37	88	22
Total	640	185[5]

Chronology
(1809–1939)

1809 Andover Theological Seminary opens; graduates first foreign missionaries.

1812 American Board of Commissioners for Foreign Mission (ABCFM) founded by Congregational, Presbyterian, and Reformed Churches.

1823 Revs. Pliny Fisk and Jonas King are first of the mostly Congregationalist missionaries to Syria; Rev. Isaac and Ann Bird and Rev. William and Abigail Goodell are first missionary couples to Syria; wives are first missionary teachers of Arab girls.

1825 Fisk dies in Beirut at age thirty-three.

1827 Rev. Eli Smith studies Arabic on Mount Lebanon.

1828 Egyptian-Ottoman War; Syria Mission suspended.

1830 Birds return to Beirut with first Presbyterian couple, Rev. George and Matilda Whiting.

1833 Dr. Asa and Martha Dodge arrive; Rev. William and Eliza Thomson arrive.

1834 Rev. Eli and Sarah Huntington Smith arrive; Eli starts Mission press; Sarah begins Beirut Female School for young Arab girls and "adopts" eight-year-old Raheel Atta.

1835 Matilda Whiting opens Jerusalem girls' school; Rebecca Williams arrives and assists Sarah in Female School; Sarah becomes ill.

1836 Eli and Sarah Smith depart; Sarah dies in Smyrna (Izmir), Turkey at age thirty-four; Rebecca Williams takes over Beirut Female School; Betsey Tilden assists in Jerusalem school.

1837 Rev. Story Hebard and Rebecca Williams marry and "adopt" Raheel.

1840 Rebecca Williams Hebard dies at age thirty-three; Betsey Tilden takes over Beirut Female School.

1842 Dr. Henry and Kitty De Forest arrive and "adopt" and teach Raheel.

1843 Matilda Whiting closes Jerusalem School; returns home for a year.

1844 Raheel marries Butrus al-Bustani; Matilda Whiting opens Abeih girls' school.

1845	Beirut Female School suspended; Betsey Tilden departs; De Forest "Female Seminary" begins in Burj Bird Mission House.
1846	Beirut Female School reopens briefly, led by Raheel Atta Bustani.
1851	Anna Whittlesey assists De Forests; dies 365 days after arrival at age twenty-three.
1853	De Forests depart; "seminary" under charge of Sarah Cheney; Rufka Gregory teaches day school for girls in Beirut schoolhouse.
1856	Daniel and Abby Bliss and Henry Jessup arrive; Sarah Cheney departs to Aleppo.
1858	Abeih School closed; Matilda Whiting departs; Blisses reopen "Female Seminary" in Abeih with Rufka Gregory as teacher; Female Seminary moved to Suq el-Gharb with Amelia Temple and Jane Johnson as teachers.
1859	Jane Johnson departs.
1860	Adelaide Mason arrives; Mount Lebanon civil war breaks out; Suk seminary closed; Americans evacuate to Beirut; missionaries engage in relief work.
1861	U.S. Civil War begins.
1862	Amelia Temple departs; Adelaide Mason opens girls' day school in Sidon; Rufka Gregory reopens Beirut girls' day school.
1863	William Thomson, Cornelius Van Dyck, and Rev. Henry Jessup hire Rufka Gregory to launch an all-Syrian Beirut Female Seminary as an independent girls' boarding school taught in English.
1865	Caroline Jessup dies; Henry Jessup raises $10,000 in U.S. for seminary building.
1866	Beirut Female Seminary opens in renovated Burj Bird; Syrian Protestant College (SPC) opens with Daniel Bliss as president.
1867	Rufka Gregory falls ill and departs to Egypt.
1868	Jessup recruits Eliza Everett as new principal; Everett begins Arabic study and, assisted by Ellen Carruth, takes over BFS.
1870	Presbyterian Church takes over Syria Mission and Female Seminary.
1871	Eliza Everett, Ellen Jackson, and Sophie Loring upgrade academics and teacher training.
1872	Eliza Everett opens Primary Department/teacher training laboratory.
1873	First BFS diplomas awarded; Tripoli Girls' School opens.
1876	Sidon Girls' School opens.
1879	BFS offers chemistry for girls.

Sarah and Her Sisters | *365*

1882	Ras Beirut Female School opens.
1885	Turkish harassment of schools begins.
1887	Eliza Everett suddenly "retires" but returns two years later.
1890	Mission meetings opened to "lady mission workers".
1892	Ellen Law arrives to upgrade teacher training.
1895	Eliza Everett resigns; Alice Barber heads BFS with Emilia Thomson and Ellen Law.
1897	Ellen Law is replaced by Anna Jessup.
1898	Alice Barber leaves; Anna Jessup withdraws.
1899	Mary Bliss Dale joins faculty; Harriet La Grange raises, and Henry Jessup rebuts, the "Schools Question"; Rachel Tolles joins faculty.
1902	Board Secretary Arthur Brown visits Mission and BFS; Ottora Horne replaces Alice Barber; "Schools Question" is laid to rest; Eliza Everett dies at age sixty-three.
1903	Beirut "Troubles" begin; American Navy protects missionaries.
1904	Beirut Female Seminary renamed American School for Girls.
1905	Rev. James Nicol joins Syria Mission; Mary Bliss Dale heads SPC Nurses Training program; Rachel Tolles and Ottora Horne visit graduates in Egypt.
1907	Rachel Tolles takes two-year family leave.
1909	SPC protests don't affect ASG; "Young Turks" Revolt.
1910	Henry Jessup dies at age seventy-eight; basketball debuts at ASG.
1911	Italian bombardment of Beirut.
1913	ASG's fiftieth anniversary; Emilia Thomson retires.
1914	Emma Baker Kennedy pledges $15,000 for new building; World War I begins.
1915	Famine and chaos envelop Syria; Kennedy Hall opens; ASG is day school only.
1916	ASG is cut off from outside world due to the war.
1917	Rachel Tolles is evacuated; Ottora Horne carries on; ASG is forced to close.
1918	Ottora Horne reopens school; all three seniors graduate; liberation by Allies.
1919	Rachel Tolles returns; Mission considers adding a college for women; ASG to add college prep year.

1920	Syria under French Mandate; women and girls liberated under new laws; inflation spikes and emigration results in many Syrians leaving for jobs elsewhere; AUB (formerly SPC) admits women in pharmacy and dentistry; ASG adds advanced classes.
1921	Rachel Tolles resigns; Emilia Thomson dies at age eighty-two; acting principal Horne helps launch a Muslim girls' school; Horne disqualifies herself to lead women's college.
1922	Frances Irwin is hired to head women's college; begins Arabic study.
1923	Women's college to affiliate, but not merge, with AUB.
1924	Frances Irwin becomes ASG principal; Alice Barber returns; ASG admits first freshmen to begin American Junior College for Girls (AJCG); AUB graduates first woman in pharmacy and admits women "above freshman year" to Arts and Sciences.
1925	AJCG has its first freshman graduates and first sophomore class; Ottora Horne retires.
1926	Winifred Shannon arrives; AUB awards first BA degrees to women; first annual Girls' Conference; Republic of Lebanon established.
1927	AJCG separates from ASG and is licensed by New York Board of Regents; opens in Sarrafian House as American Junior College for Women (AJCW); Frances Irwin takes furlough for rest and graduate studies; Winifred Shannon becomes acting principal.
1928	$40,000 Harkness endowment; 100 percent increase in enrollment; faculty apartment rented.
1929	Architect draws up plans for new building and campus; Wall Street stock market crash.
1930	Mission begins acquiring army camp for Ras Beirut campus; Winifred Shannon takes study furlough in U.S.
1931	Presbyterian Church Women launch campaign for AJCW; Great Depression.
1932	Campaign falls short, but Sage Fund makes up the difference; Sarrafian House is overcrowded; nursery school opens; first annual College Girls' Conference; first summer welfare camp.
1933	Property purchase completed; cornerstone laid and construction begins; student hostel rented; AJCW Ras Beirut campus opens to much acclaim.
1934	Frances Irwin resigns to care for her mother and resume graduate studies; Winifred Shannon takes over college; new dormitory becomes urgent.
1935	Dormitory construction begins; unrest in Palestine.

Sarah and Her Sisters | 367

1936   Growing nationalism; first dean of women; Iran Fund loan for dormitory; dorm wing opens.

1937   Winifred Shannon visits Tehran, finishes school year at AJCW, and starts as principal of Sage Junior College for Women; Frances Irwin's mother dies; Frances becomes assistant professor of history at Macalester College; gives her Beirut letters to Presbyterian Historical Society as would Winifred Shannon her diaries and letters.

1938   William Stoltzfus named AJCW president.

1939   Frances Irwin hospitalized and dies on October 12 at the age of forty-four.

Notes

PREFACE

[1] Ussama Makdisi, *The Artillery of Heaven: American Missionaries and the Failed Conversion of the Middle East* (Ithaca: Cornell University Press, 2008), 6.

[2] Makdisi, *Artillery of Heaven*, 8.

[3] Jean Said Makdisi, *Teta, Mother, and Me* (New York: W. W. Norton, 2006), 182.

PROLOGUE

[1] Alvan Bond, *Memoir of The Rev. Pliny Fisk, A.M.: Late Missionary to Palestine* (Boston: Crocker and Brewster, 1828, Reprinted by Hard Press Publishing), 317.

[2] Bond, *Memoir of Pliny Fisk*, 317, 426. Inspired by the Second Great Awakening, New England Congregationalists, in partnership with the Presbyterian and Dutch Reformed Churches, organized the ABCFM in 1810 as the first American agency to send missionaries abroad. http://www.philanthropyroundtable.org/almanac/religion/1810_american_board_of_commissioners_for_foreign_missions; David Finnie, *Pioneers East: The Early American Experience in the Middle East* (Cambridge, MA: Harvard University Press, 1967), 151–152, 190–196; *Instructions from the Prudential Committee of the A.B.C.F.M. to the Rev. Levi Parsons and the Rev. Pliny Fisk, Missionaries Designated for Palestine. Delivered in the Old South Church, Boston, Sabbath Evening, Oct. 31, 1819.* (n.s: n.d.), 2.

[3] Edward Prime, *Forty Years in the Turkish Empire; or, Memoirs of Rev. William Goodell, D.D.* (New York: Robert Carter and Brothers, 1876, Reprinted by Elibron Classics, 2005), 79, 81.

[4] Samir Kassir, *Beirut* (Berkeley: University of California Press, 2010), 98.

[5] Prime, *Forty Years in the Turkish Empire, 81–83, 85;* Isaac Bird, *Bible Work in Bible Lands; or, Events in the History of the Syria Mission* (Philadelphia: Presbyterian Board of Publication, 1872), 136–37.

[6] Prime, *Forty Years in the Turkish Empire*, 83–85.

[7] Adnan Abu-Ghazaleh, *American Missions in Syria: A Study of the American Missionary Contribution to Arab Nationalism in 19th Century Syria* (Brattleboro, Vermont: Amana Books, 1990), 28–29; "Kuttab," http://www.encyclopedia.com/humanities/encyclopedias-almanacs-transcripts-and-maps/kuttab.

370 | *Robert D. Stoddard, Jr.*

8   Rufus Anderson, *History of the Missions of the American Board of Commissioners for Foreign Missions to the Oriental Churches* (Boston: 1872, reprinted by BiblioBazaar, 2008), 39; Bird, *Bible Work in Bible Lands*, 184; Anderson, *History of the Missions*, 39; Prime, *Forty Years in the Turkish Empire*, 93, 104.

9   Peter Mansfield, *A History of the Middle East* (New York: Penguin Books, 1991), 53–55; Prime, *Forty Years in the Turkish Empire*, 103–105; Bird, *Bible Work in Bible Lands*, 269–272, 275; Anderson, *History of the Missions*, 43.

10 Finnie, *Pioneers East*, 194.

CHAPTER ONE

1   The chapter epigraph is from a letter from Sarah L. Smith to her parents, Beirut, April 2, 1834. The imagined arrival is based on the "Landing at Beyrout" scene described by the Rev. William Goodell in his *Memoir* of "half-naked, barbarous Arabs leap(ing) out and carry(ing) us… through the billows to the dry land, amidst the multitude who ran to witness so novel a scene." Edward D. G. Prime, *Forty Years in the Turkish Empire* (New York: Robert Carter and Brothers, 1876, Replica Edition, Elibron Classics, 2005), 79. Henry Jessup reiterates how the first missionaries came ashore, Henry Jessup, *Fifty-three Years in Syria: Volume I* (1910; reprint, Milton Keynes: Lightning Source, 2007), 26.

In her first letter home, Sarah describes how, "On the 28th of January… we approached our destined home" and then describes looking upon "the famed (Mount) Lebanon" from aboard their ship. Once ashore, they were "most cordially greeted by their friends." She goes on to describe "the small city enclosed by a wall" and later refers to riding on her donkey. http://www.solidere.com/ city-center/history-and-culture/archeology.

2   Edward William Hooker, *Memoir of Mrs. Sarah L. Huntington Smith* (Boston: American Tract Society, 1845), 182–183, 165; David Finnie, *Pioneers East: The Early American Experience in the Middle East*, (Cambridge: Harvard University Press, 1967), 119.

3   Fawwaz Traboulsi, *A History of Modern Lebanon* (New York: Pluto Press, 2007), 12; Samir Kassir, *Beirut* (Berkeley: University of California Press, 2010), 101.

4   Kassir, *Beirut*, 102–107.

5   Hooker, *Memoir*, 180–181.

6   Hooker, *Memoir*, 11–18; Frances Caulkins, *History of Norwich Connecticut* (Reprinted, New London County Historical Society, 2009) 547–548; https:// www.poetryfoundation.org/poets/lydia-huntley-sigourney. In the early nineteenth century "there was rapid growth in secondary education… for women. Secondary schools called academies began to flourish." They "did not require the students to stay for any set period and the curriculum varied depending on the school. The Female Seminary Movement began around 1815 ("seminaries" referred to female schools that were more serious than finishing schools) and

was led by women such as Catharine Beecher, Mary Lyon and Emma Willard. Their goal "was to form schools that would offer women an education equal to that of men by holding their pupils to the same high standards." "The History of Women and Education," National Women's History Museum, http://www.nwhm.org/online-exhibits/education/1800s_1.ht; *Portraits of American Women Writers That Appeared in Print Before 1861* (Library Company of Philadelphia, 2005).

7   Hooker, *Memoir*, 18, 23, 78, and 81. For a detailed analysis of early female education in America, see Margaret A. Nash, *Women's Education in the United States*: 1780–1840 (New York: Palgrave Macmillan, 2007).

8   William Warren Sweet, *The Story of Religion in America* (New York: Harper & Row, Publishers, 1950), 225–226.

9   The Mohegan ("Wolf People") Indian Tribe migrated from Lake Chaplain in New York to southeastern Connecticut in search of better hunting and shellfish and lived in peace and prosperity until the late seventeenth century when their sanctuary was disrupted by a series of wars ending with the English Puritan settlers victory over the Native Americans in King Philips War. The native culture of New England tribes, including the Mohegans, was dishonored, their lands seized, and their numbers decimated by diseases introduced by the whites. Melissa Jayne Fawcett, *The Lasting of the Mohegans* (Uncasville, Connecticut: The Mohegan Tribe, 1995) 16, 20, 22; Jon Meacham, *American Lion: Andrew Jackson in the White House* (New York: Penguin Random House, 2008), 91–97, 122–23, and 141–45.

10 Hooker, *Memoir*, 107–113.

11 Hooker, *Memoir*, 113–126; https://www.nytimes.com/1996/10/06/nyregion/a-huntington-s-mohegan-mission.html.

12 Hooker, *Memoir*, 106–110; Gerald Anderson, ed., *Biographical Dictionary of Christian Missions* (Grand Rapids, MI: Eerdmans, 1998), 626; Eli Smith, *Researches of the Rev. E. Smith and Rev. H. G. O. Dwight in Armenia including a Journey through Asia Minor, and into Georgia and Persia, Vols. I and II*, Elibron Classics Replica Edition).

13 Lisa Joy Pruitt, *A Looking Glass for Ladies: American Protestant Women and the Orient in the Nineteenth Century* (Atlanta: Mercer University Press, 2005), 50–51.

14 Hooker, *Memoir*, 127–33; Margaret Leavy, *The Making of a Missionary: Eli Smith at Yale, 1817–1821* (New Haven Museum and Historical Society Journal, 1995).

15 Hooker, *Memoir*, 360.

16 http://inaminuteago.com/articles/samplerhist.html; Hooker, *Memoir*, 374 and 186.

17 Hooker, *Memoir*, 373–74, 383.

18 Hooker, *Memoir*, 364, 379, 84.

19 Hooker, *Memoir*, 185–186, 190. The quotation is from Dr. Christine Beth Lindner.

20 Hooker, *Memoir*, 190, 184–185, 364.

21 Hooker, *Memoir*, 187, 374–375.

22 Hooker, *Memoir*, 377–378.

23 Hooker, *Memoir*, 188–192.

24 Adee Brown, "Looking to Quell Sexual Urges? Look No Further Than the Graham Cracker," *The Atlantic*, January 15, 2014, https://www.theatlantic.com/health/archive/2014/01/looking-to-quell-sexual-urges-consider-the-graham-cracker/282769/.

25 Hooker, *Memoir*, 360–361, 366–369.

26 Christine B. Lindner, *Rahil Ata al-Bustani: Wife and Mother of the Nahda* (Melbourne: Phoenix Publishing, 2014), 4; Hooker, *Memoir*, 370–73, 193–94.

27 Hooker, *Memoir*, 195–97, 199–201.

28 Hooker, *Memoir*, 375.

29 Hooker, *Memoir*, 218–219.

30 https://www.merriam-webster.com/dictionary/benighted.

31 Hooker, *Memoir*, 219.

32 Hooker, *Memoir*, 220.

33 Hooker, *Memoir*, 224, 230.

34 Hooker, *Memoir*, 321; Henry Jessup, *Fifty-three Years in Syria: Volume I* (1910; reprint, Milton Keynes: Lightning Source, 2007), 42.

35 Jean Said Makdisi, *Teta, Mother, and Me: Three Generations of Arab Women* (New York: W. W. Norton, 2006), 156–161. Jean Makdisi's imagining of her great-grandparents' mid-eighteenth-century home in Homs suggested some of these "imaginings" and provided the Arabic names of two items, the water jug and the "water house."

36 Hooker, *Memoir*, 379–80.

37 Hooker, *Memoir*, 379, 265.

38 Hooker, *Memoir*, 233, 263, 266.

39 Hooker, *Memoir*, 386, 264, 272, 232. Sarah first refers to the woman as a "Jewish lady," but later as a "Jewess," which is today considered an offensive term. Sarah may not have previously known any Jews in antebellum Connecticut, but her use of this term suggests she still may have been tainted by anti-Semitism. https://www.jewishvirtuallibrary.org/connecticut-jewish-history.

40 Hooker, *Memoir*, 264–267.

41 Isaac Bird, *Bible Work in Bible Lands* (Philadelphia: Presbyterian Board of Publication, 1873), 318; Hooker, *Memoir*, 279, 268.

42 Hooker, *Memoir*, 274–280; Bird, *Bible Work*, 319.

43 Bird, *Bible Work*, 319; Hooker, *Memoir*, 278; George Sabra, *Truth and Service* (Beirut: Antoine, 2009), 14–15.

44 Hooker, *Memoir*, 284, 375.

45 "The Lancasterian Monitorial System of Education: Portrait of Joseph Lancaster," http://www.constitution.org/lanc/monitorial.htm; Prime, *Forty Years in the Turkish Empire*, 93; Bird, *Bible Work*, 319,167, 228.

46 "Report of Schools at Beyroot and Vicinity," *Missionary Herald*, Vol. 32 (1836): 97; Hooker, *Memoir*, 374.

47 Hooker, *Memoir*, 287, 289, 318.

48 Samuel Wilderspin, *On the Importance of Educating the Infant Poor, 2nd Edition* (London: Goyder, Printer, 1824) (Reprinted by Bibliolife), https://www.britannica.com/biography/Samuel-Wilderspin.

49 Wilderspin, *Infant Poor*, 37; Hooker, *Memoir*, 376–377.

50 Wilderspin, *Infant Poor*, 23, 30, 195–199.

51 Hooker, *Memoir*, 265, 377; Wilderspin, *Infant Poor*, 43–Ï48.

52 Wilderspin, *Infant Poor*, 48–50, 57–60.

53 Hooker, *Memoir*, 281, 289–292.

54 Hooker, *Memoir*, 298–300.

55 Hooker, *Memoir*, 321.

56 Hooker, *Memoir*, 361–62, 365.

57 Hooker, *Memoir*, 314–15.

58 Hooker, *Memoir*, 385, 300–01.

59 Miron Winslow, *A Memoir of Mrs. Harriet W. Winslow, Combining a Sketch of the Ceylon Mission* (London: John F. Shaw, 1838), 171–72.

60 Thomas Woody, *A History of Woman's Education in the United States* (New York: The Science Press, 1929), 363.

61 http://www.livingplaces.com/CT/New_London_County/Norwich_City/Jail_Hill_Historic_District.html; Hooker, *Memoir*, 303–310.

62 "Syria and the Holy Land –Letter from the Missionaries," *Missionary Herald 33* (November 1837): 444–45; Hooker, *Memoir*, 310.

63 Hooker, *Memoir*, 139, 310–312; Thomas Laurie, *Historical Sketch of the Syria Mission* (New York: American Board of Commissioners for Foreign Mission, 1864), 23; Bird, *Bible Work*, 319.

64 Journal of W. M. Thomson, "Testimony to the Missionary Character of the Late Mrs. Smith," *Missionary Herald 33* (November 1837): 443–44.

65 Hooker, *Memoir*, 313.

66 "Letter from Messers Temple and Adger, Dated June 1836," *Missionary Herald 32* (December 1836): 467; Hooker, *Memoir*, 318.

67 Hooker, *Memoir*, 321, 391, 393.

68 http://www.webmd.com/a-to-z-guides/tuberculosis-tb-topic-overview); Hooker, *Memoir*, 11, 129; https://www.nobelprize.org/educational/medicine/tuberculosis/readmore.html.

69 Hooker, *Memoir*, 316, 377, 321.

70 Bird, *Bible Work*, 318–320; Hooker, *Memoir*, 26, 321.

71 Acts of the Apostles, Chapter 32; Hooker, *Memoir*, 316, 321–323, 327; Letter from Mr. Smith, 328, 465.

72 The site was later identified as Lisan el Kahbeh on the Bay of Sighajik. Hooker, *Memoir*, 328; "Letter from Mr. Smith," 465–466.

73 Hooker, *Memoir*, 330–337; "Letter from Mr. Smith," 465–467.

74 Hooker, *Memoir*, 339–351.

[75] Hooker, *Memoir*, 358. NOTE: The engraved stone Eli Smith had placed on Sarah's grave can still be seen in the former Anglican (now Baptist) graveyard in Izmir, Turkey. It reads: "The Monument of Sarah Lanman Smith, wife of The Rev. Eli Smith, who was born in Norwich, Conn. U.S.A., June 18, 1802. To Benevolent Efforts for the Youth and Ignorant of her Native City, for the Neglected Remnant of its Aboriginal Inhabitants, and for the Benighted Females of Syria: She Devoted all Her Ardent and Untiring Energies, As a Servant of Christ, Until Sinking Under Missionary Labors at Beyroot, She Was Brought Hither and Died in Triumphant Faith, September 30, 1836, Age 34."

CHAPTER TWO

[1] Edward William Hooker, *Memoir of Mrs. Sarah L. Huntington Smith* (Boston: American Tract Society, 1845), 319.

[2] The information on Rebecca Williams is drawn from Samuel H. Williams, *Rebecca Williams Hebard of Lebanon, Connecticut, Missionary in Beirut, Syria and to the Druzes of Mount Lebanon 1835–1840* (Glastonbury, CT: n.s. 1950), 5; Rufus Anderson, *History of the Missions of the American Board of Commissioners for Foreign Missions to the Oriental Churches* (Boston: 1872; reprinted by BiblioBazaar, 2008), 151; Henry H. Jessup, *Women of the Arabs* (1873, reprinted by Titis Digital Publishing Private Limited, Great Classic Series, 2008), 34.

[3] Sampler by Raheel Atta, 1838, on display in the Perkins-Rockwell House, Norwich, Connecticut.

[4] "Syria and the Holy Land: Letter from the Missionaries," *Missionary Herald* 33:11 (November 1836), 417, 444-445.

[5] Williams, *Rebecca Williams Hebard*, 5–6.

[6] http://www.westminsterconfession.org/confessional-standards/the-westminster-shorter-catechism.php.

[7] "Syria and the Holy Land: Letter from the Missionaries," 444–445; Williams, *Rebecca Williams Hebard*, 7–8.

[8] Williams, *Rebecca Williams Hebard*, 8–9.

[9] William McClurg Paxton, *The Paxtons: Their Origins in Scotland and Their Migrations* (Landmark Print, Platte City, Missouri 1903), 165–166; http://www.levantineheritage.com/pdf/CB-Lindner-PhD-2009.pdf.

[10] The spelling "Beyroot" was used only by the very earliest missionaries, and was quickly succeeded by "Beirut," which is the spelling adopted in this book.

[11] https://archive.org/stream/vintonbookarmeni03vint#page/n255/search/Tilden; "Statistical View of the Board and it Missions: Syria and the Holy Land," *Missionary Herald* (January 1840), 21; "Syria and the Holy Land: Report of the Syria Mission," *Missionary Herald* 35:11 (November 1839), 405; Jessup, *Women of the Arabs*, 34. In the antebellum era many New England women either married late or not at all and needed to support themselves, usually as teachers.

Excluded from most colleges, more young women sought "pre-teaching training" in female academies or seminaries. Their education was much like that provided in the all-male academies, high schools, and colleges. Over time "future teachers required higher learning and specialized training " As the standards for teachers rose there was a "trend toward credential requirements for teachers... and genuine professionalism." Margaret A. Nash, *Women's Education in the United States 1780–1840* (New York: Palgrave Macmillan, 2005) 54, 60, and 66–67.

[12] "Syria and the Holy Land: Report of the Beyroot Station," *Missionary Herald* 36:8 (August 1840) 351, 314–315. The grave for Rebecca Williams, along with those of many other American Missionaries, was relocated to the Anglo-American Cemetery in 1960. Christine B. Lindner's "History," *Anglo-American Cemetery, Beirut, Lebanon*, blog, 5 May 2014, http://anglo-americancemeterybeirut.blogspot.com/p/history.html.

[13] Isaac Bird, *Bible Work in Bible Lands* (Philadelphia: Presbyterian Board of Publication, 1873), 340; American Board of Commissioners for Foreign Missions Report,1840, 98–100.

[14] Bird, *Bible Work*, 341–342; Samir Kassir, *Beirut* (Berkeley: University of California Press, 2010), 107–108; "Report of the Beyroot Station," *Missionary Herald* 36:8 (August 1840), 351; "Syria and the Holy Land: Report of the Station at Beyroot," *Missionary Herald* 37:7 (July 1841), 302; Fawwaz Traboulsi, *A History of Modern Lebanon* (London: Pluto Press, 2012), 13.

[15] "Syria and the Holy Land: Report of the Syria Mission," *Missionary Herald* 38:6 (June 1842), 227.

[16] Hooker, *Memoir*, 378.

[17] "Letter from Dr. H. A. De Forest, Obituary of Mrs. Smith," *Missionary Herald* 38:9 (September 1842), 364.

[18] Traboulsi, *Modern Lebanon*, 15; British and Foreign State Papers, Vol. 35, Great Britain Foreign and Commonwealth Office, 304; *Persecution of Maronites and other Eastern Christians, the Massacres of 1840–1860*, http://phoenicia.org/persecution1860.

[19] https://archive.org/stream/vintonbookarmeni03vint#page/n255/search/Whiting.

[20] Henry Jessup, *Women of the Arabs*, 37–38; Hooker, *Memoir*, 278.

[21] Jessup, *Women of the Arabs*, 37; Hooker, *Memoir*, 278.

[22] Jessup, *Women of the Arabs*, 34–35; George Whiting, Journal of Mr. Whiting, *Missionary Herald*, 32:9 (September 1836), 347; Letter from the Missionaries, *Missionary Herald* 33:11 (November 1837), 493.

[23] George Whiting, Letters from Mr. Whiting, *Missionary Herald* 41:1 (January 1842); "Syria and the Holy Land: Report of the Jerusalem Station," *Missionary Herald* 41:8 (August 1842), 324.

[24] George Whiting, "Female Education," 1841, Presbyterian Church in the U.S.A. Board of Foreign Missions Correspondence and Reports, 1833–1911, Syria Mission, (PHS MF10 F761a).

376 | *Robert D. Stoddard, Jr.*

[25] Isaac Bird, *Bible Work*, 371–376; Jessup, *Women of the Arabs*, 38–39, 40–46; "Report of the Jerusalem Station," *Missionary Herald* 41:1 (August 1842), 324. Matilda Whiting's Jerusalem School is mentioned in Ela Greenberg's *Preparing the Mothers of Tomorrow: Education and Islam in Mandate Palestine* (Austin: University of Texas Press, 2010), 20–21.

[26] George Sabra, *Truth and Service*, 17; Daniel Bliss, *The Reminiscences of Daniel Bliss: Edited and Supplemented by His Eldest Son* (1920; reprint, Lexington, KY: Cornell University Library Digital Collection, 2011), 112–13.

[27] Bliss, *Reminiscences of Daniel Bliss*, 119; Jessup, *Women of the Arabs*, 36, 138; *Amerikan Bord Heyeti* (American Board), Istanbul, "Personnel records for George B. Whiting," American Research Institute in Turkey, Istanbul Center Library, online in *Digital Library for International Research Archive*, Item #15816, http://dlir. org/archive/items/show/15816 (accessed 6 September 2015); Henry Jessup, *Fifty-three Years in Syria: Volume I* (1910; reprint, Milton Keynes: Lightning Source, 2007), 23; Jessup, *Women of the Arabs*, 51; William Bird, "Journal, Jan. 1, 1854– Dec. 10, 1865," ABC 76, Box 1, Folder 1, courtesy of Houghton Library, Harvard University.

Chapter Three

[1] Hooker, *Memoir of Mrs. Sarah L. Huntington Smith*, 313.

[2] *Report of the American Board of Commissioners for Foreign Missions, presented at the Thirtieth Annual Meeting, held in the city of Troy, New York, Sept. 11, 12 and 13, 1839* (Boston: Crocker and Brewster, 1839), 83; "Syria and the Holy Land: Report of the Beyroot Station," *Missionary Herald* 36:9 (September 1839), 348.

[3] *Biographical Memoranda Respecting All Who Ever Were Members of the Class of 1832* (New Haven: Tuttle, Morehouse and Taylor, 1880); Henry Jessup, *Fifty-three Years in Syria: Volume I* (1910; reprint, Milton Keynes: Lightning Source, 2007), 95.

[4] *Report of the American Board of Commissioners for Foreign Missions*, 83; "Syria and the Holy Land: Report of the Beyroot Station," *Missionary Herald* 36:9 (September 1839), 348.

[5] Henry H. Jessup, *Women of the Arabs* (1873, reprinted by Titis Digital Publishing Private Limited, Great Classic Series, 2008), 84–85; "Syria—Letter from Mr. Smith," *Missionary Herald* 39:7 (July 1843), 281–284; Isaac Bird, *Bible Work in Bible Lands* (Philadelphia: Presbyterian Board of Publication, 1873), 354–355; Christine B. Lindner, "Rahil Ata al-Bustani: Wife and Mother of the Nahda" in Adel Beshara, ed., *Butrus al-Bustani: Spirit of the Age* (Melbourne: IPhoenix Publishers, 2014), 49–67.

[6] "Letter from Mr. Thomson dated at Beyroot, March 16, 1838," *Missionary Herald* 34, December 1.

[7] Jessup, *Women of the Arabs*, 21, 54–59.

[8] George Sabra, *Truth and Service: A History of the Near East School of Theology* (Beirut: Antoine, 2009), 13–18; Margaret Nash, *Women's Education in the United States, 1780–1840* (New York: Palgrave MacMillan, 2005).

[9] John William De Forest, *Oriental Acquaintance; or, Letters from Syria* (New York: Dix, Edwards and Co., 1856), 38–39.

[10] Womack Deana Ferree, "Lubnani, Libanais, Lebanese: Missionary Education, Language, Policy and Identity Formation," *Studies in World Christianity* 18:1 (2012): 12.

[11] "Beirut Mission Library with H. A. De Forest," December 31, 1852 (PHS MF10 F 761a).

[12] "Dr. De Forest's Report: Education: Beirut Station," 1850 (PHS MF10 F 761a).

[13] Jessup, *Women of the Arabs*, 53.

[14] Jessup, *Women of the Arabs*, 54–57.

[15] "Letter from Dr. De Forest: The Death of Miss Whittlesey," *Missionary Herald* 48:7 (July 1852), 201–202.

[16] Physicians' Desk Reference, pdr.health.com/ diseases/heatstroke-sunstroke; Jessup, *Fifty-three Years*, 96.

[17] "Dr. De Forest: Education Department (Dictated to Mrs. De Forest)," 1853, (PHS MF10 F 761a); Jessup, *Women of the Arabs*, 55.

[18] Report of the American Board of Commissioners for Foreign Missions, 44th Annual Meeting (Boston: Press of T. R. Marvin, 1853), 73; "Dr. De Forest: Education Department (Dictated to Mrs. De Forest)," 1853 (PHS MF10 F 761a).

[19] "Dr. De Forest: Education Department (Dictated to Mrs. De Forest)," 1853 (PHS MF10 F 761a).

[20] Jessup, *Women of the Arabs*, 52–53.

[21] Syria Mission Report, 1858 (?), Female Seminary 3 (PHS MF10 F761a). For more on the Abeih Academy see George Sabra, *Truth and Service: A History of the Near East School of Theology* (Beirut: Antoine, 2009), 17–21.

[22] Bliss, *Reminiscences*, 62, 65, 79, 110–111, 113–114, 157–159; Sabra, *Truth and Service*, 17–21.

[23] Bliss, *Reminiscences*, 123; Jessup, *Fifty-three Years*, 222; Syria Mission Report 1858 (?) Female Seminary 3 (PHS MF10 F761a).

[24] Bliss, *Reminiscences*, 128, 130, 133; Jessup, *Fifty-three Years*, 64. Daniel Bliss, who at the age of twenty-three taught a class of "sixteen to twenty-year-old young women in a little red school house" in Ohio, remained a strong advocate for female schools throughout his career. *Reminiscences*, 48–50.

[25] Jessup, *Fifty-three Years*, 166; Vol. II, Appendix I 798.

[26] Jessup, *Fifty-three Years*, 175; Bliss, *The Reminiscences of Daniel Bliss*, 146, 150.

[27] Jessup, *Fifty-three Years*, 175; Appendix I 798; Jessup, *Women of the Arabs*, 61–62; Leila Tarazi Fawaz, *An Occasion for War: Civil Conflict in Lebanon and Damascus in 1860* (Berkeley: University of California Press, 1995), 106–07; Traboulsi, *Modern Lebanon*, 37–39, 43; Kassir, *Beirut*, 91–93.

[28] Bliss, *Reminiscences*, 162–67.

378 | *Robert D. Stoddard, Jr.*

29 See Warren Street, *The Story of Religion in America*, revised edition (New York: Harper and Row, 1950), Chapter 18, "Slavery, Controversy and Schisms," 285–311 and Chapter 19, "The Churches North and South and the Civil War," 312–326.

Chapter Four

1   Henry Jessup, *Fifty-three Years in Syria*: Volume I (1910; reprint, Milton Keynes: Lightning Source, 2007), Vol. I, 335.

2   Jessup, *Fifty-three Years*, 175; Vol. II, Appendix I 798; Henry H. Jessup, *Women of the Arabs* (1873, reprinted by Titis Digital Publishing Private Limited, Great Classic Series, 2008), 6. The Sidon school carried on for two more years with native instructors under Mrs. Hannah Eddy's supervision. It was taken over in 1867 by Mrs. E. H. Watson, an English lady who came to Syria in 1858 and, with the support of the London Society for the Promotion of Female Education, opened her own girls' schools in Beirut and Shemlan; Robert Elliott Speer, "The Mission in Syria," Presbyterian Foreign Missions: An Account of the Missions of the Presbyterian Church in the USA, 203 (Presbyterian Board of Publications and Sabbath School Work: Philadelphia, 1901).

3   Jessup, *Women of the Arabs*, 64–65; Jessup, *Fifty-three Years*, 237. For more on Elizabeth Bowen Thompson's schools at this time, see Elizabeth Maria Bowen Thompson, *The Daughters of Syria: A Narrative of the Efforts of the Late Mrs. Bowen Thompson for the Evangelization of Syrian Females*, Chapter VII, 1864–1865, 181–191.

4   Jessup, *Fifty-three Years*, 19, 21, 147,166, 193.

5   Jessup, *Women of the Arabs*, 63–64; Jessup, *Fifty-three Years*, 222.

6   Jessup, *Fifty-three Years*, 155.

7   William Warren Sweet, *The Story of Religion in America* (Harper & Row, Publisher: New York, 1950), 324; Jessup, *Women of the Arabs*, 64.

8   Jessup, *Fifty-three Years*, 222; http://www.schenectadyhistory.org/families/ hmgfm/vanrensselaer-3.html; http://info.med.yale.edu/library/news/exhibits/hospitals/expansion.html; www.litchfieldhistoricalsociety.org/ledger/students/7015.

9   Jessup, *Fifty-Three Years*, 335; Mark Twain, *The Innocents Abroad* (Hartford: American Publishing Company, 1869), Chapter 41; Captain Charles C. Duncan, Journal entry, September 10, 1868, published in the *New York Sun; Mark Twain's Letters: 1867-1868*, Volume 2: VII (New York: Harper & Brothers 1917) 97, footnote 3.

10 Jessup, *Women of the Arabs*, 64.

11 Jessup, *Women of the Arabs*, 58, 64–65; Jessup, *Fifty-three Years*, 227, 222; Alice S. Barber, "Beirut Seminary After Forty Years," *Woman's Work for Woman* 17:12 (December 1902), 358.

12 http://www.in2013dollars.com/1864-dollars-in-2018?amount=10000.

Sarah and Her Sisters | 379

13 Jessup, *Fifty-three Years*, 225, 278–280; Jessup, *Women of the Arabs*, 77.

14 Jessup, *Fifty-three Years*, 280, 282; Carlos Martyn, ed., *William E. Dodge: The Christian Merchant* (New York) 145, 157–60; "William A. Booth," James, T. White, ed., *The National Cyclopedia of American Biography*, Vol. X; https://todayinsci.com/B/Baldwin_Matthias/BaldwinMatthias-NCAB.htm; John A. Brown obituary, *New York Times*, January 2, 1873; http://www.browsebiography.com/bio-jay_cooke.html.

15 Jessup, *Fifty-three Years*, 283–284, 290–297, 316, 310; https://www.measuringworth.com/datasets/exchangepound/result.php; http://www.in2013dollars.com/1865-dollars-in-2016?amount=3000; Jessup, *Women of the Arabs*, 77.

16 Barber, "Beirut Seminary After Forty Years," 358.

17 Henry Jessup's Memorial Letter, September 10, 1891 (PHS MF10 F 761a); Jessup, *Fifty-three Years*, 330.

18 Jessup, *Fifty-three Years*, 333; Jessup, *Women of the Arabs*, 65, 67, 106–107.

19 Jessup, *Women of the Arabs*, 12; Christine Lindner, "Rahil Ata al-Bustani," 49–67.

20 Jessup, *Women of the Arabs*, 64.

CHAPTER FIVE

1 Henry Jessup, *Fifty-three Years in Syria: Volume I* (1910; reprint, Milton Keynes: Lightning Source, 2007), 300.

2 Jessup, *Fifty-three Years*, 335.

3 Jessup, *Fifty-three Years*, 335–339; "A Detailed History," www.mtholyoke.edu/about/history/detailed; *Lake Erie College: The First 150 Years, 1856–2006*, https://www.lec.edu/Content/uploads/Historical-Insert.pdf.

4 "Not Death, Translation," *Woman's Work for Woman* (WWW), Published by Woman's Foreign Missionary Societies of the Presbyterian Church (New York) Volume 17, April 1902, 106.

5 https://archive.org/stream/vintonbookarmeni03vint#page/n257/search/Everett, 112; Eliza D. Everett to Dr. Irving, Secretary, Presbyterian Board of Foreign Missions, Beirut, October 19, 1871 (PHS MF10 F761a). Appended to this letter is a list of sources "Supporting Pupils in the School." Fourth on the list is "Cong. S. School, Painesville, Ohio," likely Miss Everett's home church and the class she taught before leaving for Beirut. Lake Erie Female Seminary became known as Lake Erie College when it awarded its first college degrees in 1898, http://www.ohiohistorycentral.org/w/Lake_Erie_Female_Seminary; Henry Jessup, *Fifty-three Years*, 336–339. Eliza Everett may have contemplated marriage and children, but prospects for young women in her era were appreciably diminished as a result of the American Civil War. Approximately 35,000 men from Ohio died and 30,000 were wounded, many disabled for life. Miss Everett and the single American women who would become her colleagues in Beirut surely lost beaus as well as brothers, cousins, childhood friends, and even fathers and

uncles. The trauma of America's deadliest war undoubtedly had a profound impact on them. http://americancivilwarinstitute.blogspot.com/[2013]/09/ohio-in-civil-war.html.

[6] Jessup, *Fifty-three Years*, 339–341.

[7] Eliza Everett, "Letter from Syria (Beirut, January 15, 1869)," *Painesville Telegraph* (May 6, 1869), 3.

[8] Eliza Everett to the "lady to take charge of the department for Missionaries' daughters," (Beirut, June 17, 1871); Sophie Loring to Dr. Irving, Beirut, April 1, 1871 (PHS MF10 F761a).

[9] Henry H. Jessup, *Women of the Arabs* (1873, reprinted by Titis Digital Publishing Private Limited, Great Classic Series, 2008), 67.

[10] Annual Report of Beirut Female Seminary, 1892, Eliza Everett for the Faculty, Beirut, February 27, 1893 (PHS MF10 F761a).

[11] "American Board of Commissioners for Foreign Missions: Overview, 1810–1985," http://www.congregationallibrary.org/finding-aids/ABCFMOverview; James Nichols, *History of Christianity: 1650–1950* (New York: The Roland Press 1956) 318.

[12] Minutes of Special Meeting of the Syria Mission, November 22–28, 1870 (PHS MF!): F761a n88); Eliza Everett to the Gentlemen of the Presbyterian Board of Mission, [PBM], Beirut, December 8, 1870, (PHS MF10 F761a).

[13] Annual Report BFS—1892, Eliza Everett, Beirut, February 27, 1893; Salaries etc. of Missionaries, 1875–76; Report of BFS Executive Committee to the Board of Missions of the Presbyterian Church [BMPC] 2 (Beirut, 1870); BFS, E. D. Everett, Beirut, 1873, (PHS MF10 F761a).

[14] Eliza Everett to the "lady to take charge," ibid; BFS Executive Committee Report to BMPC (PHS MF10 F761a:v86).

[15] BFS Annual Reports, 1873–1875, 1877–1880, 1882–1885, 1889 and 1892; native agents' salaries 1877 (PHS MF10 F761a).

[16] BFS, E. D. Everett, Beirut, 1873 (PHS MF10 F761a); Alice Barber, Tabular View No. 1, Pastors, licensed Preachers, and Other Helpers (1873?) BFS, Beirut, June 1890, (PHS MF10, F761a r88).

[17] Eliza D. Everett, Beirut, 1873; Annual Reports of BFS for 1873, 1874, 1875, 1877, 1878, 1879, 1880, 1882 1883, 1814, 1885 and 1892 (PHS MF10 F761a).

[18] Rev. D. Stuart Dodge to Dr. Ellinwood, Beirut, February 20, 1872; BFS Annual Reports of BFS for 1873, 1874, 1875, 1877, 1878, 1879, 1880, 1882 1883, 1814, 1885 and 1892 (PHS MF10 F761a).

[19] Nada Abdelsamad, Wadi Abou Jamil, "Stones for the Jews of Beirut" (Beirut: Dar al-Nahar, 2009); Annual Reports of BFS for 1873, 1874, 1875, 1877, 1878, 1879, 1880, 1882 1883, 1814, 1885 and 1892 (PHS MF10 F761a); http://www.solidere.com/city-center/urban-overview/districts-main-axes/wadi-abou-jamil-zokak-el-blatt; Alice S. Barber, "Beirut Seminary After Forty Years," *WWW*, Vol. 17, December 1902, 359.

Sarah and Her Sisters | 381

[20] Alice Barber, Beirut, June 1890; Emilia Thomson, Report of the American School for Girls [ASG], Beirut, October 1903 to July 1904; Eliza Everett to the "lady to take charge," ibid.

[21] Eliza Everett to the Gentlemen of Presbyterian Board of Missions, Beirut, December 8, 1870; Eliza Everett, BFS, Beirut, 1873 (PHS MF10 F761a).

[22] Eliza Everett to Dr. Irving, Sec. P.B.F.M, Beirut, November 19, 1871 (PHS MF10 F761a); Emilia Thomson, Report of ASG, Beirut, October 1903 to July 1904 (PHS 115 RG 3:2); "Inventory and Cash Value of Books Belonging to the Mission in Stock," December 31, 1876 (PHS MF10 F 761a); Report of BFS for 1874; Eliza Everett to Dr. Irving, ibid.

[23] Eliza Everett, Report of BFS for 1879 Beirut, January 21, 1880, (PHS MF10 F 761a).

[24] "Inventory and Cash Value of Books," December 31, 1876; Eliza Everett, *Mukhtasar 'Ilm al-Hay'a* (Beirut: American Mission Press, 1875); Abdul Latif Tibawi, *American Interests in Syria, 1800–1901: A Study of Educational, Literary and Religious Works* (Oxford: Clarendon Press, 1996), 249, 251.

[25] Julia Hauser, *German Religious Women in Late Ottoman Beirut: Competing Missions* (Leiden and Boston; Brill, 2015); Eliza Everett to Dr. David Irving, Beirut, July 17, 1871; Henry Jessup to Rev. D. Irving, Abeih, June 17, 1871.

[26] Henry Jessup to Rev. D. Irving, Abeih, August 30, 1871 (PHS MF10 F761a); Alice S. Barber, "After Forty Years," WWW, Vol. 17, 359. The Tripoli Girls' School was opened in temporary facilities in 1873 and moved to a permanent building in 1876. In Sidon a permanent building was acquired first and the school there opened also in 1876. Both were taught in Arabic only and accepted local day pupils and boarding students from nearby villages. Like BFS, both operated independently of the Mission.

[27] S. B. Loring to Dr. Irving, Beirut, February 24, 1871 (PHS MF10 F761a); Rev. William Holliday, *Historical Sketch of the Missions in Syria* (Philadelphia: Woman's Foreign Missionary Society of the Presbyterian Church, 1881) 19–20; Emilia Thomson, Report of ASG, Beirut, October 1903 to July 1904 (PHS RG 115 3:2). Teacher training in America was done in "normal schools" modeled after the *école normale* in France. William Morris, ed., *The American Heritage Dictionary of the English Language* (Boston: Houghton Mifflin, 1969), 894.

[28] Holliday, *Historical Sketch of the Missions in Syria*, 19–20; Statistics of the American Presbyterian Mission in Syria, #7 and # 6, 1881; Henry Jessup to Rev. A. Mitchell, Beirut, January 12, 1885 (PHS MF10 F761a).

[29] Annual Reports of BFS for 1872, 1874, 1877, 1882, 1883, 1884 and 1885 (PHS MF10 F 761a); Alice S. Barber, "After Forty Years," WWW, Vol. 17, 359; Christine B. Lindner, "'Burj Bird' and the Beirut Mission Compound: Researching Women in the Protestant Church of Ottoman Syria," May 31, 2016, https://www.history.pcusa.org/blog/2016,burj-birdand-beirut-mission-compound.

[30] Jessup, *Fifty-three Years*, 227; Alice Barber, "After Forty Years," WWW, Vol. 17, 359.

31 Henry Jessup to Dr. Ellinwood, Beirut, October 11, 1881 (PHS MF10 F 761a); http://www.in2013dollars.com/1881-dollars-in-2018?amount=60000.

32 Alice Barber, "After Forty Years," *WWW*, Vol. 17, 359.
Miss S. B. Loring to Dr. Irving, Beirut: August 1, 1871, (MF10 F761a); Nada Abdelsamad, *Wadi Abou Jamil: Stories About the Jews of Beirut* (Beirut: Dar Ammahar, 2010); Jessup, *Fifty Three Years*, 424–425; [Eliza] Everett and Faculty to Board of Foreign Missions, Beirut, December 1873; Henry Jessup to Ellinwood, July 25, 1877.

33 Report of Beirut Seminary for 1882, Beirut, December 14, 1882; Ellen Jackson, Report of the Beirut Seminary, 1883 (PHS MF10:F761a).

34 Eliza Everett to Dr. Dennis, Beirut, May 17, 1892; Eliza Everett, BFS Annual Report, Beirut, February 27, 1893; Eliza Everett to Dr. Gillespie, Beirut, July 31, 1894 (PHS MF10 F 761a).

35 Eliza Everett, BFS Annual Report for 1893, ibid.

36 E. Thomson, Report of Beirut Seminary for 1880, Beirut, January 1881; BFS Annual Reports for 1889 and 1893 (PHS MF10 F 761a).

37 Annual Meeting Report, Turkish Missions' Aid (London, 1892); Ras Beirut Day Schools Report, 1892 (PHS MF10 F 761a).

38 Eliza Everett, "From Syria," *Painesville Telegraph* (14 April 1870), 2. Written in Beirut February 28, 1870.

39 Eliza Everett, BFS Annual Report, Beirut, February 27, 1893 (PHS MF10 F 761a).

40 BFS Executive Committee Report to BMPC, (1870?) (PHS MF10 F 761a).

41 Eliza Everett to Gentlemen of PBM, Beirut, December 8, 1870; Eliza Everett, Report of BFS for 1874, Beirut, February 11, 1875 (PHS MF10 F 761a).

42 Eliza Everett, Report of BFS for 1878, Beirut, January 16, 1879 (PHS MF10 F 761a).

43 E. Thomson, Report of BFS for 1880, Beirut, January 1881; Report of Beirut Seminary for 1882 (PHS MF10 F 761a).

44 Whereas Mrs. Walter Baker was Miss Everett's original sponsor and likely would have continued to give general support, we have no record of it. Henry Jessup confirmed in a eulogy letter that she died in 1891.

45 Eliza Everett to Dr. Irving, Beirut, October 19, 1871; BFS Executive Committee Report to BMPC (Beirut, 1870?); Whole No. Pupils, Beirut Seminary during 1889; Henry Jessup to Rev. Edward G. Porter, Abeih, September 10,1891(PHS MF10 F761a).

46 BFS Executive Committee Report to BMPC (Beirut, 1870?); Eliza Everett to Board of Missions, Beirut, December 8, 1870 (PHS MF10:F761a).

47 Henry Jessup, *Fifty-three Years*, 448–49; Henry Jessup to Dr. Ellinwood, Beirut, June 22, 1876 (PHS MF10 F761a).

48 George Post to Mr. Jessup, Sidon, May 16, 1890 (PHS MF10 F 761a).

49 Samuel Jessup to Dr. Ellinwood, Tripoli, January 29, 1876; Eliza Everett, Report of Beirut Seminary for the year 1878, Beirut January 16, 1879 (PHS MF10 F 761a); Henry Jessup, *Fifty-three Years*, 473; Henry Jessup to Dr. Ellinwood, Beirut,

October 11, 1881: Henry Jessup to Dr. Mitchell, Beirut, November 18, 1885; Emilia Thomson, Report of Beirut Seminary for 1889 (PHS MF10 F 761a).

50 Henry Jessup to Dr. Mitchell, Beirut, November 18, 1885; Beirut, January 12, 1885; Beirut, November 17, 1886; Beirut, October 25, 1887 (PHS MF10 F 761a).

51 Henry Jessup to Rev. Mitchell, November 17, 1886; January 4, 1888; February 28, 1888; April 25, 1887; "1885 and 1886 Expenditures of the Syria Mission" (PHS MF10 F 761a).

52 Ecclesiastes 4:10 and 12 "Woe to one who is alone and falls and does not have another to help... Though one might prevail against another, two will withstand one. A three-fold cord is not quickly broken." Wayne Meeks, ed., *The Harper Collins Study Bible: New Revised Standard Version* (London: 1993), 992.

53 Eliza Everett, BFS Report for 1879, Beirut, January 21, 1880 (PHS MF10 F 761a).

54 Henry Jessup to Arthur Mitchell, Beirut, April 25, 1887; BFS Executive Committee Report to BMPC (Beirut, 1870?); Henry Jessup to Arthur Mitchell, Beirut, January 17, 1888; Eliza Everett to Arthur Mitchell, Aurora, Illinois, May 4, 1888 (PHS MF10 F 761a).

55 Eliza Everett to Rev. Arthur Mitchell, Beirut, March 8, 1892; BFS Annual Report, Beirut February 27, 1892 (PHS MF10 F 761a).

56 Henry Jessup to Rev. Mitchell, Beirut, January 12, 1885; William Nelson to Arthur Brown, Beirut (?), September 4, 1889; William Bird to Rev. J. S. Dennis, Abeih, June 13, 1892; Eliza D. Everett, BFS Annual Report–1892, Beirut, February. 27, 1893 (PHS MF10 F 761a).

57 Ellen Jackson, Report of the Beirut Seminary for 1883 (Beirut, 1883) (PHS MF10 F 761a).

58 Henry Jessup to Rev. Mitchell, Beirut, April 25, 1887 (PHS MF10 F 761a).

59 W. W. Eddy to Dr. John Gillespie, Beirut, June 11, 1894; Eliza Everett to Dr. Gillespie, Suq el Gharb, July 31, 1894 (PHS MF10 F 761a).

60 Eliza Everett to the Brethren of the Presbyterian Board of Foreign Missions [PBFM], Beirut, February 7, 1895 (PHS MF10 F 761a).

CHAPTER SIX

1 E. Everett to Presbyterian Board of Foreign Missions, February 7, 1895 (PHS MF 10 F 7616).

2 Annual Report BFM, PCUSA (New York: Presbyterian Building 1896), 238; Alice S. Barber, "After Forty Years," *WWW*, Vol. 17, 359; Alice S. Barber, "Beirut Seminary," Beirut, March 13, 1902 (PHS MF 10, F7619); Josiah Fiske obituary, *New York Times*, December 24, 1892; Henry Jessup to Arthur Brown, Beirut, January 18, 1898.

3 Ellen Law to Arthur Brown, Brooklyn, NY, March 30, 1898; Emilia Thomson to Arthur. Brown, Beirut, August 19, 1898 (PHS MF10 F 761a).

384 | *Robert D. Stoddard, Jr.*

[4] Samuel H. Adams, *Life of Henry Foster, M.D., Founder of the Clifton Springs Sanitarium* (Rochester,: 1921); Alice Barber to Arthur Brown, Clifton Springs, NY, August 8, 1898; Alice Barber to Brown, Clifton Springs, NY, August 8, 1898 (PHS MF10 F 761a).

[5] Henry Jessup to Arthur Brown, Beirut, April 19, 1898 (PHS MF10 F 761a).

[6] Anna Jessup to Arthur Brown, Beirut, November 7, 1898; Henry Jessup to Arthur Brown, Beirut, October 5, 1898 (PHS MF10 F 761a).

[7] W. S. Nelson to Arthur Brown, Beirut, December 20, 1898; Henry Jessup to Brown, Beirut, December 20, 1898 (PHS MF10 F 761a).

[8] Mary Bliss Dale to Arthur Brown, Beirut, January 17, 1899; Henry Jessup to Brown, Beirut, December 20, 1898 (PHS MF10 F 761a).

[9] W. W. Eddy to Arthur Brown, Beirut, December 22, 1898; Henry Jessup to Brown, Beirut, December 20, 1898 (PHS MF10 F 761a); Harriet La Grange to Arthur Brown, Union, New York, June 30, 1899 (PHS MF10 F 761a).

[10] Arthur Brown to Syria Mission, New York, NY, July 27, 1899 (PHS MF10 F 761a).

[11] Henry Jessup to Syria Mission, "in response to Dr. Brown's letter of July 17, 1899" (PHS MF10 F 761a).

[12] Henry Jessup to Arthur Brown, Aleih, August 19, 1899; (PHS MF10 F 761a).

[13] Williston Walker, *A History of the Christian Church* (Charles Scribner's Sons: New York, 1959), 518; Franklin Hoskins, The Syria Mission, Beirut, December 1905; W. W. Eddy to Arthur Brown, Beirut, December 22, 1898; Henry Jessup to Arthur Brown, Aleih, August 19, 1899 (PHS MF10 F 761a).

[14] Henry Jessup to Arthur Brown, Aleih, August 19, 1899; Henry Jessup to Arthur Brown, Aleih, September 2, 1899 (PHS MF10 F 761a).

[15] Arthur Brown to Syria Mission, New York, October 4, 1899 (PHS MF10 F 761a).

[16] Harriet La Grange to Arthur Brown, Tripoli, Syria, December 30, 1899; W. S. Nelson to Brown, Tripoli, December 20, 1899 (PHS MF10 F 761a).

[17] Notes on a Conference of the Executive Council and Mr. John Stewart with the Rev. Dr. Daniel Bliss, of Beirut, regarding the Syrian Boarding School question, November 1899 (PHS MF10 F 761a).

[18] Henry Jessup, *Fifty-three Years in Syria: Volume I* (1910; reprint, Milton Keynes: Lightning Source, 2007), 686; Alice S. Barber to Arthur Brown, Clifton Springs, MY, August 5,1899 (PHS MF10 F 761a).

[19] Rachel E. Tolles, "Syria Today," *WWW*, Vol. 32, December 1899, 260.

[20] Rachel Tolles to Arthur Brown, Beirut, October 9, 1899; Mary Dale to Arthur Brown, Beirut, October 16, 1899 (PHS MF10 F 761a).

[21] Rachel Tolles to Arthur Brown, Beirut, April 13, 1900; Alice Barber to Arthur Brown, Beirut, October 9, 1900; Rachel Tolles to Arthur Brown, Beirut, November 20, 1900 (PHS MF10 F 761a).

[22] Samir Kassir, *Beirut* (Berkeley: University of California Press, 2010), 147–158; Franklin Hoskins to friends, Beirut, February 25, 1900 (PHS MF10 F 761a).

[23] Undated and unsigned letter, Beirut Seminary, 1901 (PHS MF10 F7619).

Sarah and Her Sisters | 385

24 Alice S. Barber, "Beirut Seminary," Beirut, March 13, 1902 (PHS MF 10, F7619); Annual Report of Beirut Seminary, Dec. 1901–Dec. 1902, Rachel E. Tolles; Report of ASG, October 1903 to July 1904; Emilia Thomson, Annual Report of Beirut Seminary, Dec. 1901–Dec. 1902, Rachel E. Tolles (PHS MF10 F 761a).

25 "Arthur Judson Brown," http://www.bu.edu/missiology/missionary-biography/a-c/brown-arthur-judson-1856-1963; Henry Jessup, *Fifty-three Years*, 709; Rachel Tolles, Annual Report of Beirut Seminary, Dec. 1901–Dec. 1902 (PHS MF10 F 7619).

26 Henry Jessup, *Fifty-three Years*, 711; "Not Death, Translation," *WWW*, Vol. 17 (April 1902), 106; "A Memorial Service in Beirut," *WWW*, Vol. 17 (August 1902), 203.

27 Henry Jessup, *Fifty-three Years*, 709–10; "Dr. Brown's Visit," ibid.

28 Mission Circular Note, May 7, BFMPC in USA; Alice Barber, "Forty Years," *WWW*, December 1902, 658–60.

29 Rachel Tolles, Annual Report of Beirut Seminary, Dec. 1901–Dec. 1902 (PHS MF10 F 761a).

30 Rachel Tolles to Arthur Brown, Beirut, May 9, 1902 (PHS MF10 F 761a).

31 M. B. Dale, "Report of Beyrout Girls School, 1902–1903," Beirut, December 1903 (?).

32 Dale, "Report of Beyrout Girls School, 1902–1903"; Emilia Thomson, Report of ASG, Beirut, October 1903 to July 1904; Franklin Hoskins to Arthur Brown, Beirut, September 5, 6, 7, 10, 11 and 12, 1903; Franklin Hoskins to Arthur Brown, Beirut, October 6, 19, and 26, 1903; Franklin Hoskins to Arthur Brown, Beirut, November 3 and 21, 1903; Franklin Hoskins to Arthur Brown, Beirut, December 19, 1903 Alice Barber to Arthur Brown, Joliet, December 17, 1904 (PHS MF10 F 761a).

33 Franklin Hoskins to Arthur Brown, Beirut, January 12, 19, and 30, 1904; Ottora Horne to Arthur Brown, December 7, 1905; Franklin Hoskins to Arthur Brown, Beirut, June 20 and 27, 1904 (PHS MF10 F 761a).

Chapter Seven

1 *Woman's Work for Woman*, Volume 20 (December 1905): 288.

2 Rachel Tolles to Dr. Brown, Beirut, October 27, 1905 (PHS MF10 F 761a); "Emma Hart Willard: A Pioneer for Women's Education," https://www.emmawillard.org/page/about-emma-hart-willard.

3 Henry Jessup to Dr. Brown, Aleih, October 2, 1904; W. K. Eddy to Brown, Sidon, December 19, 1904 (PHS MF10 F 761a); "Sublime Porte: Ottoman Government," Encyclopedia Brittanica, https://www.britannica.com/topic/Sublime-Porte

4 Rachel Tolles to Arthur Brown, Beirut, October 27, 1905; George Doolittle to Arthur Brown, Aleih, January 14, 1905 (PHS MF10 F 761a).

[5] "The Johanniter Hospital in Beirut," https://www.goethe.de/ins/lb/en/kul/sup/spu/20919610.html; https://www.arabicbible.com/for-christians/the-bible/148-fifty-three-years-in-syria/1454-light-after-darkness.html?start=3.

[6] Stephen Penrose, *That They May Have Life: The Story of the American University of Beirut 1866–1941* (New York: The Trustees of the American University of Beirut, 1941), 34–35; 110–111, 233; Jessup, *Fifty-Three Years*, 613.

[7] Ottora Horne, 1905 report to Dr. Brown, Beirut, December 7, 1905; Henry Jessup to Dr. Brown, Beirut, February 14, 1905; Ottora Horne, ASG Annual Report, December 1908 (PHS MF10 F 761a); http://www.ncbi.nlm.nih.gov/pubmedhealth/PMH0001643;/.

[8] S. White to H. Jessup, Beirut, January 27, 1909; Ira Harris to White, Tripoli, November 12, 1909; Rachel Tolles, ASG, Beirut, Syria, 1908–1909 (PHS MF10 F 761a). Although the faculty of medicine at St. Joseph University dates back to 1888, the Hôtel-Dieu de France Medical Center did not open until 1923. The Al Makassed General Hospital opened in 1925. http://www.hdf.usj.edu.lb/histoire.htmlhttp://makassedhospital.org/history-2025/.

[9] Penrose, *That They May Have Life*, 112–113.

[10] Rachel Tolles to Brown, Beirut, October 27, 1906; Ottora Horne, 1905 report to Brown, Beirut, December 7, 1905; Rachel Tolles, ASG, Beirut, December 6, 1906 (PHS MF10 F 761a); Ottora Horne, "A Trip to Egypt," *WWW*, Vol. 25, No. 12 (December 1910), 278.

[11] Rachel Tolles, ASG, Beirut, Syria, 1908–1909 (PHS MF10 F 761a).

[12] Rachel Tolles to Dr. Brown, Attica, February 23, 1907 (PHS MF10 F 761a); https://books.google.com/books?id=R8wpAQAAMAAJ&pg=PA533&lpg=PA533&d-q=Edward+Tolles+Attica+New+York+obituary&source=bl&ots=WViXyN6PM-w&sig=zI.

[13] http://www.newspaperabstracts.com/link.php?action=detail&id=7935; Rachel Tolles to Dr. Brown, Attica, November 26, 1907; Rachel Tolles to Dr. Brown, Attica, January 20, 1908 (PHS MF10 F 761a).

[14] Ottora Horne (unsigned but in her hand), Report of ASG, 1906–1907 (PHS MF10 F 761a).

[15] Ottora Horne, 1905 report to Brown, Beirut, December 7, 1905; Rachel Tolles ASG, Beirut, December 6, 1906; http://www.sfmuseum.net/1906/ew15.html; https://cameronhouse.org/about-us/history/; Ottora Horne, ASG, Annual Report, December 1908; Rachel Tolles, ASG, Beirut, 1908–1909; http://www.bu.edu/missiology/eddy-mary-pierson-1864-1923/ (PHS MF10 F 761a); http://www.armenian-genocide.org/adana.html.

[16] Penrose, *That They May Have Life, 134–138*; Rachel Tolles, ASG, Beirut, 1908–1909 (PHS MF10 F 761a).

[17] Rachel Tolles, ASG, Beirut, 1908–1909 (PHS MF10 F 761a).

[18] Ottora Horne, ASG, Annual Report, December 1908; Rachel Tolles, ASG, Beirut, 1908–1909 (PHS MF10 F 761a).

[19] "The Young Turk Revolution of 1908," https://www.britannica.com/place/Ottoman-Empire/The-empire-from-1807-to-1920#ref482235; Franklin Hoskins to Brown, Beirut, November 21, 1908; Rouben Paul Adalian, http://www.armenian-genocide.org/adana.html.

[20] Franklin Hoskins to Dr. White, Beirut, October 12, 1910; Franklin Hoskins to Dr. White, Beirut, May 28, 1909; Ira Harris to Dr. White, Tripoli, November 12, 1909; Franklin Hoskins to Dr. White, Beirut, October 12, 1910 (PHS MF10 F 761a).

[21] Penrose, *That They May Have Life*, 134–138; F. Hoskins's Political Report, Beirut, December 1910 (PHS MF10 F 761a).

[22] Rachel Tolles to Dr. Brown, Beirut, September ?, 1908; Ottora Horne, ASG, Annual Report, December 1908.

[23] Rachel Tolles to Dr. Brown, Beirut, October 27, 1905; Ottora Horne, ASG, Annual Report, December 1908; Rachel Tolles, ASG, Beirut, 1908–1909 (PHS MF10 F 761a); *WWW*, Vol. 27 (1912), 271; *WWW*, Vol. 26, No. 12 (December 1911), 274; Rachel Tolles, ASG, Beirut, December 6, 1906.

[24] George Doolittle to Arthur Brown, Aleih, January 14, 1905 (PHS MF10 F 761a).

[25] Samir Kassir, *Beirut* (Berkeley: University of California Press, 2010), 120; James Nicol, "Tidings from Syria," Vol. 1, Dec. 30, 1905 (PHS MF10 F 761a); Dr. Mary Eddy, *WWW*, Vol. 28 (January 1913), 41; Henry Jessup to Dr. Brown, Beirut, February 14, 1905; Ira Harris to Dr. White, Tripoli, March 21, 1910; Samuel Jessup to Stanley White, Beirut, January 12, 1909; Emilia Thomson, Report of ASG, December 1909–December 1910; Henry Jessup to Arthur Brown, Aleih, July 6, 1906; George Doolittle to Arthur Brown, Zahleh, June 23, 1906 (PHS MF10 F 761a).

[26] Rev. George Doolittle, "The Struggle in Syria," *WWW*, Vol. 29 (1914), 270.

[27] "The Italo-Turkish War, 1911–1912," https://www.britannica.com/event/Italo-Turkish-War; Timothy W. Childs, *Italo-Turkish Diplomacy and the War Over Libya 1911–1912* (Leiden: E. J. Brill, 1990), 122; George Doolittle to Stanley White, Sidon, June 1912; Franklin Hoskins to Stanley White, Beirut, 1913 (PHS MF10 F 761a).

[28] "War and White Plague in Syria," *WWW*, Vol. 28 (1913), December, 276 and June, 132; "News from the Front, Syria," *WWW*, Vol. 29 (1914), 268–69; *WWW*, Vol. 27 (June 1912), 32.

[29] Ottora Horne, ASG, Annual Report, 1920–1921, Ottora Horne, ASG, Annual Report, 1913–1914; Ottora Horne for the Faculty, ASG, Annual Report, Dec 1914–Dec. 1915 (PHS MF10 F 761a).

[30] Elizabeth Eddy, "Back Among the Women of Syria," *WWW*, Vol. 29 (1914), 267–68.

[31] Report of ASG, Beirut, 1913–1914 (PHS MF10 F 761a).

388 | *Robert D. Stoddard, Jr.*

CHAPTER EIGHT

[1] *WWW*, Vol. 30 (January 1915), 66; September 1915, 209.

[2] Carlton J. H. Hayes, Marshall Whitehead Baldwin, and Charles Woolsey Cole, *History of Europe* (New York: The Macmillan Company, 1956), 903–08; Peter Mansfield, *History of the Middle East* (New York: Viking, 1991), 135; "The Ottoman Empire Enters WWI on the Side of the Central Powers," http://www.thenagain.info/webchron/easteurope/turkeycentral.html; Fawwaz Traboulsi, *A History of Modern Lebanon* (London: Pluto Press, 2012), 71–72; Samir Kassir, *Beirut* (Berkeley: University of California Press, 2010), 245.

[3] "The Struggle in Syria," *WWW*, Vol. 29 (December 1914), 270–71; Dr. F. E. Hoskins, "Editorial Notes," 266.

[4] 1913–1914: Report of ASG. Beyrout; Account of Building of ASG, O.J. Hardin (PHS RG 115 3:2).

[5] Ottora M. Horne, Annual Report. ASG, Beirut, Syria: Dec 1914–Dec. 1915 (PHS RG 115 3:2).

[6] Ottora M. Horne, "News from the Front," WW, Vol. 30, January 1915, 1; 66.

[7] Traboulsi, *Modern Lebanon*, 72; (Mrs. F. E.) Harriett M. Eddy Hoskins, "Cheerful News from Far Off Lebanon," *WWW*, Vol. 30 (September 1915), 276.

[8] Kassir, *Beirut*, 245; Hoskins, "Cheerful News from Far Off Lebanon," 279.

[9] Horne, "News from the Front," 209.

[10] Franklin Hoskins to Arthur Brown, March 2, 1915 (PHS RG 115 3:2).

[11] Account of Building of ASG, O.J. Hardin (PHS RG 115 3:2); Rachel Tolles, "Syria Today," *WWW*, Vol. 32 (August 1917), 262; Annual Report. ASG, Beirut, Syria: Dec 1914–Dec. 1915 (PHS RG 115 3:2).

[12] Ottora M. Horne, Biennial Report, ASG, Beirut, Syria December 1916–December 1918 (PHS RG 115 3:2).

[13] Mrs. Franklin Hoskins, "Women Workers in Troublous Times," *WWW*, Vol. 31 (1916), 269.

[14] Tolles, "Syria Today," 262; Rachel Tolles, Report of ASG, 1919–1920; Annual Report. ASG, December 1915 (PHS RG 115 3:2).

[15] Tolles, "Syria Today," 262.

[16] Hoskins, "Women Workers in Troublous Times," 269.

[17] Tolles, "Syria Today," 261 (photos); "News from the Front," *WWW*, Vol. 31 (1916), 136.

[18] Hoskins, "Cheerful News from Far Off Lebanon," 275–76; From Miss Ottora Horne, Beirut, 242.

[19] Tolles, "Syria Today," 263; (Rev.) George Scherer, *WWW*, Vol. 31 (February 1916), 25, 280; "Editorial Notes," *WWW*, Vol. 34 (1919), 74.

[20] Traboulsi, *Modern Lebanon*, 71–72; Kassir, *Beirut*, 245.

[21] "Editorial Notes," *WWW*, Vol. 31 (1916), 267; Tolles, "Syria Today," 261–62; "Message from Syria," 222.

[22] Biennial Report, ASG, 1916–1918 (PHS RG 115 3:2).

Sarah and Her Sisters | *389*

[23] Rouben Paul Adalian, *Woodrow Wilson and the Armenian Genocide*, Armenian National Institute, www.armenian-genocide.org/Wilson; https:\\turkey.usembassay.gov\us-dipolmatic_interactive-turkey.html; Stephen Penrose, *That They May Have Life: The Story of the American University of Beirut, 1866–1941* (Beirut: American University of Beirut, 1941), 161–62; "Message from Syria," *WWW*, Vol. 32 (Oct. 1917), 222.

[24] "Message from Syria," 222; Biennial Report, ASG, 1916–1918 (PHS RG 115 3:2).

[25] Tolles, "Syria Today," 262; "Editorial Notes," 98.

[26] "News from the Front," *WWW*, Vol. 31 (1916), 136; "Message from Syria," *WWW*, Vol. 32 (October 1917), 222.

[27] Biennial Report, ASG 1916–1918, (PHS RG 115 3:2); R. R. Palmer. (ed.) *Rand McNally Atlas of World History* (New York: 1957) 176; *WWW*, Vol. 32 (1917), 262–63; "Editorial Notes," 98; December, "From Statement of the Assembly's Board," 260–261.

[28] Biennial Report, ASG 1916–1918, 2 (PHS RG 115 3:2); "Message from Syria," 222.

[29] Raymond Kevorkian, *The Armenian Genocide: A Complete History* (New York: I. B. Tauris, 2011), 382ff; Biennial Report, ASG 1916–1918 (PHS RG 115 3:2); Tolles, "Syria Today," 262.

[30] Alasdair Soussi, "The Spanish Flu Pandemic and Its Impact on the Middle East," The National Lifestyle, February 10, 2018, https://www.thenational.ae/lifestyle/the-spanish-flu-pandemic-and-its-impact-on-the-middle-east-1.703289.

[31] Biennial Report, ASG 1916–1918, 11 (PHS RG 115 3:2).

[32] Kassir, *Beirut*, 245–247.

[33] "Syria Once More on the Map," *WWW*, Vol. 33 (1918), 250; "Editorial Notes," 243.

[34] "Editorial Notes," *WWW*, Vol. 34 (August 1919), 170: December, "Editorial Notes," 242; Ottora Horne, "Schoolgirls in Beirut," 250.

[35] *WWW*, Vol. 33, No. 1 (December 1918), 243.

[36] "News from the Front: Syria," *WWW*, Vol. 34 (February 1919), 243; Ottora Horne, December, "Our Missionaries in Moslem Lands," 243; Rachel Tolles, Report of ASG, 1919–1920, July 26, 1920 (PHS RG 115 3:2).

[37] http://www.collinsdictionary.com/dictionary/english/kaimakam; Rachel Tolles, Report of ASG, 1919–1920, July 26, 1920.

[38] Report of ASG, 1919–1920, (PHS RG 115 3:2).

CHAPTER NINE

[1] The chapter epigraph is from Roberts, *Short History*, II:3 (Beirut, 1958) (PHS: F TU72 B396s) 1.

[2] Samir Kassir, *Beirut* (Berkeley: University of California Press, 2010), 258–59; 265–69; Fawwaz Traboulsi, *A History of Modern Lebanon* (London: Pluto Press, 2012), 88; Rachel Tolles, Report of ASG 1919–1920; Ottora Horne, Annual Report

1920–1921; Alice Barber, ASG Report, 1921–1922, Ottora Horne, ASG Annual Report, 1922–1923; Ottora Horne, Annual Report 1923–1924 (PHS RG 115 3:2).

[3] Lanice Paton Dana, "Reconstruction Problems in Syria: After the Captivity," *WWW*, Vol. 35 (December 1920), 241–43.

[4] Arthur J. Brown, *One Hundred Years: A History of the Foreign Mission Work of the Presbyterian Church in the USA* (New York: Revell, 1936) 1005.

[5] Dana, "Reconstruction Problems in Syria," 243; http://www.elcjhl.org/department-of-education/schools/beit-jala/history/.

[6] Stephen Penrose, *That They May Have Life: The Story of the American University of Beirut, 1866–1941* (New York: The Trustees of the American University of Beirut, 1941), 252; James Nicol, "An Outline History of the American Junior College for Women and Beirut College for Women" (unpublished: Nassar Library, Lebanese American University), Chapter 2.

[7] Tolles, Report of ASG, 1919–1920; Horne, Annual Report 1920–1921 (PHS RG 115 3:2).

[8] Horne, Annual Report 1920–1921 (PHS RG 115 3:2).

[9] Alice Barber, "Servant of God, Well Done!", *Woman's World*, Vol. 37, December 1921, 271.

[10] Nicol, "Outline History," Chapter 2; Horne, Annual Report 1920–1921 (PHS RG 115 3:2); Tolles, Report of ASG, 1919–1920; Alice Barber, Syria Annual Report–1922–1923; Horne, Annual Report (PHS RG 115 3:2); Thomas Russel, *Women Leaders in the Student Christian Movement: 1880–1920* (Maryknoll, NY: Orbis Books, 2017), Chapter 1.

[11] Nicol, "Outline History," Chapter 2; "Only a Teacher," http://www.pbs.org/onlyateacher/timeline; "Normal School," http://www.newworldencyclopedia.org/entry/Normal school.

[12] Barber, ASG Report 1913–1914 and 1921–1922 (PHS RG 115 3:2 and PHS MF10 F 761a).

[13] Penrose, *That They May Have Life*, 252–53; Nicol, "Outline History," chapters 1–2.

[14] Minutes of Syria Mission, American Girls' School, Beirut, Board Action, February 16, 1925 (PHS RG 115 3:2)

[15] Obituary of Frances P. Irwin, Minneapolis Star Tribune, October 14, 1939; *The Gopher*, 1917, University of Minnesota, 352; Candidates for Degrees program, Master of Arts, March 27, 1923, 43. Frances Irwin's master's thesis was titled "Land Speculation by Virginians in the Trans-Allegheny Region 1737–1763." Chapter 3 of James Nicol's "Outline History" claims that Irwin did further graduate work at the University of Chicago, but there is no record of her enrollment.

[16] Nicol, "Outline History," chapter 3; Letters of Frances Pryor Irwin, Beirut, November 6, 1922 (PHS RG 186–1); Horne, Annual Report–1922–1923 (PHS RG 115 3:2); History of the American Community School, Beirut, http://www.acs.edu.lb/page.cfm?p=1064.

[17] Nicol, "Outline History," Chapter 2; Horne, Annual Report, 1922–1923 (PHS RG 115 3:2).

Sarah and Her Sisters | *391*

18 Horne, Annual Report 1923–1924 (PHS RG 115 3:2).

19 Frances Irwin, Annual Report of ASG, 1924-1925; Contract for Short Term Workers (PHS RG 115-3-2).

20 *The Jayhawker*, University of Kansas, 1921, 352.

21 F. P. Irwin to Mr. J. H. Nicol, Beyrouth, March 2, 1927 (PHS RG 115–3–2); Contract for Short Term Workers (PHS RG 115–3–2).

22 Roberts, *Short History*, II:3 (PHS: F TU72 B396s); Annual Report ASG,1924–1925 (PHS RG 115-3-2); Winifred Shannon Diaries, December 8, 1925 (Winifred Shannon Papers 1924–1936, PHS RG 165-1-I).

23 Annual Report of ASG,1924–1925 (PHS RG 115-3-2).

24 Nicol, "Outline History," chapter 4; American School for Girls, Beyrouth, 1924–1925 (PHS RG 115-3-2).

25 Penrose, *That They May Have Life*, 253; Annual Report, ASG 1925–1926 (PHS RG 115-3-2).

26 Penrose, *That They May Have Life*, 253; Roberts, *Short History*, II:3 (PHS: F TU72 B396s); Annual Report, ASG 1925–1926; Frances Irwin to Rev. J. H. Nicol, Beyrout, May 28, 1926 (PHS RG 115-3-2).

27 American School for Girls, Beyrouth, 1924–1925 (PHS RG 115-3-2); Shannon Diaries, November 6, 1925 (PHS RG 165-1-I); Ellen Goodrich Bushwell to Mrs. Irwin, Beirut, February 6, 1926 (PHS RG 186-1).

28 http://www.columbia.edu/~sss31/Turkiye/ata/hayati.html#women; Traboulsi, *Modern Lebanon*, 88–90; Kassir, *Beirut*, 258.

29 Nicol, "Outline History," chapter 2; Shannon, Annual Report of ASG 1926–27; Frances Irwin to J. H. Nicol, May 28, 1926; Frances Irwin to Dear Friend, AJCG, Beirut, July 26, 1927 (PHS RG 115-3-2).

30 Frances Irwin's master's thesis lists "American Diplomatic History" and "American Foreign Relations," both taught by "Mr. Wright."

31 Frances Irwin to Dear Friend, Beirut, July 26, 1927; James Nicol to Dr. George Trull, Beirut, June 24, 1927; Shannon, Annual Report of ASG 1926–27 (PHS RG 115-3-2); Nicol, "Outline History," chapter 2; http://sites.psu.edu/ global/2018/02/08/mustafa-kemal-ataturk-and-his-reforms/.

32 School Report ASG, 1926-27

33 School Report, ASG, 1925–1926 (PHS RG 115-3-2); Penrose, *That They May Have Life*, 253; Frances Irwin to J. H. Nicol, May 28, 1926; Syria Mission Report, 1926–27 (PHS RG 115-3-2).

34 School Report, ASG 1925–1926 (PHS RG 115-3-2); Shannon Diaries, December 6, 1925 (PHS RG 165-1-I); Frances Irwin to J. H. Nicol, Beyrout, May 28, 1926 (PHS RG 115-3-2).

35 Nicol, "Outline History," chapter 2; AJCG Annual Report, Beirut, 1926–27; Frances Irwin to J. H. Nicol, May 28, 1926; Syria Mission Report, 1926–27 (PHS RG 115-3-2).

36 Frances Irwin to J. H. Nicol, Beyrout, May 28, 1926 (PHS RG 115-3-2); "Introduction to the Girls of the American Junior College, Beirut," Fall 1926 (PHS RG 115-3-2).

CHAPTER TEN

1 Ottora Horne, Annual Report of the American School for Girls for the Year 1927–1928 (PHS RG115:3:3).

2 James Nicol to Miss Irwin, April 19, 1927; Frances Irwin to Dear Friend, Beirut, July 26, 1927 (PHS RG 115:3:3); James Nicol, "An Outline History of the American Junior College for Women and Beirut College for Women" (unpublished: Nassar Library, Lebanese American University), Chapter 3.

3 New York State Education Department: Board of Regents, https://www.regents.nysed.gov/; extract of letter from President Dodge confirming conversation with the Regents of the University of the State of New York, November 3, 1927; Frances Irwin to Dear Friend, July 26, 1927; James Nicol to Miss Irwin, July 26, 1927; Special Announcement, Transfer of the Junior College for Girls to Ras Beirut (PHS RG 115-3-3).

4 Annual Report, AJCG (1926–27); Frances Irwin to Dear Friend, July 26, 1927 (PHS RG 115-3-2).

5 Roberts, *Short History* (Beirut, 1958), II:8; James Nicol to Miss Irwin, July 26, 1927 (PHS RG115:3:3); Frances Irwin to her parents, October 9, 1927 (PHS RG 186-1).

6 Frances Irwin to her parents, September 20 and September 28, 1927, and October 9, 1927 (PHS RG 186-1); Shannon Diaries, September 12 to October 5, 1925 (PHS RG 165-1-I).

7 It is important to point out here that the American School for Girls continued to grow and prosper on its own. Eventually the girls-only school evolved into today's Beirut Evangelical School for Girls and Boys in Rabieh, Lebanon. The author hopes that another writer will complete the rich legacy of BESGB.

8 Winifred Shannon to My Dear Friends, January 16, 1928; Annual Report, American Junior College for Women (AJCW), 1927–28 (PHS RG115:3:3); Frances Irwin to J. H. Nicol, May 28, 1926, F. P. Irwin to Mr. J. H. Nicol, March 2, 1927 (PHS RG 115-3-2).

9 Winifred Shannon to Mr. Nicol, December 26, 1928 (PHS RG 115:3:3); Roberts, *Short History*, II:3 (PHS: F TU72 B396s); Annual Report, AJCG, 1926–27 (PHS RG 115-3-2).

10 Frances Irwin to her parents, October 9 and November 1, 1927 (PHS RG 168); Shannon Diaries, November 1, November 2, and November 7, 1925 (PHS RG 165-1-I); http://cunard-whitestarline.wikia.com/wiki/RMS_Aquitania; Frances Irving to Irene Sheppard, March 9, 1939 (PHS RG115:3:3).

11 Shannon Diaries, November 4, November 7, and November 9, 1927 (PHS RG 165-1-I); Frances Irwin to James Nicol, May 20, 1928; James Nicol to Frances Irwin, July 2, 1928 (PHS RG115:3:3).

12 Shannon Diaries, September 12, October 5, October 6, and October 26, 1925 (PHS RG 165-1-I).

13 Winifred Shannon to Mr. Nicol, September 1928; James H. Nicol to Chief Engineer, November 26, 1928 (PHS RG 115:3:3).

14 Winifred Shannon to Mr. Nicol, November 7, November 19, and December 26, 1928; Annual Report of AJCW 1928–29 (PHS RG 115:3:3).

15 Winifred Shannon to My Dear Friends, January 16, 1929 (PHS RG 115:3:3).

16 Annual Report of AJCW 1929–1930; unsigned final examinations memo (PHS RG 115:3:3); Roberts, *Short History*, II:21; American Junior College for Women enrollment and graduation statistics 1927–1937 (PHS RG 115:3:3).

17 Annual Report of the American Junior College for Women for the Year 1929–1930; American Junior College for Women, Annual Report 1930–1931 (PHS RG 115 3:3).

18 Annual Report of AJCW, 1929–1930 (PHS RG 115:3:3).

19 Irene Sheppard to Winifred Shannon, November 21, 1929; Miss Katharine Tubbs to Syria Mission, August 7, 1932; Irene Sheppard to Miss Kerr, February 4, 1930; Irene Sheppard to Frances Irwin, February 5, 1930 (PHS RG 115:3:3).

20 Fawwaz Traboulsi, *A History of Modern Lebanon* (London: Pluto Press, 2012), 93–97; Paragraph from Rev. J. H. Nicol's letter to Miss I. Sheppard, April 1, 1930 (PHS RG 115:3:3).

21 Roy Creighton to Miss Irwin, June 21, 1929, Estimate on administration building (PHS RG 115 3:3).

22 James Nicol to Robert Speer and Irene Sheppard, May 23, 1930; Roberts, *Short History*, II: 9–10.

23 James Nicol to Robert Speer, December 2, 1930; Paul Erdman to Irene Sheppard, January 12, 1935; Nicol to Frances Irwin, Beirut, May 7, 1930; Nicol to Frances Irwin, June 21, 1930 (PHS RG 115 3:3); Roberts, *Short History*, II: 10–11.

24 Irene Sheppard to Robert Speer, June 4, 1930 (PHS RG 115 3:3).

25 Frances Irwin to R. L. Creighton, October 24, 1930; Irwin to Nicol, Beirut, October 2, 1930 (PHS RG 115 3:3).

26 Frances Irwin to James Nicol, August 8, October 2, November 6, and December 1, 1930 (PHS RG 115 3:3).

27 Annual Report of AJCW, 1929–1930 (PHS RG 115:3:3).

28 Annual Report of AJCW, 1930–1931 (PHS RG 115 3:3); Roberts, *A Short History*, II:6.

29 Irene Sheppard to Roy Creighton, January 13, 1931; James Nicol to Irene Sheppard, January 12, 1931; Roy Creighton to Irene Sheppard, February 13, 1931; Irene Sheppard to Miss Kerr, February 4, 1930; Irene Sheppard to Frances Irwin, May 11, 1931; *Training Christian Womanhood in Bible Lands* (brochure) (PHS RB 115 3:3).

30 AJCW, Annual Report 1930–1931(PHS RG 115 3:3).

31 Irene Sheppard to James Nicol, March 17, 1931 (PHS RB 115 3:3).

32 James Nicol to Irene Sheppard, May 5, 1931 (PHS RB 115 3:3).

33 Irene Sheppard to Frances Irwin and James Nicol, May 11, 1931; Nicol to Sheppard, May 5, 1931; Lateefeh Daoud to Winifred Shannon, July 12, 1931 (PHS RB 115 3:3).

34 Specific Work Department to Irene Sheppard, November 17, 1931.

35 Irene Sheppard to Frances Irwin and James Nicol, December 11, 1931; May 11, 1931; August 18, 1931; Sheppard to Irwin, April 26, 1932; Sheppard to Irwin and Nicol, December 11, 1931 (PHS RB 115 3:3).

36 James Nicol to Irene Sheppard, August 4, 1931 (PHS RB 115 3:3).

37 Irene Sheppard to Frances Irwin, April 26, 1932; Frances Irwin to Irene Sheppard, October 16, 1931; AJCW, Beirut Station, September 1932; James Nicol to Mrs. Charles Corbett, January 18, 1932; AJCW Report for 1931–32; Dear Friends Report for 1931–32; Frances Irwin to Irene Sheppard, October 16, 1931; Winifred Shannon to Roy Creighton, March 18, 1931 (PHS RB 115 3:3).

38 Irene Sheppard to Miss Margaret Doolittle, May 31, 1932; Irene Sheppard to Frances Irwin, April 26, 1932; Russell Carter to James Nicol, February 18, 1931 (PHS RB 115 3:3).

39 Irene Sheppard to Dr. Speer, Miss Schultz, and Miss Elliott, March 8, March 14, and June 23, 1932 (PHS RB 115 3:3).

40 ASG Girls, Beyrouth, 1924–1925; ASG School Report 1925–1926; Annual Report, AJCW 1926–1927; Excerpt from Frances Irwin to Miss Sheppard, October 16, 1931 (PHS RB 115 3:3).

41 BFM, Station Letter, Beirut, Fall 1932 (PHS RB 115 3:3).

42 Samir Kassir, Beirut (Berkeley: University of California Press, 2010), 322; The American Junior College for Women, Beirut Station, Syria Mission, September 1932 (PHS RB 115 3:3).

43 Samir Kassir, Beirut, 272; AJCW, Beirut Station, September 1932 (PHS RB 115 3:3).

44 Lateefeh Daoud to Winifred Shannon, July 12, 1931; Winifred Shannon to Ann Reid, July 14, 1931; Irene Sheppard to Winifred Shannon, August 5, 1931 (PHS RG115:3:3).

45 Frances Irwin to Irene Sheppard, October 28, 1931; Lateefeh Daoud to Miss Shannon, July 12, 1931; Irene Sheppard to Frances Irwin, December 12, 1931 (PHS RG115:3:3).

46 BFM Station Letter, Beirut, Fall 1932 (PHS RG115:3:3).

47 James Nicol to Irene Sheppard, June 2, 1932 (PHS RB 115 3:3).

48 AJCW Annual Report, 1932–33; Frances Irwin to Irene Sheppard, June 22, 1933; Frances Irwin, January 4, 1933 (copy) (PHS RG115:3:3).

49 AJCW Catalogue 1932–1933, 8, 9, 16, 17, 18 (Near East School of Theology Special Collection).

Sarah and Her Sisters | 395

50 Station Letter, Beirut, Spring 1933; Annual Report 1932–33, AJCW (PHS RG115:3:3); AJCW Catalogue, 1932–1933, 6 (Near East School of Theology Special Collection); "To Ladies of Presbyterian Women's Guild, Parsons, Kansas," December 29, 1932 (PHS RG 165-2-2).

51 Frances Irwin, January 4, 1933 (copy); Robert Speer to Irene Sheppard, March 8, 1933; Irene Sheppard to Miss Kittredge and Mrs. Duguid, March 15, 1933; Irene Sheppard to Robert Speer, April 6, 1933; Irene Sheppard to James Nicol and Frances Irwin, April 17, 1933 (PHS RG115:3:3).

52 Frances Irwin to Irene Sheppard, June 22, 1933 (PHS RG115:3:3).

53 Frances Irwin to her parents, February 20, 1933 (PHS RG 186-2-9).

CHAPTER ELEVEN

1 Annual Report, 1933–34, American Junior College for Women (PHS RG 115 3 2).

2 Daniel Roberts, *Short History* (Beirut, 1958), II:13, 16.

3 Winifred Shannon to Dear Daddy, March 5, 1933 (PHS RG 165-2-4).

4 Roberts, *Short History*, II:11–12, 13–14; Irene Sheppard to Robert Speer, April 6, 1933; Station Letter, Beirut, Spring 1933; Annual Report 1932–33, AJCW (PHS RG115:3:3).

5 Annual Report, 1932–33, AJCW (PHS RG115:3:3).

6 Roberts, *Short History*, II:13, 16.

7 Winifred Shannon to Dear Dad, May 21, 1933 (PHS RG 165-2-4).

8 Frances Irwin Letters, July 2, 1933 (PHS RG 186-6-10).

9 Frances Irwin Letters, August 16, 1933 (PHS RG 186-6-10).

10 James Nicol to Irene Sheppard, February 16, 1934; Mr. Tower to Robert Speer and Irene Sheppard, June 20, 1934; Memo to Dr. Speer, Mr. Carter, Miss Schultz, and Miss Kittredge, March 12, 1935; Irene Sheppard to William Greenslade, September 18, 1934; Frances Irwin to Irene Sheppard, November 27, 1934; January 10, 1934; Irene Sheppard to Robert Speer, March 2, 1934; Mr. Tower to Irene Sheppard, March 12, 1934 (PHS RG 115:3:3).

11 Winifred Shannon to Dearest Little Bear, August 28, 1933 (PHS RG 165-2-4); Irene Sheppard to Herman Otto, August 25, 1933; Winifred Shannon to Irene Sheppard, September 24, 1933 (PHS RG115:3:3).

12 Winifred Shannon to Dear Daddy, March 5, 1933 (PHS RG 165-2-4).

13 Frances Irwin Letters, September 4 and 11, 1933 (PHS RG 186-6-10).

14 Frances Irwin Letters, September 24, 1933 (PHS RG 186-6-10).

15 Frances Irwin Letters, October 3, October 8, and October 15, 1933 (PHS RG 186-6-10).

16 Frances Irwin Letters, October 15, 1933 (PHS RG 186-6-10).

17 Frances Irwin Letters, October 25 and 29, 1933 and November 8, 1933 (PHS RG 186-6-10).

18 Frances Irwin Letters, November 26, 1933 (PHS RG 186-6-10).

19 Annual Report, 1933–1934, AJCW; Frances Irwin to Irene Sheppard, January 10, 1934 (PHS RG115:3:3); Roberts, *Short History*, II:14-15, 18; Frances Irwin photos (PHS RG 186-2-9).

20 Tenth Annual Report AJCW, 1934–1935 (PHS RB 115 3:3); Frances Irwin to her parents, January 27, 1935 (PHS RG 186-2-12).

21 Mission Actions on Dormitory, AJCW; Paul Erdman to Irene Sheppard, Beirut, March 6, 1935 (PHS RG115:3:3).

22 Tenth Annual Report AJCW (PHS RG115:3:3); Frances Irwin to her parents, January 13, 1935; January 27, 1935; Roberts, *Short History*, II:16.

23 Tenth Annual Report AJCW (PHS RG115:3:3); James Nicol to Irene Sheppard, Beirut, November 5, 1935; Mission Actions re: Dormitory AJCW (PHS RB 115 3:3).

24 H. W. Glockler to Irene Sheppard, September 17, 1935.

25 Peter Mansfield, *A History of the Middle East* (New York: Penguin Books, 1991), 205–206; http:// www.palestinefacts.org/pf_mandate_riots_1936-39.php; Tenth Annual Report AJCW; Winifred Shannon to Irene Sheppard, November 1, 1935; James Nicol to Irene Sheppard, November 5, 1935 (PHS RG115:3:3).

26 Fawwaz Traboulsi, *A History of Modern Lebanon* (London: Pluto Press, 2012), 97–102.

27 Winifred Shannon to Irene Sheppard, November 1, 1935; Eleventh Annual Report of American Junior College for Women (PHS RG 115 3:3); Roberts, *Short History*, II:21.

28 Eleventh Annual Report of AJCW (PHS RG 115 3:3).

29 Irene Sheppard to Frances Irwin, March 4, 1936; Frances Irwin to Irene Sheppard, March 9, 1936; Mr. Pattison to Irene Sheppard and Mr. Carter, May 26, 1936; Eleventh Annual Report of AJCW; Minutes of the Sage College Committee, March 1936 (?) (PHS RG115:3:3).

30 Irene Sheppard to James Nicol and Winifred Shannon, November 27 and 28, 1936; Traboulsi, *A History of Modern Lebanon*, 99; Details of D6009, December 31, 1936, AJCW; Details of D6710, March 23, 1937, AJCW Equipment Account; Final Statement, Equipment Account, Dormitory, June 3, 1937 (PHS RG115:3:3).

31 Winifred Shannon letter to alumnae, January 1, 1937, Irene Sheppard to Mr. Trull, May 3, 1937 (PHS RG115:3:3).

32 Irene Sheppard to Mr. Trull, May 3, 1937; Irene Sheppard to James Nicol and Winifred Shannon, November 27 and 28, 1936 (PHS RG115:3:3).

33 Winifred Shannon to Irene Sheppard, December 6, 1936; Irene Sheppard to James Nicol and Winifred Shannon, May 29, 1936 (PHS RG115:3:3); "Mohammed Reza Shah Pahlavi," https://www.britannica.com/biography/Mohammad-Reza-Shah-Pahlavi; A. Reza Arasteh, *Education and Social Awakening in Iran* (Leiden: E.J. Brill, 1962), 120; "Alborz College," Encyclopedia Iranica, http://www.irani-caonline.org/articles/alborz-college.

34 Winifred Shannon to Sage Committee, February 11, 1937; Jane Doolittle to Sage Committee, February 11, 1937 (PHS RG115:3:3).

35 Irene Sheppard to James Nicol and Winifred Shannon, November 27, 1936; Twelfth Annual Report of AJCW (1936-1937) (PHS RG115:3:3).

36 Irene Sheppard to James Nicol and Winifred Shannon, November 27, 1936; Twelfth Annual Report of AJCW (PHS RG115:3:3

37 James Nicol, "An Outline History of the American Junior College for Women and Beirut College for Women" (unpublished: Nassar Library, Lebanese American University), Chapter 3; *The Mac Weekly*, Macalester College, October 28, 1937, September 23, March 24, and May 5, 1938, October 5 and October 5, 1939; Obituary of Frances P. Irwin, *Minneapolis Star Tribune*, October 14, 1939. Frances Irwin's Lakewood Cemetery plot is in Section12, Lot 52, Grave 1.

EPILOGUE

1 Edward William Hooker, *Memoir of Mrs. Sarah L. Huntington Smith* (Boston: American Tract Society, 1845), 311.

AUTHOR'S NOTE

1 Jean Said Makdisi, *Teta, Mother, and Me: Three Generations of Arab Women* (New York: Norton, 2006), 191–194.

APPENDIX B

1 Compiled from Reports of Beirut Female Seminary for the years 1874, 1875, 1877, 1878, 1880, 1882, 1885, and 1890 (PHS MF10 F761a).

2 Rachel Tolles, Report of the American School for Girls, Beirut, Syria, 1919–1920, July 26, 1920; Ottora Horne, Annual Report 1920–1921, July 15, 1921 (PHS RG 115 3:2).

3 Ottora Horne, Annual Report of the American School for Girls, Beirut, Syria, 1922–1923; Frances P. Irwin, Annual Report of the American School for Girls, Beirut, 1924–1925; Contract for Short Term Workers (PHS RG 115 3:2).

APPENDIX C

1 Roberts, *Short History*, II.

2 Annual Reports of AJCW, 1926–27, 1931–32, 1932–33, 1934–35 (PHS RG115:3:3); Roberts, *Short History*, II:19.

3 Annual Reports of AJCW, 1926–27, 1927–28, 1928–29, 1929–30, 1931–32, 1932–33, 1933–34, 1934–35, 1935–36 (PHS RG115:3:3).

4 Annual Reports of AJCW, 1926–27, 1931–32, 1932–33, 1934–35 (PHS RG115:3:3)

5 Roberts, *Short History*, II:21.

Index

A

Abbott, Peter 22, 49
Abd el Karim, Mufid 310
'Abdu'l-Bahá 213
Abdul Hamid II 152, 177, 205
Abeih 84, 88, 89, 90, 97, 101, 103, 105, 110, 112, 113, 115, 122, 137, 204, 363, 364
Abyssinian 39, 56, 77
academic standards 274, 280, 282, 296
Aftimus, Joseph 221
Aiken, Edward 105
Aiken, Susan 105
Alay 49, 77, 80
Alborz College 336
Aleppo 95, 150, 204, 209, 291, 340, 345, 364
Aleppo College 340
Alexandria 59, 118, 126, 150, 178, 189, 204, 237
Allenby, General 239
alma mater 181, 302, 310
American Board of Commissioners for Foreign Missions 13, 25, 135
American Community School 253, 325
American schools 189, 192, 204, 247
American Tract Society 63
American University Hospital 283
American University of Beirut 105, 110, 244, 245
American University of Cairo 337
Amherst 103, 355
Andover Theological Seminary 13, 25, 92, 103, 363

Anglicans 59, 71, 135
Apparatus (Science) 162
Arab Revolt 229
Araman, Iskandar 286
Araman, Lulu Shebly 96, 182
Araman, Michaiel 122, 125, 357
Argentina 247
Arthington, Robert 121
Artimus, Yusef Bek 309
astronomy 97, 122, 141, 184, 248
Ataturk, Kemal 266
athletics 255, 334, 360
Atta, Raheel 40, 76, 77, 82, 93, 356, 363, 364
Auburn Theological Seminary 209
Australia 126, 158, 194
automobile 211, 340
Azzeddin, Najla 255, 261, 323

B

al-Bustani, Butrus 93, 363
Baalbek 76, 123, 173, 297, 321
Badger, Roberta 81, 82, 83
Badre, Albert 346, 353
Baghdad 240, 261, 270, 288, 291, 299, 323
Bahá'í Faith 213
Baker, Eleanor Williams 123
Baker, Walter 123, 216
Baldwin, Matthias 119
Bamdoon 41, 97, 106
baseball 287, 288
basketball 255, 264, 273, 278, 287, 288, 365

Batroun 122, 204
Beach, Moses 114
Beadle, Hannah 93
Beck, Eva 278, 281, 359
Beirut Boys Seminary 59, 81
Beirut Evangelical Church 126, 207
Beit Loring 145, 177, 200
Berbir, Munira 261
Bint Jebeil 298, 313
Bird, Ann 16, 49, 355, 363
Bird, Isaac 13, 14, 16, 18, 19, 21, 35, 37, 51
Bird, Sarah 101
Bird, William 14, 137, 158
Bliss, Abby 92, 103, 105, 106, 110, 112, 119, 135, 164, 206, 355, 364
Bliss, Daniel 92, 103, 105, 106, 109, 110, 112, 117, 119, 137, 173, 195, 206, 211, 233, 364
Bliss, Frederick 108
Bliss, Howard 206, 229
Bliss, Mary 112, 136, 157, 164, 176, 193, 195, 356, 365
blockade 82, 219, 222, 228, 232, 233, 240
Board of Managers 113, 114, 117, 151, 332, 338
Board of Regents 274, 366
Boojah 70, 71
Booth, Martha 283, 359
Booth, William 118, 121
Boston 21, 25, 31, 71, 92, 130, 139
botany 122, 184
Brazil 182, 194, 247
Britain 82, 109, 219, 243, 247
British Army 158, 328
British Syrian schools 112, 249
Brooklyn 162, 189, 356
Brooklyn, USS 186
Brown, Arthur 163, 164, 165, 168, 171, 179, 191, 199, 245, 365
Brown, John 119
Brumana 235

Burj Bird 19, 22, 96, 100, 119, 121, 226, 364
Bustani, Sarah Huntington 95, 101, 125

C
Caesar, USS 232
Cairo 17, 126, 179, 180, 198, 204, 255, 291
Calhoun, Emily 101
Calhoun, Simeon 137
Calvinist 24, 37, 347
Calvin, John 9, 135
Carabet, Salome 86
Carruth, Ellen 131, 133, 135, 136, 156, 356, 364
Castello Rosso 68
Catechism 89
Cedars 76, 123
Ceylon 57, 61
chemistry 141, 184, 258, 262, 268, 275, 281, 287, 295, 296, 301, 333, 359, 364
Cheney, Sarah 92, 101, 103, 105, 106, 355, 364
Chicago 180, 192, 199, 292
Child Welfare 301
China 99, 133, 168, 179, 201, 255, 340
Chios 68
cholera 29, 39, 89, 119, 154, 184, 189, 212, 215, 223
Christian Endeavor Society 201
Church of Scotland 144
church women 122, 150, 151, 171, 230, 275, 291, 298
Churi, Josef, Madame 207
Clifton Springs 163, 181
College Medical School 195
Columbia University 323
common schools 35, 51, 82, 96, 100, 143
Conference, School Girls' 264
Congregational Church 26, 31, 130
Connecticut 13, 19, 23, 27, 29, 31, 50, 65, 76, 92, 114, 151, 351
conscription 214, 215, 221

Sarah and Her Sisters | *401*

conversion 26, 57, 148
Cooke, Jay 119
Cotton, Charles 186
crash, stock market 293, 366
Creighton, Roy 285, 291, 293, 325
Curtis, Jessie M. 216, 356
Cyprus 34, 66, 67, 82, 113, 117, 178, 188, 193, 194, 300

D
Dabbas, Charles 262
Damascus 17, 59, 103, 123, 150, 156, 178, 179, 209, 229, 264, 330
Danish 229
Daoud, Lateefeh 301, 359
Debbas, Mme. 321
De Forest, Henry 92, 97, 99, 113, 296, 345, 355, 363
De Forest, Kitty 92, 96, 99, 105, 106, 182, 296, 363
Deir Mama 331
dengue fever 119, 196, 212, 276, 279, 293
Dennis, James 147
Dennis, Mary 147
dentistry 245, 260, 366
Denver 157
Dickinson, Emily 105
dietetics 283
diplomacy 186
diplomat 106
discipline 11, 42, 97, 203, 236, 242, 280, 322
Djamal Pasha 235
Dodge, Asa 19, 22, 92
Dodge, Bayard 227, 249, 274, 330
Dodge, Cleveland 230
Dodge, Ellen Phelps 118, 122
Dodge, Harriet 131
Dodge, Martha 19, 34, 36, 37, 40, 41, 44, 64, 76, 80, 84, 88, 355, 363
Dodge, Stuart 118
Dodge, William E. 118, 131

Dog River 264, 337
Donaldson, Lillian 262, 276, 278, 359
Doolittle, George 211
Doolittle, Jane 336
Doolittle, Margaret 249, 295
Druze Rebellion 270
dysentery 83, 331

E
early childhood education 304
earthquake 201
Eddy, Hannah 101
Eddy, Mary Pierson 201
Eddy, William 165, 171, 217
electric 186, 227, 234, 246
Ellinwood, Frank 146
Elliot, Ruth 312
Elmore, Mary 183
emigration 158, 194, 366
English Department 142, 143
English Society 34, 183
epidemics 154, 212, 223
Eramian, Miss 323
Erdman, Mable 304, 360
erysipelas 196
European, Joint Commission 109, 114
evangelizing 101, 111, 172
Everett, Eliza 129, 130, 131, 135, 136, 139, 140, 142, 143, 151, 156, 157, 160, 161, 168, 180, 207, 216, 342, 356, 364, 365

F
Faisal I, King 299
famine 14, 222, 223, 228, 240
Farnum, Anna Whitman 114
Farnum, Henry 114, 121
Field, Athletic 278, 313
Fisher, Charles, Mrs. 333, 360
Fisher, Helen 136, 356
Fiske, Josiah 162
Fiske, Martha 162
Fisk, Pliny 13, 363

Flendrich, Mademoiselle 248
Fosdick, Harry Emerson 266
France 109, 219, 243, 329, 334
Franklin, USS 152
Frazer, A. S. 114
French Army 109
French High Commission 262, 285
Fuad Pasha 109
Fuaz, Asine 139, 357

G

Gallup, Marilla 129
Gaskell, Agnes 283
General Assembly 181, 294
Germans 189, 209
Ghoreyeb, Stella 200, 201
Glen Lake Sanatorium 343
Gliddon, Miss 41
Glockler, Jessie 200, 207, 356
Goodell, Abigail 16, 355, 363
Goodell, William 13, 16, 17, 51
Goodrich, Ellen 261, 268, 298
Graham, Sylvester 39
Gray, Frances 345
Great Depression 285, 294
Greater Lebanon 110, 243, 262
Greensboro College 323
Greenslade, Vivian 304, 360
Greenslade, William 310
Gregory, Sada 89
gymnasium 285, 287, 289

H

al Haddad, Sarah Smith 95
al Haddad, Tannoos 36, 95, 144
Habaica, Feridy 139, 357
Habboub, Sunneyeh 261, 268
Haddad, Asin 122
Haddad, Farha 139, 157, 161, 207, 357
Hammana 223
Harden, O. J. 221
Harkness Endowment Fund 299
Harkness Legacy Fund 294

Harpoot 233
Harris, Ira 209, 212
Harvard 25
Hazlett, Edith 248, 356
Hebard, Story 59, 60, 61, 76, 81, 82,
122, 363
Hekimiah, Henriette 255
Hersey, Eileen 333, 338
Hitti, Habib 281
Holenkoff, Olga 258, 281, 358, 359
Home Economics 338, 345, 360
Homs 103, 105, 201, 209, 261
Hooker, Edward 71, 351
Hoskins, Franklin 184, 206, 211, 224,
229
Hoskins, Harriette Eddy 215
hostel 288, 315, 317, 329, 366
Houghton Female Seminary 129, 130,
131, 143
Huntington, Jabez 55, 345
Husayn, Sharif 229
Hyde, Nancy 24
hygiene 262, 278, 281, 296, 298, 301,
304, 313, 323, 332, 359
hymns 37, 101, 106, 152, 179

I

Ibrahim Pasha 18, 22, 40
Iddi, Emile 329
immigrants 228, 347
immigration 247, 328
India 122, 168, 179, 340
infant schools 52
Influenza 154, 196, 237, 247, 258, 333
Innocents Abroad 115
insurance 146, 317
Iran 135, 327, 331, 332, 334, 336, 338, 367
Iran Fund 331, 367
Iraq 135, 243, 256, 274, 291, 299, 300,
319, 322, 328, 336
Irwin, Anna White 342
Irwin, Frances 252, 254, 255, 256, 258,
262, 266, 268, 269, 270, 273, 274, 275,

276, 278, 282, 285, 287, 292, 295, 298,
308, 316, 318, 323, 325, 329, 331, 338,
340, 342, 343, 351, 359, 360, 366, 367
Italian 14, 22, 34, 47, 56, 77, 122, 144,
155, 214, 220, 222, 347, 360, 365
Italy 214, 219, 276, 326

J

Jabbra, Joseph 346, 352
Jackson, Ellen 136, 141, 151, 152, 156,
260, 356, 364
Jaffa 178, 179, 182, 204, 237
Jamal Pasha 229
Jasmine, Malory 178, 179
Jerusalem Girls' High School 245
Jerusalem Girls' School 84
Jessup, Anna 112, 136, 157, 163, 181,
356, 365
Jessup, Caroline 112, 364
Jessup Hall 224, 227, 234, 241, 260, 268
Jessup, Harriet 131
Jessup, Henry 11, 111, 112, 114, 117,
119, 126, 127, 129, 131, 137, 144, 146,
149, 152, 154, 157, 163, 164, 165, 167,
168, 171, 172, 180, 191, 201, 207, 209,
226, 334, 351, 364, 365
Jessup, Samuel 154, 211
Jessup, Theodosia 180, 207
Jessup, William 235
Jesuits 17, 144, 196
Johns Hopkins University 294
Johnson, Jane 106, 108, 356, 364
Junishian, Yacob 207

K

al-Kulliya 312
el Khuri, Jeboor Saad 158
Kennedy, Emma Baker 216, 365
Kennedy Hall 221, 224, 226, 227, 232,
233, 365
Khouri, Kareemeh 255, 357
Kikano House 221
kindergarten 147, 180, 204

King, Jonas 13, 14, 363
King's Daughters 201
kosher 150
Kurds 360

L

La Grange, Harriet 159, 165, 167, 168,
172, 174, 356, 365
Lancaster, John 50
Lanneau, Julia 93
Larnaca 82
Latakia 150, 204
Laubach Method 338
Law, Ellen 136, 147, 159, 161, 162, 163,
356, 365
Lebanese Republic 262
Lecerf, Esther 278, 281, 360
Lee, Mary E. 329, 359
Levy, Sara 251
Lewis, Edward 141
Library Books 162
Liverpool 118, 119, 131, 174, 252
Loring, Sophie 136, 142, 145, 151, 356,
364

M

Macalester College 342, 367
Mackie, Daisy 199, 212
Mahmud II, Sultan 18
mail 56, 59, 151, 228, 230, 239, 331, 340
malaria 177, 331
Malta 18, 29, 31, 34, 82
Mandate 262, 278, 328, 366
Manley, Ida 256, 258
manners 98, 148, 212, 238
Mansourieh 61
March, Amy 212
March, Frederick 212
March, Jennie 212
Markle, Elizabeth 283, 360
Marseilles 119, 122, 232, 278
Mason, Adelaide 108, 109, 111, 112,
356, 364

massacres 108, 109, 195
mathematics 81, 97, 246, 258, 262, 278, 281, 301, 359
measles 108, 154, 196
medicine 59, 67, 80, 194, 200, 255, 260, 261
Mehmed V 205
Melbourne 126
Ministry of Education 206, 328
Minneapolis 252, 261, 279, 313, 325, 326, 342, 343, 345
Missionary Society 29, 162, 212
Mission Compound 145, 226, 231, 252
Mission Press 29, 64, 141, 145, 215, 226, 228, 233, 242
mission schools 17, 82, 110, 113, 188, 206, 226, 229, 233, 238, 245, 255
Missouri 205, 266, 280, 301
Miss Taylor's Muslim Girls' School 144
Mitchell, Mildred 329, 330, 335, 359, 360
Mohegans 27, 29, 347
Montrose 112, 118
Morgenthau, Henry 229
Moseitbeh 222
motto 253, 337
Mount Holyoke 130, 131
Mr. Schneller's School 212
Mugreditchian, Armenouhi 261
Muir, Henry 126
Murr, Ilias 293
music 27, 54, 64, 101, 123, 145, 174, 184, 204, 241, 266, 270, 275, 357

N

Nasiriyeh 323, 331, 337
Nassar, Riyad 346, 353
Nassar, Salwa 346
Nassar, Shakir 321
nationalism 328, 330, 367
Nazim Pasha, Waly 188, 190
Near East Relief 255, 278, 283
Near East School of Theology 310

Nickoley, Edward 258, 338
Nickoley, Kathryn 360
Nicol, Catherine 337, 338
Nicol, James 209, 211, 246, 249, 251, 266, 269, 275, 281, 285, 286, 310, 317, 327, 345, 359, 360, 365
Nile 197, 198
Normal Schools 227, 244, 249
North Fork 29
Norwich 19, 23, 24, 25, 26, 27, 31, 36, 47, 53, 57, 58, 59, 70, 77, 151, 351, 355
Nurbakhsh School for Girls 336
Nurse's Diploma 337
nursery school 304, 316, 321, 322, 332, 333, 366
nursing 195, 337

O

Ohio 130, 151, 205, 216, 240, 261
Ottoman Empire 22, 152, 201, 219, 230

P

Pahlavi, Reza Shaw 336
Painesville 130, 151
Palestine 13, 22, 29, 44, 123, 135, 162, 180, 196, 237, 243, 251, 268, 284, 291, 292, 328, 366
Paris 130, 131, 261
Park College 280, 301
Parliament 205, 284
Paul, Saint 66, 176
Paxton, John 81
Penrose, Jr., Stephen 250
pharmacy 245, 260, 281, 366
Philadelphia 11, 55, 119, 149, 342, 352, 356
physics 97, 184, 281
physiology 97, 141, 184, 296
Pittsburgh 268, 294
plague 18, 65, 196
playground 122, 145, 184, 194, 227, 258, 261, 264
political science 252, 283, 321, 333

Sarah and Her Sisters | 405

Post, George 137
practice teaching 143, 179, 198
Presbyterian Board of Foreign Missions 136, 274
Presbyterian Church 110, 135, 136, 216, 291, 294, 298, 340, 364, 366
Princeton Theological Seminary 19, 35
Protestantism 9, 13, 57, 88, 97, 143
protests 285, 365
Prussia 109
Prussian Deaconesses 142, 179
Prussian Hospital 196
psalms 179
psychology 283, 322, 333, 345, 360

R

railroads 114, 173, 178, 209, 217, 256
Ramadan 242
Ramiz Bey, Waly 185
Ras Beirut Female School 147, 365
Rashid Bey, Waly 185, 186
recruitment 192, 284
Red Cross 205, 241
refugees 49, 109, 110, 111, 177, 188, 223, 244, 264
Rex, USS 326
Rhoades 68
Rignault, Madame 323
Roosevelt, Theodore 185, 205
Russia 109, 219

S

Sabri, Marie 346
Sabunjy, Sada 98, 100, 103
Sage College 332, 336, 340
Sage Fund 293, 298, 299, 306, 308, 327, 331, 332, 336, 366
Sage, Russell, Mrs. 298
salaries 117, 136, 137, 149, 151, 164, 168, 197, 220
Salisky, Lulu 184
San Francisco 189, 201
San Francisco, USS 186

Sarkis, Sara 122
Sarrafian, Samuel 274, 278
Schechter, William 346
School of Arts and Sciences 249, 251, 254
Scottish Presbyterian 135, 252
Scranton 118, 151, 356
Second Great Awakening 25, 170
security 192, 287, 288, 292, 327, 328
Seelye, Kate 283
Seelye, Laurens 242
sewing 35, 53, 77, 83, 87, 95, 99, 145, 179, 183, 338
Shannon, Margaret 321, 330, 360
Shannon, Winifred 256, 258, 264, 276, 278, 282, 286, 292, 295, 296, 309, 312, 313, 315, 318, 326, 329, 331, 332, 336, 338, 340, 359, 360, 366, 367
Shekkur, Luciyah 122, 135
Sheppard, Irene 284, 299, 315, 327, 331, 342
Sherman, Charles 86
Sherman, Martha 86
Shidiak, Assad 17
Shweir 182, 333
Sidon Girls' School 364
Sigourney, Lydia Huntley 24, 27
singing 45, 55, 77, 122, 152, 174, 200, 215, 227, 264, 310, 326
sirocco 119, 337
slavery 36, 39, 110
small pox 154
Smith, Charles Henry 83
Smith, Eli 9, 18, 21, 29, 31, 34, 83, 93, 96, 101, 114, 181, 233, 363
Smith, Hetty 101
Smith, Maria 83, 355
Smith, Sarah 9, 19, 21, 23, 29, 35, 44, 45, 48, 51, 58, 71, 75, 76, 84, 86, 91, 92, 95, 99, 111, 121, 151, 152, 168, 182, 248, 345, 346, 347, 351, 355, 363
Smyrna 48, 52, 65, 66, 68, 71, 174, 205, 216, 363

Social Gospel 171
social science 278, 283, 359
sociology 258, 321, 338, 360
Sophomore Sneak 330
sports 264, 288, 333
steamships 228
Stoltzfus, Ethel 345
Stoltzfus, William 340, 345, 367
student council 322, 330
Sublime Porte 192
Sunday schools 48, 117
Suq el-Gharb 103, 108, 110, 111, 112, 122, 145, 197, 253, 279, 364
swimming 337
Switzerland 232
Syrian Female Seminary 111, 113
Syrian Protestant College 103, 110, 117, 118, 136, 176, 178, 190, 195, 201, 202, 229, 230, 245, 364
Syrian Revolt 262
Syrian Training College 249, 268

T
Tantaquidgeon, Lucy Occum 27
Taylor, Howell 325
Tayyebat 340
Tehran 255, 256, 332, 336, 338, 367
Temple, Amelia 106, 108, 109, 111, 356, 364
Temple, Daniel 70
Temple, Martha 70
tennis 253, 273, 278, 287, 304, 319, 322
textbooks 140
Third French Republic 243
Thomson, Eliza 19, 22, 34, 37, 41, 84, 86, 355, 363
Thomson, Maria Abbott 49
Thomson, William 19, 22, 37, 43, 49, 50, 59, 60, 80, 82, 110, 112, 122, 137, 363, 364
Tilden, Betsey 59, 76, 81, 82, 83, 87, 88, 92, 95, 355, 363, 364
Tod, Alexander 121

trachoma 313, 331
transportation 173, 209, 228
Tripoli Girls' School 90, 146, 293, 364
Trireme 337
Troy Female Seminary 192
tuberculosis 212
Turkish 14, 44, 109, 125, 148, 152, 154, 155, 184, 186, 191, 192, 195, 205, 211, 214, 215, 220, 229, 230, 231, 234, 237, 238, 240, 244, 266, 275, 304, 347, 360, 365
Twain, Mark 115
typewriter 211
typhoid 125, 154, 162, 184

U
United Presbyterian Church 135
Université Saint-Joseph 196, 244
University of Chicago 261, 266, 323
University of Kansas 256
University of Minnesota 209, 252, 276, 279, 329, 342, 345

V
Vacation Bible School 233, 236
Van Dyck, Cornelius 112, 137, 181, 233, 364
Van Dyck, Eliza 136, 152, 156, 356
Van Rensselaer, Alexander 114
Van Zandt, Jane Elizabeth 195, 196
Veils Up 298, 310
Victrola 266, 334
Village welfare 322, 331

W
Wadi Abou Jamil 140
War
  - American Civil War 113, 118
  - Italo-Turkish War 214
  - Mount Lebanon Civil War 109
  - World War 214, 336, 365
Wassa Pasha 155
White, Stanley 231, 239
Whiting, George 84, 86, 182

Sarah and Her Sisters | 407

Whittlesey, Anna 92, 99, 100, 101, 355, 364
Wilderspin, Samuel 51, 52
Wilhelm II, Kaiser 219
Williams, Rebecca 29, 37, 48, 50, 51, 56, 61, 64, 76, 81, 83, 87, 88, 91, 92, 93, 355, 363
Wilson, Lois 248, 253, 255, 356
Wilson, Woodrow 230, 239
Winslow, Harriet Lathrop 57, 61
Witwat, Khozma Ata 95
Woman's Work for Woman 182
Women's Board of Missions 151
Woods, Sadie 255, 268

Wortabet, Gregory, Mrs. 34
Wortabet, Hanna 86
Wortabet, John 141
Wright, Quincy 266, 297

Y

Yale 25, 26, 83, 92, 114, 130
Young Turks 205, 213, 365
YWCA 238, 255, 266, 300

Z

Zahleh 168
Zionists 246
zoology 275, 281, 287, 296, 360
Zwilling, Mlle. 321

Credits

Fig. 1: Presbyterian Historical Society • Fig. 2: From the *Memoir of the Rev. Pliny Fisk, A.M.: late missionary to Palestine* by Bond, Alvan, 1793-1882; Fisk, Pliny, 1792-1825 • Fig. 3: Henry Jessup, *Fifty-Three Years in Syria,* vol. I, Fleming H. Revell Company, 1910 • Fig. 4: Connecticut Digital Archive • Fig. 5: Presbyterian Historical Society • Fig. 6: Special Collections, Yale Divinity School Library • Fig. 7: Duxbury Rural and Historical Society, original watercolor by Felice Polli • Fig. 8: Illustration by Aldo Cherini • Fig. 9: De Agostini Picture Library/Bridgeman Images • Fig. 10: American University of Beirut/Library Archives • Figs. 11-13: Library Company of Philadelphia • Fig. 14: Public domain • Fig. 15: Created by Rarelibra for public domain use • Fig. 16: Photo by Christine B. Lindner, 2006, used by permission • Fig. 17: Photo by Jon Chapman, used by permission • Fig. 18: Item is in the public domain • Fig. 19: Special Collections, Yale Divinity School Library • Fig. 20: American University of Beirut/Library Archives • Fig. 21: The Stapleton Collection/Bridgeman Images • Fig. 22: Henry Jessup, *Fifty-Three Years in Syria,* vol. I • Fig. 23: Public domain • Fig. 24: Henry Jessup, *Fifty-Three Years in Syria,* vol. I • Fig. 25: Special Collections, Yale Divinity School Library • Fig. 26: Presbyterian Historical Society • Fig. 27: Amherst College Archives & Special Collections. Public domain • Fig. 28: American University of Beirut/Library Archives • Fig. 29: Wash drawing by Clary Ray, circa 1900. Public domain. Courtesy of the Navy Art Collection, Washington, DC. • Fig. 30: Abdullah frères. Public domain • Fig. 31: By Contemporary portrait. Public domain • Fig. 32: David McNeely Stauffer collection on Westcott's History of Philadelphia • Fig. 33: By New York, N.Y. : M. King – Notable New Yorkers of 1896-1899 : a companion volume to King's handbook of New York City, Public domain • Fig. 34: Public domain • Fig. 35: Source unknown • Fig. 36: Presbyterian Historical Society • Fig. 37: Presbyterian Historical Society • Fig. 38: Special Collections, Yale Divinity School Library• Figs. 39-40: American University of Beirut/Library Archives • Figs. 41-42: Presbyterian Historical Society • Fig. 43: US Naval History and Heritage Command • Fig. 44-45: Special Collections, Yale Divinity School Library • Fig. 46: Presbyterian Historical Society • Fig. 47: Alinari Archives, Florence/Bridgeman Images • Fig. 48: USS *Brooklyn* by Robert Enrique Muller – Collection of the New York Naval Shipyard. U.S. Naval Historical Center Photograph • Fig. 49: National Archives and Records Administration, Still Pictures Division, College Park, Md. • Fig. 50: Courtesy Susquehanna County Historical Society, Montrose, PA • Fig. 51: Photo © Gusman/Bridgeman Images • Fig. 52: © Archives Charmet/Bridgeman Images • Fig. 53: Presbyterian Historical Society • Fig. 54: Courtesy of University of Minnesota Archives, University of Minnesota – Twin Cities • Fig. 55: Courtesy of Kansas University Archives • Figs. 56-65: Presbyterian Historical Society • Figs. 66-67: American University of Beirut/Library Archives • Figs. 68-69: Presbyterian Historical Society • Fig. 70: Courtesy of Lebanese American University • Figs. 71-77: Presbyterian Historical Society • Fig. 78: American University of Beirut/Library Archives • Figs. 79-83: Presbyterian Historical Society • Fig. 84: Bain News Service, publisher/Public domain • Figs. 85-90: Presbyterian Historical Society • Fig. 91: Macalester College • Fig. i: Photo by Dave Oat, Graven Images, Preston, CT • Fig. ii: CLK Hatcher/CC BY-SA (https://creativecommons.org/licenses/bysa/2.0) • Fig. iii: Photo taken by author in Tantaquidgeon Museum, Uncasville, CT • Fig. iv: Historic Buildings of Connecticut https://historicbuildingsct.com • Fig. v: JJBers/CC BY (https://creativecommons.org/licenses/by/4.0) • Fig. vi: Courtesy of Park Congregational Church, Norwich, CT. Photo by David Oat, Graven Images, Preston, CT • Fig. vii. Courtesy of The Faith Trumbull Chapter, DAR, Inc, Norwich, CT, Photo by Dave Oat, Graven Images, Preston, CT • Fig. viii: Photo by the author • Figs. ix-xx: Courtesy of Lebanese American University.